Springer Series on Behavior Therapy and Behavioral Medicine

Series Editor: Cyril M. Franks, Ph.D.

Advisory Board: John Paul Brady, M.D., Robert P. Liberman, M.D., Neal E. Miller, Ph.D., and Stanley Rachman, Ph.D.

DANIEL B. FISHMAN, Ph.D. (Harvard University) is Professor of Psychology in the Graduate School of Applied and Professional Psychology at Rutgers University. Prior to his Rutgers appointment, he was Associate Director for Administration and Evaluation at a comprehensive community mental health center in metro Denver, Colorado. His fifty articles and book chapters and forty invited addresses span interests in philosophy of science, behavior therapy, organizational behavior management, behavioral medicine, program evaluation, cost-effectiveness analysis, community mental health, and professional psychology training. A past President of the Eastern Evaluation Research Society and Board Member of the Association for Advancement of Behavior Therapy, he is currently President-Elect of the newly formed Society for Studying Unity Issues in Psychology. A former Consulting Editor for the *Journal of Community Psychology* and *Professional Psychology: Research and Practice,* Dr. Fishman's books include *A Cost-Effectiveness Methodology for Community Mental Health Centers: Development and Pilot-Test,* and *Assessment for Decision* (with D.R. Peterson). He is presently working on a volume entitled *Work, Health, and Organizational Competitiveness: New Challenges for Psychology* (with C. Cherniss).

FREDERICK ROTGERS, Psy.D. (Rutgers University) is presently a psychologist with the Impaired Professionals Project of the Rutgers University Center of Alcohol Studies, a consultant at the Carrier Foundation in Belle Mead, New Jersey, and an adjunct faculty member of the Graduate School of Applied and Professional Psychology at Rutgers University. He also conducts an active private practice. An expert in forensic psychology, Dr. Rotgers spent over 10 years working in correctional institutions, first as Chief Psychologist in one of New Jersey's maximum security penitentiaries and then as Chief Psychologist of the New Jersey State Parole Board. Dr. Rotgers is also on the Editorial Board of the journal *Correctional Theory and Practice.* Dr. Rotgers' interests include the clinical application of social learning theory to addictive behavior, the philosophical foundations of behavior therapy, and the exploration of unity issues in psychology.

CYRIL M. FRANKS, Ph.D. (University of London Institute of Psychiatry) is a senior Professor of Psychology in the Graduate School of Applied and Professional Psychology at Rutgers University. He is co-founder and first President of the Association for Advancement of Behavior Therapy; founder and first Editor (1970–1979) of the journal *Behavior Therapy;* senior author of the series *Annual Review of Behavior Therapy;* and Editor of the Springer Series on Behavior Therapy and Behavioral Medicine. Professor Franks also holds a B.Sc. from the University of Wales and an M.A. from the University of Minnesota. In addition to being Editor of the journal *Child and Family Behavior Therapy* and Senior Associate Editor of the *Journal of Compliance in Health Care,* Professor Franks is the author of some 300 articles and book chapters and the editor of numerous books in his field. His earlier publications were primarily in the area of laboratory conditioning and personality variables in normal and abnormal subjects. His current interests pertain to the conceptual and theoretical foundations of behavior therapy and their historical determinants.

Paradigms in Behavior Therapy: Present and Promise

Daniel B. Fishman
Frederick Rotgers
Cyril M. Franks
Editors

SPRINGER PUBLISHING COMPANY
New York

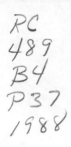

Springer Publishing Company, Inc.
536 Broadway
New York, NY 10012

88 89 90 91 92 / 5 4 3 2 1

Library of Congress Cataloging-in-Publication

Paradigms in behavior therapy.

(Behavior therapy and behavioral medicine series ;   19)
Includes bibliographies and index.
1. Behavior therapy. I. Fishman, Daniel B.
II. Rotgers, Frederick. III. Franks, Cyril M.
IV. Series: Springer series on behavior therapy and
behavioral medicine. [DNLM: 1. Behavior Therapy.
WM 425 P222]
RC489.B4P37   1988   616.89'142   87-32214
ISBN 0-8261-5130-2

Printed in the United States of America

Contents

**PART IV: Behavior Therapy Paradigms:
Integrationist Approaches**

PART V: Overview and Commentary

Contributors

Leonard Krasner, Ph.D. (Columbia University) is Clinical Professor of Psychiatry and Behavioral Sciences at Stanford University, and Professor Emeritus of Psychology at the State University of New York at Stony Brook. He has published books and papers, theoretical, historical, and clinical, on the origins of behavior therapy and behaviorism in America. Most recently (1987), he has authored (with A.P. Goldstein) a text on *Modern Applied Psychology*. He established at SUNY Stony Brook, in 1965, the first behaviorally oriented doctoral training program in clinical psychology. He has been and continues to be involved in a wide range of research in and applications of psychology, including behavior modification, environmental design, verbal conditioning, token economy, "abnormal" behavior, health behavior, and issues of values in science.

Hans J. Eysenck, Ph.D., D.Sc. (University of London) is Professor Emeritus of Psychology in the Institute of Psychiatry at the University of London (Maudsley Hospital). He is co-founder and first President of the International Society for the Study of Individual Differences; founder and first Editor (1964-1978) of the journal *Behaviour Research and Therapy;* founder and Editor of the journal *Personality and Individual Differences;* and founder and Co-editor with S. Rachman of *Advances in Behaviour Research and Therapy*. He is also Editor of the *International Series of Monographs in Experimental Psychology*. Author of some 900 articles and author or editor of over 40 books on psychology, his main interests are in personality and individual differences, intelligence, behavior genetics, behavior therapy, and the psychology of politics.

Howard Rachlin, Ph.D. (Harvard University) is Professor of Psychology at the State University of New York at Stony Brook. His research interests include the study of choice and self-control in people and animals. His theoretical interests include the development of an economic model of choice and the relation between studies of animal choice and studies of human decision. In addition to numerous articles and chapters, he is the author of *Introduction to Modern Behaviorism, Behavior and Learning,* and *Behaviorism in Everyday Life,* and of two books in press, *Judgment, Decision, and Choice: An Introduction* and *Behaviorism and Freedom.* He has been on the editorial board of several journals, such as the *Journal of the Experimental Analysis of Behavior* and the *Journal of Experimental Psychology: General,* and is one of the Co-editors of the annual series *Quantitative Analysis of Behavior.*

Edward Erwin, Ph.D. (The Johns Hopkins University) is Professor of Philosophy at the University of Miami. His published work is mainly in epistemology, philosophy of science, and philosophy of psychology. He is author of two books, *The Concept of Meaninglessness* and *Behavior Therapy: Scientific, Philosophical and Moral Foundations.* At its publication, the latter was described by David Barlow, then president of the Association for Advancement of Behavior Therapy, as perhaps "the most important book yet written on behavior therapy" for its critical analysis of the philosophical underpinnings of the field. Dr. Erwin's current interests include epistemological issues pertaining to behavior therapy and psychoanalysis.

Philip C. Kendall, Ph.D. (Virginia Commonwealth University) is Professor of Psychology and Head of the Division of Clinical Psychology at Temple University. He is also a Professor of Research in Psychiatry at Eastern Pennsylvania Psychiatric Institute of the Medical College of Pennsylvania. Dr. Kendall serves as Editor of the journal *Cognitive Therapy and Research* and the serial publication *Advances in Cognitive-Behavioral Research and Therapy,* and he serves on the editorial board of numerous professional journals (e.g., *Behavior Therapy* and *Journal of Consulting and Clinical Psychology*). The author of numerous research papers and monographs, Dr. Kendall has also co-authored *Clinical Psychology: Scientific and Professional Dimensions* (with J. Ford) and *Cognitive-Behavioral Therapy for Impulsive Children* (with L. Braswell). In addition, he is one of the co-editors of the *Annual Review of Behavior Therapy* (with Franks, Wilson, and Foreyt). Dr. Kendall's interests lie in cognitive-behavioral assessment and treatment, especially with children.

Steven F. Bacon, B.A., is a Ph.D. candidate in clinical psychology at the University of Minnesota and a research staff member of the Minnesota Twin Registry Project. His current interests include cognitive behavior therapy, behavioral medicine, psychophysiology, the psychology of pain, personality assessment, and computerized testing.

Robert L. Woolfolk, Ph.D. (University of Texas at Austin) is currently Professor of Psychology at Rutgers University. He has served on the faculties of Princeton University, the University of Texas at Austin, and the University of Medicine and Dentistry of New Jersey. The author of numerous scientific papers, monographs, and book chapters, he has conducted empirical research on psychological stress, skilled motor performance, and the effects of psychotherapy. His books include *Stress, Sanity, and Survival* and *Principles and Practice of Stress Management* (with P. Lehrer). He has also written on the philosophical and sociocultural foundations of psychology and psychotherapy. This work has appeared in such journals as *American Psychologist, Behaviorism,* and *Journal of the American Psychoanalytic Association.*

Arthur Staats, Ph.D. (University of California at Los Angeles) is Professor of Psychology at the University of Hawaii at Manoa. Author of many journal articles, book chapters, and books, he is on the editorial board of a number of journals. Co-founder, first President, and Newsletter Editor of the Society for Studying Unity Issues in Psychology, for over 30 years he has focused on constructing a comprehensive, unified theory for psychology; on conducting research at selected places in the various fields included in his theory; and on formulating an indigenous methodology and philosophy of psychology, as a foundation for making psychology into a unified, advanced science. His latest three books are *Child Learning, Intelligence, and Personality; Social Behaviorism;* and *Psychology's Crisis of Disunity: Philosophy and Method for a Unified Science.*

Gary E. Schwartz, Ph.D. (Harvard University) is Professor of Psychology and Psychiatry at Yale University and Director of the Yale Psychophysiology Center. He has published extensively in the areas of biofeedback and self-regulation, psychophysiology of emotion, and stress and, most recently, in research linking defensive coping styles and cerebral laterality with physiological disregulation and disease. He is on the editorial boards of *Health Psychology* and *Biological Psychology,* and he is past President of the Biofeedback Society of America and the Health Psychology Division of the American Psychological Association. Recent edited books include *Consciousness and Self-Regulation: Advances in Research, Volume IV* (with Davidson and Shapiro), and *Placebo Theory, Research and Mechanisms* (with White and Tursky).

To Claire, Jo, and Violet

I

Introduction

1

Setting the Scene

Daniel B. Fishman
Frederick Rotgers
Cyril M. Franks

In essence, behavior therapy involves the direct or indirect application of learning theory and related experimentally derived principles to change a wide variety of undesirable or maladaptive behaviors at individual, group, organizational, and community levels. In recent years, much work has been done on the technology and theory of circumscribed elements within behavior therapy. However, little has been written about the philosophical and conceptual foundations of behavior therapy and their relevance for either theory or practice.

Even a superficial review of the field reveals a wide and, at times, conflicting diversity of positions and assumptions concerning such focal issues as the role of mental concepts and cognitive variables in behavior therapy, the extent to which behavior therapy techniques should and could be directly tied to laboratory-based theoretical principles of learning, and the extent to which behavior therapy should be integrated within the more general areas of psychology and psychotherapy practice.

One of the very few major works on the philosophy of behavior therapy and related conceptual matters to appear to date is Erwin's (1978) *Behavior Therapy: Scientific, Philosophical, and Moral Foundations*. Erwin, it might be noted, is a philosopher by training and identification, not a psychologist. To collate and possibly update recent developments in this area, one of us (Franks) organized a symposium at the 1983 combined meeting of the Second World Congress on Behavior Therapy and the annual convention of the Association for Advancement of Behavior Therapy. This symposium was titled, "The Paradig-

matic Status of Behavior Therapy: Grand Illusion or Today's Reality?"
The participants and their respective topics were: Cyril Franks, "Paradigms, Pre-paradigms, and Paradigm Shifts"; Leonard Krasner,
"Paradigms Lost"; Arthur Staats, "Pre-Paradigms within Pre-Paradigms"; Hans Eysenck, "Paradigms in Behavior Therapy"; Irene Martin and A.B. Levey, "Two Paradigms in Search of Authority"; and
Edward Erwin, discussant.

The present book, a direct outcome of that symposium, has two
general purposes: to articulate the basic assumptions underlying modern behavior therapy within a philosophy-of-science context, and to
sample and compare the views of systematically selected, prominent,
exemplar behavior theorists with regard to the status of behavior
therapy on various dimensions of the concept "paradigm." To accomplish these aims, the book is divided into five major sections: Part I,
Introduction; Part II, Behavior Therapy Paradigms: Conditioning
Models; Part III, Behavior Therapy Paradigms: The Cognitive Revolution; Part IV, Behavior Therapy Paradigms: Integrationist Approaches; and Part V, Overview and Commentary. Part I starts with
the present chapter, which introduces the reader to the major issues
involved, explains how they arose, and sets the scene for what is to
follow. In Chapter 2, we raise and explore the implication of a variety
of paradigmatic questions and issues of importance for behavior therapy. These are grouped around three major perspectives: (1) the concept of a "scientific paradigm" as set forth by Kuhn in his landmark
book, *The Structure of Scientific Revolutions* (1970); (2) the epistemological, theoretical, technological, ethical, and sociological-political-
historical arenas, or dimensions, of a scientific paradigm; and (3) the
contrast between those paradigms that presently exist in the field and
those paradigms that could, realistically or otherwise, come into being
in the near future.

In Parts II–IV a prominent group of behavior therapists who have
given much thought to these matters respond to the fundamental
questions and issues articulated in Chapter 2. These individuals were
selected on the basis of their demonstrated interest in and contributions to the study of fundamental issues in behavior therapy. Thus,
Erwin and Woolfolk were selected for their work in epistemology. Another group were selected for their particular theoretical approaches:
applied behavior analysis (Rachlin); neobehaviorism (Eysenck); social-
learning theory (Rotgers); cognitive behavior therapy (Kendall and
Bacon); general-systems theory (Schwartz); and "social behaviorism,"
now called "paradigmatic behaviorism" (Staats). Fishman was chosen
for his work in the area of behavioral technology, and Krasner, for his

knowledgeable political, historical, and sociocultural contributions over the years.

Each author was given considerable leeway to decide which issues were most important for him and which deserved the most attention. In reviewing the final manuscripts, it became clear that the chapters could be grouped into three sections. These roughly follow the historical development of behavior therapy, beginning with a focus on conditioning, followed by a turn toward cognition, and then proceeding to contemporary concerns about consolidation and integration. In addition, there is a sequential theme within each section. Part II, "Conditioning Models," is organized historically. Krasner describes the ground-breaking paradigmatic behavior therapy model of the post-World War II years—a model that emphasized "outer" concerns, such as overt behavior, environmental contingencies, and social change, as opposed to the traditional model in clinical psychology at that time, with its emphasis upon such "inner" concerns as personality, traits, mind, disease, and pathology. Eysenck presents his neobehaviorist, classical conditioning model. Then Rachlin offers a perspective based on one of the most recent and striking developments in operant-conditioning theory, that of molar behaviorism.

Part III, "The Cognitive Revolution," is organized in terms of the degree of "conservatism" in the authors' approach to the introduction of cognitive concepts into behavior therapy. Erwin, the most conservative, argues that while, or perhaps because, cognitive approaches are possibly efficacious, these approaches should be investigated through rigorous scientific methods. Kendall and Bacon's more middle-of-the-road cognitivism emphasizes the role that cognitive factors play in the scientist's efforts to understand the world and the importance of cognitive factors as causal agents in the genesis of emotional and behavioral disturbances. Woolfolk, the most "liberal," advocates extending present-day cognitive behavior therapy to consider such inferential and phenomenological concepts as "identity," "self," "freedom," and "the lived experience."

Part IV, "Integrationist Approaches," is organized by the scope of the authors' integrationist perspective. Rotgers, with the most focused scope, concentrates on Bandura's social-learning theory and its attempt to integrate conditioning and cognitive theories within the domains of traditional behavior therapy. Staat's integration is more broad—no less than the linking of the conditioning and cognitive models of behavior therapy with the concepts and methods of general psychology in such areas as neuropsychology, intelligence, personality theory and measurement, child development, and group process. Fishman reconsiders behavior therapy's traditional epistemology of positivism and replaces it with social constructionism. In contrast to the more usual identification of social constructionism with a hermeneutic, qualitative approach to psychology, Fishman's technologically focused version of social constructionism retains what he argues are the basic characteristics of behavior therapy, such as quantification, empiricism, functional analysis, and analysis of complex problems into smaller and simpler parts. Lastly, Schwartz presents the broadest integrative perspective of all, proposing that behavior theory and practice be viewed as a subclass of general-systems theory. Schwartz describes the systems approach in the widest possible terms as a "metatheory," a cognitive framework for viewing the whole of nature rather than just as a discipline-specific theory per se.

Finally, in Part V, we attempt to place these various positions in perspective. The positions are first compared and contrasted in terms of the question and issues raised in Part I. From this review, two main conclusions are reached: first, that while there are some dominant, overarching themes and sources of identity within the general field of behavior therapy today, there is, in fact, a wide diversity of paradigmatic assumptions and positions; and second, that each of these positions presents a particular combination of gains and tradeoffs. To provide a more rational manner for making decisions about paradigmatic issues, we develop an analogy between a geographic region and the domain of paradigmatic positions. Just as a conventional roadmap helps guide an individual to a particular physical place, so a conceptual roadmap can help an individual route himself or herself to a particular conceptual position. Along the way, the roadmap presents certain choicepoints. One purpose of a conceptual roadmap is to inform the reader as to where the conceptual choicepoints are and what the possible conceptual consequences might be of taking one path rather than another.

Overall, then, the goal of this book is not to advocate for the advantages of one paradigm over another. Rather, our aim is to present descriptions of and rationales for the various paradigms and to articulate the strengths and weaknesses of each of them.

References

Erwin, E. (1978). *Behavior therapy: Scientific, philosophical, and moral foundations.* New York: Cambridge University Press.

Kuhn, T.S. (1970). *The structure of scientific revolutions* (2nd ed.). Chicago: University of Chicago Press.

2

Paradigms in Wonderland: Fundamental Issues in Behavior Therapy

Daniel B. Fishman
Frederick Rotgers
Cyril M. Franks

> "When I use a word," Humpty Dumpty said, in a rather scornful tone, "it means just what I choose it to mean—neither more nor less."
> "The question is," said Alice, "whether you *can* make words mean so many different things."
> "The question is," said Humpty Dumpty, "which is to be master—that's all."
> LEWIS CARROLL, *Through the Looking Glass*
> (Gardner, 1960)

In theoretical terms, behavior therapy may be viewed as an approach to the understanding of behavior and behavior change that relies upon the methodology of behavioral science within a learning-theory or other appropriate experimental psychology framework. Contemporary behavior therapists tend to define *behavior* broadly to include both overt actions and observable manifestations of more covert affective and cognitively mediated processes. These processes may occur at several levels: psychophysiological, individual, small group, organizational, and community. In practical terms, behavior therapy may be conceptualized as the data-based application of this theoretical approach to generate a technology whose primary goal is cost-effective, constructive behavior change. By constructive, we mean behavior change that is desired by all concerned and considered ethical. From either point of view, theory or practice, a number of basic paradigmatic issues must be addressed by behavior therapists if behavior therapy is to retain its originally envisioned position as a conceptual and scientific advance rather than as simply another therapeutic innovation.

In a general sense, the various concepts of "paradigm," as developed by Kuhn (1962) and others, revolve around the body of explicit and implicit assumptions to which a discipline adheres in its conduct. Many psychologists and observers of psychology (e.g., Kimble, 1984; Koch, 1981; Krasner & Houts, 1984; Staats, 1983) have attempted to delineate and explore the philosophical assumptions underlining various aspects of psychological practice. Prompted by concern about the adequacy of psychological activity *qua* science (e.g., Gergen, 1982; Toulmin, 1972), many psychologists have begun to question the empiricist and logical-positivist underpinnings of experimental psychology. Behavior therapy is not immune to this process of philosophical soul-searching. As Erwin (1978) points out, it is a prime example of the application of logical-positivist–empiricist philosophy to the social sciences.

In analyzing the scope of paradigm-related questions in behavior therapy, we have found it conceptually useful to distinguish three dimensions: (1) the *concept of paradigm* developed by Kuhn; (2) the different behavior therapy *arenas* in which paradigmatic issues emerge and are played out; and (3) the dimension of present versus future *time.* These three dimensions are outlined in Figure 2-1 and described in detail below. The dimensions create a 4 × 5 × 2 matrix with, at least in theory, 40 possible contexts in which the nature of paradigms in behavior therapy might be discussed. While such discussions cannot, of course, be neatly pigeonholed into one or even a few of the matrix cells, Figure 2-1 is helpful in orienting the reader to the multi-dimensional contexts of paradigm discussions.

In selecting contributors to this book, we chose individuals with particular expertise in one of the paradigmatic arenas outlined in Figure 2-1: Erwin and Woolfolk, in the epistemological arena; Eysenck, Rachlin, Kendall and Bacon, Rotgers, Staats, and Schwartz, in the scientific/theoretical arena; Fishman, in the technological arena; and Krasner, in the sociological/political/historical arena; all were asked to address the ethical arena. Each author was invited to address the same set of questions from his distinctive perspective, a design predicated on the belief that a comparative analysis of multiple perspectives would yield new insights and thereby help clarify issues that could easily become obscured by single-perspective reviews.

Following the outline in Figure 2-1, the purpose of this chapter is to lay out the core paradigmatic issues to be addressed. We will discuss

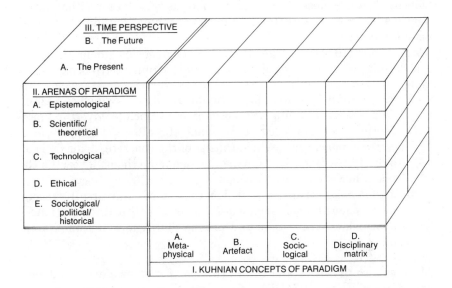

FIGURE 2.1 Three dimensions of paradigms in behavior therapy.
The three dimensions create a 4 × 5 × 2 matrix, which suggests at least 40 possible contexts in which the nature of paradigms in behavior therapy might be discussed. While of course such discussions cannot typically be pigeonholed into one or even a few of the matrix cells, the figure is designed to be helpful in orienting an author and reader to the multiply dimensioned contexts of paradigm discussions.

each dimension in turn, beginning with the various concepts of paradigm, proceeding through consideration of the arenas, and concluding with the time perspective. Our discussion, focused on what we see as the basic dilemmas or questions associated with each dimension, serves as an initial guide to some of the fundamental issues with which behavior therapy must eventually come to grips.

Kuhnian Concepts of ''Paradigm''

The broad concept of "paradigm" in scientific disciplines has been popularized by Kuhn in the *Structure of Scientific Revolutions* (Kuhn, 1970; Pollie, 1983). Unfortunately, Kuhn used the term paradigm in diverse and often vague senses, as he himself later acknowledged. Furthermore, he confined his discussion of paradigms to the natural sciences. Nevertheless, it is Kuhn's notions of paradigm that have spearheaded critical scrutiny of the philosophical foundation of the social sciences.

Masterman (1974) identifies three broad categories among the multiple definitions and senses of "paradigm" in Kuhn's 1970 book:

1. *Metaphysical paradigms,* or "metaparadigms," which consist of "a new way of seeing," "an organizing principle governing perception itself," or a cognitive "map" of reality.
2. *Artefact paradigms,* which consist of the concrete, basic tools of a discipline, such as its instruments and methods, its textbooks and other exemplary writings.
3. *Sociological paradigms,* which consist of "universally recognized scientific achievements," "a set of political institutions," or legislation and judicial decisions that help to define a discipline.

In response to critics and in the service of greater clarity and systematization, Kuhn (1974) developed a fourth sense of paradigm:

4. *Paradigm as a disciplinary structure.* Catalano (1979) concisely describes this fourth way of looking at "paradigm":

Kuhn insisted that a paradigm could not be separated from the people who used it. So, while the concept had an abstract sense, . . . it also had a sociological sense which reflected a discipline's need for communication, organization, and perpetuation through teaching students. To capture both the abstract and sociological senses, Kuhn suggested that a paradigm be conceptualized as consisting of four elements. The first of these is the *basic assumptions* about the discipline's subject, . . . usually in the form of general laws. . . . The second paradigm element is the *analogies* the discipline uses to clarify its basic assumptions. . . . The third element of a paradigm is the *conventions* its adherents adopt to facilitate experimentation and communication. These conventions include epistemology (e.g., empirical vs. intuitive), descriptive mode (e.g., qualitative vs. quantitative), research setting (e.g., naturalistic vs. laboratory), and unit of analysis (e.g., individual or group). . . . The fourth element of Kuhn's paradigm is *exemplars,* . . . the classic works of a discipline." (pp. 8–9)

In analyzing the history of the natural sciences, Kuhn (1962) contended that knowledge does not always accumulate in a gradual, step-by-step fashion. Rather, progress often takes place through sudden and fundamental shifts in the very foundations of the science's theory and methods. Examples of these shifts are such frequently cited scientific "revolutions" as Copernican astronomy and Einsteinian physics.

From his historical analyses, Kuhn developed a new, four-stage, cyclical theory of knowledge progression in a scientific field. The first is called the "pre-normal" or "pre-paradigmatic" stage. It exists when individuals or small groups of researchers pursue knowledge of the same phenomenon in an independent manner, without communicating among themselves. Since they do not communicate, each typically uses different terms, measures, and theories. This lack of coordination tends greatly to slow the development of the field.

The second stage, called "normal science" or "paradigmatic science," takes place when a group of researchers mutually decide to work cooperatively with one another, using a single framework or paradigm with common terms, methods, theories, and criteria for deciding what are the "relevant problems" to be studied. This mutuality of interests and practices defines a discipline. Continuation of the discipline over time takes place by training students to continue to work within it. Working with existing knowledge within the framework of the paradigm, researchers attempt to solve the next logical problem growing from the last found solution. Since this process is similar to puzzle solving, the second stage is sometimes characterized as the "normal puzzle solving" stage.

The normal stage gives way to a third, "crisis" stage, when new observational methods and research designs yield "anomalous" data, that is, data that cannot be explained by the paradigm of the second stage. During this stage, the discipline searches for a new paradigm that will better encompass existing data.

When the crisis of the third stage is resolved by the adoption of a new paradigm, the fourth "revolution" stage has begun. Thus, the movement to the fourth stage involves a "paradigm shift" from the second stage. This shift leads to a new stage of normal science, and the cycle begins again.

Kuhn's work remains controversial, both in its substance and in his style of writing and presentation (e.g., Lakatos & Musgrave, 1970). However, all critics agree that he has developed important new concepts, such as the distinction between "pre-paradigmatic" and "paradigmatic" science. His theory raises important questions for behavior therapy theorists to address. In the context of this book, the following types of questions are of particular interest:

1. In the past, has behavior therapy ever been a paradigm in Kuhn's sense of the word?
2. Is behavior therapy a paradigm today?

3. Was the "cognitive revolution" in behavior therapy a "paradigm shift"?
4. How useful are Kuhn's theory and concepts in assessing the present status and future direction of behavior therapy?

Arenas of Paradigm

Within the context of the above, behavior therapy involves the adoption of a particular *epistemology* to generate *scientific theories* of behavior, which, in turn, are used to develop and apply *technology,* whose primary goal is cost-effective, constructive, *ethical* behavior change. As the discipline has evolved, a *community of individuals*—behavior therapists—has been created with particular sets of knowledge, skills, attitudes, values, and interests. Viewed in this way, there are at least five arenas in which behavior therapy must address paradigmatic issues either explicitly or implicitly: (1) the epistemological arena, (2) the scientific and theoretical arena, (3) the technological arena, (4) the ethical arena, and (5) the political, sociological, and historical arena. Each of these will be addressed in turn.

The Epistemological Arena

Epistemology is the branch of philosophy that investigates the origin, nature, methods, and limits of human knowledge. An epistemological theory sets forth the criteria according to which the relevance and validity of a particular body of knowledge are judged. In other words, no knowledge is simply *given* in an absolute sense. To illustrate this, consider the epistemological theory of solipsism, which asserts that only the individual self of the knower can be proven to exist—the existence of all other potential realities is questionable. From the perspective of solipsism, the vast majority of the world's cumulative knowledge about the external "real world" is valid only to the extent that it corresponds to the individual's personal belief system.

The bottom line in epistemology is that there is no *à priori* criterion for judging the truth value of statement X. There is a wide variety of possible, coherent epistemological systems that have been set forth—one of them being logical positivism—and the evaluator of statement X's truth value can choose among these systems. To a substantial extent, the truth or falsity of statement X will depend upon the system chosen rather than the content of the statement itself (Messer & Winokur, 1984). In the end, it is an individual's or group's ability to persuade others of the merit of adopting its epistemological system that will determine whether those others will accept the system (Bartley, 1962; Gergen, 1982). For example, imagine a contemporary behavior therapist being transported to fifth-century Italy and trying to "sell" an empiricist epistemology to a scholastic scholar as the best means of determining a statement's truth!

In a similar vein, Woolfolk and Richardson (1984) comment on the relativity of epistemological criteria, including those of the natural sciences:

> Behavior therapy [is] . . . conceived of as a [value] neutral structure, a body of "objective" knowledge, verified by experimental test. . . . Recent work in the philosophy and history of science, however, has undermined seriously the view of science on which behavior therapy's self-image is based. Attempts to equate scientific knowledge with that which is empirically verifiable or to identify scientific progress with some inflexible standard of verification have proven lacking. (p. 777)

Since it is true that logical positivism, the main underlying epistemology of behavior therapy, is only one of many epistemological systems and that many today are questioning whether it is the best one either philosophically or practically, we must be much more clear about the epistemological options open to the behavior therapist and the rationale for choosing among them. This leads to an examination of epistemological options typically confronting a psychologist. These are set forth, in part, in recent articles in the *American Psychologist* by Kimble (1984) and Krasner and Houts (1984). For example, the epistemological options these authors identify include: determinism vs. indeterminism; objectivism vs. intuitionism; nomothetic vs. idiographic laws; elementism vs. holism; factual vs. theoretical orientation; behavioral vs. experimental content emphasis; biological vs. environmental determinism; and quantitative vs. qualitative orientation.

Within the context of this *zeitgeist* of epistemological debate and uncertainty, the following types of questions are raised with regard to behavior therapy:

1. What model of epistemology best meets the needs of contemporary behavior therapy? Some version of logical positivism, such as Popper's falsificationism or Hempel's model? Alternatives to logical positivism, such as Harre and Secord's realism or Feyerabend's proliferationism? Or perhaps a neorationalist model, such as Gergen's sociorationalism or the more hermeneutic approaches of Ricoeur or Gadamer?
2. Is there one "best" epistemological approach for behavior therapy? Or is some combination of approaches or some type of

alternating among approaches more meaningful and useful?

The Scientific/Theoretical Arena

An important set of issues in this arena is raised by Erwin (1978), who concludes:

> Learning theories do not constitute an adequate foundation for behavior therapy. . . . [Then what does?] The position taken here is that there is no known theory or law of any kind that is of sufficient scope to serve as a foundation and that has also been empirically confirmed. We cannot even be certain that such a theory or law will ever be developed. . . . Well, it just might happen that, try as we may, we will never be able to formulate relatively simple general laws of human behavior. (p. 127)

A related and very striking quote is found in Koch (1959):

> Consider the hundreds of theoretical formulations, rational equations, and mathematical models of the learning process that have accrued; the thousands of research studies. And *now* consider that there is still no wide agreement, even at the crassest descriptive level, on the empirical conditions under which learning takes place. (p. 731)

Koch expressed this view in 1959, a time at which behavior therapy started to develop and grow, supposedly on the rock-solid base of scientific knowledge about human learning!

One of us (DBF) had a similar experience as a graduate student in the early 1960s. After studying the various learning theories from Hilgard's (1956) classic textbook and from original source readings—including Tolman, Guthrie, Hull, Skinner, and Pavlov—he had a personal reaction that learning theory, as exemplified in these writings, was a new medieval scholasticism. He had a hard time seeing how these theories might be clinically and practically germane to the pressing needs of the day.

All this suggests that political and sociological reasons for the development of behavior therapy may be of more relevance than the view that behavior therapy is a predictable, direct, logical outgrowth of learning theory. In addition, this raises the issue of what is and should be the scientific and theoretical base of behavior therapy.

Another set of questions is raised in Barlow, Hayes, and Nelson's (1984) *The Scientist Practitioner.* These authors review the clinical literature and conclude that not only do practitioners (both behavioral and nonbehavioral) not perform research, they do not even consume it! Barlow et al. further conclude that "research has little influence on practice" (p. 31). Where, then, do practitioners get their techniques? From "intuitive eclecticism" (p. 35).

What implications do these findings have for the theoretical bases of behavior therapy? If behavior therapy is not tied to behavioral research, then the logical interconnectedness of the "discipline" of behavior therapy as defined earlier would seem to break down. Related issues also emerge. In light of the problems in linking theory with practice, what is the proper form of theory for it to influence practice? Is such an influence possible and, if so, is it practical?

In the above context, the following types of questions seem particularly important:

1. What is the theoretical basis of behavior therapy?
2. How do behavior therapists derive techniques?
3. What theoretical framework can best meet the needs of behavior therapy?
4. Can a single framework accomplish all of this and, at the same time, succeed in both stimulating and guiding practice?

The Technological Arena

As Fishman and Neigher (1982) describe, science (basic research) can be differentiated from technology (applied research) in a variety of ways. For example, basic research tends to involve individualistic researchers who employ controlled, laboratory-like conditions to derive general laws and theories about human behavior. In contrast, technological research tends to involve mission-oriented groups of investigators who employ real-world, field conditions to derive particular, decision-focused, or managerial knowledge about specific behavioral problems.

Behavior therapy combines both the scientific and technological perspectives. Which of these one employs in practice influences the nature of the knowledge one seeks and the means by which it is sought. This differentiation between science and technology poses clear questions for behavior therapy as a technology:

1. What evaluative criteria should behavior therapists adopt to determine the cost-efficiency and effectiveness of their technique?
2. What is the documented cost-efficiency and effectiveness of current procedures?
3. What are ideal forms for the linkages between the theory of behavior therapy and the strategies for technological implementation?
4. What are the gaps that exist between theory and practice in

behavior therapy, and how can they be bridged more effectively?
5. What are or what should be the links among epistemology,
theory, and practice to effect an ideal behavioral technology?

The Ethical Arena

Gergen (1982) argues convincingly that the epistemological position
held in theory inevitably influences the value judgments made in
practice. Although one of the tenets of a logical-positivist approach to
science is that scientific activity is value-free, hence objective, it seems
fair to say that most behavior therapists would affirm that values
form an important part of clinical practice. Woolfolk and Richardson
(1984) argue that behavior therapy cannot be separated from the times
in which it is practiced and that, in fact, behavior therapy as practiced
has committed itself to certain values that seem typical of twentieth-
century modernism, such as individual freedom, self-development,
self-determination, social tolerance, social equality, collaborative rationality for solving interpersonal conflict, and belief in the essential
goodness of human nature and its capacity for positive change.

The issues surrounding questions of values and ethics in behavior
therapy are extraordinarily complex, so much so that, in the interest
of focusing this book, we limited the emphasis placed in the guidelines
to our contributors with respect to this arena. However, the issues in
this arena are some of the most socially relevant and important ones
that ultimately face behavior therapists (e.g., issues surrounding the
model-of-a-person that is implicit in behavior therapy). Also, ethical
issues intertwine substantially with positions taken in the other arenas we have outlined. Therefore, as space permitted, we encouraged
all contributors to address ethical issues. Possible questions to be
considered include:

1. What is the *actual* role of ethical values in contemporary paradigms of behavior therapy?
2. How does this compare with what *should* be the role of ethics in
   behavior therapy paradigms?
3. How are ethical issues related to those in the other paradigmatic arenas—epistemological, scientific/theoretical, technological, and sociological/political/historical?

The Sociological/Political/Historical Arena

Behavior therapists consist of a community of individuals with special knowledge, skills, attitudes, and values. This entity can be conceptualized in a variety of ways. For example, as described earlier, Kuhn introduced the concept for "normal science" to describe the activities of a discipline during periods of stable paradigm. This activity is devoted largely to solving mundane puzzles within the paradigm and to maintaining the paradigm itself. Assuming that behavior therapy is in a period of "normal science," the following types of questions become important:

1. What are the special attitudes that behavior therapy has to contribute both to its own maintenance (assuming this is desirable) and to society at large?
2. What are the determinants of behavior therapy's continuation as a politically viable, internally coherent force?
3. Is behavior therapy's continued political viability and visibility good? Why or why not?
4. Is behavior therapy in some form or another likely to continue?
5. What are the factors associated with behavior therapy's "political success" and acceptance by the public and by service decision makers?
6. How adequate is Kuhn's model for behavior therapy as a political entity? What other approaches to this arena might you suggest?
7. What effects do the contemporary social and political climates in society at large have on behavior therapy? For example, how do patterns of funding or political emphasis on "hot" social problems influence the practice of behavior therapy?

Assuming, instead, that behavior therapy is in a period of "paradigm shift," as opposed to "normal science," the following types of questions become important:

8. What is the nature of this shift?
9. What are the political and social implications of this state of affairs for the field?

The Time Perspective and Implications for Action

The questions posed about paradigms in behavior therapy can be viewed from three general time perspectives: past, present, and future. In this book, focus is placed upon the latter two. Thus the various contributors consider the paradigmatic issues outlined above in terms of the structure and process of behavior therapy as it presently *is*, how it *should be* in the future, and how it is *likely to be* in the future. Therefore, in the context of this book, the following sorts of questions emerge in the domain of time perspective:

1. What is the present paradigmatic status of behavior therapy?
2. What should be the future course of behavior therapy?
3. What steps are needed to facilitate these desired directions of development?
4. How likely is it that this ideal will actually obtain? If it is unlikely, what is likely to occur?

Summary

Behavior therapy as a paradigm can be viewed from at least three different perspectives: Kuhn's concept of paradigm; the various arenas of a paradigm, including the epistemological, scientific/theoretical, technological, ethical, and sociological/political/historical; and the viewpoint of present versus future time.

The interelationships among these three perspectives are probably as relevant as their individual components. For convenience, we break our questions into discrete areas. Nevertheless, we recognize that the decisions and assumptions made in each area have profound influences on how the issues are viewed in other areas. For all contributors the task was twofold: (1) to articulate their positions with respect to the specific parameters of the paradigm concept as outlined above; and (2) to consider the interrelationships among these seemingly disparate areas and the implications of these relationships for behavior therapy.

References

Barlow, D.H., Hayes, S.C., & Nelson, R.O. (1984). *The scientist practitioner: Research and accountability in clinical and educational settings.* Elmsford, NY: Pergamon.

Bartley, W.W., III. (1962). *The retreat to commitment.* New York: Knopf.

Catalano, R. (1979). *Health, behavior, and the community; An ecological perspective.* Elmsford, NY: Pergamon.

Erwin, E. (1978). *Behavior therapy: Scientific, philosophical, and moral foundations.* New York: Cambridge University Press.

Fishman, D.B., & Neigher, W.D. (1982). Psychology in the eighties: Who will buy? *American Psychologist, 37,* 533–546.

Gardner, M. (1960). *The annotated Alice.* New York: Forum.

Gergen, K.J. (1982). *Toward transformation in social knowledge.* New York: Springer-Verlag.

Hilgard, E.R. (1956). *Theories of learning.* New York: Appleton-Century-Crofts.

Kimble, G.A. (1984). Psychology's two cultures. *American Psychologist, 39,* 833–839.

Koch, S. (1959). Epilogue. In S. Koch (Ed.), *Psychology: A study of a science (Vol. III).* (pp. 729–788). New York: McGraw-Hill.

Koch, S. (1981). The nature and limits of psychological knowledge. *American Psychologist, 36,* 257–269.

Krasner, L., & Houts, A.C. (1984). A study of the "value" systems of behavioral scientists. *American Psychologist, 39,* 840–850.

Kuhn, T.S. (1970). *The structure of scientific revolutions* (2nd ed.). Chicago: University of Chicago Press.

Kuhn, T.S. (1974). Reflections on my critics. In I. Lakatos & A. Musgrave (Eds.), *Criticism and the growth of knowledge* (pp. 231-278). New York: Cambridge University Press.

Lakatos, I., & Musgrave, A. (1974). *Criticism and the growth of knowledge.* New York: Cambridge University Press.

Masterman, M. (1974). The nature of a paradigm. In I. Lakatos & A. Musgrave (Eds.), *Criticism and the growth of knowledge* (pp. 59–89). New York: Cambridge University Press.

Messer, S.B., & Winokur, M. (1984). Ways of knowing and visions of reality. In H. Arkowitz & S.B. Messer (Eds.), *Psychoanalytic therapy and behavior therapy: Is integration possible?* (pp. 63–100). New York: Plenum.

Pollie, R. (1983). Brother, can you paradigm? *Science 83, 4,* 76–77.

Staats, A.W. (1983). *Psychology's crisis of disunity: Philosophy and method for a unified science.* New York: Praeger.

Toulmin, S. (1972). *Human understanding (Vol. I).* Princeton, NJ: Princeton University Press.

Woolfolk, R.L., & Richardson, F.C. (1984). Behavior therapy and the ideology of modernity. *American Psychologist, 39,* 777–786.

II

Behavior Therapy Paradigms: Conditioning Models

3

Paradigm Lost: On a Historical/Sociological/ Economic Perspective

Leonard Krasner

Prologue

In the beginning, in a very ancient time called the sixties, there was created a new Paradigm among those who were ordained by the Lord to heal psyches and It was called Behavior Therapy, and about a dozen of the ordained came together from many parts of the land and said, "Let us organize and advance our Paradigm, for it is indeed new, and we shall change behavior and create a better society. There are many in the land who are our Antagonists who have another Paradigm and would destroy us, so let us go forth and spread our Paradigm because Ours is the Truth. When one holds a Paradigm, it is a sacred trust and our new Paradigm requires us to do very different things than they do in order to heal and bring about change."

And so the ordained formed this new cult for the Advancement of Behavior Therapy and it grew and grew and spread throughout the land and prospered. And some said, "Let us trade with the other Paradigm," and some said, "Let us combine with the other Paradigm." And, lo and behold, what soon occurred was that the Antagonists had infiltrated and taken over, and there was sadness in the land for suddenly the ancient Paradigm had indeed been lost and was no more.

On Being a Participant-Observer

Can a view of behavior therapy in a paradigmatic context be written objectively by a participant-observer in some of the events? Put in terms of a model that defies "objectivity," the answer is clearly "no." However, my view is that placing material in broad social/historical contexts is not an objective restoration of *fact* but is affected by and is a function of the current influences on the writer, his or her biases/ values, and the broader society in which the writer functions. It is necessary for an author to identify and specify his or her theoretical views and goals, particularly in a volume on paradigms. The aim of an evaluation of the past is to understand the present so that we may be guided in our decisions affecting future behavior. The examination of a "scientific" movement such as behavior therapy is itself subject to the influences on and biases of the investigator (Krasner, 1971, 1978; Mitroff, 1974). I confess, a little sadly and a little proudly, that I have been a *participant-observer* in the development of the post–World War II behavior therapy movement, as per the prologue, and whatever bias that has been generated must be taken into consideration in evaluating the remainder of this chapter.

Before we even touch upon developments in behavior therapy, we must expand this theme of participant-observation to a broader level, since it is very much related to my views on the process of invention/ creation that takes place in the evolution of paradigms.

To understand the social/historical context of behavior therapy, we must describe views about the writing of history itself, the field of historiography, an important element of which is a belief held by many psychologists and by some historians. It is sharply expressed by the philosopher Popper (1950):

> . . . all scientific descriptions of fact are highly selective, in that they always depend upon theories . . . a scientific description will depend, largely, upon our point of view, our interests which are as a rule connected with the theory or hypothesis we wish to test; although it will also depend upon the facts described. Indeed, the theory or hypotheses could be described as the crystallization of a point of view . . . in history no less than in science, we cannot avoid a point of view; and the belief that we can must lead to self-deception and to lack of critical care. . . . History has no meaning . . *although history has no meaning, we can give it a meaning.* (pp. 444–461)

This point of view, as it involves the history of psychology, has been expressed by Marx (1977), a professor of psychiatry and sociomedical science who offers, in his review of the history of psychology in the last decade, a set of biases about approaches to the writing of history with which I am in close agreement:

I view history as a creative projective enterprise. . . . I view history as interaction between the historian and the past . . . there are no permanent solutions, only tentative constructs . . . there are lasting ethical values. . . . I think that in history, as in psychology . . . we need to reintroduce the doer into the doing. In order to discuss history of psychology, we have to ask about historians of psychology . . . the historian of psychology is not a passive observer or collector, but a very active participant in the creation of the history of his discipline. . . . I believe that historians of psychology will have to come to grips with their aims, purpose and ideology. The myth of disinterested science or of objective social science is no longer tenable. (pp. 41–47)

In terms of putting material into perspective, the historian Halle (1977) offers a similar concept. His argument is that in relatively short historical periods it may be that chance, accident, and the uncertainty principle may apply, but that in longer perspectives, the broader principles of evolutionary selectivity would apply. In the era of the development of behavior therapy, which is so recent and, in cosmic terms, so brief, it is likely that *chance* happenings (e.g., Reyna spending a leave in South Africa and carrying the virus of Hull, which was caught by Wolpe and developed into "reciprocal inhibition") may well be an important factor in understanding this period.

In effect, we are dealing with the behavior of individuals. Writers of all sorts tend to reify metaphors and to write about or talk of or conceptualize "psychology" or "behavior therapy" as if they were entities. "Psychology" does not speak, but Skinner or Watson or Dewey or Freud speak or write, and sometimes they sound as if they indeed speak for "psychology."

Thus we emphasize the behavior of those creating behavior therapy and those reacting to the creations. My view posits a process of continuous creation as the core of behavioral science. Talented, brilliant, and creative individuals are continually inventing new ideas, models, hypotheses, experiments, ways of observing and conceptualizing human behavior. The act of observing is also the act of influencing and participating. We are all participant-observers.

Even the writing of a history of behavior therapy (Kazdin, 1978) is an act that influences development and interpretation of the field.

On Paradigms

In this chapter we explore the historical development of those two pervasive terms, *behavior therapy* and *paradigm*. My view, succinctly stated, is that, when put into the social/historical/political/economic context both of American society and of the "mental health" professions, the approach to and concept of human behavior eventually labeled as behavior therapy did indeed represent an alternative paradigm at its inception. And to a large extent, because of influencing events within both society and the profession, that paradigmatic model has changed, developed, and merged with the model to which it was originally proposed as an alternative.

Currently, there is controversy as to whether or not behavior therapy can be conceptualized within Kuhn's model of revolutions in science through paradigmatic shifts. There is even broader controversy as to whether or not psychology itself is at a paradigmatic stage, that is, possesses a broad model of human nature that is generally acceptable in the discipline. Some historians take the position that mainstream psychology itself has passed through a series of major paradigms. The best estimates, which go up to five, include structuralism, psychoanalysis, humanism, cognition, and, of course, behaviorism. Others argue that psychology itself is still at a pre-paradigmatic stage (e.g., Staats, 1983).

Actually, the concept of "paradigm" has been used loosely even by Kuhn. A popular occupation is to count the ways in which the concept was used by Kuhn and others. Since the publication of *The Structure of Scientific Revolutions* in 1962, there has been a deluge of citations of his work and references to the concept of "paradigms" in order to justify a wide range of theories, models, and historical interpretations. This chapter and this volume now join the growing paradigmatic parade.

Kuhn's views were affected by a then obscure monograph by Fleck (1935/1979) that had studied the impact of the *social* basis of knowledge on the scientific study of syphilis. Fleck stressed the impact of the community "thinking" about the nature and solution to specific scientific problems and the dialectic between what was known about a particular problem and the *act of knowing it.*

Kuhn's approach was that of a social historian placing the behavior and belief systems of the scientists of the era in a context of the social, political, and economic developments of that era. A major element in Kuhn's approach involved the analysis of the "scientific community" at any given time. Basic to the development of his ideas was an analysis of community structure: the origins, education, and professional initiation of members, as well as the types of working consensus they bring to bear in approaching their subject matter.

Influenced by Fleck's classic book, Kuhn himself came to stress two usages of the term *paradigm.* "On the one hand, it stands for the entire constellation of beliefs, values, techniques, and so on, shared by the members of a given community. On the other, it denotes one sort of element in the constellation, the concrete puzzle solutions which, employed as models or examples, can replace explicit rules as a basis for the solutions of the remaining puzzles of normal science" (1962, p. 11). These interrelated aspects are encompassed by the term *disciplinary matrix*, which incorporates symbolic generalizations, beliefs in models, shared values (e.g., accuracy, quantification), and "exemplars," or recognized puzzle solutions.

The historian of psychology, Leahey (1980), offers a framework from which we can approach the question of behavior therapy as a Kuhnian revolution. Was there normal science and an established paradigm to revolt against? Were there anomalies? Was there a crisis? Did a rival paradigm emerge to solve the anomalies? Did the new paradigm attract adherents? Was there a period of struggle? These issues in the history and philosophy of science are an integral part of understanding the original and current paradigmatic status of behavior therapy. My opinion is that there is an affirmative answer to all of Leahey's questions as regards behavior therapy's development and flourishing in the 1950s and 1960s.

On Behavior Therapy

A major integrating theme of the early post–World War II group of behavior therapy investigators was a broad model of human behavior that emphasized social/environmental causation. The basic theoretical framework of the emerging behavior therapy movement of the 1960s was its *social-learning* alternative to the then-current, pathology-oriented *medical* model (Ullmann & Krasner, 1965).

In very broad, perhaps oversimplified, terms, the clashing conceptual models of human nature can be designated as "inner" and "outer" explanations of locus of causation of behavior (the perennial nature-vs.-nurture controversy, which has been with us as a society for a very long time). There are theorists and investigators who conceptualize in terms of *inner* concepts, variables, or metaphors—such as disease, pathology, traits, personality, mind, cognitions, and mind–body or health–illness dichotomies. Others, primarily but not exclusively identified as behaviorists, focus on the outer, environmental, social consequences, on a social-learning emphasis, and on a "Utopian" stream—the planning of social environments to elicit and maintain the best of human behavior.

As behavior therapy developed and became successful in attracting adherents to its paradigms, the very nature of the model began to shift, and there developed a merger with the model to which it had been a genuine alternative. Behavior therapy was an "outer" (social/

environmental) model of human nature as distinct from the then-predominant "inner" (personality/biological/mental/cognitive/disease) models. Behavior therapy has, to a large extent, been co-opted by and merged into the "inner" model. Thus it no longer represents the paradigm in which many of its early adherents believed. The term *cognition* has returned to a predominant position in psychology. I view these developments not as another paradigm shift but rather as a *paradigm lost.*

Implicit in the "outer" model is, of course, the notion that change in human behavior is possible, even desirable, since human nature is plastic, not fixed and immutable. It is appropriate that each of the two most influential "outer"-model behaviorists of this century, Watson (1929) and Skinner (1948), has offered his own version of a "Utopian" society.

I will now briefly trace the history of behavior therapy in terms of the social, historical, and economic contexts, both conceptual and practical in which it developed, as well as the community of scholars and scientists who developed it. Behavior therapy, as it developed in the post-World War II period, did indeed represent a paradigmatic shift (using the term in the disciplinary matrix context) in terms of the model, shared values, and exemplars of the community involved. Even the name of the major organization in the field, the Association for Advancement of Behavior Therapy (AABT), presents a strong point for arguing that a paradigmatic state in the behavioral community existed, at least in the 1960s.

It is especially crucial to determine the scope and limitation of the field of behavior therapy, since too comprehensive a view (e.g., equating it with all of psychology) renders it meaningless and too narrow a view (e.g., equating it with a specific technique, such as desensitization) renders it virtually useless. As one plods through the vast literature of behavior therapy, one is reminded of the parable of the blind men who described the elephant solely on the basis of their touching parts of the animal. They gave excellent accounts of tusks, legs, trunk, and ears, but no version of a complete elephant. Our task is to present a picture of the whole elephant and to demonstrate how it differs from other animals, for it is clear, to me at least, that the elephant of *behavior therapy* did indeed exist and that, at least prior to its sad demise, it could be discriminated from other creatures of the psychological jungle.

The first use of the term *behavior therapy* in the literature was in a 1953 status report by Lindsley, Skinner, and Solomon, referring to their research on operant conditioning of a plunger-pulling response in psychotic patients. Lindsley suggested the term to Skinner, based on its simplicity and linkage to other treatment procedures. It often comes as a surprise to modern behavior therapists, with their emphasis on the one-to-one relationship, that the term was initially used by Skinnerians. After this early usage, "behavior therapy" was generally replaced by "behavior modification" or "behavior analysis" by those who identified their efforts with operant conditioning.

Independently of this early usage, and of each other, Lazarus (1958) used the term to refer to Wolpe's application of reciprocal-inhibition techniques to neurotic patients, and Eysenck (1959) used the term to refer to the application, based in large part on the procedures of a group of investigators then working at the Maudsley Hospital in London, of what he called "modern learning theory" to the behavior of neurotic patients.

In his 1969 volume, *Behavior Therapy: Appraisal and Status,* Franks highlighted the disagreements that existed even then among self-identified behavior therapists as to the definition of behavior therapy. He pointed out that: "Responses alone are the data available to the student of human behavior, and all else is a matter of inference and construct" (p. 1). He noted that at that point most behavior therapists linked their work with the learning theories that were then called stimulus-response or SR (e.g., Pavlov, Skinner, Guthrie, and Hull). Franks noted and attributed theoretical importance to the base of a "common, explicit, systematic and a priori usage of learning principles to achieve well-defined and pre-determined goals" (p. 2).

Perhaps the most completely agreed-upon concept in this ever-growing community was that of "learning," although, of course, there were subtle and sharp differences in the use of the term. Some investigators have consistently defined behavior therapy in terms of learning theory. Wolpe (1969) offered an illustrative definition: "Behavior therapy, or conditioning therapy, is the use of experimentally established principles of learning for the purpose of changing unadaptive behavior. Unadaptive habits are weakened and eliminated; adaptive habits are initiated and strengthened" (p. xi).

In the introduction to his paper "Why I Am Not a Cognitive Psychologist," Skinner (1977) nicely summarized the outer/environmental model:

The variables of which human behavior is a function lie in the environment. We distinguish between (1) the selective action of that environment during the evolution of the species, (2) its effect in shaping and maintaining the repertoire of behavior which converts each member of the species into a person, and (3) its role as the occasion upon which behavior occurs. Cognitive psychologists study these relations between organism and environment, but they seldom deal with them directly. Instead they invent internal surrogates which become the subject matter of their science. (p. 1)

A more encompassing framework comes from those who viewed behavior therapy in the broader context of social learning (Bandura, 1969) or behavior influence (Krasner & Ullmann, 1973). Ullmann and Krasner (1965) described behavior therapy as treatment deducible from the sociopsychological model that aims to alter a person's behavior directly through application of general psychological principles. This was contrasted with "evocative psychotherapy," which is treatment deducible from a medical or psychoanalytic model that aims to alter a person's behavior indirectly by first altering intrapsychic organizations.

During the 1960s, there was much discussion and drawing up of lists of the ways in which behavior therapy differed from traditional psychotherapy. These lists ranged from those having a dozen or more clear differences (pointing to behavior therapy as a clear alternative model) to those deemphasizing the differences or even calling for a bridging of the two approaches. Whether it is possible, or even desirable, to combine the two approaches was a major controversy of the period. Eysenck (1959), for example, took the position that bridging between behavior therapy and psychoanalysis was undesirable. My position was and is that the bridging of two paradigmatic models that have historically developed as clear *alternatives* to each other would generally show a misunderstanding of the basic principles of both.

In preparing the first *Annual Review* chapter on behavior therapy in 1971, I noted some of the elements of the belief system then common to behavior therapy (Krasner, 1971):

a. the statement of concepts so that they can be tested experimentally.
b. the notion of 'laboratory' as ranging from the animal mazes or shuttle boxes through basic human learning studies to hospitals, schoolrooms, homes and the community.
c. research as treatment and treatment as research.
d. an explicit strategy of therapy.
e. demonstration that the particular environmental manipulation was indeed responsible for producing the specified behavior change. This is the basis of those who argue that behavior therapy is really an experimental approach in which each individual is an experiment in which N = 1. Even in desensitization the hierarchy is individualized by virtue of the individuals learning history.
f. the goals of the modification procedure are usually determined by an initial functional analysis or assessment of the problem behaviors. In effect, what are the environmental determinants, maintainers, and consequences of current behavior, and what possible alternatives can be developed? (p. 487)

Thus the unifying factor in behavior therapy was its basis in derivation from experimentally established procedures and principles. The specific experiments varied widely but had in common all of the attributes of scientific investigation, including control of variables, presentation of data, replicability, and a probablistic view of behavior.

I cannot resist quoting golden words from an earlier paper given at an AABT meeting, since they are pertinent to the theme of this volume. I was on a panel devoted to a retrospective of behavior therapy and a look toward the then-impending eighties (which I understand have arrived and will probably soon depart). I remarked about behavior therapy (Krasner, 1981):

> I realize that these combinations of words are sacred since this is indeed the 14th convention of the AABT. Having been among the founding fathers and mothers of this august organization I confess to having erred in acquiescing to the use of the term of "behavior therapy" in the title. The label has enhanced the co-opting of "behavior therapy" by the medical model. However, this is still retrospective and I will be more optimistic in my prospective observations.

Thus, I am arguing that behavior therapy as developed in the 1960s represented a clear alternative in the mental health industry to the then-predominant paradigm with its focus on inner processes. This is, of course, not to say that there was no usage of "inner" concepts and terminology in behavioral thinking, such as awareness, self, anxiety, phobia, conditioning, bias, expectancy, and so forth. However, the major focus was on outer, environmental influences and consequences rather than hypothesized inner processes.

In preparing this chapter I reviewed seven major influential books of the 1960s. The topics, concepts, techniques, models, and individuals covered, in effect, the disciplinary matrix and exemplars of a community of scholars, to return to Kuhn's terms. The authors are Bandura (1969), Eysenck (1959, 1960), Eysenck and Rachman (1965), Franks (1969), Kanfer and Phillips (1970), Krasner and Ullmann (1965), Staats (1964), Ullmann and Krasner (1965), and Wolpe (1969). My opinion, and I stress the word *opinion,* is that the disciplinary matrix and exemplars manifested in these books did indeed represent a new paradigm that was a clear *alternative* to the focus on inner pathology then current in the healing professions. Bandura (1978) amply demonstrated the recycling and reemergence of the medical ideology/model in the behavior therapy of the 1970s. Albee (1980, 1982) has presented cogent social/humanistic arguments for the replacement of the "mental illness" inner "defect" model by a social learning "competency" model.

We are pointing out the changes and implications of the paradigmatic shift from an "outer" to an "inner" model. In 1971, I argued that the history of the behavioral approach included a utopian stream, involving an ethical concern for the social implications of behavior control as well as offering blueprints for a better life, such as Skinner's (1948) *Walden Two*. This stream can be traced from Plato's *Republic* to the setting up of a token economy on a psychiatric ward or in a community setting. A subsequent series of papers, emphasizing social inequities as the focus for behavior modification, research on diffusion of innovations, and the comments they engendered, were implicit and explicit expressions of utopianism (Michael, 1980; Stolz, 1981).

Cognitive Behavior Therapy

The concept of "cognitive behavior therapy," a term appearing very frequently in recent publications and research, is a puzzle. It is, in effect, a *symptom* of the loss of the sacred paradigm of the founding community of scholars. I am tempted to label this label the "oxymoron of the year." Lest the reader feel that I am somehow denigrating the label, giving it a DSM III category, we are doing nothing of the sort. *Oxymoron* is a perfectly good English word, defined by the dictionary as "a rhetorical figure in which an epigrammatic effect is created by the conjunction of incongruous or contradictory terms, for example, a mournful optimist.

The reader can have fun developing other oxymorons. Thus if cognitive behavior therapy means an integration of cognitive "inner" concepts with "outer" concepts, such as behavior, you should have objections from two sets of purists. Those who view behavior therapy as an "outer," alternative paradigm to the old "inner" paradigm would argue that the term is indeed an oxymoron, two antithetical concepts that are genuine alternatives, hence, not combinable. Others would argue that behavior therapy in its original paradigm included cognitive variables; hence, to add this new adjective is redundant and unnecessary. In "The Current Status of Behavior Therapy," Kazdin and Hersen (1980) express nicely some of the paradigmatic issues I am describing:

> Considerable ambiguity surrounds the current status of behavior therapy and behavior modification. [They note that they are using the two terms synonymously in this paper.] The lack of a clear definition of behavior therapy is a major source of the ambiguity. At the inception of the field, major definitions frequently distinguished behavior therapy as the attempt to alter behavior based upon the application of principles and theories of learning . . . or from psychology and the social sciences more

generally. . . . Over the years the definitions of behavior therapy have
expanded. . . . Debate about the central features of behavior therapy naturally had led to ambiguity about what the field is currently.

Part of the ambiguity of what behavior therapy is also derives from the
major different variations that have been identified. Variations include
multimodal behavior therapy, cognitive behavior therapy, applied behavior analysis and others. . . . Also specific techniques within these areas
often differ dramatically by focusing on what clients imagine or say to
themselves or how they perform in treatment. The different variations or
techniques often seem to have little in common, and indeed, occasionally
are diametrically opposed in their conceptual bases. [In effect, a neat way
of saying oxymoron.] (pp. 283–284)

On Broader Contexts

It is important to place behavior therapy in a broader social, political,
and economic context. By its very nature, the concept of "paradigm"
implies such a context. However, we are actually dealing with two
separate but interrelated contexts, that of the *society*, and that of the
profession. Even though a professional context is implicit in Kuhn's
usage of the term *community of scholars*, it is only fairly recently that
real attention has been paid to the social, political, and economic
context of the profession (e.g., Mahoney, 1976). Even now, there is
generally reluctance on the part of those professionals who view themselves as scientific, particularly psychologists, to accept or acknowledge that there are social, political, and economic aspects to the profession that influence the theory, methodology, and approach to the
actual *content* of the field.

In dealing with behavior therapy we are looking at a view, a belief
system, about human nature. Many historians and psychologists contend that the basic views about the nature of man held at any period of
time, even by professionals and scholars, are influenced by the broader
zeitgeist of the society and that these, in turn, influence society as
expressed in books, newspapers, the media, and the pop culture of the
period.

Behavior therapy is a human creation and a very significant one. It
is not possible to discuss it out of the context of its creators or the
societal context in which they functioned. The behavioral movement
in American psychology and society can be viewed as a scientific/social
movement influenced by, and in turn influencing, the broader society
in which it developed (Ullmann, 1969). Behavior therapy and behaviorism, from which it developed, both evolved in the context of the
social, political, cultural, educational, economic, and intellectual his-

tory of twentieth-century America. Conversely, as the pragmatic philosophy of the behavioral movement spread beyond the bounds of the
psychological laboratory, it influenced virtually every aspect of American life. Perhaps no other systematic approach to human behavior has
been as vilified, praised, used, and misused as behaviorism (except,
perhaps, psychoanalysis!).

Behaviorism in the form of behavior therapy represented a break
with authority, a break with traditions even of its own history. It was,
in effect, something new and exciting. The professionals of the period
who were identifying either with humanism or with behaviorism (or
with both) were advocating an open society in which human behavior
could be a function of what individual human beings did, felt, and
believed *now;* individuals were not perceived as victims of a mechanical history of the society or of their own lives.

The philosophical roots of behavior therapy are generally traced to
the positivistic philosophy system founded by Comte, which radically
rejected all metaphysics, the inquiry into the ultimate causes and
nature of things. The objective of science was to discover *facts,* their
relations, and the laws governing them. Positivism strongly reinforced
the antimentalistic, and anti-introspectionist tendencies in psychology. The behaviorist tenets in American psychology seemed very much
in agreement with positivistic views. The controversy as to whether
science is value-free or value-laden has been an integral part of the
history of behavior therapy (Krasner & Houts, 1984).

Another intellectual source of influence on behavior therapy was
the mechanical approach to human behavior that dates back at least
to the eighteenth century, when some philosophers called for an entirely mechanistic approach to human behavior. Even in the physiology of the period, the *reflex* concept of the nervous system was becoming predominant. One of the early criticisms of behavior therapy was
that it was indeed too "mechanical."

Still another context was that of other mental health/philosophical
movements. In much the same manner as was to occur in the latter
half of the century, early psychoanalytic thought in the United States
played an important role in the early development of behaviorism:
that of "the opposition," the theoretical model for which behavior
therapy became an alternative. Bakan (1966) neatly captures the relationship between the two social movements:

> Psychoanalysis has played the role of "temptation" to the behaviorists.
> This temptation largely centered round two features of the American
> culture and its articulation with psychoanalysis. The first was the seem-
> ing confirmation of Freudian thought of the deeply rooted Calvinistic
> notion of the natural depravity of man. The second was the reaction

against the social forces of sexual repression. . . . The tendency to ferret
out hidden motives in mankind is a feature of the culture of America
which harks back to the Puritan origins of America. (p. 23)

Watson, an important progenitor of behavior therapy, viewed behaviorism as coming onto the American scene to rescue the country from
psychoanalysis. Freud had visited the United States in 1909 and apparently had completely captured the imagination of the American
public and intelligentsia. And so Watson rushed to the rescue of the
American mind (and soul), in much the same way as Skinner, Wolpe,
and their colleagues were to do in the latter half of the century.

The American Context of Behavior Therapy

In this section, I focus on the development of behavior therapy within
an American context. This is not to say that behavior therapy is or was
an exclusively American phenomenon. Many of the key contributions
to the behavior therapy paradigm of the 1950s and 1960s came from
investigators in many parts of the world, including the United King-
dom, the Soviet Union, and South Africa. However, in my biased view,
the key element in the paradigm that has been lost is a societal
sensitivity that was typically, if not uniquely, American. It has been
repeatedly argued by historians, psychologists, and historians of psychology that the origins of behaviorism, the philosophical progenitor
of behavior therapy, lie deep within basic aspects of American society.
For example, both Watson and Skinner, the two major influences on
behaviorism in the twentieth century, were born in rural America,
emphasizing the linkage between certain aspects of rural/farm life—
the raising of animals, the tinkering with machinery, and the development of a highly idealistic approach to life—and such developments in
psychology as the apparatus-laden psychology laboratory, with its emphasis on animal subjects, and a utopian orientation to society, all of
which have been basic ingredients of behaviorism in America.

Historians of the late nineteenth and early twentieth centuries emphasize the growth of *materialism, determinism, mechanism,* and *anti-
intellectualism* as pervasive forces in American society as it moved
from a predominantly rural to an urban base. These trends were compatible with the major philosophical tenets of behaviorism. Many of
these characteristics are often considered to be typified in the person
of Watson, perhaps the first psychologist who could legitimately be
labeled a behavior therapist. For example, Watson was born into a
deeply religious, southern, rural family, and his ideas about life repre-

sented a break with most of the characteristics of a rural society. His writings became a major influence in the urban society of a changing America (Cohen, 1979).

As a historian of psychology, Bakan (1966) has clearly linked behaviorism with American society via Watson:

> Behaviorism must be understood as a cultural expression; and a number of the important features of the complex which behaviorism represented enjoyed a special confluence in the personality and background of this one individual. John B. Watson, "American,". . . . We hypothesize that a major cultural contextual feature for appreciating the nature of behaviorism is that of rural American as it confronted the growing urbanization and industrialization of America in the late 19th and 20th centuries. (p. 8)

Another important stream of influence in American society with which behaviorism has been linked is that of progressivism. Leahey (1980) argued that:

> Behaviorism is also the product of progressivism, a widespread political reform movement that began in the 1890's. It sought to replace the old bosses and hack politicians with an elite bureaucracy that would scientifically manage society. It was mildly utopian and its goal was societal control . . . . Behaviorism seemed to many progressives to provide the scientific tools with which they could rationally and efficiently manage society. Social control through behavioral technology is one of the longest lived of progressive ideas. (p. 287)

Thus there was in existence in America the social/philosophical/ psychological bases for the postwar development of behavior therapy. I highlight those social, cultural, and political events in the post–World War II era that were to influence or be influenced by the development of the behavioral paradigm out of which behavior therapy grew.

There was a strong sense of idealism on the part of the returning GIs. Harold Russell, a popular World War II hero, is quoted as saying, "The guys who came out of World War II were idealistic. They sincerely believed that this time they were coming home to build a new world" (Goulden, 1976, p. 40). This theme of idealism finds expression in such "utopian" novels as *Walden Two* (Skinner, 1948), a major behavioral product of this period, but I contend that the theme of a better world was part of the belief system of the early professionals attracted to behavioral approaches. In my 1971 article on behavior therapy I listed 15 streams of development that had come together in the latter part of the 1960s to form a distinctive approach to helping individuals. The last of these streams was described as follows:

There is an increasingly important stream that can be labeled *utopian* in its emphasis on planning the social environment to elicit and maintain the best of man's behavior. It includes an ethical concern for the social implications of behavior control, as well as offering blueprints for a better life such as Skinner's *Walden Two*. This stream can of course be traced from Plato's *Republic* to the setting up of a token economy on a psychiatric ward or in a community setting. (p. 491)

Thus, an important stream of ideas becoming increasingly evident in that period was that of the social responsibility that derives from science or the pursuit of knowledge—a stream in which the early behaviorists were involved. Gregg (1948) expressed this warning eloquently in an invited speech on "The Profession of Psychology as Seen by a Doctor of Medicine" to the American Psychological Association:

Lastly, psychology as well as medicine must realize this inescapable sequence: study discovers knowledge, knowledge brings power, power entrains responsibility, and responsibility must be prepared to survive praise or blame, dependence or passionate resentment. One can see this sequence in the history of physics, from Archimedes to the atomic bomb; study, knowledge, power, responsibility. If this is the sequence in our knowledge of the physical world, can we expect the history of psychology to follow a different course? I think not. It may be a tragic history or it may be magnificent. Whatever its future may be, psychology will sooner or later have to face the responsibility that comes from power. (p. 401)

The late 1940s and 1950s also saw an outburst of growth in income and employment. Psychology began its period of unprecedented growth in sheer numbers as a field with an idealistic goal of helping others and society. With a strong scientific underpinning, it became the ideal field to attract bright, ambitious students who were to become the behavior therapists of the future. This growth culminated in the 1950s and 1960s with the introduction of new concepts, research, and applications—and behavior therapy, the ultimate in effecting social good.

The theme of optimism ran through both American society ("we can do anything, having won this war") and behaviorism, in which the model of environmental change, whether that of the earlier Watson or the then-current Skinner, had always been optimistic. This was expressed by the last sentence of Mailer's (1948) *The Naked and the Dead*—"The spirit of the world is ours for the taking."

In the twentieth century, an organized body of knowledge, referred to as the discipline of "psychology," has evolved to a point at which the theories and applications of its practitioners have had influence on virtually every aspect of American life. The historian Curti (1980) has traced the changing conceptions of human nature as they interacted with American thought from the seventeenth century to the present. In devoting a chapter to the behavioral movement, he describes behaviorism as an "idea" about the nature of man. We agree and would contend that the "idea" has taken on a life of its own. Curti succinctly describes the impact of this "idea" in noting that, "Exponents of behaviorism, which led to a view of human nature less comprehensive than Freudianism, claimed that it was the first really scientific view of man and that in origin and character it was truly American. It began as a revolt in professional psychology. It came to influence the social sciences, education, business, government, views about sex, and indirectly, religion and the humanities" (p. 373). This observation again points up the contrast between these two basic *alternative* views of the nature of humankind.

The broad concept of behaviorism touches upon most issues in the study of human behavior—philosophical, psychological, sociological, moral, social, intellectual—that have stirred and plagued mankind not only in our own era but at least back to the ancient Greeks, if not to biblical times: the nature of man and of consciousness, free will vs. determinism, nature vs. nurture, evolution vs. creationism, the impact of value and ethical systems. Behaviorism as a paradigmatic view of human life has been integrally related to every aspect of the science of psychology as well as every aspect of American life in the twentieth century. Although this view at first seems to imply an imperial grandiosity, it merely illustrates that there is a mutual influence between paradigmatic views of human nature and the society in which the purveryors of the views function. In recent years the issues dealt with from a behavioral perspective have become more sophisticated. The big issues have not been resolved, but they are being fought at more subtle levels. Current behavior therapy cannot be divorced from these controversial roots. Unfortunately, there is little awareness of the existence of these roots among many current practitioners of behavior therapy.

One impact of the paradigmatic shift is nicely expressed by London (1983):

> In fact, the early social consciousness and utopian tendencies of behavior therapy, extending it beyond the clinic and consulting room into the broader domains of the classroom, the prison, and potentially the reconstruction of society, à la Skinner and the radical behaviorists of the late 1960s, did it far more harm than good. Retreating from those positions did more for the establishment's good will than undertaking them ever could have. Psychoanalysis did not have this trouble because it was never connected with social reform. (p. 25)

On Behavior Therapy and Social Control

A central theme of this approach to behavior therapy as a paradigm is its mutual influence on American society and, related to this theme, its influence on the goal or direction of psychology itself as involving the *control* and *prediction* of human behavior. Samelson's (1980) reappraisal of Watson places this theme in focus:

> After all, Watson's call for a revolution in psychology had been largely programmatic. His main thrust had aimed at a redefinition of scientific standards and a redirection of psychology. Put simply, this redefinition proceeded at three different levels: first was the change in method: the call for objective procedures and the elimination of "unscientific" introspection. . . . The second level concerned the *subject matter* of psychology, changing it from mental contents and/or processes to movement and behavior, with its attendant peripheralism rejection of central process, and associated metaphysical connotations. . . . I would like to propose, however, that the crucial argument occurred at a third level and dealt with the goal for psychology. According to Watson, this goal was to be the "prediction and control of behavior." (p. 417)

It is the issue of behavior control that, more than any other, was to pervade the psychological and social scene of the latter part of this century and is/was the core of the behavior therapy paradigm. Behaviorism's goal of controlling behavior for social betterment, or utopianism, created the most controversy about, enthusiasm for, and criticism of early behavior therapy. If your goal as a psychologist is the prediction and control of behavior, the immediate issues are: For what purpose? And whence came your mandate to control others?

Woodworth (1938), one of the acknowledged founders of modern psychology, had earlier captured this underlying spirit of behaviorism when he contended that:

> It is the moral qualities of the behavioristic movement, rather than its scientific achievements, that give it its present public significance. It is its boldness, freedom, tough-mindedness, and unlimited faith in the ability of science to take charge of human affairs. As one of my students, representing the generation that has grown up since the War, has said to me, behaviorism means for many a new hope and a new orientation when the old guide posts have become hopelessly discredited. It is a religion to take the place of religion. (p. 92)

This issue of the purpose of behavior control manifests itself in various subtle ways, both professionally and societally. On a broad level, we are currently witnessing two related phenomena in American psychology. First, there is an uneasiness, or malaise, about where we are going as a science and as a profession (Phillips, 1982). At the same time, and often from the same individuals, there is a clarion call for change and for psychology explicitly to take the leader in applying its basic science to broader social and policy issues—in effect, to develop a "better world." Sarason (1981) has cogently argued that psychology as a science and profession has become "misdirected" because of its focus on the individual (e.g., personality, dynamics) as an entity without consideration of the social context that influences that individual. Sarason's critique sharply rebukes the direction of postwar, mainstream psychology because of its avoidance of social issues. In effect, the behavior therapy paradigm, with its "outer" emphasis on environmental and social change, never really became predominant in American psychology. Its absorption into the predominant "inner" model, emphasizing, disease or personality, was a deterrent to an emphasis on social reform.

The notion of a paradigm lost is nicely expressed in the headline of *The New York Times* (Section B) of April 7, 1981: "B.F. Skinner Now Sees Little Hope for the World's Salvation." The high hopes and optimism of the postwar period, in part generated by the victorious war over an evil enemy and in part generated by the ever-optimistic view of an environmental–behaviorist model of human nature, appear to have faded in frustration.

Skinner followed in a direct line from his utopian progenitors by boldly asking the question, "Why Are We Not Acting to Save the World?", in the title of his 1982 APA invited address.

> Our only hope is to change the behavior of those, mainly in governments, religion, or industry and trade, who control the contingencies under which people live. . . . A much more promising strategy would be to induce people to act to promote a better world. The Utopian literature approaches the problem of the future in that way. But Utopianism which merely portrays a better way of life with no indication of how it is to be achieved is no help. (pp. 22–23)

I do not contend, however, that the paradigm loss has had only negative consequences. To its critics, behavior modification became synonymous with brainwashing, or behavior change for undesirable or evil purposes. Perhaps the best example of this comes from Huxley's *Brave New World* (1932), in which he satirically applied his version of Pavlovian conditioning in a society whose value system decreed that certain individuals destined to become workers should not be distracted by literature. To be sure that this occurred, Huxley's planners would put a child on the laboratory floor near a few attractive books. As the child moved to the books or touched them, he was frightened by loud noises or electrically shocked. This was repeated as necessary, and books remained aversive objects for the rest of his life. Today, we rarely observe in popular or professional literature the equation of behavior therapy with evil control such as brainwashing or manipulation.

On the Future

I noted in my 1971 article that:

> The decade of the 1960's covered the childhood and adolescence of behavior therapy, its birth was in the 1950's. The 1970's should see its development into adulthood and perhaps even maturity. Ahead will almost certainly lie old age and senility in the 1980's, but by that time it will have given birth to a newer and at this point (at least by this observer) unpredictable paradigm. (p. 519)

In effect then, this chapter confirms this prediction (since it was my own, why not?). To summarize, the behavior therapy paradigm, as it developed in the 1960s, has indeed grown, matured, and lost its identity. Since I helped bury "behavior modification" (Krasner, 1976), I feel free to mourn the demise of such a nice paradigm. However, since in paradigms we are dealing with the behavior of individuals in a particular scientific community at a particular historical time, perhaps the paradigm lost can yet be re-created?

What would I like to see happen? I would hope for a reemergence of the clinical psychologist/behavior therapist/ scientist–practitioner/participant-observer/prevention/empirical-clinical science/social learning/ environmental design/utopian role. These terms are deliberately linked together philosophically and historically. Does this mean another organization or journal? I hope not. But it does mean an informal network among individuals with this orientation (paradigm), and there are many out there.

The reemergence of this old paradigm would have considerable influence on psychology and the mental health professions. However, in contrast to what I would like to see, what is likely to happen is that the mental health industry, supported by third-party payments, is likely to grow even more powerful, since money is indeed a powerful reinforcer; and clinical psychology/behavior therapy is likely to continue to be "misdirected" inward—a classic case of blaming the victim. This would not be good news for the consumer/patient/client (or even the old paradigmatic behavior therapist). Behavior therapy and empirical clinical science would indeed become fractionated. The scientist would disappear from the scientists–practitioner model.

Come back, come back, ye olde paradigm, wherever you are!

References

Albee, G.W. (1980). A competency model to replace the defect model. In M.S. Gibbs, J.R. Lachenmeyer, & J. Sigal (Eds.), *Community psychology: Theoretical and empirical approaches* (pp. 213–238). New York: Gardner.

Albee, G.W. (1982). Preventing psychopathology and promoting human potential. *American Psychologist, 37,* 1043–1050.

Bakan, D. (1966). Behaviorism and American urbanization. *Journal of the History of the Behavioral Sciences, 2,* 5–28.

Bandura, A. (1969). *Principles of behavior modification.* New York: Holt, Rinehart & Winston.

Bandura, A. (1978). On paradigms and recycled ideologies. *Cognitive Therapy and Research, 2,* 79–103.

Cohen, D. (1979). *J.B. Watson: The founder of behaviourism.* London: Routledge & Kegan-Paul.

Curti, M.E. (1980). *Human nature in American thought.* Madison, WI: University of Wisconsin Press.

Eysenck, H.J. (1959). Learning theory and behaviour therapy. *Journal of Mental Science, 195,* 61–75.

Eysenck, H.J. (1960). *Behaviour therapy and neuroses.* London: Pergamon.

Eysenck, H.J., & Rachman, S. (1965). *The causes and cures of neuroses.* San Diego: Knapp.

Fleck, L. (1979). *Genesis and development of a scientific fact.* Chicago: University of Chicago Press. (Original work published 1935)

Franks, C.M. (Ed.). (1969). *Behavior therapy: Appraisal and status.* New York: McGraw-Hill.

Goulden, C. (1976). *The best years: 1945–1950.* New York: Atheneum.

Gregg, A. (1948). The profession of psychology as seen by a doctor of medicine. *American Psychologist, 3,* 397–401.

Halle, L.J. (1977). *Out of chaos.* Boston: Houghton Mifflin.

Huxley, A. (1932). *Brave new world.* New York: Harper.

Kanfer, F.H., & Phillips, J.S. (1970). *Learning foundations of behavior therapy.* New York: Wiley.

Kazdin, A.E. (1978). *History of behavior modification: Experimental foundations of contemporary research.* Baltimore: University Park Press.

Kazdin, A.E., & Hersen, M. (1980). The current status of behavior therapy. *Behavior Modification, 4,* 283–302.

Krasner, L. (1971). Behavior therapy. In P.H. Mussen (Ed.), *Annual review of psychology* (Vol. 22). (pp. 483–532). Palo Alto, CA: Annual Reviews.

Krasner, L. (1976). On the death of behavior modification: Some comments from a mourner. *American Psychologist, 31,* 387–388.

Krasner, L. (1978). The future and the past in the behaviorism–humanism dialogue. *American Psychologist, 33*, 799–804.

Krasner, L. (1981). Conceptual models. Paper presented at the Annual Meeting, Association for Advancement of Behavior Therapy, Toronto, Canada, November 15.

Krasner, L., & Houts, A.C. (1984). A study of the "value" systems of behavioral scientists. *American Psychologist, 39*, 840–850.

Krasner, L., & Ullmann, L.P. (Eds.). (1965). *Research in behavior modification: New developments and implications.* New York: Holt, Rinehart & Winston.

Krasner, L., & Ullmann, L.P. (1973). *Behavior influence and personality: The social matrix of human action.* New York: Holt, Rinehart & Winston.

Kuhn, T.S. (1962). *The structure of scientific revolutions.* Chicago: University of Chicago Press.

Lazarus, A.A. (1958). New methods in psychotherapy: A case study. *South African Medical Journal, 33*, 660–664.

Leahey, T.H. (1980). *A history of psychology: Main currents in psychological thought.* Englewood Cliffs, NJ: Prentice Hall.

Lindsley, O.R., Skinner, B.F., & Solomon, H.C. (1953). *Studies in behavior therapy* (Status Report 1). Waltham, MA: Metropolitan State Hospital.

London, P. (1983). Science, culture and psychotherapy: The state of the art. In M. Rosenbaum, C.M. Franks, and Y. Jaffee (Eds.), *Perspectives on behavior therapy in the eighties* (pp. 17–32). New York: Springer.

Mahoney, M.J. (1976). *Scientist as subject: The psychological imperative.* Cambridge, MA: Ballinger.

Mailer, N. (1948). *The naked and the dead.* New York: Rinehart.

Marx, O.M. (1977). History of psychology: A review of the last decade. *Journal of the History of the Behavioral Sciences, 13*, 41–47.

Michael, J. (1980). Flight from behavior analysis. *The Behavior Analyst, 3*, 1–22.

Mitroff, I.I. (1974). *The subjective side of science.* New York: Elsevier.

Phillips, E.L. (1982). *Stress, health and psychological problems in the major professions.* Washington, DC: University Press of America.

Popper, K. (1950). *The open society and its enemies.* Princeton, NJ: Princeton University Press.

Samelson, F. (1980). J.B. Watson's little Albert, Cyril Burt's twins, and the need for a critical science. *American Psychologist, 35*, 619–625.

Sarason, S. (1981). *Psychology misdirected.* New York: Free Press.

Skinner, B.F. (1948). *Walden Two.* New York: Macmillan.

Skinner, B.F. (1977). Why I am not a cognitive psychologist. *Behaviorism, 5*, 1–10.

Skinner, B.F. (1982, Aug). *Why are we not acting to save the world?* Address presented at the annual convention of the American Psychological Association, Washington, DC.

Staats, A.W. (Ed.). (1964). *Human learning: Studies extending conditioning principles to complex behavior.* New York: Holt, Rinehart & Winston.

Staats, A.W. (1981). Paradigmatic behaviorism, unified theory construction methods, and the zeitgeist of separation. *American Psychologist, 36*, 239–256.

Staats, A.W. (1983). *Psychology's crisis of disunity: Philosophy and method for a unified science.* New York: Praeger.

Stolz, S.B. (1981). Adoption of innovations from applied behavioral research: "Does anybody care?" *Journal of Applied Behavior Analysis, 14*, 491–506.

Ullmann, L.P. (1969). Behavior therapy as social movement. In C.M. Franks (Ed.), *Behavior therapy: Appraisal and status* (pp. 495–523). New York: McGraw-Hill.

Ullmann, L.P., & Krasner, L. (Eds.). (1965). *Case studies in behavior modification.* New York: Holt, Rinehart & Winston.

Watson, J.B. (1929, June 29). Should a child have more than one mother? *Liberty,* pp. 31–35.

Wolpe, J. (1958). *Psychotherapy by reciprocal inhibition.* Stanford, CA: Stanford University Press.

Wolpe, J. (1969). *The practice of behavior therapy.* Elmsford, NY: Pergamon.

Woodworth, R. (1938). *Experimental psychology.* New York: Holt.

4

Psychotherapy to Behavior Therapy: A Paradigm Shift

Hans J. Eysenck

From Psychoanalysis to Behavior Therapy

I will suggest in this chapter that the general body of "dynamic" theory and psychotherapeutic applications of this theory by Freud and his followers have constituted a paradigm more or less in the sense in which Kuhn (1959, 1970) uses the term. I will also suggest that the demonstration that psychotherapy so defined simply did not work (Eysenck, 1952) was a precursor of a genuine revolution in the field that resulted in the adoption of a different paradigm, that is, a different set of theories, and a different set of therapies derived from these principles, which may be referred to under the generic term *behavior therapy* (Eysenck, 1959). It will, of course, be necessary to discuss the precise meaning of the term *paradigm* in its application to these movements, and to justify its use.

No one who was a student of psychology in the years just preceding or just after the Second World War will doubt that psychoanalysis possessed many of the characteristics of a Kuhnian paradigm. The great majority of psychiatrists and clinical psychologists, aided and abetted by many personality psychologists and social psychologists, accepted Freudian views as a "metaphysical paradigm" (Masterman, 1974), that is, as a "new way of seeing," "an organizing principle governing perception itself," seeing it simply as a cognitive map of psychological reality. It could also be characterized as an "artefact paradigm," consisting of the concrete, basic tools of the discipline, including methods (dream interpretation, free association) as well as its textbooks and other exemplary writings. And in the third place it was accepted as a "sociological paradigm," in that its followers (and many who were not themselves psychoanalysts) spoke of its "universally recognized scientific achievements" and acknowledged the writ of its political institutions, which alone could act as training bodies and confer the status of trained psychoanalysts on novices.

To these three perspectives recognized by Masterman as implicit in Kuhn's original writings, Kuhn himself has added the notion of the paradigm as disciplinary structure or disciplinary matrix. In this largely sociological sense, it reflects the discipline's need for communication, organization, and perpetuation through teaching students (Catalano, 1979). This is not too dissimilar to the sociological paradigm, but it assumes particular importance for psychoanalysis because of the explicit "brain washing" procedures to which it subjects its students (Eysenck, 1985).

To say there is a paradigm that is meaningfully associated with Freudian psychoanalysis is not to say that psychoanalysis is a scientific discipline. The fact that a paradigm exists does not make a discipline scientific. A great deal more is required than that. A large number of people can readily be persuaded that a given set of postulates is, in some sense of the word, "true." A recognition of the nonscientific nature of Freudian thought has led to a reevaluation in recent years by those who would wish to turn it into a hermeneutic discipline (Habermas, 1970; Ricoeur, 1970, 1981). Grünbaum (1984) has discussed the issues involved in great detail, demonstrating conclusively that the hermeneutic philosophy and approach go counter to Freud's own thinking and disavow his efforts to assume a scientific pose. A detailed examination of the degree to which psychoanalysis can be said to be scientific is given elsewhere (Eysenck, 1985).

The history of the growth of behavior therapy as a new paradigm, its opposition to Freudian psychotherapy, and its eventual emergence as an alternative paradigm, has been well traced by Kazdin (1978) and, more recently, by Schorr (1984). The early work, both theoretical and applied, of Watson, Mary Cover Jones, Salter, Jacobson, and many others must, of course, never be forgotten, but I think it would be historically accurate to say that behavior therapy as a potential paradigm emerged with the publication of my paper on "Learning Theory and Behaviour Therapy" (Eysenck, 1959). In this paper I quite consciously contrasted the old and the new paradigms in a set of ten major tenets that compared the one to the other (see Table 4.1).

It is true that some people (e.g., Wachtel, 1977; Marmor & Woods, 1980; Ryle, 1978) try to gloss over the differences listed in Table 4.1 and prefer a benevolent eclecticism, but, as I shall point out, I find

TABLE 4.1   Major Contrasting Tenets of the Freudian Psychotherapy and Behavior Therapy Paradigms

Freudian psychotherapy	Behavior therapy
1. Based on inconsistent theory never properly formulated in postulate form.	1. Based on consistent, properly formulated theory leading to testable deductions.
2. Derived from clinical observations made without necessary control, observation, or experiments.	2. Derived from experimental studies specifically designed to test basic theory and deductions made therefrom.
3. Considers symptoms the visible upshot of unconscious causes ("complexes").	3. Considers symptoms as unadaptive conditioned responses (CRs).
4. Regards symptoms as evidence of repression.	4. Regards symptoms as evidence of faulty learning.
5. Believes that symptomatology is determined by defense mechanism.	5. Believes that symptomatology is determined by individual differences in conditionability and autonomic liability, as well as accidental environmental circumstances.
6. All treatment of neurotic disorders must be *historically* based.	6. All treatment of neurotic disorders is concerned with habits existing at *present*; their historical development is largely irrelevant.
7. Cures are achieved by handling the underlying (unconscious) dynamics, not by treating the symptom itself.	7. Cures are achieved by treating the symptom itself, i.e. by extinguising unadaptive CRs and establishing desirable CRs.
8. Interpretation of symptoms, dreams, acts, and so on, is an important element of treatment.	8. Interpretation, even if not completely subjective and erroneous, is irrelevant.
9. Symptomatic treatment leads to the elaboration of new symptoms.	9. Symptomatic treatment leads to permanent recovery provided autonomic as well skeletal surplus CRs are extinguished.
10. Transference relations are essential for cures of neurotic disorders.	10. Personal relations are not essential for cures of neurotic disorders, although they may be useful in certain circumstances.

Note: From Eysenck (1959).

little to support such a view. Others (e.g., Meichenbaum, 1975) believe that a new paradigm shift has taken place with the advent of cognitive behavior therapy, but that view also can be shown to be wrong, as I will try to show presently (see also Wolpe, 1978; Ullmann, 1981.)

Criticisms of Behavior Therapy

Early critics of behavior therapy, as so conceived, directed their criticisms at issues that, curiously enough, are very much in line with the conception of behavior therapy as a new paradigm (Breger & McGaugh, 1965, 1966; see reply by Rachman & Eysenck, 1966).

The argument brought forward by Breger and McGaugh is twofold. In the first place, they challenge the theoretical basis of behavior therapy, maintaining that the "laws of learning" on which behavior therapy is said to be based remain to be established. Fundamental issues, such as the role of mediational events in behavior change, the nature of responses learned, and the limitations of a stimulus-response analysis, have not yet been resolved. They make the point that behavior therapy mistakenly assumes a monolithic learning theory as a basis of behavior therapy as an applied science. But, if learning theory itself has not resolved major issues, then how can behavior therapy rely on this theory as an established guide? (Erwin, 1978).

This situation, however, is precisely what characterizes a new paradigm. Barnes (1982) comments on the "perceived inadequacy of a paradigm as it is initially formulated and accepted . . . its crudity, its unsatisfactory predictive power, and its limited scope, which may in some cases amount to but a single application. In agreeing upon a paradigm, scientists do not accept the finished product: rather, they agree to accept it as the basis for future work, and to treat as illusory or eliminable all apparent inadequacies and defects. Paradigms are refined and elaborated in normal science. And they are used in the development of further problem-solutions, thus extending the scope of scientific competences and procedures" (p. 46).

The fact that a large number of queries remain about the application of learning theory to behavior therapy, and, indeed, about the establishment of learning theory itself, cannot be an argument against the new paradigm. Quite the contrary; it is because this is a new paradigm that these problems remain for normal science to settle. Newton's theory of gravitation was initially rejected by French physicists and has thrown up anomolies throughout its existence; it would be simple-minded to expect learning theory and behavior therapy to do better! Breger and McGaugh, and those who follow them in their criticisms, are simply ignorant of the way the physical sciences have progressed. To reject a theory because it is imperfect is to reject all scientific theories. It ill becomes those who have no theory to offer to criticize those who do have a theory because that theory is not yet perfect! The true point at issue surely is whether or not learning theory has suggested new methods of treatment that are demonstrably superior to those suggested by the displaced paradigm of Freudian psychoanalysis.

Breger and McGaugh's second point is that there is no real link between behavior therapy techniques and the principles of learning theory. The example they use is systematic desensitization using as "stimuli" anxiety-provoking scenes imagined by the client. Yet, they say, in the usual type of conditioning experiment the stimulus is an unambiguous, discrete event defined in objective terms, not a private event defined subjectively by the client.

There are two answers to this second point. The first one is rather simple. Quite clearly, Breger and McGaugh (and all the later critics follow their line of argument) have not advanced beyond the Watsonian type of learning theory; they are unaware of the large advances that have subsequently been made. No one familiar with modern learning theory (e.g. Gray, 1975; MacIntosh, 1974, 1984) would argue along these lines. Ever since Pavlov's original writings, learning theory has put forward explanations in terms of stimulus-stimulus (S-S) conditioning, incorporating cognitive elements, and the battle between this type of theory and the Watsonian stimulus-response (S-R) type of theory has long since swung in favor of the former. Here, indeed, is one issue in which the normal work of science has fairly decisively settled a longstanding argument, and it is very much to the detriment of so-called cognitive psychologists that they have not realized that contemporary learning theory is in many ways different from and superior to the kind of learning theory popular 50 years ago. Criticisms that might be acceptable as far as the older version is concerned are certainly not acceptable regarding present day learning theory.

This point, as we shall see, is also very relevant in relation to the claims of cognitive psychologists to have effected a paradigm shift from Pavlovian conditioning to cognitive explanations. As will be discussed later, this claim, too, is based on a complete misunderstanding of the facts.

Before looking at modern learning theory and the role of cognitive factors, let us consider the allegation that the principles of learning theory do not, in fact, determine current practice in behavior therapy. This point, which emerges in many different critiques (Locke, 1971; London, 1972; Breger & McGaugh, 1965), is difficult to answer for two reasons. In the first place, it is perfectly possible that certain applications of behavior therapy are based on serendipity, accidental insights, or other features that are difficult to isolate. Thus, it is not suggested that all the methods used by behavior therapists are necessarily deduced from learning theory, but rather that the majority of important applications are so deduced (Eaglen, 1978).

In the second place, the accusation is never made in a specific manner, but always as a general statement. General statements of this kind are obviously difficult to refute, but what can be done is to give examples of successful applications of learning theory to behavior therapy. It would be possible to fill this entire book with such examples. I will merely give two examples of the direct application of learning-theory principles to treatment, with the implicit challenge to critics to leave the safe ground of general statement and deal with these specific examples.

The first is enuresis (Morgan, 1978). Learning theory makes several specific predictions that go counter to those made by psychoanalysis. (1) Enuresis should be abolished in most subjects (other than those suffering from infections) by means of the bell-and-blanket conditioning technique. (2) There should be a fair number of relapses, because conditioning is stopped the moment the criterion is reached. (3) The *intensity* of the UCS would be related to the success of the treatment. (4) Intermittent (partial) reinforcement should prove superior to 100% reinforcement in preventing relapse. (5) Overlearning should be effective in preventing relapse. The evidence supports all these predictions (Morgan, 1978).

Similarly, predictions for the treatment of obsessive-compulsive neurosis were derived from the animal experiments of Solomon (Solomon & Wynne, 1953; Solomon et al., 1953) and put into practice with human patients (Meyer et al., 1974; Foa & Goldstein, 1978; Rachman & Hodgson, 1980). The usual abysmal therapeutic failure rate with this kind of neurosis was transformed into a high success rate of over 80%.

Theory in Physics and Psychotherapy

In his elaboration of reciprocal-inhibition therapy by desensitization, Wolpe (1958) also worked within the confines of modern learning theory, although later on he suggested (Wolpe, 1976a, 1976b) that, since there is no one "modern learning theory," it is meaningless to define behavior therapy in terms of such a theory. Apparently, he would prefer that treatment should instead be based on "principles and paradigms," but as Eaglen (1978) points out, "this is a superficially attractive solution, especially since the distinction between theories, principles and paradigms is rather vague." Maher (1972) would seem to adopt a similar point of view when he suggests that behavior therapy is based on the empirical observations relating to stimulus-response relations. He goes on to suggest that there is general agreement about the validity of many of these propositions, as it is only in the matter of hypothesizing processes that might account for them that disputes arise.

All this is true but, as pointed out earlier in this chapter, if scientists had to wait until perfect agreement were reached on theoretical issues, it would never be possible to apply scientific principles in any meaningful manner. We now know that, fundamentally, Newtonian physics is wrong, but it has been usefully applied for 300 years and is still being so employed in all cases where the speed of movement involved is well short of that of light. Indeed, I think it is wrong to talk about learning theory as a thing set apart, applied to psychiatric patients suffering from neurotic disorders, as a separate rubric. I would prefer to see the treatment as part of the testing of theoretical propositions, thus providing a complete integration of experiment and therapy. The studies on obsessive-compulsive patients conducted by Rachman and Hodgson (1980) are as much part of the experimental literature as are the studies by Solomon and his colleagues of dogs traumatized in the shuttle box. Both use existing theories to make predictions, both carry out experiments to test these predictions, and both use the results to improve the theories that give rise to their respective experiments.

Again, an example may be easier to follow than a theoretical discussion. In our early studies on the influence of flooding with response prevention, Rachman (1966) found that a two-minute exposure of spider phobics to spiders was followed not by extinction, but rather by an increment in the conditioned response, that is, fear and avoidance. Yet in their later work on obsessive-compulsives, Rachman and Hodgson (1980) found that, for most of their patients, flooding with response prevention resulted in marked improvement or cure. Here we have a clear paradox, with apparently similar methods of treatment leading to quite different results. Again, Wolpe (1958) has pointed out that, in the process of desensitization, high levels of anxiety should always be avoided, because when errors are made by therapists and such high levels are encountered, the patient shows marked relapse. So here, again, flooding apparently produces a worsening rather than an improvement of the patient's state! These paradoxes are difficult or impossible to resolve in terms of orthodox learning theory; but we may seek an explanation in terms of a neobehavioristic theory of neurosis, formulated in part to get past some of the difficulties into which Watson's original, rather simple-minded theory had run (Eysenck, 1979,

1980, 1982). This theory successfully resolves the paradox, pinpoints the parameters responsible for the respective success or failure of the treatment, and also suggests new ways of improving treatment when desensitization has gone wrong (Eysenck, 1978b). This illustrates well the interplay between theory and practice that I have in mind, viewing practice simply as an alternative method for testing theories and thus forming an experimental complement to theory.

Cognitive Theory as Paradigm?

Suggestions have been made more and more frequently in recent years that some reconciliation is possible between the psychoanalytic and the behavoristic approaches and that, indeed, the two may be reducible to a common set of principles (Feather & Rhoads, 1972; Goldfried, 1980; Rhoades & Feather, 1974; Wachtel, 1977); but it will be shown here that the fundamental theories or paradigms of the two approaches are quite distinct and impossible to reconcile (Messer & Winokur, 1980; Franks, 1984; Yates, 1983). Indeed, if one thing is clear, it is that if some formulation of behavior therapy such as that attempted in this chapter is accepted, the conflict is incapable of any form of resolution. As Yates (1983) puts it:

> In any area of human endeavour, whether it relates to science, to medicine, or to psychotherapy, the characteristic feature of progress seems to involve the rise of strong competing views to which the adherents tenaciously hold, often in spite of the empirical evidence available to them. That the dispute between psychoanalysis and behavior therapy belongs in this category can hardly be disputed. . . . The issues between them will not be resolved by premature attempts at reconciling the irreconcilable. Time alone will resolve the issue. (pp. 122–123)

The position is quite different with respect to cognitive psychology, which has often in recent years been suggested as providing a paradigm shift away from behavior therapy. As we shall see, there does not seem to be any reason to assume that cognitive theory presents a paradigm in the sense in which the term is used by Kuhn or in this chapter. There are points of similarity and even identity between orthodox behavior therapy, as defined above, and cognitive theory that make it impossible to speak here of a paradigm shift (Latimer & Sweet, 1984; Marzillier, 1980; Wolpe, 1981). Scharnberg (1984) should be consulted on this point.

Let us note, in the first place, that there is no "cognitive theory" to set against "learning theory" in the orthodox sense of that term. It may be true that there are several "learning theories" rather than one. As we have already seen, this is traditional in science. What is more upsetting, however, as with cognition, is when there is no theory at all! As Allport (1975) has pointed out in his comment on "The State of Cognitive Psychology," the field is characterized by:

> ... an uncritical, or selective, or frankly cavalier attitude to experimental data; a pervasive atmosphere of special pleading; a curious parochialism in acknowledging even the existence of other workers, and other approaches, to the phenomena under discussion; interpretation of data relying on multiple, arbitrary choice-points; and underlying all else a near vacuum of theoretical structure within which to interrelate different sets of experimental results, or to direct the search for significant new phenomena. (p. 143)

Unflattering as it is, this is still a true description of the state of the art. So-called cognitive theory is not a theory at all in the traditional sense; it is simply a ragbag of promissory notes on a nonexistent bank account; an appeal to processes that are seldom described and defined in a unique manner, obeying laws that are never specified and mediating behavior in ways that remain ever more mysterious. That is not a scientific theory; it is not even the beginning of a scientific theory. It is the negation of what is normally regarded as scientific practice.

To say all this is not equivalent to denying the existence, the importance, or the relevance of cognitive *processes*. Cognitive processes are intimately related to language, and it will be remembered that Pavlov clearly introduced a language system into his theory of conditioning when he contrasted the second signaling system, found in humans, with the more primitive conditioning systems found in animals. This certainly constitutes the recognition of "cognitive factors," even in the most strictly objective behavioral system. Platonov (1959) quotes Pavlov to the effect that words can be conditioned stimuli and conditioned responses, thus incorporating cognitive factors into Pavlov's conditioning system. In *The Word as a Physiological and Therapeutic Factor*, Platanov shows experimentally that words and concepts can and do enter as elements into the conditioning process in the case of human subjects. Staats (e.g., 1964, 1968) has continued this tradition in a long series of original studies, and Martin and Levey (1978) have collected evidence to show that "evaluative conditioning" is a process that uses the principles of conditioning in a specifically human context. Many other examples could be given to show that modern conditioning theory does not by any means disregard cognitive processes. On the contrary, these are central to all modern learning theory, including that part concerned with conditioning in animals (MacIntosh, 1983; Martin & Levey, 1979).

MacIntosh (1984) makes it quite clear how views have changed in recent years as far as learning theory is concerned:

> The view of conditioning as the establishment of new reflexes or the strengthening of S-R connections, a view which dominated Western learning theory for half a century, has gradually given way to a view of conditioning as the acquisition of knowledge about the relationship between events in an animal's environment, knowledge which may not be immediately apparent in any change in behavior at all. When a CS is regularly followed by a reinforcer, animals can be said to learn that the CS signals the reinforcer. This is achieved by the establishment of an association between some central representations of the two. From studies which have altered the value of a reinforcer after conditioning, it is apparent that the representation of the reinforcer associated with the CS must, in at least some cases, itself be available for modification when that value is manipulated. (p. 56)

Such "central representations" are, of course, cognitive processes as properly defined, and hence modern learning theory incorporates cognitive processes in a most explicit fashion. It is not clear why cognitive theorists should claim exclusive patronage of such processes or why they should declare that modern learning theory is incomplete because it does not take them into account, when clearly it does (Rescorla, 1972).

It may be interesting to look in more detail at one of the more recent cognitive attempts to create a "unifying theory of behavioral change" (Bandura, 1978). Bandura maintains that "given appropriate skills and adequate incentives . . . efficacy expectations are a major determinant of peoples' choice of activities, how much effort they will expend, and for how long they will sustain effort in dealing with effortful situations" (p. 173). But, of course, as Eysenck (1978a) pointed out in a symposium devoted to these concepts (Rachman, 1978), "expectations" would be regarded by learning theory as simple conditioned responses, consequent upon certain types of unconditioned and conditioned stimuli. The role of expectation in conditioning was discussed many years ago by Zener (1937), and the more recent formulations of learning theory quoted above from MacIntosh would certainly make it easy to conceive of "expectations" as cognitive representations within a learning theory paradigm. It is not clear what is gained by adopting the term in a mentalistic sense. Bandura certainly does not suggest any novel rules, other than those of associative conditioning, which would lead to the acquisition of such "expectations." But if that is so, then there has been no change, except a purely semantic one, and nothing has been gained. We still know as little or as much about the origin of behavioral change as we did before! To *label* a process cognitive rather than conditioning does not alter the facts of the case and does not advance us in an understanding of the dynamics of the situation; nor does it help devise better treatments. Such purely semantic battles are illusory at best and divisive at worst. They have no true scientific content.

What, then, shall we say to those like Beck (1976), Ellis (1974), Goldfried and Goldfried (1975), Mahoney (1977), and Meichenbaum (1975), who maintain that cognitive theory leads to new and different types of therapies, superior to the "mechanistic" ones embraced by traditional behavior therapy? The answer must surely be twofold. In the first place, we must query the evidence. Are the methods used by these authors in truth superior to the best methods that traditional behavior therapy, based on learning theory, can supply? I have avidly read the literature, but I know of no single study that has compared, say, flooding with response prevention in the treatment of obsessive-compulsive handwashing, or the bell-and-blanket method with cognitive theory based methods in the treatment of enuresis, to the advantage of the latter. What is usually done is to offer a mixture of behavioral and cognitive methods, without clarifying which produces the end effect and without introducing any proper clinical evaluation of the effectiveness of these methods as compared with others. All we have is vociferous claims without proof. What is clear is that verbal methods by themselves and without behavioral interaction do not produce good therapeutic results (Rachman & Wilson, 1980; Kazdin & Wilson, 1978).

The crucial point that may separate cognitive therapists from traditional behavior therapists is surely the question of whether cognitions are changed by changes in behavior, or vice versa? Do expectations change because circumstances have changed, or do circumstances become changed because expectations have changed? It is impossible to arrive at any definitive answer to this question, but the evidence does seem to suggest very strongly that in neurotic patients it is much easier to bring about cognitive changes by behavioral intervention than vice versa. If cognitive theorists doubt this, then it is up to them to produce good evidence, especially on an experimental level, to prove their point.

Animal and Human Conditioning: Consciousness

It may be useful at this point to come to grips with the issue of precisely what the differences are between animal and human conditioning and learning and to face directly the problem posed by consciousness (Humphrey, 1983; Wallace & Fisher, 1983). It is consciousness and its implications for cognition that has made psychology "a science in conflict" (Kendler, 1981), and clearly no discussion of the possible contribution made by cognitive theory, or its claims to constitute a paradigm shift, can omit a consideration, however cursory, of these problems.

The kind of behaviorism that cognitive psychologists appear to object to is essentially that of Watson (1930). According to Watson, "psychology, as a behaviorist views it . . . needs introspection as little as do the sciences of chemistry and physics" (p. 86). But these are the positivist excesses of *methodological behaviorism*, which have been left behind by the growth of Skinner's *radical behaviorism*. Skinner certainly allows consciousness and introspection, in their proper place, although he, like Watson, argues that, extrapolation from animals to humans is the best and certainly the most convenient way of discovering the principles governing human behavior (Boakes, 1983). This, too, is now somewhat old-fashioned, and recent trends have been toward what Lowe (1983) calls a *dialectical behaviorism*. As he points out, "the dialectical view suggests that whilst there is a great deal in common between animal and human behavior there are also qualitative differences" (p. 87). Such a view, which is entirely consistent with Skinner's radical behaviorism, does not rule out any of the phenomena of human psychology and offers an analysis of human consciousness that makes no concession to mentalism. In it, the environment remains a *primary* determinant of all behavior, both animal and human, verbal and nonverbal, but the qualitatively new effects produced by language are recognized.

There is much experimental evidence, a good deal of it from operant conditioning, to show the differences between human and animal conditioning and their dependence on language. Thus Lowe (1979), as an example, considers the use of a fixed-interval schedule with animals and with humans aged 4 and older. With animals, we find the classic scallop, but with humans we find either a continuous and high rate of responding between reinforcers or a very low response rate consisting of just one or two responses at the end of the interreinforcement interval—a very different type of reaction! Similarly, with fixed ratio (FR) schedules, the standard animal pattern of behavior is a pause following reinforcement, followed by a constant and relatively high rate of responding until the occurrence of the next reinforcer. The duration of the pause is an increasing function, and response rate a decreasing function, of FR value. In most human studies, however, the pattern of responding is very different— there are no postreinforcement pauses, and the rate of responding is unaffected by changes in the schedule parameter.

Another point of difference is that behavioral "rigidity" is usually found in human research, but hardly ever in animal experiments. Such "rigidity" in humans can be found in studies using variable-interval schedules, concurrent schedules, and other schedules, details of which are to be found in Lowe (1983).

Another example may be taken from the generalized matching law, which seems to apply to animals, but which has been found by Horne and Lowe (1982) not to be characteristic of human performance.

As far as classical conditioning is concerned, here, too, there has been much work to illustrate differences between human and animal species, depending in large measure on language. Thus, simply informing subjects of the CS-UCS relationship, with no actual pairing, has been found to produce immediate conditioning (e.g., Dawson & Grings, 1968; Katz et al., 1971; McComb, 1969; Wilson, 1968), with a similar impressive drop in responding following informing the subject of extinction (e.g., Coljan, 1970; Koenig & Castillo, 1969). Subjects are also able to influence the size of the CR following suitable instructions (Brewer, 1974).

As Davey (1983) points out:

> One of the apparently crucial factors in mediating some of these instructional effects is "awareness of contingencies." First, only Ss who can verbalize the correct CS-UCS relations in post-experimental questionnaires appear to exhibit conditioning (Bear & Fuhrer, 1968, 1970). Secondly, when level of awareness of CS-UCS relations is measured on a trial-to-trial basis throughout conditioning, differential CRs occur only after the time that contingency awareness has developed (e.g., Dawson & Biferno, 1973; Biferno & Dawson, 1977; Fuhrer & Baer, 1980). Thirdly, studies which deliberately attempted to "mask" the CS-UCS relationship and prevent Ss from becoming aware of the CS-UCS contingency have largely failed to find evidence for conditioning. (p. 97)

Work along these lines has occasionally given rise to somewhat exuberant and unlikely claims, such as those by Brewer (1974) that "there is no convincing evidence for operant and classical conditioning in humans" (p. 186). Such a belief would leave out of account the very real similarities between human and animal conditioning and extinction. The fact that cognitive variables are implicated in conditioning does not mean that conditioning does not exist or that the parameters determining its functioning cannot be discovered in humans. The general laws of conditioning in animals and humans are too similar to make Brewer's suggestion a likely one.

Altogether, the cognitive thesis is grossly overstated (Nisbett & Wilson, 1977). As Davey (1983) himself points out, there are many exceptions to the rule that awareness of CS-UCS relations is essential for successful conditioning. Most of the work has been done with UCRs of very low intensity, thus presumably reducing the effects of conditioning as such, and increasing those of cognitive factors. When really strong UCRs are used, as in scopolamine injection (Campbell et al., 1964), no amount of cognitive instruction was found to have the slightest effect on the immensely strong CR formed under these conditions.

There is an ancient Chinese saying that would seem to be quite relevant to this discussion: "a man who has been bitten by a snake is afraid of a coil of rope." It would be difficult to say that the man was not aware that the coil of rope was in fact harmless; it is the strength of the UCR that overrides conscious considerations, and it is this strength of the UCR that cannot easily be replicated in the laboratory. Relevant to this controversy is the work of Corteen and Wood (1972) and Dawson and Schell (1982) on dichotic listening; they showed that nonattended CSs could elicit a CR although the subject of the experiment was not conscious of the occurence of the CS!

Radical and Dialectical Behaviorism

It is necessary to adopt the so-called *dual-level view* of human classical conditioning (Baer & Fuhrer, 1973; Grings, 1965), which contrasts "true" primitive conditioning, in which learning occurs at an autonomic, noncognitive level, with cognitive relational learning, which involves cognitive and conscious processes? It seems more likely that we are dealing with a unitary process, in which the importance of cognitive factors increases with the evolutionary development from primitive to advanced organisms. Some form of "representation" of the UCS is always involved, but is most noticeable in humans and hence can be most easily manipulated by instructions and other ways. Unfortunately, the precise problem of exactly how cognitive factors are integrated with associationist principles of learning is one that has not been studied in sufficient detail to make any detailed conclusions possible. This is an important task for the future.

The possession of language, of course, marks an important qualitative differences between animals and humans, but it should not lead us to deny the existence of cognitive processes in subhuman animal species. The interesting work of Lowe (1983) has demonstrated that the differences observed in operant conditioning between animals and humans are not a function of species differences, but rather a function of language development. Young children who have not yet developed language show responses similar to animals, gradually shifting over, with the development of language, to behavior appropriately human. There is much to be learned from this empirical type of approach to what otherwise would be an intractable philosophical problem.

If what I have said so far sounds like an abandonment of behaviorism and an acceptance of the importance of "private events," I can only claim that such an acceptance is in excellent accord with Skinner (1974) and the doctrines of radical behaviorism. As he points out: "A science of behaviour must consider the place of private stimuli . . . the question then is this: what is inside the skin, and how do we know about it? The answer is, I believe, at the heart of radical behaviourism" (pp. 211–212). He has also pointed out that "a person becomes conscious . . . when a verbal community arranges contingencies under which he not only sees an object but sees that he is seeing it. In this special sense consciousness or awareness is a social product" (p. 213). The misunderstanding of the radical behaviorist position by many authors, including Chomsky (1975), Harré and Secord (1972), Kendell and Hollon (1979), Ledwidge (1978), Locke (1979), Strupp (1979), and Wilson (1978) is difficult to understand in view of the many occasions on which Skinner has expressed his views, consistently opposing the notion that radical behaviorism only deals with publicly observable events and that it eschews inference. As Lowe (1983) points out:

> The principal distinguishing feature of his radical behaviorism is that it considers that a science of behavior, like other sciences, *must* deal with events which are not publicly observable; inference, therefore, is held to be essential in the study of behavior, regardless of parsimony. Recognition of the importance of private events in human psychology thus poses no problems, in principle, for radical behaviorism. (p. 32)

We can see clearly from this that the paradigm shift alleged to have taken place from behaviorism to cognitive psychology is a pseudoshift, a shift in name only. It is based on a complete misunderstanding of what modern learning theory, and particularly radical behaviorism, is all about. Those who make claims for the shift disregard the explicit statements of Skinner and other behaviorists and the developments in general learning theory, with its insistence on "representations" of a cognitive kind. What we have, then, is an arbitrary distortion of reality, using semantic confusion to suggest the existence of a paradigm shift that in reality does not exist. It seems a pity that the "normal work" of science should be impeded by unnecessary and meaningless semantic battles of this kind.

Paradigms and Ordeal by Quackery

We are now in a position to address some of the major questions raised by the editors of this book. Is behavior therapy a paradigm? In one sense, the answer must be "yes"; in another, it must be "no." It would be unrealistic to imagine that all psychologists, or all behavior therapists, or even a majority of them, would be agreed on the general principles outlined here or the theory of neurosis and therapy in conditioning terms suggested by the author. In that sense, the answer clearly is "no." But this "no" must immediately be qualified by raising another question, namely, the population that should be canvassed in order to establish the existence of a paradigm.

As Bernal (1954) has pointed out, every science in its development passes through an ordeal by quackery. For a long time, the scientific and the superstitious, the rational and the irrational, exist together, often in the same person. From Ptolemy to Kepler, astronomers and astrologers were difficult to distinguish, and both these eminent astronomers were also exponents of astrology. It was only after Kepler that astrology became recognized as superstition and the path of the two disciplines separated. Similarly, chemistry and alchemy had a symbiotic relation for a long time, with the same persons being outstanding representatives of both (Newton is a good example). Psychology is still in this stage; science and quackery are only too closely related in some practitioners, and to imagine that decisions are made on rational grounds by the majority of psychologists, even as regards the adoption of theories and therapeutic practices, is itself an irrational belief.

As a consequence, there is practically no rational discourse on an empirical basis between adherents of different theories. They even lack a common base of knowledge, which must be presupposed to exist before any meaningful discourse can take place. My theory of conditioning and extinction, fundamental, in my view, to any understanding of the causes and cures of neurosis (Eysenck, 1982), is largely dependent on the distinction between Pavlovian A and Pavlovian B conditioning. Judgment of it must depend on the referee's knowledge of this distinction and the empirical material underlying it. In my experience, few behavior therapists have sufficient knowledge of conditioning principles to know of this distinction or to be able to judge its application in this particular case.

In a similar way, and to judge simply by their writings, few cognitive theorists and therapists have adequate knowledge of modern learning theory or the recent evidence on the issues discussed in the last few paragraphs. Their objections and criticisms are directed at straw men erected for the specific purpose of being overthrown, rather than dealing with existing theories and experimental results. Clinicians, in particular, are impatient with the slow gathering of empirical data necessary to unravel intricate theoretical problems and seldom keep up with the experimental literature.

Whether there does exist, within the knowledgeable but very small minority, sufficient agreement to make the paradigm acceptable as such is a difficult question that can only be answered in a subjective manner. If absence of fundamental criticism is such a criterion, then perhaps we might say that there are here the beginnings of a paradigm and that as the acceptance of the paradigm widens, the less specifically the theory is stated. Perhaps we might say that we have a paradigm in search of an audience; whether this contradicts the very notion of a paradigm is difficult to say, seeing that Kuhn certainly did not anticipate such problems in what in many ways is still a pre-paradigmatic field of study.

In this rather loose sense of the term—that is, viewing behavior therapy in the widest sense as emphasizing behavioral modification and including cognitive processes (imagery, self-instruction, expectancy, etc.) while leaving open the degree to which cognitive processes influence behavior, or behavior influences cognitive processes—I think a great majority would probably favor this paradigm, agreeing with the proposal that it be regarded as a distinct paradigm shift from the psychodynamic worldview. A majority would also favor certain methods of treatment derived from the general theory, such as modeling, desensitization, flooding; there would also presumably be a good deal of agreement that the ultimate test of any theory or method must be a pragmatic one, that is, its demonstrated ability successfully to treat patients suffering from various types of neurotic (and possibly psychotic) illness. Clearly we are here in the area of inexact concepts of "fuzzy sets and systems" (Gognen, 1968; Zadeh, 1966). Greater precision and more formal answers can only be reached through specific attempts to make people in this general area more aware of the alternatives, induce them to carry out specific experiments to reduce the "fuzziness" of concepts and sets, and consciously attempt to make the discipline more paradigmatic than it is at the moment.

How can this goal be best achieved? The answer must surely be by reducing the influence of the principle of certainly, that is, by inducing people at opposite ends of the continuum, ranging from primitive behaviorism to dogmatic "cognitionism," to abandon their certainties, look at the weaknesses in their particular positions, and begin to read and digest the empirical literature supportive of the other side. This is not to encourage eclecticism. I have elsewhere criticized current eclec-

ticism as "but a mish-mash of theories, a hugger-mugger of procedures, a gallimaufry of therapies, and a charivaria of activities having
no proper rationale, and incapable of being tested or evaluated"
(Eysenck, 1970, p. 145). Indeed, such eclecticism is exactly the opposite
of what I have in mind, namely, a sharpening of theories, a designing
of crucial experiments to set one theory against another in laboratory
and clinical tests rather than to attempt an adversarial trial along
judicial, not scientific, lines. We certainly have it in our power to
construct a proper paradigm of wide ranging importance both scientifically and practically. But by our indolence and arbitrariness we are
doing out best to throw away that chance.

Some of the worst excesses of eclecticism have been committed in
the field of evaluation of psychotherapy, where the famous statement
by Luborsky and colleagues (1975) that "everyone has won and all
must have prizes" is the fatuous summary of an Alice-in-Wonderland
attempt to disguise the fact that empirical studies failed entirely to
show any superiority of psychotherapy (a term not used here to include
behavior therapy) to placebo treatment or even, frequently, to no treatment at all (spontaneous remission). Admittedly some reviewers, like
Bergin and Lambert (1978), follow Luborsky and colleagues in this
curious belief, but Rachman and Wilson (1980) have criticized both
these sets of authors for gigantic sins of both omission and commission, namely, leaving out large bodies of data inconvenient to their
thesis and introducing irrelevant date artificially interpreted to support their thesis. The much more inclusive work of Rachman and
Wilson and the more recent study of Prioleau and colleagues (1983)
leave no doubt that the optimism of Luborsky, Bergin, and others is
entirely unjustified. These far-reaching negative results would, in any
scientific endeavor, spell the end of an easygoing eclecticism eager to
detect virtue in every passing fancy, but unwilling to submit itself to
strict scientific discipline.

Perhaps an additional word should be said about Smith and colleagues' (1980) attempt to establish *The Benefits of Psychotherapy.* On
the basis of what they call a meta-analysis of a large body of evidence,
they come to the optimistic conclusion that:

> Psychotherapy is beneficial, consistently so and in many different ways.
> Its benefits are on a par with other expensive and ambitious interven-
> tions, such as schooling and medicine. The benefits of psychotherapy are
> not permanent, but then little is. . . .
> The evidence overwhelmingly supports the efficacy of psychotherapy. . . .
> Indeed, its efficasy has been demonstrated with near monotonous regu-
> larity. . . . Psychotherapy benefits people of all ages as reliably as school-

ing educates them, medicine cures them, or business turns a profit. (p. 183)

As Eysenck (1983) has pointed out, they achieve this remarkable conclusion by a sleight-of-hand that is unique even in the history of this murky topic. They present a table comparing the effects of 18 different methods of psychotherapy (including behavior therapy) with the effects of no treatment, and they find that the former is indeed superior to the latter. However, closer inspection shows that they have included placebo treatment as one of the 18 methods of treatment! When placebo treatment is regarded, as it should be, as a control rather than a treatment, the effect of psychotherapy suddenly disappears (see also Prioleau et al., 1983). That this trick has not been detected by most reviewers, and has not prevented psychotherapists from repeating the conclusions, is an indication of the low state into which the whole field has sunk.

Two additional points may be of interest. In the first place, Smith and colleagues find that *duration of treatment* shows no correlation with *success of treatment*; thus one hour is as good as 10 years of psychoanalysis! In the second place, they find that *length of training* of the therapist is uncorrelated with *success of therapy*. It makes no difference whether a treatment is administered by a novice with just a few hours of training, or an experienced psychoanalyst with 20 years of experience! If these generalizations are indeed true, then clearly psychotherapy as we know it, involving lengthy treatment and long training for the therapist, has no place in the treatment of psychiatric disorders.

The last intriguing finding of Smith and colleagues is that behavior therapy is significantly superior to psychotherapy. Admittedly, they try to argue this away in a typically subjective and rather preposterous fashion (Eysenck, 1983), but the fact of superiority remains, agreeing well with Kazdin and Wilson (1978), Rachman and Wilson (1980), and others. If all this is, indeed, the best that can be said about traditional psychotherapy, then clearly a paradigm shift from psychotherapy to behavior therapy is more than timely!

The Future of a Paradigm

I am in no doubt, as will have become apparent, that there does exist a substantive theoretical framework that can meet the needs of contemporary behavior therapy and whether we adopt some form of radical behaviorism or its even more recent development (dialectical behaviorism), this must be one of *neobehavioristic* theory. It will undoubtedly be as difficult to persuade cognitive theorists to abandon their conditioned reactions of horror to Skinnerian ideas, unjustified as they are by Skinner's own pronouncements, as it will be to persuade Skinner's own followers to accept, as he does, the role of covert event and the transformation in human behavior brought about by language. Lowe (1983) calls this latter phenomenon "an extraordinary paradox in contemporary behaviorism" (p. 23). As he points out, in contradistinction to the methodological variety of Watson, Skinner's radical behaviorism has established its theoretical identity largely on the basis of its recognition of the importance of covert events in human behavior; Skinner, moreover, has argued that being able, through language, to describe our own behavior to ourselves has resulted in a form of "consciousness" that is unique in the animal world (Skinner, 1957, p. 140; 1974, p. 220). To see Skinner (and possibly Eysenck?) as being at the center, rather than at an extreme, of this continuum, and to regard them as prospective peacemakers rather than militant extremists, will tax the imagination of behaviorists and antibehaviorists equally. Nevertheless, this is the position, and disbelievers are invited to consult the relevant literature.

It would, of course, be necessary to widen traditional forms of radical behaviorism (or even dialectical behaviorism) by admitting factors that hitherto have not figured largely in theoretical or applied developments. One of these is the importance of personality and individual differences; the other, related, one is the importance of genetic factors (Torgersen, 1979; Rose & Ditto, 1983) and "preparedness." The literature here is so overwhelmingly positive about the importance of both these aspects of human functioning (Eysenck & Eysenck, 1985; Eaves & Eysenck, 1985) that I feel it would be gilding the lily to argue the case any further. Again, on this point Skinner and his position are often misconceived. At the public debate between Skinner and myself at the annual convention of the American Psychological Association in Montreal in 1980, Skinner explicitly agreed that both genetic factors and individual differences (personality) were important variables to take into account in any behavioristic formulation of psychological laws. Thus, here, too, there seems to be no discord, although little has been done by either behaviorist or cognitive psychologists to relate these variables and concepts to clinical theory and practice.

Another problem to be faced is the overinclusiveness of the term *neurosis*, which is often equated by psychotherapists and behavior therapist alike with the set of problems presented to them in the clinic, excluding, of course, psychotic disorders. However, many of the complaints of patients in the clinic have little if anything to do with neurosis. We have existential maladjustments, we have educational difficulties arising from a variety of sources, we have detrimental behaviors due to poverty, poor parenting, and many other similar causes; many of these need advice and practical help, but they cannot be construed as neurotic disorders in any strict sense of the term. A proper definition of *neurosis* is, of course, difficult (Gossop, 1981), but from a conceptual point of view greater clarity and agreement is obviously needed if we wish to arrive at theories of neurosis that would be useful for the advancement of better methods of treatment. Mowrer (1950) once suggested that "the absolutely central problem in neurosis . . . is a paradox—the paradox of behavior which is at one and the same time self-perpeptuating and self-defeating" (p. 180). I have attempted to suggest a solution to this problem along the lines of classical conditioning (Eysenck, 1982), and Tryon (1978) has tried to do so in terms of operant conditioning. I think a definition of *neurosis* must be based on an adequate theory of neurotic behavior; indeed, the two clearly depend on each other (Eysenck, 1982).

This type of almost-circular definition is common and even inevitable in science. Why do we use mercury and alcohol in liquid-in-glass thermometers, rather than water or linseed oil? The answer is that results achieved with the former, but not the latter, agree with predictions made by the kinetic theory, to the effect that

$$tf = \frac{m_1 t_1 + m_2 t_2}{m_1 + m_2}$$

It would, of course, be absurd to apply these principles if they did not show good agreement with common practice, but in fact they do. It would, therefore, be of great help if behavior therapists would make clearer distinctions between neurotic and nonneurotic problems, between problems better defined in terms of Pavlovian or Skinnerian conditioning, and between methods of treatment relevant to the appropriate theory. We will be in a much better position, as an organized group of scientists–practitioners, to confront our opponents and specify more clearly the precise nature of our position if we accept these proposals.

Much has been said in the preceding paragraphs about the time perspective of behavior therapy as a paradigm, that is, the present status of the art in terms of the issues discussed, the future course I would like to see behavior therapy take, and the steps needed to facilitate these desired directions of development. I think the present status of behavior therapy is confused: partly because of genuine difficulties in arriving at agreed theories, partly because of a willful disregard of contributions made by people whose theoretical orientations are inimical to one's own, and partly because of sheer ignorance.

In reading through the hundreds of books and thousands of articles that have contributed to this chapter, I was particularly impressed by the odd failure of the competitors to pay any attention to the precise nature of the position they were attacking. In my discussion I have singled out Skinner's position as being attacked, and sometimes defended, on entirely the wrong grounds. Much the same could be said of many other authors. Erwin (1980) has eloquently expounded on a similar misunderstanding by critics of my position with regard to the effectiveness of psychoanalysis and psychotherapy. I think it is unworthy of a scientific discipline to countenance rebarbative practices of this kind, that is, critiques not aimed at the true position of the opponent, critiques that obfuscate rather than illuminate. We should study in much greater detail the positive features of the opponents' positions rather than thunder away at imagined weaknesses. I know that this is a counsel of perfection unlikely to be found acceptable, but without something of the kind we will not reach the desired paradigm in our time.

Conclusions

As regards the future course of behavior therapy, I still think that what we need is better theories, better experiments, and better methods, all, of course, dependent on the recognition of the nature of our enterprise as applied science; we also need to stress similarities rather than differences and agreements rather than disagreements, building on what is common and deciding controversial questions by means of well-planned, well-executed experimental studies. The distance between clinicians and experimentalists is immense at the moment and seems hardly to be bridgeable, yet such a bridge is absolutely essential if we are to reconcile our differences and improve our methods. Theorists and experimentalists occasionally throw out comments about the possible applications of their work but hardly ever implement these or communicate with practitioners in an attempt to get cooperative work going. Similarly, clinicians disdainful of what they consider the minutiae of experimental and theoretical work fail to see its applicability to their practical problems, preferring to remain isolated from the mainstream of academic psychology.

In the future, I would like to see a coming together of these great traditions, with resulting benefit to both. I firmly believe that many of these problems of learning theory can be best tackled in relation to naturally occurring phenomena of neurotic disorder. For ethical reasons, it is impossible to produce strong emotional reactions or conditioned responses and their extinction in the laboratory.

As experimentalists, if we want to find out how these things happen, we must go to the clinic, ready to give as well as take, ready to help in the treatment as well as benefit from the experiments. Clinicians, on the other hand, should be aware that, useful as their present-day methods are when compared with earlier ones of psychodynamic origin, they are still far from perfect. Many important and vital problems remain. These can only be solved by means of better theories, more rigorous experimental tests, and clinical investigations planned along theoretical lines. Collaboration with experimentalists will be essential, leading to better understanding of theoretical issues, however recondite these may at first appear to be. Unless we speak a common language, we will not be able to get even as far as telling each other our problems. A great opportunity for improving the theoretical status of psychology, and at the same time improving its image in the eyes of the world by means of advancing better methods of treatment, will be lost. This, I think, would be a tragedy. Better education is, of course, the obvious answer to many of our problems, but what I have seen of the teachers is not reassuring. Most appear to me to be one-dimensional figures, knowledgeable in one area but ignorant in all others.

Admittedly the task is a difficult one, and the literature in enormous and constantly growing. Ideally, the teacher should be equally versed in the *Journal of Experimental Psychology*; *Personality and Individual Differences*; *Behaviour Research and Therapy*; *Psychophysiology*; *Psychometrika*; and *Behaviour Genetics*. If this seems a tall order, all one can say is that we are paid to be experts in this field, and these are the contributing streams that unite to produce the desired end-result of a strong current flowing toward greater achievement. If we cannot combine these various areas of expertise we do not deserve to aspire to a position equal on the mental and behavior side to the position of physicians on the physical side. Physicians, whatever their faults, do have a good and thorough training in many areas, ranging from physics and chemistry to physiology and anatomy. They spend years mastering an enormous amount of material, and it is not obvious to me why psychologists should not be asked to do the same in order to achieve the same social eminence and the same social status.

Perhaps the distance between the academic theoretician and the practical clinical psychologist is too wide to permit direct integration. In that case, it may be useful to take a leaf out of the book of the physicists (Gaston, 1973) who have found, by bitter experience, that a certain complex division of labor is needed. As Gaston points out, talking about high-energy physics:

The division of labor results from the very specialized task that each group of the community performs. Abstract theorists produce axiomatic theories that are not beneficial at present in explaining the behavior of elementary particles. Intermediate theorists produce theories that have more relevance for physical reality but are not yet very useful. Phenomenological theorists build and test models that are extremely useful to experimentalists. Bubble chamber experimentalists analyze photographic film to reconstruct elementary particle interactions. Counter/part chamber experimentalists monitor their detection devices as the particles are accelerated and collide with targets, providing the secondary particles and events of interest, and also analyze film from visual spark chambers. These five groups comprise a continuum of proximity to physical reality, with the abstract theorist being at the opposite end from physical reality while the counter/part chamber experimentalist not only records actual events as they are happening but are as near as safety measures allow while the experiment is taking place. Since each of these five tasks is so specialized, it is conceivable that these groups would not need to be in frequent communication with each other because of scientific necessity. (pp. 170–171)

Very few experimentalists, says Gaston, can judge the quality of an abstract theory, and few abstract theorists are able to judge the validity of experimental results. Indeed, he goes on to say that: "an abstract theorist would not ordinarily be able to suggest a crucial experiment— and if he were able, the experimentalist might not understand what he was talking about" (p. 171).

What holds this community together is the phenomenological theorists. They receive more recognition than any other group. Although relatively few in number, they are linked to more members of the scientific community than is any other subgroup. It is they who tie together the two extremes, the abstract theoreticians at the one end and the experimentalists at the other, interpreting the work of the former to the latter and reporting back results of the work of the latter to the former. Perhaps psychology needs such a group to act as intermediaries between theoreticians and clinicians. This suggestion is offered in all seriousness. Where the gap is as large as it appears to be at the moment, something drastic needs to be done, and an institutionalized form of intermediary appears to be the best available solution at this time.

Who else but such a phenomenological theorist would be able to interpret the possible role of autoshaping in the application of behavior therapy (Hearst & Jenkins, 1974), the importance of Herrnstein's mathematical statement of the law of effect for behavior therapy (McDowell, 1982), or the applicability of Pavlov's premise of equipotentiality in human classical conditioning (Ohman et al., 1976); judge Tryon's operant explanation of Mowrer's neurotic paradox; or relate the place of informational variables in Pavlovian conditioning (Rescorla, 1972) to the practice of behavior therapy? These are important theoretical concepts and contributions, but what part do they play in the practice of behavior therapy? Clearly some mediation is required.

But perhaps it will be necessary first of all for us to agree on important points in the paradigm we wish to present to the world. I can only hope that readers will agree with me that the basis for such a paradigm exists, that it is based on a paradigm shift from psychoanalysis to behavior therapy, and that the paradigm embraces behavioral and cognitive approaches in a unified theory of dialectical behaviorism. If only we can bury the hatchets of past disagreements and concentrate on what binds us together, we may yet surprise Kuhn and achieve what he thought impossible, namely, a genuine paradigm in the social sciences!

References

Achinstein, P. (1983). *The nature of explanation*. New York: Oxford University Press.

Allport, D.A. (1975). The state of cognitive psychology. *Quarterly Journal of Experimental Psychology*, 141–152.

Armstrong, D.M. (1984). *What is a law of nature?* London: Cambridge Press.

Baer, P.E., & Fuhrer, M.J. (1968). Cognitive processes during differential trace and delayed conditioning of the GSR. *Journal of Experimental Psychology*, 78, 81–88.

Baer, P.E., & Fuhrer, M.J. (1970). Cognitive processes in the differential trace conditioning of electrodermal and vasomotor activity. *Journal of Experimental Psychology*, 84, 176–178.

Bandura, A. (1978). Self-efficacy: Toward a unifying theory of behavioral change. *Advances in Behaviour Research and Therapy*, 1, 139–161.

Barnes, B. (1982). *T.S. Kuhn and social science*. London: Macmillan.

Beck, A.T. (1976). *Cognitive therapy and the emotional disorders*. New York: International Universities Press.

Bergin, A.E., & Lambert, M.J. (1978). The evaluation of therapeutic outcomes. In S.L. Garfield & A.E. Bergin (Eds.), *Handbook of psychotherapy and behavior change: An empirical analysis* (pp. 139–190) New York: Wiley.

Bernal, J.D. (1954). *Science and history* (Vols. 1-4). London: Watts.

Biferno, G.A., & Dawson, M.E. 1977). The onset of contingency awareness and electrodermal classical conditioning: An analysis of temporal relationships during acquisition and extinction. *Psychophysiology*, 14, 164–171.

Blackman, D.E. (1983). On cognitive theories of animal learning: Extrapolation from humans to animals? In G. Davey (Ed.), *Animal models of human behavior* (pp. 37–50). New York: Wiley.

Boakes, R.A. (1983). Behaviorism and the nature–nurture controversy. In G.

Davey (Ed.), *Animal models of human behaviour.* (pp. 83–94) New York: Wiley.

Breger, L., & McGaugh, J.L. (1965). Critique and reformulation of "learning theory" approaches to psychotherapy and neurosis. *Psychological Bulletin, 63,* 338–358.

Breger, L., & McGaugh, J.L. (1966). Learning theory and behavior therapy. A reply to Rachman and Eysenck. *Psychological Bulletin, 65,* 170–173.

Brewer, W.F. (1974). There is no convincing evidence for operant and classical conditioning in humans. In W.B. Weisner & H.J. Palermo (Eds.), *Cognition and the symbolic processes* (pp. 39–58) Hillsdale, NJ: Erlbaum.

Buchdahl, G. (1969). *Metaphysics and the philosophy of science.* Oxford, England: Blackwell.

Campbell, D., Sanderson, R.E., & Laverty, S.G. (1964). Characteristics of a conditioned response in human subjects during extinction trials following a single traumatic conditioning trial. *Journal of Abnormal and Social Psychology, 68,* 627–639.

Catalano, R. (1979). *Health behavior and the community: An ecological perspective.* New York: Pergamon.

Catania, A.C. (1983). Behavior analysis and behavior synthesis in the extrapolation from animal to human behavior. In G. Davey (Ed.), *Animal models of human behavior* (pp. 51–70). New York: Wiley.

Chomsky, N. (1975). *Reflections on language.* Glasgow, Scotland: Collins.

Cohen, I.B. (1980). *The Newtonian revolution.* London: Cambridge University Press.

Coljan, D.M. (1970). Effects of instruction on the skin resistance response. *Journal of Experimental Psychology, 86,* 108–112.

Conant, J.B. (Ed.). (1964). *The overthrow of the phlogiston theory.* London: Cambridge University press.

Corteen, R.J., & Wood, C. (1972). Autonomic responses to shock-associated words in an unattended channel. *Journal of Experimental Psychology, 94,* 308–313.

Davey, G. (1983). An associative view of human classical conditioning. In G. Davey (Ed.), *Animal models of human behaviour* (pp. 95–114). London: Wiley.

Dawson, M.E. (1973). Can classical conditioning occur without contingency learning? A review and evaluation of the evidence. *Psychophysiology, 10,* 82–86.

Dawson, M.E., & Biferno, M.A. (1973). Concurrent measurement of awareness and electrodermal classical conditioning. *Journal of Experimental Psychology, 101,* 55–62.

Dawson, M.E., Catania, J.J., Schell, A.M., & Grings, W.W. (1979). Autonomic classical conditioning as a function of awareness of stimulus contingencies. *Biological Psychology, 9,* 23–40.

Dawson, M.E., & Grings, W.W. (1968). Comparison of classical conditioning and relational earning. *Journal of Experimental Psychology, 76,* 227–231.

Dawson, M.E., & Schell, M.E. (1982). Electrodermal responses to attended and non-attended stimuli during dichotic listening. *Journal of Experimental Psychology, Human Perception and Performance, 8,* 315–324.

Eaglen, A. (1978). Learning theory versus paradigms as the basis for behavior therapy. *Journal of Behavior Therapy and Experimental Psychiatry 9*, 215–218.

Eaves, L., & Eysenck, H.J. (1985). *The genetics of personality.* London: Academic Press.

Ellis, A. (1974). *Humanistic psychotherapy: The rational–emotive approach.* New York: Julian.

Erwin, E. (1978). *Behavior therapy: Scientific, philosophical and moral foundations.* New York: Cambridge University Press.

Erwin, E. (1980). Psychoanalytic therapy. The Eysenck argument. *American Psychologist, 35*, 435–443.

Eysenck, H.J. (1952). The effects of psychotherapy: An evaluation. *Journal of Consulting Psychology, 16*, 319–324.

Eysenck, H.J. (1954). *The psychology of politics.* London: Routledge & Kegan Paul.

Eysenck, H.J. (1959). Learning theory and behaviour therapy. *The Journal of Mental Science, 105*, 61–75.

Eysenck, H.J. (Ed.). (1960). *Behaviour therapy and the neuroses.* Oxford, England: Pergamon.

Eysenck, H.J. (Ed.). (1964). *Experiments in behaviour therapy.* Oxford, England: Pergamon.

Eysenck, H.J. (1968). A theory of the incubation of anxiety/fear responses. *Behaviour Research and Therapy, 6*, 309–321.

Eysenck, H.J. (1970). A mish-mash of theories. *International Journal of Psychiatry, 9*, 140–146.

Eysenck, H.J. (1972) Behaviour therapy is behavioristic. *Behavior therapy, 3*, 609–613.

Eysenck, H.J. (1976a), *Behaviour therapy—Dogma or applied science?* In M.P. Feldman & A. Broadhurst (Eds.), *The theoretical and experimental foundations of behaviour therapy* (pp. 333–363). London: Wiley.

Eysenck, H.J. (1976b). The learning theory model of neurosis—A new approach. *Behaviour Research and Therapy, 14*, 251–267.

Eysenck, H.J. (1978a). Expectations as causal elements in behavioral change. *Advances in Behaviour Research and Therapy, 1*, 171–175.

Eysenck, H.J. (1978b) What to do when desensitization goes wrong? *Australian Behaviour Therapist, 5*, 15–16.

Eysenck, H.J. (1979). The conditioning model of neurosis. *The Behavioral and Brain Sciences, 2*, 155–199.

Eysenck, H.J. (1980). A unified theory of psychotherapy, behaviour therapy and spontaneous remission. *Zeitschrift für Psychologie, 188*, 43–56.

Eysenck, H.J. (1982). Neobehavioristic (S-R) theory. In G.T. Wilson & C.M. Franks (Eds.), *Contemporary behavior therapy* (pp. 205–276). New York: Guilford Press.

Eysenck, H.J. (1983). In M.L. Smith, G.V. Glass, & T.I. Miller (Eds.), The benefits of psychotherapy (special issue). *Behaviour Research and Therapy, 21*, 315–320.

Eysenck, H.J. (1985). *The decline and fall of the Freudian Empire.* London: Viking.

Eysenck, H.J., & Eysenck, M.W. (1985). *Personality and individual differences.* New York: Plenum.

Eysenck, H.J., & Rachman, S. (1965). *Causes and cures of neurosis.* London: Routledge & Kegan Paul.

Feather, B.W., & Rhoads, J.M. (1972) Psychodynamic behavior therapy. *Archives of General Psychiatry, 26,* 496–511.

Foa, E.B., & Goldstein, A. (1978). Continuous response and strict response prevention in the treatment of obsessive-compulsive neurosis. *Behavior Therapy, 17,* 169–176.

Franks, C.M. (1984). On conceptual and technical integrity in psychoanalysis and behavior therapy. In H. Arkowitz & S. B. Messer (Eds.), *Psychoanalytic therapy and behavior therapy* (pp. 223–247). New York: Plenum.

Fuhrer, M.J. & Baer, P.E. (1969). Cognitive processes in differential GSR conditioning: Effects of a masking task. *American Journal of Psychology, 82,* 168–180.

Gaston, J. (1973). *Originality and competition in science.* Chicago: University of Chicago Press.

Gognen, J.A. (1968). The logic of inexact concepts. *Synthese, 19,* 325–373.

Goldfried, M.R. (1980). Toward the delineation of therapeutic change. *American Psychologist, 35,* 991–999.

Goldfried, M.R., & Goldfried, A.P. (1975). Cognitive change methods. In F.H. Kaufer & A.P./ Goldstein (Eds.), *Helping people change* (pp. 143–172). New York: Pergamon.

Gossop, M. (1981). *Theories of neurosis.* New York: Springer.

Grant, D.G. (1964). Classical and operant conditioning. In A.W. Melton (Ed.), *Categories of human learning.* New York. Academic Press.

Gray, J.A. (1975). *Elements of a two-process theory of learning.* London: Academic Press.

Grings, W.W., & Dawson, M.E. (1973). Complex conditioning. In W.F. Prokasy & D.C. Raskin (Eds.), *Electrodermal activity in psychological research.* New York: Academic Press.

Grünbaum, A. (1984). *The foundations of psychoanalysis: A philosophical critique.* London: University of California Press.

Habermas, J. (1970). *Zur logik der sozialwissenschaften.* Frankfurt: Suhrkamp Verlag.

Harré, R., & Secord, P.F. (1972). *The explanation of social behaviour.* Oxford, England: Blackwell.

Hearst, E., & Jenkins, H.M. (1974). *Sign tracking: The stimulus reinforcer relation and directed action.* Austin, TX: Psychonomic Society.

Horne, P.J., & Lowe, C.F. (1982). Determinants of human performance on multiple concurrent variable interval schedules. *Behavior Analysis Letters, 2,* 186–187.

Humphrey, L. (1983). *Consciousness regained.* Oxford University Press.

Jardine, N. (1984). *The birth of history and philosophy of science.* London: Cambridge University Press.

Jones, M.C. (1924). The elimination of children's fears. *Journal of Experimental Psychology, 7,* 383–390.

Katz, A., Webb, L., & Stotland, E. (1971). Cognitive influences on the rate of

GSR extinction. *Journal of Experimental Research in Personality, 5,* 208–215.

Kazdin, A.E. (1978). *History of behavior modifications.* Baltimore: University Park Press.

Kazdin, A.E., & Wilson, G.T. (1978). *Evaluation of behavior therapy.* Cambridge, MA: Ballinger.

Kendall, P.C., & Hollon, S.D. (1979). *Cognitive-behavioral interventions: Theory, research and procedures.* New York: Academic Press.

Kendler, H.H. (1981). *Psychology: A science in conflict.* Oxford, England: Oxford University Press.

Koenig, K.P., & Castillo, D.D. (1969). False feedback and longevity of the conditioned GSR during extinction: Some implications for aversion therapy. *Journal of Experimental Psychology, 74,* 505–510.

Kuhn, T.S. (1959). *The Copernican revolution.* New York: Vintage.

Kuhn, T.S. (1970). *The structure of scientific revolutions.* Chicago: University of Chicago Press.

Kuhn, T.S. (1974). Second thoughts of paradigms. In F. Suppe (Ed.), *The structure of scientific theories* (pp. 459–482). London: University of Illinois Press.

Lakatos, I. (1976). *Proofs and refutations.* London: Cambridge University Press.

Latimer, P.R., & Sweet, A.A. (1984). Cognitive versus behavioral procedures in cognitive behavior therapy: Critical review of the evidence. *Journal of Behavior Therapy and Experimental Psychiatry, 15,* 9–22.

Ledwidge, B. (1978). Cognitive-behavior modification: A step in the wrong direction? *Psychological Bulletin, 85,* 353–375.

Locke, E.A. (1971). Is "behavior therapy" behavioristic? *Psychological Bulletin, 76,* 318–327.

Locke, E.A. (1979). Behavior modification is not cognitive and other myths. A reply to Ledwidge. *Cognitive Therapy and Research, 3,* 119–125.

London, P. (1972). The end of ideology in behavior modification. *American Psychologist, 27,* 913–920.

Lowe, C.F. (1979). Determinants of human operant behavior. In M.D. Zeiler & P. Harzem (Eds.), *Advances in analysis of behavior: Vol. 1. Reinforcement and the organization of behavior* (pp. 159–192). Chichester: Wiley.

Lowe, C.F. (1983). Radical behaviorism and human psychology. In G. Davey (Ed.), *Animal models of human behaviour* (pp. 71–94). New York: Wiley.

Luborsky, L., Singer, B., & Luborsky, L. (1975). Comparative studies of psychotherapies: Is it true that "everyone has won and all must have prizes?" *Archives of General Psychiatry, 32,* 995–1008.

MacIntosh, N.J. (1974). *The psychology of animal learning.* London: Academic Press.

MacIntosh, N.J. (1984). *Conditioning and associative learning.* Oxford, England: Clarendon Press.

MacKinnon, E.M. (1982). *Scientific explanations of atomic physics.* London: University of Chicago Press.

Maher, B. (1972). Scientific aspects of behavior therapy. *Seminars of Psychiatry, 4,* 121–128.

Mahoney, M.J. (1977). Reflections on the cognitive learning trend in psychotherapy. *American Psychologist, 32*, 5–13.

Maier, N.R.F. (1949). *Frustration: The study of behavior without a goal.* New York: McGraw-Hill.

Maier, N.R.F., & Ellen, P. (1951). Can the anxiety-reduction theory explain abnormal fixations? *Psychological Review, 58*, 435–445.

Marmor, J., & Woods, G.M. (1980). *The interface between the psychodynamic and behavioral therapies.* New York: Plenum.

Martin, I., & Levey, A. (1978). Evaluative conditioning. *Advances in Behavior Research and Therapy, 1*, 57–101.

Martin, I., & Levey, A. (1979). Classical conditioning. In M. Christie & P. Mellett (Eds.), *Psychosomatic approaches in medicine: Vol. 1. Behavioural approaches.* London: Wiley.

Marzillier, J.S. (1980). Cognitive therapy and behavioural practice. *Behaviour Research and Therapy, 18*, 249–258.

Masterman, M. (1974). The nature of a paradigm. In I. Lakatos & A. Musgrave (Eds.) *Criticism and the growth of knowledge* (pp. 59–90). New York: Cambridge University Press.

Mays, D.T., & Franks, C.M. (1986). *Negative outcome in psychotherapy and what to do about it.* New York: Springer.

McComb, D. (1969). Cognitive and learning effects in the production of GSR conditioning data. *Psychonomic Science, 16*, 96–97.

McDowell, J.J. (1982). The importance of Herrnstein's mathematical statement of the law of effect for behavior therapy. *American Psychologist, 37*, 771–779.

Meichenbaum, P.H. (1975). Self-instructional methods. In F.H. Kanfer & A.P. Goldstein (Eds.), *Helping people change.* New York: Pergamon.

Mendelsohn, K. (1966). *The quest for absolute zero.* London: Weidenfeld & Nicolson.

Messer, S.B., & Winokur, M. (1980). Some limits to the integration of psychoanalytic and behavior therapy. *American Psychologist, 35*, 818–827.

Meyer, V., Levey, R., & Schnurer, A. (1974). The behavioural treatment of obssessive-compulsive disorder. In H.R. Beech (Ed.), *Obsessional states.* London: Methuen.

Morgan, R.T.T. (1978). Relapse and therapeutic response in the conditioning treatment of enuresis: A review of recent findings on intermittent reinforcement, overlearning and stimulus intensity. *Behaviour Research and Therapy, 16*, 273–279.

Mowrer, O.H. (1950). *Learning theory and personality dynamics.* New York: Arnold.

Newton-Smith, W.H. (1981). *The rationality of science.* London: Routledge & Kegan Paul.

Nisbett, R.E., & Wilson, T. (1977). Telling more than we can know: Verbal reports on mental processes. *Psychological Review, 84*, 231–259.

Öhman, A., Fredrikson, M., Hugdahl, K., & Rimmö, P. (1976). The premise of equipotentiality in human classical conditioning: Conditioned electrodermal responses to potentially phobic stimuli. *Journal of Experimental Psychology: General, 105*, 313–337.

Platonov, K. (1959). *The word as a physiological and therapeutic factor.* Moscow: Foreign Languages Publishing House.

Popper, K. (1935). *Logik der forschung.* Vienna: J. Springer.

Popper, K. (1965). *Conjectures and refutations.* New York: Basic Books.

Prioleau, L., Murdock, M., & Brody, N. (1983). An analysis of psychotherapy versus placebo studies. *The Behavioral and Brain Sciences, 6,* 275–285.

Rachman, S. (1966). Studies in desensitization. 11. Flooding. *Behaviour Research and Therapy, 4,* 1–6.

Rachman, S. (Ed.) (1978). Perceived self-efficacy. *Symposium in Advances in Behaviour Research and Therapy, 1,* 37–269.

Rachman, S., & Eysenck, H.J. (1966). Reply to a "critique and reformulation" of behavior therapy. *Psychological Bulletin, 65,* 165–169.

Rachman, S.J., & Hodgson, R.J. (1980). *Obsessions and compulsions.* Englewood Cliffs, NJ: Prentice-Hall.

Rachman, S., & Wilson, G.T. (1980). *The effects of psychological therapy.* London: Pergamon.

Rescorla, R.A. (1972). Informational variables in Pavlovian conditioning. In G.M. Bower (Ed.), *The psychology of learning and motivation.* New York: Academic Press.

Rhoads, J.M., & Feather, B.W. (1974). Application of psychodynamics to behavior therapy. *American Journal of Psychiatry, 131,* 17–20.

Ricoeur, P. (1970). *Freud and philosophy.* New Haven, CT: Yale University Press.

Ricoeur, P. (1981). *Hermeneutics and the human sciences.* New York: Cambridge University Press.

Rose, R.J., & Ditto, W.B. (1983). A developmental genetic analysis of common fears from early adolescence to early childhood. *Child Development, 54,* 361–368.

Ross, L.E., Ferreira, M.C., & Ross, S.M. (1974). Backward masking and conditioned stimuli: Effects on differential and single cue classical conditioning performance. *Journal of Experimental Psychology, 103,* 603–616.

Ryle, A. (1978). A common language for the psychotherapies. *British Journal of Psychiatry, 132,* 585–594.

Scharnberg, M. (1984). The myth of paradigm-shift, or how to lie with methodology. Uppsala: Aluguist & Wikersell.

Schorr, A. (1984). *Die verhaltenstherapie.* Weinheim: Beltz.

Skinner, B.F. (1957). *Verbal behavior.* New York: Appleton-Century-Crofts.

Skinner, B.F. (1974). *About behavourism.* London: Jonathan Cape.

Smith, M.L., Glass, G.V., & Miller, T.I. (1980). *The benefits of psychotherapy.* Baltimore: John Hopkins University Press.

Solomon, R.L., Kamin, L.J., & Wynne, L.C. (1953). Traumatic avoidance learning: The outcomes of several extinction procedures with dogs. *The Journal of Abnormal and Social Psychology, 48,* 291–302.

Solomon, R.L., & Wynne, L.C. (1953). Traumatic avoidance learning: Acquisition in normal dogs. *Psychological Monographs, 67* (4, Whole No. 354).

Staats, A.W. (1964). *Human learning.* New York: Holt, Rinehart & Winston.

Staats, A.W. (1968). *Learning, language and cognition.* New York: Holt, Rinehart & Winston.

Strupp, H.H. (1979). Psychotherapy research and practice: An overview. In S.L. Garfield & G.E. Bergin (Eds.), *Handbook of psychotherapy and behavior change: An empirical analysis* (pp. 3–22). New York: Wiley.

Strupp, H.H., Hadley, S.W., & Gomes-Schwartz, B. (1977). *Psychotherapy for better or worse: The problem of negative effects.* New York: Aronson.

Suppe, F. (Ed.). (1974). *The structure of scientific theories.* London: University of Illinois Press.

Thouless, R.H. (1935). The tendency to certainty in religious beliefs. *British Journal of Psychology, 26,* 16–31.

Torgersen, S. (1979). The nature and origin of common phobic fears. *British Journal of Psychiatry, 134,* 343–351.

Tryon, W.W. (1978). An operant explanation of Mowrer's neurotic paradox. *Behaviorism, 6,* 203–211.

Tweney, R.D., Doherty, M.E., & Mynatt, C.R. (Eds.). (1981). *On scientific thinking.* New York: Columbia University Press.

Ullmann, L.P. (1981). Cognitions: Help or hindrance? *Journal of Behavior Therapy and Experimental Psychiatry, 12,* 19–23.

Wachtel, P.L. (1977). *Psychoanalysis and behavior therapy.* New York. Basic Books.

Wallace, B., & Fisher, L.E. (1983). *Consciousness and behaviour.* London: Allyn & Bacon.

Watson, J.B. (1930). *Behaviorism.* New York: Norton.

Watson, J.B., & Rayner, R. (1920). Conditioned emotional reactions. *Journal of Experimental Psychology, 3,* 1–14.

Wilson, G.D. (1968). Reversal and differential GSR conditioning by instruction. *Journal of Experimental Psychology, 26,* 491–493.

Wilson, G.T. (1978). Cognitive behavior therapy: Paradigm shift or passing phase? In J. Forey, T., & D. Rathjen (Eds.), *Cognitive behavior therapy: Research and application* (pp. 7–37). New York: Plenum.

Wolpe, J. (1958). *Psychotherapy by reciprocal inhibition.* Stanford, CA: Stanford University Press.

Wolpe, J. (1976a). Behavior therapy and its malcontents—I. Denial of its bases and psychodynamic fusionism. *Journal of Behavior Therapy and Experimental Psychiatry, 7,* 1–5.

Wolpe, J. (1976b). Behavior therapy and its malcontents—II. Multimodel eclecticism, cognitive exclusionism and exposure empiricisim. *Journal of Behavior Therapy and Experimental Psychiatry, 7,* 109–116.

Wolpe, J. (1978). Cognition and causation—human behavior in therapy. *American Psychologist, 33,* 437–446.

Wolpe, J. (1981). The dichotomy between classical conditioned and cognitively learned anxiety. *Journal of Behavior Therapy and Experimental Psychiatry, 12,* 35–42.

Yates, J. (1983). Behaviour therapy and psychodynamic psychotherapy. Basic conflict or reconciliation and integration? *British Journal of Clinical Psychology, 22,* 107–125.

Zadeh, L.A. (1965). Fuzzy sets and systems. In J. Fox (Ed.), *System theory* (pp. 29–37). New York: Polytechnic Press.

Zener, K. (1937). The significance of behavior accompanying conditioned salivary secretion for theories of the conditioned response. *American Journal of Psychology, 50,* 384–403.

5

Molar Behaviorism *

Howard Rachlin

During the past 15 years, those of us studying the behavior of rats and pigeons in Skinner boxes and publishing in the *Journal of the Experimental Analysis of Behavior* have developed a molar form of behaviorism. The methods and concepts we have come to use and the theories we argue about are, we believe, not only interesting but important and, what is more, applicable to the concerns of everyday life.

Yet most behavior therapists, the people who first saw how radical behaviorism could revolutionize clinical psychology, have ignored molar behaviorism. Some, loyal to Watson, Hull, Pavlov, or Skinner, continue to rely on molecular behavioral principles. They have learned that cumulative response rates scallop on fixed-interval schedules and that punishment does not work; and these "facts" (both of which are probably false), plus one or two others, underly their practices. The principles upon which their therapy is based, developed prior to Herrnstein's (1961) crucial work on choice, are overly simplistic, if not disproven outright.

Other behavior therapists, tired of applying techniques based on simplistic theories to complex problems or having tried and failed, have joined the cognitive revolution and became cognitive behavior therapists. Because the cognitive vanguard has adopted the computer metaphor, one might expect cognitive behavior therapy to make use of that metaphor. Dysfunctional behavior might be viewed as faulty push-down storage, information loss in processing, output malfunc-

* This chapter was prepared with the help of a grant from the National Science Foundation. I thank Marvin Frankel, Marvin Goldfried, Leonard Krasner, and K. Daniel O'Leary for their many helpful comments and suggestions.

tion, and so forth. But this vocabulary does not seem to have been adopted. Instead, cognitive behavior therapy has become a straightforward return to mentalism. When these therapists abandoned radical behaviorism, they abandoned science as well.

This chapter suggests that molar behaviorism may be a useful paradigm in therapy. Unlike cognitivism or Freudianism or other explanatory theories, molar behaviorism does not require that the client be convinced to accept any particular view of his or her behavior or of the world. While molar behaviorism is strictly behavioral, it is easily translated into everyday mentalistic terms. The client may maintain one view of a client–therapist interaction, along with one vocabulary, and the therapist another, along with another vocabulary.

The Function of Theory in Psychology

What is a theory supposed to do in the first place? Consider two possible roles; one I shall call Aristotelian, the other, platonic.

The Aristotelian role of theory is to mirror reality. According to Randall (1960), a generally accepted authority, "Aristotle's aim is to understand, to find out why things are as they are. It is not to control things, not to make them different from what they are. . . . Aristotle sought intelligibility rather than power. Or better, we can say that for Aristotle the highest power a man can exercise over the world is to understand it" (pp. 2–3). For Aristotle, "we can be said to 'know' a thing only when we can state in precise language what a thing is and why it is as it is" (Randall, p. 7). In other words, understanding is achieved through explanation. Explanation requires two components, a functioning world and a language with which to describe it. The language Aristotle used for this purpose was Greek. We might use English or logic or mathematics. In any case, a theory would be a set of words, sentences, which reflect the world. The more precise the reflection, the better the theory. In this view, truth and falsity mean a better or worse fit, or match, between the world and the language with which it is described.

Transferring this conception to our present concern, the purpose of theory in clinical psychology would be to provide a model of human behavior. An ideal theory would be one that matched human behavior in every respect. This theory could then be said to explain and thereby provide understanding of human behavior. Once the initial job of explanation was done, it would be a trivial exercise, according to this view, to use the theory in therapy to change human behavior. Prediction and control would follow from a true explanation.

For this program to work there must exist a clear and undisputed dividing line between the world that is described by language and the language that describes the world. Otherwise, arguments will arise about what belongs to the world itself and what belongs to the description of it. As applied to the behavior of physical objects, this division seems valid. There is, on the one hand, a stone and, on the other, our description in English or mathematics of the stone's behavior. The Aristotelian point of view can be applied to the behavior of nonhuman animals as well as stones. On one hand, there is the frog flapping out its tongue and catching a fly in midair: on the other hand, there is an English or mathematical description of this process. The frog itself does not know what it is doing, but we humans may know because we are capable of mirroring the frog's behavior by our language. A neat division is thus possible. The stone or the frog *behaves,* but we *understand.* Given such understanding, prediction of the frog's tongue-flapping behavior would indeed follow in a straightforward way and control would be made possible.

However, when applied to human behavior, this point of view runs into trouble. People not only behave as stones and frogs do, we also speak and write. It is not always easy to distinguish between a person's verbal and nonverbal behavior. Is it language or behavior when a mother coos to her baby or a man says "pass the salt"? Is one child's pushing another aggressive behavior, but that same child's saying "I hate you" a description of an internal state?

Even if we could always decide between language and other behavior, is language itself to be left unexplained, understood? Would simply repeating what a person says constitute adequate understanding or explanation of it? Obviously not. To be explained, one language would have to be *translated* into another, more precise, language—mathematics, say, or logic (the goal of positivism). But many such mathematical or logical translations are possible. To evaluate one against another we would need a set of independent rules (translation rules) by which each logical or mathematical theory could be related to the verbal behavior it was intended to describe. As Wittgenstein (1958) showed, however, it is no easier to decide which of several translation rules is best than it is to decide which of several theories is best in the first place. In any case, behavior therapists want to understand human behavior by predicting and controlling it, not merely by explaining it. (Otherwise they would have been content with Christian, Freudian, Jungian, or any of a host of theories that, historically, have provided comprehensive explanations.) Even if a true explanation and true translation were agreed upon, there is no guarantee that they could be used to predict and control human behavior.

Let us, therefore, go back and consider a different starting point, that of Plato. For him, the ultimate object of a theory was not to explain the world but to help us live a better life: "Of all inquiries . . . the noblest is that which concerns . . . what a man should be, and what he should practice and to what extent both when older and when young." (*Gorgias*, 487e). This is a purpose congruent with that of behavior therapy.* Knowledge, for Plato, is entirely at the service of this goal. When language helps us to live a better life, it may be true understanding. When language does not help us in living a better life it is false, regardless of how it may seem to reflect, mirror, or match the world. From the Platonic viewpoint there is no boundary between language and the rest of life. According to Friedlander (1964, p. 200), Plato sees words "as instruments after the model of tools in the crafts." Language is behavior with a special function, not to *model* or *reflect* other behavior but to *control* other behavior. Language is a tool in the service of control where "control" includes self-control. (Nothing in Plato's dialogues contradicts Skinner's view of verbal behavior as a discriminative stimulus for other reinforced behavior, including other verbal behavior. A theory for Skinner, as for Plato, is a complex discriminative stimulus. It function in our lives is that of a discriminative stimulus—to control or own behavior and that of other people so as to maximize reinforcement.)

Underlying this notion of the purpose of theory is Plato's concept of what constitutes a good life. In forming this concept, one rule is applied consistently—what is good in the long run is better than what is pleasurable in the short run. The 'good' is not simply the sum of immediate pleasures but consists of certain combinations or patterns of behavior. People achieve good lives when the patterns of their behavior as whole persons, not just their verbal behavior, conform to patterns in the world. For others, especially tyrants, Plato says, "the penalty they pay is the life they lead" (*Theatetus*, 177a).

It makes no sense to ask, in this context, whether a theory is "objective" or uninfluenced by our motives. A theory, in Plato's view, is not just influenced by our motives, it is an *artifact* of our motives (i.e., our long-term goals). It is entirely at the service of our motives. Should our

---

* I have argued elsewhere (Rachlin, 1985a) that Plato may be interpreted in wholly behavioral terms and that his theory of human behavior is essentially behavioral maximization theory.

motives change, our theories must change along with them. But, for Plato, our *longest-term* motives will never change.

From this point of view, one theory cannot be tested against another by how well it conforms to reality (in modern terms, by stating an hypothesis, collecting "objective" data, and performing a statistical test). Such hypotheses were the kind that Newton rejected and Skinner (1950) claimed were unnecessary. From this point of view, an experiment that does no more than "confirm" a theory is useless. An experiment, to be useful, must advance not our explanation of the world, but our ability to live good lives—our ability to predict and control our own behavior and that of others so that short-term pleasures will be avoided when they conflict with our happiness in the long run.

For a person holding this view, a theory would be a guide to empirical investigation but it would never be disconfirmed by the results of one or two "crucial" experiments. The test of a theory would be its utility as it was modified by the evidence, not whether it remained inviolate. From this viewpoint, Hull's (1943) S-R behaviorism died not because it was proved wrong but because it became unwieldy as it was modified to account for data. If the Platonic function of theory were accepted, Krasner and Houts (1984) would be justified in their dismay when they discovered that most behaviorists agreed with the statement: "Scientific observation provides us with hard data independent of our subjective desires, wishes, and biases" (p. 845). Such data would be utterly useless. No data would be neutral. Data would be viewable only *through* the observer's theory. Possibly, the behaviorists who agreed with the statement interpreted "subjective" as "immediate," thereby making the statement meaningful in Platonic terms.

The second (the Platonic) of the two functions of theory is clearly more congenial to the goals of behavior therapy than is the first (the Aristotelian). Behaviorism, in its molecular form, especially as conceptualized by Skinner, does seem generally to have adopted this goal. In recent years, however, molecular behaviorism has run up against several conceptual and empirical difficulties. Many behavior therapists have abandoned molecular behaviorism and adopted cognitivism in one form or another. I will argue that this was a poor trade, that it was a mistake. Behavior therapists, in making this trade, have inadvertently abandoned the Platonic for the Aristotelian view without coming to grips with its problems. The mistake is understandable—explanation is easy, prediction and control are hard. It would have been avoided, however, if behavior therapists had paid attention to developments within the behavioral laboratory, particularly the development of molar behaviorism.

Molecular Behaviorism, Cognitivism, and Physiologism

All human behavior beyond instincts carried directly through the genes may be explained in terms of classical and instrumental conditioning. The former process consists of the pairing of a discrete conditioned stimulus with a discrete unconditioned stimulus. The conditioned stimulus, by virtue of the pairing, comes to elicit a conditioned response. For instance, the ongoing behavior of a rat repeatedly exposed to a tone, the conditioned stimulus, and then shocked, the unconditioned stimulus, may be disrupted when the tone alone is sounded. The disruption is said to be an index of an internal conditioned response, often labeled "fear" or "anxiety." Application to everyday human behavior involves tracing instances of fear (disruptive of normal behavior) to previous pairing of a stimulus now contiguous with the fear (the putative conditioned stimulus) with some primary aversive stimulus (the putative unconditioned stimulus). When such disruption is dysfunctional, a behavior therapist might attempt to extinguish the fear by methods developed in the laboratory—systematic desensitization, for example.

As most commonly studied, instrumental conditioning consists of the pairing of a discrete response, such as a rat's lever press, with a discrete positive or negative reinforcer, such as eating a pellet of food or the removal of an electric shock. Both positive and negative reinforcement procedures result in increases of response rates. Thus, a rat's rate of lever pressing increases when lever presses are repeatedly followed by eating pellets of food (or reduction of shock intensity). Application to human behavior involves tracing instances of a response presently occurring at a high rate to prior pairings of that response with a positive or negative reinforcer, for instance, pairing a baby's crying with reduction of the aversive stimulation from a cold, wet diaper. When such a response is dysfunctional, a behavior therapist might attempt to reduce its rate by removing its reinforcement, or reinforcing other behavior incompatible with the dysfunctional response, or both. For instance, a teacher might treat a boy's hyperactivity in the classroom by ignoring it (extinction) and paying more attention to the boy when he is sitting quietly in his seat or peacefully cooperating with others. Such treatment assumes the hyperactive behavior, whatever its origin, had been maintained (reinforced) by the teacher's attention.

Within the molecular behavioral paradigm, to predict or control a response of a person in a real-world environment it is necessary to discover either stimuli that reliably elicit the response or stimuli that reliably reinforce it. To conform to the molecular conception of conditioning, such eliciting and reinforcing stimuli must furthermore be contiguous with the response. In the case of classical conditioning, when eliciting stimuli are not found in the immediate environment, chains of second- or third-order conditioned stimuli must be found in the environment to bridge the temporal gap between the primary eliciting stimulus and the response. For instance, a person's normal behavior might begin to be disrupted by fear of a dentist hours before an appointment. To explain such fear in terms of classical conditioning, one would have to find environmental chains of stimuli that reliably occur between the first signs of fear and the drilling itself. When such stimuli are not found, they are often merely supposed to occur inside the person in terms of a sequence of physiological events, or a sequence of ideas or images, or perhaps an internal clock, the readings of which lead in chainlike (contiguous) fashion from present stimuli to later stimuli (in the dentist's office). By hypothesizing the existence of such events we apparently explain the workings of the mind, but, in practice, we lose prediction and control.

In the case of instrumental conditioning, when reinforcing stimuli do not exist in the immediate environment, chains of conditioned reinforcers must be found in the environment to bridge the temporal gap between a response and primary reinforcement. For instance, a person works at a job not for food, clothing, and shelter directly but for money, which is differentially paired with these primary reinforcers. But almost never is each act of work followed by payment. A series of stimuli, conditioned reinforcers and discriminative stimuli, must be found between a discrete work response and eventual payment—approval from the boss, sight of a pile of completed work next to a machine, a tally of work done, sight of the office clock, and so forth. Where such stimuli are not found they must be hypothesized to exist inside the person. These hypothetical events have taken many forms: physiological response proprioception, a memory of work completed, an internal clock, an r_s-s_g connection, an internal operant or respondent, a thought, a hope, a wish, a dream. Hypothesizing their existence trades prediction and control for explanation, trades the Platonic for the Aristotelian conceptions of science—progress, perhaps, in philosophy, but regress in attainment of the goals of behavior therapy.

It may be fairly claimed that molecular behaviorism demands such a trade, that without postulating internal mechanisms we would lose both explanation *and* prediction and control of those actions that cannot be explained by molecular behaviorism alone. Furthermore, those unexplained actions seem to represent important and extensive areas of human behavior. With the inference of internal connections, at least explanation is salvaged.

This problem (with molecular behaviorism) and this solution (phy-siologism or cognitivism) are not unique to behavior therapy. It oc-curred quite early in the development of molecular behaviorism in the laboratory—mostly in its attempt to deal with aversive control.

In attempting to explain (without the negative law of effect) why punishment works, Thorndike (1932) postulated an internal mecha-nism—negative reinforcement of behavior other than that being pun-ished. Mowrer's (1960) two-factor theory of avoidance holds that overt avoidance responses not immediately followed by reduction of a pri-mary aversive stimulus are nevertheless immediately reinforced by reduction of an internal state labeled "fear." Correspondingly, posi-tively reinforced responses, not immediately followed by a primary positive reinforcer, are immediately reinforced by the increase of an internal state labeled "hope."

In the late 1960s, two articles, one by Rescorla and Solomon (1967) and one by Herrnstein (1969), reviewed the evidence and found no empirical support for two-factor theory. Herrnstein went on to argue that two-factor theory was a hindrance to control of behavior in the laboratory because it suggested control of avoidance behavior by inter-nal processes that proved impossible to discover, whereas precise con-trol of avoidance behavior could actually be achieved by varying an external (but molar) property of the environment—the overall rate of aversive stimulation. The variable that best predicts and controls the avoidance responding of a rat or a pigeon in the laboratory is not some covert process (however "explainable" as due to conditioning) but rather the degree to which rate of responding is (negatively) correlated with rate of overt aversive stimulation. In other words, Herrnstein showed that when molecular behaviorism fails to explain instrumen-tal responding in terms of *overt* reinforcers immediately following *overt* responses, it is not necessary to postulate *covert* reinforcers. Whatever benefits such explanatory fictions might provide, prediction and control are certainly sacrificed.

Subsequently, Herrnstein (1970) and his students extended the mo-lar conception further. Avoidance behavior was shown to be a subcate-gory of a more general molar law, the matching law (Baum, 1973), applicable to all instrumental behavior. Starting from Herrnstein's conception of choice and Premack's (1965) conception of the relative nature of reinforcement and punishment, a field of behavioral eco-nomics has emerged in which behavior is said to obey molar economic laws (Rachlin et al., 1981).

These laboratory conceptions have obvious extensions outside of the laboratory, some of which have already been proposed (McDowell, 1984: Rachlin, 1985b). The people who might have been expected to adopt them are behavior therapists, perhaps discouraged by the problems with molecular behaviorism and looking for an alternative. Yet behavior therapists have generally not done so. They seem to be divided into two camps, those sticking resolutely to molecular behaviorism (Eysenck and Wolpe, for example) and those having been swung around by the cognitive revolution (Bandura and Mahoney, for example). Neither camp is congenial to the aims of behavior therapy (prediction and control of behavior). Before expanding further upon this argument, I will attempt to define more concretely the issues involved with respect to a crucial concept—self-control.

Self-Control

In the molar-behavioral conception (Rachlin, 1974), "self-control" is another expression for control of behavior by distant consequences. For instance, consider again a visit to the dentist. The immediate consequences of a visit versus a nonvisit (more or less immediate pain), let us assume, favor a nonvisit; the distant consequences (possible loss of teeth and more extensive pain) favor a visit. Given these assumptions, visiting the dentist is "self-controlled," while not visiting the dentist is, let us say, "impulsive."

Molecular behaviorism has an easy explanation for "impulsive" behavior—it is immediately reinforced. But people (and even other animals: see Mazur & Logue, 1978; Rachlin & Green, 1972) do not always behave impulsively. Sometimes people do visit dentists, even without current toothaches. Molecular behaviorism cannot easily explain such actions because there are neither immediate overt stimuli preceding them nor immediate overt reinforcers following them. Any molecular theory, whether molecular behaviorism or the equally molecular physiologism or cognitivism, must then postulate *internal* events contiguous with the action (visiting the dentist) so as to better explain it. The difference between molecular behavioral, physiological, and cognitive theories in their explanations of such behavior is only on the nature of those internal events.

The molecular-behavioral theorist relies on internal surrogates of conditioning processes, originally defined in terms of the organism as a whole: internal self-reinforcement, fear reduction, hope augmentation, and so forth. However, before this century began, Dewey (1896) pointed out that concepts such as stimulus and response (correspondingly, the concepts of operant and respondent) lose their meaning when transferred to the interior of the behaving organism. If, as some behaviorists argue, the system under study is the organism as a whole, a stimulus is an input to that system and a response is an output. An event taking place wholly inside the system cannot be either a stimulus *or* a response as these concepts have been defined (except by constructing a homunculus, another person residing within a person, who can receive private stimulation and emit private responses invisible to an observer). Thus, going to the dentist may be reinforced even though no reinforcers are observed. This sort of rationale does not work in the laboratory (Herrnstein, 1969; Rescorla & Solomon, 1967); it works still less well in the real world—as philosophers have been quick to point out (Block, 1981; Geach, 1957; Putnam, 1980).

The alternative offered by the philosophers takes two forms—physiologism and cognitivism. Physiologism argues that all higher mental processes (invoked to explain behavior unaccompanied by contiguous overt stimuli) are nothing but physiological processes in the brain; the mind will eventually be explained in physiological terms. Such a declaration cannot, of course, be proved false (and as research in brain physiology develops, may be proved entirely correct), but its current usefulness is questionable. Nor is it clear why philosophers who promote this view (Searle, 1980, for example) do not conceive of all mental states in terms of atomic physics. Why stop at physiology when even more molecular theories are available? The vacuity of physiologism is revealed when you abandon the quest for explanation and focus on prediction and control. Self-control, in this view, is control by one part of the brain (presumably a "higher" part) over another. We go to the dentist because of the action of those higher mechanisms. We behave impulsively because of their failure to act. When we gamble away the rent, for instance, those mechanisms are asleep or inactive or stunned. Psychosurgery, drug therapy, and vitamin therapy may be said to rely on physiologism. However, at this stage of our knowledge of brain physiology, use of these therapeutic techniques is like groping in the dark. Most behavior therapists, fortunately not licensed to perform operations or to dispense drugs, have not attempted to use physiologism in their practice.

Many behavior therapists claim, however, to have become cognitive psychologists. Cognitive psychology, like physiologism, is an attempt to explain, in terms of contiguous events, behavior not preceded by immediate overt eliciting stimuli or followed by immediate overt reinforcers. If all behavior were impulsive, there would be no point in adopting cognitive psychology. If none of us ever went to the dentist except to relieve immediate pain, if immediate escape from aversive stimulation or immediate consumption of primary positive reinforcers were our only criterion for action, we would not need cognitive psychology to explain it. But then, as Plato claimed (*Philebus,* 21c), our behavior would be like that of an oyster—an animal supposedly without self-control.

According to cognitive psychology, thoughts may cause behavior. Thus a man who goes to the dentist when not in pain may be said to be impelled by the thought that going to the dentist is good for his health. His thought is "information" that comes to him from either his direct experience or (more commonly) from the instructions or example of another person. The information, when it is not being used, is stored as in a computer. The storage mechanism is supplemented by various internal information-processing devices designed to access it, update it, and use it, along with other items of information, in making decisions. These processing devices act much like the logic mechanisms or calculating mechanisms of a computer.

Finally, the output of the decision-making mechanism is somehow (in a way rarely specified by cognitive psychologists) converted into behavior. Unlike physiologism, cognitive psychology is not committed to any particular physiological instantiation of the computer mechanism. Just as the very same computer program may be instantiated by electronic impulses or bubbles or relay settings or chemical states, so the very same cognitive events might be instantiated by a host of different actual physiological states. What the particular physiological state is at any given time does not matter to the cognitivist. It is the cognitive mechanism, the computer flow diagram, that counts. (Cognitivists do not seem to realize that the same argument that they use against physiologism may be used against them by behaviorists: Any given set of overt events—stimuli from the environment and behavioral outputs—may be instantiated by a host of different computer programs. Which it is in any particular case does not matter to the behaviorist. It is the behavior that counts.)

Cognitivism and Mentalism

The nature of the cognitive mechanism has been uncovered in three ways. One way is by introspection—a person may look inward, observe his own cognitions, and report them to others. Introspection's main problem is its assumption of privacy. A true introspection is a report that perfectly matches an internal state. Since observers cannot confirm whether the match is a good one or a poor one, they must accept whatever a person claims to be introspection as a valid report. Philosophers only recently came to realize that the absolute certainty of a person's introspections is a social convention rather than a fact of nature (Wittgenstein, 1958). When a person's introspections are contradicted by his other behavior, this method says that his introspections are correct. Overt behavior is only a messenger or ambassador of what Skinner (1953) calls autonomous man, an homunculus known only by the person within which it dwells.

Freud (1953/1900) and Watson (1924) had little in common except their rejection of the validity of a person's introspections as direct revelations of an internal mental state. Modern cognitive psychology also rejects introspection. One reason for such rejection is that when we introspect we do not see the sort of events that modern cognitive psychology says are in our minds (Nisbett & Wilson, 1977). The things we introspect upon are not computer mechanisms. They seem to be immediate and unitary—unconnected (on the surface) with other mental events. However well they may serve for explanations ("I did it because I wanted to"), they are unreliable for purposes of prediction and utterly useless for control. This is not to say that a person's introspections should be ignored—any more than the person's other behavior should be ignored. What Freud, Watson, and modern cognitive psychology reject is introspection's privileged status as a behavior especially revealing of mental processes.

According to modern cognitive psychology, introspection does not reveal the true state of the mind any more or any less than other behavior does. The child who says "I hate you" is not revealing a mental state any more than is the child who strikes out. Even those cognitive psychologists who value explanation above prediction and control reject the sort of explanation that introspection provides. The fundamental requirement of scientific explanation, that there be a language, on the one hand, and a thing that the language matches, on the other hand, is met by introspection only in a trivial sense. All that an observer can see is the language itself. The match of verbal behavior to internal state has to be taken on faith. No conceivable evidence can contradict it. Thus, introspection is too simple, too tenuously related to other behavior, hence, too unscientific to be useful, either in the laboratory or in behavior therapy.

A second method of cognitive psychology, artificial intelligence (or AI) has much more to recommend it. It consists of the attempt to simulate human thought by a digital computer (Simon, 1956). After the simulation is perfected, AI will assume that the mind works just like the computer (or the computer program) by which it is simulated. If AI were successful, we would be able to have a conversation with a computer by, say, typing in a message and getting back messages on the screen, messages impossible to distinguish verbally from those another person would give us. For instance, a computer program may eventually design responses that are verbally indistinguishable from those of a schizophrenic person. Another program might produce responses verbally indistinguishable from those of a depressed person. The differences in the two programs would then constitute a valid theory of schizophrenia and depression, testable by further interaction between the program and real people.

As explanation, AI has scientific validity. It is, in fact, a perfect case of explanation. It provides a clear language (the language of computer design and computer programming), clearly defined behavior for the language to match (the verbal behavior of a schizophrenic or depressed person), and a clear test for the match (indistinguishability of computer output and human output). There are several problems, however, in adopting it for behavior therapy. One problem is that AI is still very far from adequate simulation of the language of a dysfunctionally behaving person. Another problem with AI is that, even if perfect simulation were attained, it is not clear how "reprogramming" of a person's mind could be accomplished. (Remember, AI is not a physiological theory.) A behavior therapist would find a computer program that would aid him in interaction with clients more useful than one that just simulated another client. Even if AI were to attempt to simulate a behavior therapist rather than a behavior therapist's client, an *ideal* behavior-therapist program could hardly be attained merely by simulating *actual* behavior therapists (I am sure most behavior therapists will agree with me here—at least as regards their colleagues). Before constructing a therapist program, AI would first have to discover what therapeutic methods were most effective. But a *coherent* system of effective therapeutic methods would constitute a theory already in place, and AI would be superfluous.

Still another problem with AI is that, however important it may be, verbal behavior is only one part of our behavior. AI will never convincingly simulate pain, for instance, unless it simulates more than verbal behavior. A machine that emits verbal behavior indistinguishable from that of a person in pain is unlikely to be mistaken for a person in pain unless it also simulates the functional aspects of pain. Thus a squeaky wheel that seems to demand oiling is a better metaphor for a person crying for help than a computer terminal that prints out the message "ouch!"

A third method of cognitive psychology, the one in most common use, is to observe behavior in natural conditions and under controlled conditions in the laboratory and, from those observations, to infer the existence of and the nature of internal cognitive processes. A good example of this sort of cognitive psychology is decision theory (Wallsten, 1980). Decision theorists observe people making real and hypothetical decisions and infer from their behavior what the cognitive mechanism must be. For instance, Kahneman and Tversky (1984) propose that probabilities, as objectively presented in alternatives ("prospects"), are internally converted by a person into "decision weights." Correspondingly, prospective rewards are converted into internal values. These conversions are specified by approximate functional forms. The product of decision weight and outcome value then determines the value of the prospect, which is compared (internally) with the value of other prospects, resulting in a decision. Decisions are influenced in turn by "framing effects" due to the action of *context* on a central decision mechanism. Finally, behavior is emitted as the product of the central cognitive mechanism and the various contextual alterations. Among cognitive theories, Kahneman and Tversky's prospect theory is among the most precisely formulated. It does make some predictions and offer some control. For instance, it predicts, within a limited sphere, when a group of decisions will be consistent among themselves and when they will be inconsistent. My colleagues and I (Rachlin et al., 1986) have recently shown that prospect theory may be translated into wholly behavioral terms. (The central feature of our translation is the conversion of probabilities to delays of reinforcers.) We argue that such translation is desirable because once it is made the arena of prediction and control of behavior is much expanded. One need not accept our translation, however, to see the general applicability of decision theory to everyday life. It was long ago pointed out (by Tolman, 1938, among others) that all of life may be viewed as a series of decisions. Cognitive decision theory systematically explains the decisions people make—both those that seem rational to an observer and those that seem irrational. When dealing with dysfunctional behavior inadequately explained by molecular behaviorism, behavior therapists could have turned to modern cognitive decision theory for a respectably scientific explanation and perhaps even a few suggestions as to prediction and control. (For instance, people normally undervalue stated probabilities. That is, their decision weights are lower than the physical probabilities of outcomes. A depressed person might exaggerate this normal underevaluation and thus take no risks, even quite moderate ones. Treatment might consist in training a person to evaluate prospects more accurately or at least more normally.)*

According to Kendall and Bemis (1983), the first basic tenet of cognitive behavioral therapy is: "The human organism responds primarily to cognitive representations of its environments rather than to those environments per se" (p. 565). If this were true, cognitive behavior

---

* Another possible aspect of decision theory applicable to therapy might be the various cognitive limitations on rationality postulated by Simon (1956). Dysfunctional behavior would consist of the exaggeration of one or another form of irrationality.

therapists should be able to use the best current theories of how the environment is cognitively represented. Yet cognitive behavior therapists have ignored not only prospect theory but all decision theory, as they have ignored other areas of experimental cognitive psychology, as they have ignored molar behaviorism. In other words, cognitive behavior therapists, in abandoning an inadequate molecular behaviorism, have abandoned the experimental base that made behavior therapy successful in the first place. Of the above techniques of cognitive psychology, they have resorted most to introspection—the easiest to apply but the least useful.

Cognitive Behavior Therapy

This is not the place to provide a history of cognitive behavior therapy or a detailed analysis of its basic concepts. My object is just to illustrate the claim that cognitive behavior therapy, in abandoning molecular behaviorism, has come to rely on introspection.

In a discussion of cognitive behavioral techniques, Kendall and Bemis (1983) say at the outset that "the parameters of the approach are not yet fully established, and the relationship between the various cognitive-behavioral schools remains unclear" (p. 565). But they add later that Bandura's concept of self-efficacy has been proposed "as a unifying mechanism that can account for the gains achieved through very different modes of treatment" (p. 584). Self-efficacy is seen by Bandura as a description (or part of an explanation) of a cognitive state that is actually supposed to exist inside a person. Various treatment procedures are said to alter a person's self-efficacy. Self-efficacy, in turn, alters the person's behavior. The first step in evaluating self-efficacy as an explanatory concept is to draw a dividing line between the language of explanation and the thing being explained.

It might be supposed that the language of explanation in this case is mathematics. However, in a recent debate in *Psychological Review,* Staddon (1985) has argued that the mathematical language with which Bandura's theory is sometimes expressed [e.g., Behavior = f (Person & Environment)] is not mathematical in the sense that it does not fit properly into the computational system that mathematics provides. As I understand it, Bandura's (1985) answer is that his mathematical descriptions are not intended as descriptions of behavior in another language (mathematics) but as shorthand English descriptions of behavior. The laws of interaction among cognitive terms, then, must be expressible in grammatical English rather than mathematics. The thing being explained by these terms is a cognitive state. The problem is that the only available measure of this cognitive state is the verbal behavior of the person in whom it resides.

Self-efficacy has been proposed as "the final common pathway through which different treatments are considered to produce change" (Kazdin, 1983, p. 279). As a cognitive concept it cannot be the same as "efficacy," which directly describes an observable relation between behavior and environment. It must be possible for self-efficacy as an internal state to be high or low while observed efficacy is low or high. Otherwise self-efficacy would be just another name for efficacy. But self-efficacy and efficacy are hard to distinguish from each other. Various cognitive treatments are said to improve self-efficacy. Improved self-efficacy results somehow in improved efficacy: "Expectations of mastery [self-efficacy] are proposed to influence a person's initiation and persistence of coping behavior [efficacy]" (Kazdin, 1983, p. 279). What, then, is the difference in practice between self-efficacy and efficacy? As far as a noncognitive behavior therapist can determine, "self-efficacy" describes either people's introspective reports or their answers to questions about their expectations, while "coping" or "efficacy" describes their other overt behavior.

The outcome of the research on the topic of self-efficacy is to show that, as people improve in efficacy, they also improve in self-efficacy. Thus their verbal behavior is generally consistent with their other overt behavior. But whether that verbal behavior describes an internal state, which then (in some unspecified way) causes efficacy, whether verbal behavior itself (without the cognition) serves as a discriminative stimulus for efficacious behavior, whether the verbal behavior merely describes efficacy, or whether the verbal behavior and the efficacy are both the result of some third process is all unknown.

Introspections of English-speaking people are typically expressed in English. Any system that attempts to explain human behavior using everyday English vocabulary and grammar should, it would seem, be especially careful to avoid slipping into the easy and inaccurate introspective mode. It does not seem as if "self-efficacy" as a concept avoids this trap.

It may be argued that, in evaluating cognitive behavior therapy, one should focus not on a largely theoretical construct such as "self-efficacy" but on actual techniques of treatment. Since, as I indicated previously, there has been much research on the cognitive mechanisms underlying how people make decisions, cognitive behavior therapists who treat people's decision-making behavior might be expected to rely on, or at least refer to, this research. Again, this does not seem to be the case. For instance, Beck and colleagues (1978) list indecisiveness as the first of a series of "cognitive" symptoms of depression

(p. 185). However, they refer to no research on decision making and they suggest no treatment for indecisiveness. Instead, the therapist is encouraged to tell the patient that "it is inadvisable to make major decisions when one is depressed" (p. 186). When depression is cured, indecisiveness is expected to go away by itself. Only when a decision must be made are Beck and colleagues willing to help. Then, they suggest writing out a list of advantages and disadvantages (hardly a new technique) or, where this does not work, flipping a coin. A reluctant client was told that her panic at making a decision was "the result of her obsessiveness" (p. 187). Other clients are indecisive because of "guilt." There is no reference anywhere to a coherent conception for decision making or of cognition in general. Here, as elsewhere where cognitive behavior therapy deviates from behavior therapy, the difference consists in the therapist's either verbally lecturing the client or asking the client to introspect ("to monitor negative automatic thoughts," for example). The language, the rationale, and the method of treatment of cognitive behavior therapists are more closely connected to those of pastoral counselling or to the writings of Carlos Castanada (see Meichenbaum, 1974, for specific acknowledgement of this connection) than they are to any scientific endeavor.

Beck and colleagues' (1978) *specific* cognitive techniques for treating depression consist of first giving clients a book to read, then "defining cognition for the patient," then "teaching" the client how thoughts affect behavior, then training the client to introspect ("detection of automatic thoughts") and to "reattribute" (i.e., relabel) events. It is not surprising that these techniques have strong effects on clients' *verbal* behavior. Like Freud, Beck and colleagues make converts out of their clients. At the beginning of therapy, clients say they are depressed. At the end, they say they are not depressed. What is wrong with this treatment? Verbal behavior *is* important, and what clients say about themselves is an important part of their behavior. The problem with this sort of therapy is that the cognitive (verbal) treatments are often tacked onto inadequate behavioral (nonverbal) treatments and the claim is made that the cognitive addition constitutes an improvement or refinement in the behavioral techniques. Thus the development of nonverbal behavioral technique languishes in cognitive behavior therapy; behavioral techniques that might be improved are not improved. Clients are sent out into the world with a new vocabulary in the vain hope that nonverbal behavior will thereby be altered. The harm this does is that, in relabeling their internal states, clients' language may well lose whatever function it once served as a guide and organizer of behavior (as a discriminative stimulus). Admittedly, in a depressed client this function may be only minimally operative.

However, by insisting that mental terms are labels for internal states rather than discriminative stimuli for overt behavior, (including verbal behavior), cognitive behavior therapy insures the dysfunction of language. In telling "the truth" about their cognitions, clients are taught to lie about their behavior. Telling yourself that your hand feels cool will not substitute for pulling it out of the fire.

But is this condemnation too severe? Does a fundamental behavioral change simply follow from a change in vocabulary? There is no evidence for such a change. On the basis of comparisons of the effects of behavior therapy and cognitive behavior therapy, Latimer and Sweet (1984) have argued that the cognitive revolution has produced nothing of therapeutic value. Erwin (Chapter 6, this volume) disputes this claim on the grounds that, in certain cases, cognitive principles may *explain* why certain behavioral techniques work or do not work. But even if explanation (without prediction or control) were a valid goal of theory, the principles of cognitive behavior therapy are themselves not part of a systematic view of the mind. They constitute a simple relabeling, no better able to explain a behavioral technique than saying a procedure works because it is a "good procedure" and does not work because it is a "bad procedure." If, with the aid of cognitive principles, it were possible to predict in advance which behavioral procedures would work or to design truly effective procedures that were not primarily behavioral, the cognitive revolution would have been valuable to behavior therapy. But a paradigm such as cognitive psychology, which relies wholly on explanation and rejects prediction and control as trivial, is unlikely to facilitate prediction and control.

Latimer and Sweet were too mild in their conclusions. Just as an ineffective medical therapy (such as Laetril therapy) is harmful because it may draw attention away from effective ones, an ineffective view of the mind is harmful if a potentially effective one is available. As Lacey and I (1978) have argued elsewhere, molar behaviorism is such an effective view of the mind.

Molar Behaviorism

The critical difference between a behavioral paradigm and a cognitive or physiological one is that the former makes no inference about events going on internal to its point of reference, whereas the latter two paradigms do make such inferences. Thus, insofar as Hull infers r_g-s_g occurring inside the organism, and insofar as Skinner infers the occurrence of internal operants or respondents, and insofar as an individual intact organism is the point of reference, these theorists are postulating the existence of cognitive or physiological events—not behavioral ones. This is the case even when the inferred internal behavior corresponds to that of the organism as a whole; the logical status of an inferred internal operant is the same as that of an inferred internal cognitive mechanism (dissonance, for instance) or an inferred neural network (a cell assembly, for instance). This is not to say that internal operants, internal cognitive mechanisms, or internal neural networks do not exist—just that *they are not part of a behavioral theory.* To the extent that a theory makes use of such inferences, it is not wholly behavioral.

In defense of internal operants, Skinner has maintained that the skin is unimportant as a dividing line between a person and the world. It is true that any dividing line is arbitrary. One might speak of the behavior of an arm, or the behavior of a man aside from his arm, or, to cite a common example in philosophy, the behavior of a man aside from his diseased tooth. But once an individual intact organism is chosen as a point of reference the skin *becomes* important. It is the (quite arbitrary) place where stimuli end and responses begin (Dewey, 1896).

A consistent behavioral viewpoint does not preclude inference or theory. Recent behavioristic theory is, in fact, elaborate in this respect. It is true that behaviorism precludes inference of internal entities or events. What is left then? Inference of external entities or events—external patterns of behavior. The making of such inferences is no simple task (as Erwin, in chapter 6, this volume) points out. But these inferences may be confirmed by the repetition of overt patterns of behavior. The application of such knowledge in a therapeutic context does not require the employment of hypothetical entities but instead rests on the experimental manipulations of overt behavior.

Molar behaviorism, like molecular behaviorism (Skinner, 1953), offers interpretations of mental terms and is as much a theory of the mind as a cognitive psychology. From the molar-behavioral viewpoint, a person's knowledge of cars would not be separable from his or her verbal and nonverbal behavior with respects to cars. A driver's knowledge of cars would be different from a mechanic's knowledge of cars exactly to the extent that driving a car is different from repairing it. At a given instant, the driver and the mechanic may be doing the same exact thing. Molecular theories must distinguish between the two individuals in terms of current internal states (of knowledge). Even molecular behaviorism must employ the concept of differing current "dispositions" (Ryle, 1949) or "probabilities" (Skinner, 1953) underlying actual behavior. Molar behaviorism, however, distinguishes between the knowledge of the driver and the mechanic wholly on the basis of behavior, not of current behavior (presumably identical in the two cases) but of temporally extended behavior. The driver's knowledge differs from that of the mechanic because of differing long-term interactions with cars. If their car-related histories are the same, however, the two individuals' knowledge *cannot* be different. In spatial terms, we make such molar distinctions all the time. A triangle that touches a square at a point is a *triangle* because of its pattern of points in space and not because its triangleness is somehow encoded in a point of overlap with the square. Two triangles are identical when their points form the same pattern, not because one or two of their points overlap. Correspondingly, in temporal terms, a driver's knowledge of cars is a *driver's* knowledge because of the driver's pattern of car-related behavior in time and not because the knowledge is encoded in the driver at a given moment when he or she happens to be doing the same thing as a mechanic.

The same conception applies to emotions, perceptions, even sensations. (Skinner's molecular behaviorism requires him to conceive of these events as internal behaviors.) Molar behaviorism sees the emotion of love, for instance, as inseparable from loving behavior. It agrees with the wife who refuses to believe that her husband loves her "deep down inside" despite his philandering, his rudeness, his disregard of her needs.*

Once, after I delivered a lecture on the behavioral nature of emotions, a well-known philosopher in the audience asked me to suppose a beautiful woman were, from all outward signs, in love with me. How would I feel, he wondered, were I to discover that she was not a real woman but an ingenious mechanical doll. My answer to him was another question: "How far did we go?" If I had discovered her mechanical nature after the first 10 minutes or impassioned conversation I would, of course, feel badly (but no worse than when flesh-and-blood women prove to be equally unresponsive to me); there was no chance for her to love me. If, on the other hand, we had courted, married, had (half-mechanical) children, and during all this time she had acted perfectly lovingly, and on her deathbed (having aged beautifully to 90

---

* While it is generally recognized that introspections are invalid indicators of most cognitions, it is generally unrecognized that introspections are no more valid as reports of sensations, perceptions, and emotions than they are of cognitions. Even Skinner (1953) supposes emotions to be private internal states. In philosophical discussion, *pain* has come to stand for the single most obviously private event (Putnam, 1980). I recently argued (Rachlin, 1985b) that, consistent with molar behaviorism, pains are *not* properly private events but (like cognitions, perceptions, sensations, and emotions) are more usefully regarded as temporally extended patterns of overt behavior, modifiable, like other operants, by reinforcement and punishment. Few commentators agreed with me.

years) she warned me against allowing an autopsy to be performed because steel rods, foam rubber, machine oil, and electric wires would be found instead of bones, flesh, blood, and nerves, would I be disappointed then? I don't think so. Would you?

Consider the behavioristic treatment of chronic pain as developed by Fordyce (1976). *Pain* is a prototypical mentalistic term—a "raw feel." The concept of pain seems to defy behavioral analysis. If ever an internal event were necessary as an explanation of behavior it would be in the case of pain. However, instead of inferring the existence of events (physiological or cognitive) *inside* the person, Fordyce infers the existence of events *outside* the person or, more precisely, at the border between the person and the environment—the environmental consequences of the pain. These range from pain-contingent access to narcotic medication, to time off from work, to attention and concern from others, to avoidance of temptation (avoidance of small, immediate rewards). Treatment consists of breaking the contingent relationship between pain and its consequences either by scheduling the consequences independent of the behavior (as in the case of narcotic medication, initially), reducing them (as in the case of inactivity and narcotic medication, ultimately), or making them contingent on behavior other than pain (as in the case of attention and concern from family members). This behavioral treatment, obvious and crude as it may seem, works at least as well as, and in most cases better than, surgery, drugs, or cognitive therapy.

Everyone agrees that there must be more to pain than a tear or a whimper or a heart-rending cry of agony. What could that extra thing be? For the physiologist and the cognitivist there is only one answer—an internal mechanism, emotional or physiological—a ghost in the machine or a machine in the machine.

For the behaviorist, too, there can be only one answer—other behavior (Rachlin, 1985b). In addition to the tear there are other tears at other times, screams, cries, whimpers, verbal descriptions—in short, an inferred behavioral pattern occurring over time (Brunswik, 1952). Such behavioral patterns are usually inferred (rather than presently observed), but, unlike inferred cognitive and physiological entities, they can be observed in the future and have been observed in the past. They are the very patterns by which we distinguish between real pain and fake pain: correspondingly, real joy and fake joy, real love and fake love. In making these distinctions, in our own behavior as in that of others, we refer to no internal state. The actor on the stage knows that he is acting, not because he is in touch with some internal mental event, but because he observes (just as the public does) that his onstage behavior is inconsistent with his offstage behavior. The actor, of course, could be wrong. His wife could say that he was not acting at all—that indeed he was really like that (offstage as well). Better knowledge of our mental lives comes not from *deep* observation (introspection) but from *wide* observation of behavior over long periods of time.

Identification of temporally extended patterns of behavior with our mental vocabulary is called *molar* behaviorism, as distinct from *molecular* behaviorism, such as that of Skinner. Molecular behaviorism needs to trace behavioral chains between events so that there will be no temporal gaps. Thus, according to molecular behaviorism, for a respondent to occur, an immediate stimulus must occur; for an operant to increase in rate, an immediate reinforcer must occur. When these immediate events are not observed, molecular behaviorism must infer their existence. Since molecular behaviorism is forbidden, by its own self-restriction, to infer temporal gaps in causal chains, it must assume those chains to exist where they cannot be observed—inside of the organism.

In this way, molecular behaviorism carries the seeds of its own destruction. Molecular behaviorism is required by its own restrictions to infer the existence of internal events but, to the extent it does so, it is not behavioristic. This self-contradiction, I believe, lies at the core of most philosophical objections to behaviorism. The objections do not apply to molar behaviorism. However, the price you have to pay, if you accept molar behaviorism, is the acceptance of causation at a temporal distance. Such causation is admittedly counterintuitive, but, in physics, causation at a spatial distance has been accepted since Newton and, at a temporal distance, since Einstein. Because behavior of organisms would seem to be at least as complicated as behavior of planets, explanatory principles in psychology need to be at least as unrestricted as those in physics.

The Imperialization of Self-Control

According to Tolman (1938), the first psychologist to call himself a molar behaviorist, all instrumental behavior is choice. Like Skinner, Tolman was uninterested in elicited responses. While Skinner viewed a nonelicited response (an emitted response) as another kind of reflex (an operant), Tolman viewed a nonelicited response as a choice. Thus, for Tolman, a rat in a Skinner box whose lever presses are reinforced by the delivery of a food pellet is choosing between pressing the lever and getting the pellet versus not pressing the lever and not getting the pellet. While molar behaviorism, in its various forms, has been developed by students of Skinner, while it uses Skinnerian vocabulary and

Skinnerian techniques of experimentation and analysis (all of which are far more powerful than those developed by Tolman), it has adopted Tolman's conception of instrumental behavior as choice behavior rather than Skinner's conception of operant behavior as another kind of reflex.

If all instrumental behavior is choice behavior, what kinds of choices are worth studying? Let us consider two kinds: (1) where each outcome would arrive at the same time, say choosing between vanilla, chocolate, and strawberry ice-cream cones at the ice-cream parlor; and (2) where outcomes arrive at different times, say choosing between one ice-cream now and two ice-cream cones tomorrow. Both kinds of choices may be difficult to make, as both involve, in Lewin's (1938) terms, approach–approach conflict. Both are analyzable by the specific molar-behavioral theories so far proposed, for instance, melioration (Herrnstein & Vaughan, 1980) or maximization (Rachlin et al., 1981). But the case where alternatives arrive at different times holds a special interest in psychology because such choice is seen in both behavioristic jargon and everyday language as a test of "self-control." Avoidance–avoidance conflict and approach–avoidance conflict may also be tests of self-control if (and only if) alternatives arrive at different times. An example of the former might be the choice between going to the dentist (small pain now) and not going to the dentist (large pain later). An example of the latter might be smoking a cigarette (small pleasure now and large pain later) or not smoking (no pleasure now, no pain later).

While both laymen and behaviorists see such choices as tests of self-control, they differ as to the way in which those choices may be explained. In the approach–approach case (which we will stay with as an example), self-control is demonstrated by choice of the larger, more delayed reward; lack of self control (impulsiveness) is demonstrated by choice of the smaller, more immediate reward. The layman views self-control itself as an internal process (exercise of willpower) and the choice as a mere indication of that process. In this, the layman agrees with the cognitive psychologists or the physiological psychologists who see self-control as a thought process or a neural (inhibitory) process. The molar behaviorist, contrary to the others, sees self-control as a pattern of choices. This conception may be expressed in terms of Baum's generalized version of Herrnstein's matching law:

$$\frac{B_1}{B_2} = \left(\frac{A_1}{A_2}\right)^{S_A} \cdot \left(\frac{R_1}{R_2}\right)^{S_R} \cdot \left(\frac{D_2}{D_1}\right)^{S_D}$$

where, with two alternatives (1 and 2), B stands for a measure of behavior, A for amount of reinforcement, R for rate of reinforcement, D for delay of reinforcement, and the exponents, s_A, s_R, and s_D for the sensitivity of behavior to the respective reinforcement parameters. The degree of self-control in a given case may be measured by the ratio of s_A and s_R to s_D (Logue et al., 1984). When s_A and s_R are high and s_D is low, the pattern of choices will maximize overall rate of reinforcement. As s_D grows relative to s_A and s_R, delay of reward begins to exert its effect on behavior. The effect of delay is, essentially, to *discount* reward (much as a 30-year bond sells at a discount because receipt of principal is delayed). The degree of this discount becomes great as s_D grows relative to s_A and s_R.

It is possible to view virtually all of psychology in terms of self-control, hence, in terms of these parameters. The great advantage of this conception is that it provides a measure (for an individual in a given situation) of the span of time over which reinforcement is maximized. Learning, development, socialization, and all of clinical psychology, however diverse individual situations may be, may be seen as variations of that time span (variation of s_D relative to s_A and s_R). This conception is nothing drastically new, of course. It is an essential element in one form or another in all theories of maturation, development, and clinical psychology. Nor, I hasten to point out, does it imply that individuals may be characterized by a set of exponents. Obviously, none of us is equally impulsive in all situations. But, so long as the consequences (for a response, in a situation) can be measured, degree of self-control can be determined. The advantage of this conception is that it provides a measure of the self-control of a person in a situation, while the measure (not the value of the exponent itself) applies across people and across situations. As far as I know, no other corresponding technique has been proposed.

Clinical Psychology

What would the imperialization of self-control mean in clinical psychology? Where clinical problems are labeled "self-control," behavioristic interpretation is obvious and guides current practice. For instance, overeating constitutes immediate reward to a currently overweight person, but dieting, for that person, is rewarded only after a long delay. Common weight-control techniques, such as calorie counting and daily weighings, provide overt secondary reinforcers bridging the gap between current behavior and future reward. Encouragement and social support from families or groups provide relatively small but more immediate rewards for dieting that may somewhat counterbalance the immediate reward of the food itself. Such clinical techniques and others based on behavioristic principles have been successful with problems currently understood in terms of self-control. From the point of view of molar behaviorism, those nonsuccesses that occur must be due not to failure by the therapist to consider physiological or cognitive factors but to failure to account (in the widest sense) for all of the reinforcers, for instance, overweight as avoidance of sexual temptation or as conformity with contingencies imposed by (a more immediate if not the larger) society. Such motivational factors are often considered nonbehavioral because they are not focused on immediate eating behavior, but they are behavioral in the molar sense advocated here.

For clinical problems not usually labeled "self-control," behavioristic interpretation may not be so obvious. An example of extension of the self-control model to problems not ordinarily considered in those terms is the previously discussed pain treatment by Fordyce. Pain would seem to be the very model of a short-term negative effect, but a pattern of chronic pain, in the absence of an easily identifiable pain stimulus, is considered by Fordyce to be a positively reinforced operant. As indicated previously, pain behavior (ie., pain) does produce relatively immediate rewards. Society is, in fact, geared to provide such rewards without question. The long-term consequences of chronic pain, however, may be decidedly negative. The worst of them is probably the habituation of friends and family members to the person's pain, escalating the amount of pain required to produce the rewards (like the story of the boy who cried wolf). Such a pattern of behavior and reward has been identified by the economists Stigler and Becker (1977) as a negative addiction. In their economic model (congruent with molar behaviorism: see Rachlin et al., 1981), negative addictions occur when the use of a commodity entails an increase of its effective price (by habituation) and when the demand for the commodity is inelastic. Most people's demand for attention and affection seems indeed inelastic, and if these commodities are withheld except on occasions of extreme demand (e.g., pain behavior) chronic pain must be a consequence.

A similar sort of analysis may be applied in other cases of behavior not obviously interpretable as self-control. Agoraphobia, for instance, is not easily treatable by common behavioral techniques. Again, before inferring that cognitive or physiological factors must be considered in treatment of agoraphobics, it might be worthwhile to examine more thoroughly the consequences of being homebound. An agoraphobic cannot go out to work or shop. The agoraphobic is much more than normally dependent on another person (usually a spouse), and such dependence might be rewarded (subtly or unsubtly) by the spouse.

Also, agoraphobics (like overweight people) are less subject to sexual advances by others and less likely than others to be able to make advances successfully. In such cases, agoraphobia (like obesity) might be reinforced and therapy opposed by a spouse. Those cases, furthermore, might be expected to be more common in societies (or subsocieties) with a sexual double standard (except, of course,where a veil serves a similar purpose). Panic attacks and the agoraphobic's fear of them might thus serve only as mediators—excuses to stay home. In this conception, the concentration of therapy on those panic attacks (ignoring what is reinforcing them) would be misguided.

Finally, clinical psychology is currently supposed to be directed at "dysfunctional" behavior. But how can we decide what behavior is dysfunctional? Under present circumstances diagnostic judgments remain arbitrary. They change with public opinion. In 1940 homosexuality was regarded as pathological. In 1985 homosexuality is pathological only under certain conditions. Freud convinced the twentieth century that sexual behavior is intrinsically healthy. By his standards, the behavior of a woman who engaged in sex only at the behest of her husband would be unhealthy, even without other symptoms. The view that certain overt actions stem from *internal* dysfunctions and are thus *in themselves* undesirable (regardless of their external function) is unfortunately not confined to psychoanalysis. Wolpe (1973, p. 24, Table I) lists homosexuality as only one of some 40 consequences of a single internal disturbance—neurotic anxiety. Others include dizziness, spastic colon, peptic ulcers, migraine headaches, stuttering, asthma, amnesia, and impaired sexual function. The molar-behavioral model points to a more consistent mode of diagnosis. It suggests a hunt, not into the person but into the person's past, for patterns of behavior and reinforcement of which the current behavior forms only a part. Once such patterns are identified, they may be changed.

Consider the recurrent question in clinical psychology of whether homosexuals should be changed to heterosexuals (given that effective techniques exist). Sometimes this issue is dealt with in general terms—they should or should not, they should if they want to, they should if they are also pederasts, and so forth. But the molar-behavioral model brings the issue around to the one that should always be foremost for behavior therapy—*what are the consequences, distant as well as immediate, for this person in this situation?* If they could be identified, it would be clear to both therapist and client whether immediate consequences excessively predominate over distant ones. Such an analysis anticipates that health and sickness, in general, and diagnostic classifications, in particular, will indeed vary as reinforcement contingencies vary. Thus it should come as no surprise that novel pathological behavioral patterns (borderline personality, for instance) were not acknowledged 50 years ago—the relevant reinforcing contingencies simply did not exist at that time.

The above remarks are admittedly vague and possibly ill informed. They are speculations by a nonclinical psychologist about clinical problems. They are intended merely as examples of how complex problems can be discussed wholly within a behavioristic framework. It is not necessary under such circumstances to resort either to cognitive or physiological explanations.

Behaviorism will lead to effective clinical procedures only when behaviorists remain consistent in their behavioral approach to complex as well as simple clinical problems. Extensive behavioral analysis of such problems is needed. It seems to me that behavior therapists have recently been avoiding the effort that such analyses would demand and retreating into a cosy and intuitively comfortable mentalism. In this respect it is the behavior therapists themselves who show lack of self-control. An immediate consequence for them is the bond established with the client, the empathy, the possession of a common paradigm. The long-term consequence is the failure of clients to make fundamental changes in their lives.

References

Bandura, A. (1985). Representing personal determinants in causal structures. *Psychological Review, 91,* 508–512.

Baum, W.M. (1973). The correlation based law of effect. *Journal of the Experimental Analysis of Behavior, 20,* 137–153.

Beck, A.T., Rush, A.J., Shaw, B.F., & Emery, G. (1978). *Cognitive therapy of depression.* New York: Guilford.

Block, N. (1981). Psychologism and behaviorism. *Philosophical Review, 30,* 5–43.

Brunswik, E. (1952). The conceptual framework of psychology. In *International Encyclopedia of Unified Science* (Vol 1, No. 10). Chicago: University of Chicago Press.

Dewey, J. (1896). The reflex arc concept in psychology. *Psychological Review, 3,* 357–370.

Fordyce, W. E. (1976). *Behavioral methods for chronic pain and illness.* St. Louis: Mosby.

Freud, S. (1953). The interpretation of dreams. In *The standard edition of the complete psychological works of Sigmund Freud* (Vols. IV and V). London: Hogarth (Original work published 1900).

Friedlander, P. (1958, 1964, 1969). *Plato* (3 Vols.). Princeton, NJ: Princeton University Press.

Geach, P. (1957). *Mental acts.* New York: The Humanities Press.

Herrnstein, R.J. (1961). Relative and absolute strength of response as a function of frequency of reinforcement. *Journal of the Experimental Analysis of Behavior, 4*, 267–272.

Herrnstein, R.J. (1969). Method and theory in the study of avoidance. *Psychological Review, 76*, 49–70.

Herrnstein, R.J. (1970). On the law of effect. *Journal of the Experimental Analysis of Behavior, 13*, 243–266.

Herrnstein, R.J., & Vaughan, W., Jr. (1980). Melioration and behavioral allocation. In J.E.R. Staddon (Ed.), *Limits to action: The allocation of individual behavior* (pp. 143–176). New York: Academic Press.

Hull, C.L. (1943). *Principles of behavior.* New York: Appleton-Century.

Kahneman, D., & Tversky, A. (1984). Choices, values and frames. *American Psychologist, 39*, 341–350.

Kazdin, A.E. (1983). Treatment research: The investigation and evaluation of psychotherapy. In M. Hersen, A.E. Kazdin, & A.S. Bellack (Eds.), *The clinical psychology handbook* (pp. 265–288). New York: Pergamon.

Kendall, P.C., & Bemis, A.M. (1983). Thought and action in psychotherapy: The cognitive-behavioral approaches. In M. Hersen, A.E. Kazdin, & A.S. Bellack (Eds.), *The clinical psychology handbook* (pp. 565–592). New York: Pergamon.

Krasner, L., & Houts, A. (1984). A study of the "value" systems of behavioral scientists. *American Psychologist, 39*, 840–850.

Lacey, H.M., & Rachlin, H. (1978). Behavior, cognition and theories of choice. *Behaviorism, 6*, 177–202.

Latimer, P., & Sweet, A. (1984). Cognitive versus behavioral procedures in cognitive-behavior therapy: A critical review of the evidence. *Journal of Behavior Therapy and Experimental Psychiatry, 15*, 9–22.

Lewin, K. (1938). *The conceptual representation and the measurement of psychological forces.* Durham, NC: Duke University Press.

Logue, A.W., Rodrigues, M.L., Pena-Correal, T., & Mauro, B. (1984). Choice in a self-control paradigm: Quantification of experience-based differences. *Journal of the Experimental Analysis of Behavior, 14*, 53–69.

Mazur, J.E., & Logue, A.W. (1978). Choice in a "self-control" paradigm: Effects of a fading procedure. *Journal of the Experimental Analysis of Behavior, 30*, 11–19.

McDowell, J.J. (1984). The importance of Herrnstein's mathematical statement of the law of effect for behavior therapy. *American Psychologist, 37*, 771–779.

Meichenbaum, D. (1974). Self-instructional methods. In F.H. Kanfer & A.P. Goldstein (Eds.), *Helping people change* (pp. 390-423). New York: Pergamon.

Mowrer, O.H. (1960). *Learning theory and behavior.* New York: Wiley.

Nisbett, R.E., & Wilson, T.D. (1977). Telling more than we can know: Verbal reports on mental processes. *Psychological Review, 84*, 231–259.

Plato. (1961). *The collected dialogs.* E. Hamilton and H. Cairns (Eds.). Princeton, NJ: Princeton University Press.

posium on motivation: 1965 (pp. 123–180). Lincoln: University of Nebraska Press.

Putnam, H. (1980). Brains and behavior. In N. Block (Ed.), *Readings in philosophy of psychology* (Vol. 1) (pp. 24–36). Cambridge, MA: Harvard University Press.

Rachlin, H. (1974). Self-control. *Behaviorism, 2,* 94–107.

Rachlin, H. (1985a). Maximization theory and Plato's concept of the Good. *Behaviorism, 13,* 3–20.

Rachlin, H. (1985b). Pain and behavior. *Behavioral and Brain Sciences, 8,* 43–83.

Rachlin, H., Battalio, R., Kagel, J., & Green, L. (1981). Maximization theory in behavioral psychology. *Behavioral and Brain Sciences, 4,* 371–388.

Rachlin, H., & Frankel, M. (1969). Choice, rate of response and rate of gambling. *Journal of Experimental Psychology, 80,* 444–449.

Rachlin, H., & Green, L. (1972). Commitment, choice and self-control. *Journal of the Experimental Analysis of Behavior, 17,* 15–22.

Rachlin, H., Logue, A.W., Gibbon, J., & Frankel, M. (1986). Cognition and behavior in studies of choice. *Psychological Review, 93,* 33–45.

Randall, J.H., Jr. (1960). *Aristotle.* New York: Columbia University Press.

Rescorla, R.A., & Solomon, R.L. (1967). Two-process learning theory: Relationships between Pavlovian conditioning and instrumental learning. *Psychological Review, 74,* 151–182.

Ryle, G. (1949). *The concept of mind.* London: Huchinson House.

Searle, J.R. (1980). Minds, brain and programs. *Behavioral and Brain Sciences, 3,* 324.

Simon, H.A. (1956). Rational choice and the structure of the environment. *Psychological Review, 63,* 129–138.

Skinner, B.F. (1950). Are theories of learning necessary? *Psychological Review, 57,* 193–216.

Skinner, B.F. (1953). *Science and human behavior.* New York: Macmillan.

Skinner, B.F. (1975). *Verbal behavior.* New York: Appleton-Century-Crofts.

Staddon, J.E.R. (1985). Social learning theory and the dynamics of interaction. *Psychological Review, 91,* 502–507.

Stigler, G.J., & Becker, G.S. (1977). De gustibus non est disputandum. *The American Economic Review, 67,* 76–90.

Thorndike, E.L. (1932). Reward and punishment in animal learning. *Comparative Psychological Monographs, 8,* (39).

Tolman, E.C. (1938). The determiners of behavior at a choice point. *Psychological Review, 45,* 1–41.

Wallsten, T.S. (Ed.). (1980). *Cognitive processes in choice and decision behavior.* Hillsdale, NJ: Erlbaum.

Watson, J.B. (1924). *Behaviorism.* Chicago: University of Chicago Press.

Wittgenstein, L. (1958). *Philosophical investigations* (3rd ed.). New York: Macmillan.

Wolpe, J. (1973). *The practice of behavior therapy.* New York: Pergamon.

III

Behavior Therapy Paradigms: The Cognitive Revolution

6

Cognitivist and Behaviorist Paradigms in Clinical Psychology

Edward Erwin

It is common in clinical psychology to speak of behaviorist, cognitivist, and psychoanalytic paradigms. On this usage, there can be a paradigm in a discipline despite fundamental and widespread disagreement.* I will adhere to this usage, and stipulate that a paradigm exists if a scientific group shares an empirical theory, some distinctive philosophical or methodological views, and one or more exemplars (shared examples of a successful research strategy). This definition closely resembles Kuhn's definition of a "disciplinary matrix" (Kuhn, 1970, p. 182). The key difference is that, unlike Kuhn (p. 15), I will not require a research consensus for the entire discipline of clinical psychology. The main reason for using paradigm in this nonconsensus sense is that some term is needed to characterize what psychoanalysts, behaviorists, and cognitivists are disagreeing about. The term *theory* is too narrow for this purpose. The disagreements are partly about empirical theories, but they are also about scientific values, the utility of certain exemplars, and philosophical and methodological assumptions.

The existence of rival paradigms has stimulated a vigorous debate that has persisted over a decade. Are there solid, rational grounds for preferring either the old (behaviorist) or new (cognitivist) behavior therapy paradigm—or for preferring either to psychoanalysis? Or can a paradigm be defended only relative to its own internal standards? These questions raise fundamental epistemological issues, as well as

* I would like to thank Hans Eysenck and Harvey Siegel for helpful comments.

conceptual and empirical ones. The epistemological issues are discussed in the first part of this paper; the empirical and conceptual
issues in the second part.

Epistemological Issues

Relativism

Behavior therapists are sometimes said to be committed to an empiricist epistemology. For example, the editors of this volume point out
that behavior therapy is a prime example of the application of a logical-positivist–empiricist philosophy to the social sciences (Fishman et
al., Chapter 2, this volume). There is some empirical evidence, moreover, that behavior therapists are more likely than nonbehavior therapists to accept empiricist doctrines. In their valuable study of the
values of psychologists, Krasner and Houts (1984) used the Epistemological Style Questionnaire with two groups: (1) a behavioral group
composed of those who launched the "behavior-modification" movement in the 30-year period following the Second World War, and (2) a
randomly selected comparison group of nonbehavioral psychologists
from the same period. They found that the behavioral group was more
inclined to reject both rationalist and anti-empiricist doctrines.

If behavior therapy is based on an empiricist epistemology, is this a
strength or a weakness? It is a severe weakness if, as the editors
suggest, relativism is true. They point out that there is a wide variety
of possible, coherent epistemological systems besides empiricism and
that the evaluator of statement X's truth value can chose among these
systems. To a substantial extent, they argue, the truth or falsity of a
statement will depend upon the system chosen (Fishman et al., Chapter 2, this volume). If this sort of relativism is true, it is difficult to see
how one can rationally choose between competing paradigms. The
behavior therapist can try to substantiate his or her theoretical and
therapeutic claims by appeal to experimental evidence, but the psychoanalyst, for example, can choose an epistemic system that downgrades this type of evidence and guarantees the truth of psychoanalytic claims.

Krasner and Houts (1984) also argue in favor of relativism. They
conclude (p. 841) that the epistemological status of scientific claims
may be no less relativistic than the comparable status of value claims
in philosophical ethics.

Woolfolk and Richardson (1984) also appear to endorse relativism,
although I am uncertain about this interpretation. They point out that

recent work in the philosophy and history of science has undermined seriously the view of science on which behavior therapy's self-image is based; attempts to equate scientific knowledge with that which is empirically verifiable or to identify scientific progress with some inflexible standard of verification have proven lacking. The form and content of scientific knowledge, they argue (p. 777), are strongly influenced by sociopolitical factors and the attitudes and sensibilities of scientists.

Because relativism comes in different forms, it is helpful to specify the exact doctrine that is being advocated. Fishman and colleagues (Chapter 2, this volume) appear to be endorsing, or at least are asking about the truth of, the following principle:

(R): The truth or falsity of any statement X will depend on the epistemological system that is chosen.

If (R) implies that the mere adoption of an epistemological principle, whether or not the principle is true, can make a statement true (or false), then this sort of relativism can be easily refuted. A nonrelativist can simply accept an epistemological principle, such as (S), that guarantees the falsity of (R):

(S): Whatever the nonrelativist believes to be true is true.

The nonrelativist believes that (R) is false; so by merely accepting (S), he can guarantee that (R) is false. It does not matter that (S) itself is not true. Suppose that the relativist replies that (S) must be true if it is to be used to refute relativism. He then renders (R) trivial. That is, he interprets it as saying that a statement X will be true if it entails a true epistemological principle (or principles) plus other true assumptions. On this interpretation, (R) is not relativistic and is wholly trivial. Any nonrelativist can agree that if a statement X is implied by true premises, then X is true.

To avoid both easy refutation and the charge of triviality, the relativist might argue that the *justification,* rather than the truth value, of a statement X will depend upon one's epistemological system. That is, the relativist might reject (R) and substitute (R_1):

(R_1): The justification of any statement X will depend on the epistemological system that is chosen.

(R_1) encounters a problem analogous to that faced by (R). The nonrelativist can again appeal to (S) (whatever the nonrelativist believes is true) to justify his belief that (R_1) is false. If the adoption of any consistent epistemological principle is sufficient to justify whatever it entails, or whatever it plus other justified assumptions entail, then one can justify any belief, including the belief that relativism is false. The relativist might reply that the epistemological principles that are adopted must themselves be justified if they are to be used to refute relativism, but, once again, this renders relativism trivial. Any nonrelativist can agree that if an epistemological principle is justified, and it (plus other justified assumptions) entails statement X, then statement X is justified (provided that we see the logical connection between the premises and conclusion).

I do not think that Krasner and Houts (1984) are trying to defend either of the above kinds of relativism. I think that their claim is that: (1) one must begin with what they call "an assumptive framework" and (2) there are no neutral standards for justifying this framework. They are not saying, or at least they do not have to say, that whatever is justified on the basis of this framework is itself justified; that is, they can agree that because the basic framework is unjustified, what it supports is also unjustified. This view may also be the kind of relativism that Fishman and colleagues have in mind.

Is this third kind of relativism defensible? Siegel (1980, p. 115) provides a precise formulation of the doctrine as follows:

(R_2): For any knowledge-claim p, p can be evaluated (assessed, established, etc.) only according to (with reference to) a set of background principles and standards of evaluation, $s, \ldots s_n$; and, given a different set of background principles and standards, $s'_1 \ldots s'_n$, there is no neutral (that is, neutral with respect to the two or more alternative sets of principles and standards) way of choosing between the two or more alternative sets in evaluating p.

If we add to (R_2) the assumption that there will always be rival background principles and that there must be some neutral way to choose between them if p is to be established, then there will be no way to establish p. The most we will be able to do is to justify p on the assumption that the background principles are true; but that will not suffice to justify p, for the background principles will always be unjustifiable.

Is there any good reason to accept (R_2)? No. As Siegel (1980) points out, we can substitute any proposition for "p"; hence, we can substitute (R_2). What follows is that (R_2) is itself unjustifiable. This is not surprising. If a relativist argues that any claim X must ultimately rest on an unjustifiable "assumptive framework," and the lack of justification for the framework renders the claim unjustifiable, then the claim of the relativist is also unjustifiable. But, then, there is no good (epistemic) reason to accept it. Relativism of this type is rationally self-defeating in that its truth guarantees that it is unwarranted. Pointing this out does not prove that relativism is false, but rather that there is no good reason to think it true.

There are various options open to the relativist at this point. He might try to exempt his own doctrine from itself, or try to define "truth" relativistically, or even deny the principle of noncontradiction. Siegel (1986) explores some for the options and shows how they lead either to incoherence or triviality. There is, of course, a great deal more that must be said before one can justifiably claim to undermine all interesting kinds of relativism. My goal has been a more modest one: to show that certain relativistic claims made recently in the behavior therapy literature are either trivial or unfounded.

Empiricism

At this point, the relativist might reply as follows: "Even if I cannot defend relativism, I challenge the behavior therapist to provide a (nonrelativistic) defense of his or her empiricist epistemology. Even if I cannot prove this, I predict that the challenge will not be met."

It must be conceded that meeting such a fundamental challenge is often difficult. At the most basic level of belief, one quickly runs out of cogent evidence and argument—which is exactly the relativist's point. Nevertheless, I think that the challenge is answerable. My basic strategy will be to pare to a minimum the empiricist doctrines that behavior therapists are logically committed to and then to show how the remaining core can be justified without begging any questions against the rival psychoanalytic paradigm.

In considering the empiricist foundations of behavior therapy, it is important to distinguish between doctrines that many (or most) behavior therapists do accept and those that they logically must accept given other assumptions that are crucial to their position. Although the kind of inquiry undertaken by Krasner and Houts (1984) is important, it can tell us only what behavior therapists *do* accept, at least if the inquiry is restricted to the use of questionnaires; it does not tell us what they *should* accept. For example, should behavior therapists, given their other views, accept logical empiricism? I do not see why, although it depends on what doctrines we have in mind. Some of the most distinctive logical-empiricist views include: a rejection of all synthetic *a prioricity*, a verifiability criterion of meaningfulness, and a partial interpretation view of theoretical terms. There may be good arguments for one or more of these views, but I see nothing in the overall position of most behavior therapists that logically compels them to accept any of these doctrines.

What about other empiricist doctrines that have been attributed to behavior therapists? Consider the following. The first two are taken from Krasner and Houts's (1984) Epistemological Style Questionnaire; the third is suggested by remarks of Woolfolk and Richardson (1984, p. 777); and the fourth is discussed by Krasner and Houts (p. 841).

(1) Observation of raw data is both prior to and independent of theory.
(2) Scientific observation provides us with hard data independent of our subjective desires, wishes, and biases.
(3) The form and content of scientific knowledge are strongly influenced by sociopolitical factors as well as those related to the attitudes and sensibilities of the community of scientists.
(4) There can be no neutral observation language.

Why did the behavior therapists questioned by Krasner and Houts tend to accept (1) and (2)? A reasonable conjecture is that they felt compelled to by virtue of their commitment to an objective study of clinical phenomena. Most behavior therapists, be they cognitivists or behaviorists, accept the need for empirical—and, in particular, experimental—evidence to answer questions about theory or therapy. Some behavior therapists even define behavior therapy as the application of experimental methods to clinical psychology (Davison & Neale, 1974, p. 485). If (1) or (2) is false, however, then the whole enterprise of providing objective answers to clinical questions by appeal to experimental evidence appears threatened. Similar reasoning would seem to require a rejection of (3) and (4). Woolfolk and Richardson (1984, p. 777) point out that the truth of (3) plus other facts undermines behavior therapy's self-image. Krasner and Houts (1984, p. 841) argue that because (4) is true, the fundamental assumption of objectivism is untenable.

It would seem, then, that behavior therapists are logically compelled to accept (1) and (2) and to reject (3) and (4). Whether that is actually so, however, depends on the content of these theses. As with relativistic doctrines, these statements admit of both interesting and trivial interpretations (which raises a problem for using questionnaires to find out if behavior therapists do accept them). Consider, for example, (1): Observation of raw data is both prior to and independent of theory. If "raw data" means *pure sense data* (data free from all theoretical influence), then the thesis is trivial, although behavior therapists need not believe in pure sense data. If "raw data" means *observational data* relevant to the testing of a theory, then the thesis is implausible if we are talking about *all* raw data. Suppose that a psychoanalyst and behavior therapist disagree as to whether or not the use of the bell-and-blanket method for treating enuresis will typically result either in failure to solve the problem or in symptom substitution. Suppose that the technique is used with a child who then stops wetting the bed and starts having temper tantrums. The psychoanalyst, let us suppose, sees the temper tantrums as symptom substitution. The behavior therapist rejects this description if it implies that the new behavior is caused by an unresolved id–ego conflict; he sees the behavior as a new conditioned response. The observations of each theorist, we might say, are "theory-laden"; they are influenced by the theories and concepts employed by each one. If (1) implies that this sort of thing never occurs, then (1) is false. Why, however, should a behavior therapist want to defend (1) when interpreted in this extreme way? For experimental purposes, it is sufficient that *some* relevant observations are not laden with either theory being tested. For example, the behavior therapist and psychoanalyst could agree to a list of maladaptive behaviors, including bedwetting, temper tantrums, refusal to eat dinner, and fighting with a sibling. The failure for any maladaptive behavior on the list to follow the cessation of the bedwetting within a specified time would then count as a case where symptom substitution did not occur, unless an unlisted maladaptive behavior occurred. In the latter case, if both sides agreed, the new type of maladaptive behavior would be added to the list; if there were disagreement, the case could be counted as irrelevant to the symptom-substitution hypothesis.

Someone who accepts (1) might argue that even the observation that bedwetting has occurred is theory-laden. One would not, for example, see something as "bedwetting" unless one possessed that concept. A behavior therapist, however, can concede this point but reply that the observation of bedwetting does not require the acceptance (or the rejection) of psychoanalytic or conditioning theory. Both the behavior therapist and psychoanalyst in our example can observe *that* bedwetting has occurred, and they both can see it *as* bedwetting. They can do the same for other maladaptive behaviors, such as throwing a temper tantrum, refusing to eat dinner, or fighting with a sibling. The fact that the observation of each item is theory-laden in some way or other poses no threat to the experimental evaluation of theories, as long as the observations are not determined by the theory being tested. As Von Eckardt (1981) points out, to obtain relevant, objective data, it is sufficient that the following be possible: that data relevant to a given theory T can be collected by someone whether or not he or she believes in T, or even whether or not he or she has any knowledge of T.

Statements (2), (3), and (4) also admit of both trivial and nontrivial interpretations. For example, (2) might be read as saying that our desires, wishes, and biases *never* influence our observation of hard data. The statement is then not particularly plausible, but the behavior therapist has no motivation to defend it. However, (2) could be read as implying that *sometimes* we can make objective evaluations of data; that is, sometimes what we observe is not distorted by our desires, wishes, and biases. For example, whatever their biases and desires, the behavior therapist and the psychoanalyst can both observe that a child is not eating his dinner or is fighting with his sister. Once again, on the second reading, the statement is trivial.

Statement (3) is also trivial if it says merely that scientific knowledge (or, rather what scientists believe) is *sometimes* strongly influenced by sociopolitical factors and the attitudes and sensibilities of scientists. However, (3) might imply that the influence of these factors is so strong and so ubiquitous that scientists can never (or rarely) make objective, rational assessments of empirical data. When interpreted in this extreme way, the behavior therapist has reason not to accept it. But why should this present a problem? There is no evidence that it is true.

If the second, extreme version of (3) were true, how could Woolfolk and Richardson (1984) accomplish their goal of analyzing the moral and epistemological underpinnings of behavior therapy? As scientists, they, too, have to assess evidence, at least the evidence that behavior therapists really do hold the views that Woolfolk and Richardson attribute to them. If Woolfolk and Richardson cannot make rational, objective assessments of the evidence, then they cannot tell if their own judgments are true—including the judgment that scientific knowledge is strongly influenced by sociopolitical factors and attitudes. The same kind of problem arises for Krasner and Houts (1984). They claim that (4) is true (that there can be no neutral observation language) and that, therefore, the fundamental assumption of objectivism is untenable. Suppose that some extreme version of (4) were true, one that did imply that it is impossible to decide on rational grounds if any judgment is true. How, then, could Krasner and Houts pursue the psychology of science in the manner they intend? They would be incapable of making rational assessments of the evidence they accumulate about the epistemological views of scientists. If the assumption of objectivism is untenable, as they say, then the objectivity of their own enterprise is undermined.

Is (4) true? Again, that depends on what (4) says. It might mean that the language we commonly use to describe what we observe can never be free from all interpretation. For example, even when we describe what we see as "a wet bed," the description is not entirely neutral. We are interpreting what we see, and someone who lacked the concept of a "bed" would not describe his or her observation in the same way. This interpretation renders trivial the statement, "there can be no neutral observation language." It is compatible with the "objectivist" assumption that observational language relevant to a theory T can be neutral in the sense that it can be used to describe what one observes whether or not one accepts T. "Wetting the bed" is thus neutral in this sense; it can be used by both the behavior therapist and psychoanalyst to describe what may be relevant to psychoanalytic theory. If (4) states the more extreme doctrine that there is no language neutral between two theories that can be used to describe relevant observations, then (4) runs into the same problem as (1). The phrase "the bed is not wet" is neutral between psychoanalysis and conditioning theory; but it can describe an observation relevant to the disconfirmation of the former.

So far, I have questioned whether behavior therapists need to be committed to any interesting empiricist doctrines. They need not accept the distinctive epistemological views of logical empiricism; they are not compelled to accept (1) or (2) unless each is interpreted so as to make it defensible but relatively trivial; and they need not reject (3) or (4) unless each is interpreted to state an extreme doctrine that is indefensible.

Is there no nontrivial empiricist doctrine lying at the foundation of behavior therapy? What about the view of some neobehaviorists that all theoretical terms must be operationally defined? I would agree that this is a nontrivial empiricist doctrine and that it is indefensible (Erwin, 1978, pp. 54–60), but I doubt that it is essential to a behavior therapy paradigm. Cognitivists do not generally accept it, nor is there reason why they ought to. What about the commitment to experimental testing? This does seem to be a nontrivial empiricist commitment, one that would be rejected by many psychoanalysts (as well as many humanists, existentialists, and phenomenologists). The question arises, then, as to how it is to be justified. Or, is it part of the "assumptive framework" that Krasner and Houts (1984) claim is unjustifiable?

In considering its defense, we first have to ask: what exactly does this commitment to experimental testing consist of? I am referring to an acceptance of

(5) Experimental testing is generally necessary for the confirmation of theoretical and therapeutic *causal* claims in clinical psychology (unless some suitable substitute is used).

The phrase "generally necessary" is inserted in (5) to make room for certain exceptions to be discussed later. The addition of the phrase "suitable substitute" threatens to trivialize the thesis, but it need not succeed. It can be understood that, for example, epidemiological studies may serve as a suitable substitute for experimentation, but uncontrolled case studies generally can not.

Can (5) be rationally defended? One way of doing so is to appeal to the differential nature of confirmation (Erwin & Siegel, 1987). For evidence E to confirm hypothesis H *differentially* is for E to afford at least some reason for believing that H is true and not to afford equal (or better) reason for believing some rival hypothesis that is at least as plausible. For example, if the evidence from an experiment, plus our background evidence, rules out one of the only three plausible hypotheses that explain certain data, but is neutral between the remaining two hypotheses, then the evidence does not *differentially* confirm either of the remaining hypotheses. Does it provide any sort of confirmation for each? In answering this question some philosophers of science would distinguish between a weak and strong sense of "confirmation" [what some writers call a "relevance" and "absolute" sense; see Salmon (1982)]. A hypothesis is *weakly* confirmed by certain evidence if the evidence provides at least some grounds for thinking the hypothesis true; it is *strongly* confirmed only if the evidence is weighty enough to warrant belief in the hypothesis. Some writers, then, hold that a hypothesis is weakly confirmed even when the evidence is not differential. In the example just cited, the evidence that rules out one rival hypothesis increases the probability of the remaining two and, consequently, weakly confirms both. In reply, Erwin and Siegel (1987) argue that an increase in probability is not sufficient for confirmation; they conclude that *all* confirmation is differential. Whether this conclusion is right or not, there is reason to believe that strong confirmation, at least, is differential. We want to rule out the possibility of E strongly confirming H_1 and H_2 even though they are equally plausible and logically inconsistent; otherwise, we are warranted in believing what we know is a contradiction. This possibility is ruled out by the requirement that E strongly (or absolutely) confirms H_1 only if E does not afford equal or greater reason to believe some rival hypothesis of equal or greater plausibility.

Why argue that confirmation, or at least strong confirmation, is differential? This is something that behavior therapists are likely to take for granted. However, some psychoanalysts appear implicitly to deny it. For example, Hall (1963, p. 344) asks whether his results could have been predicted by some theory other than psychoanalysis and replies that the question is irrelevant. The question is not irrelevant, however, if confirmation is differential. If it is, and some equally plausible theory explains his results just as well as psychoanalytic theory, then his results do not confirm the latter (at least, not "strongly").

Once it is agreed that confirmation is differential, then the need for experimentation can be defended by arguing in specific cases that plausible rivals to the hypothesis being considered can only be ruled out (i.e., discounted) by the imposition of experimental controls. Grünbaum (1984) has demonstrated that this is so for Freud's causal claims; behavior therapists have done the same for their own therapeutic claims, as well as those of others.

The need for experimentation can be rationally defended, then, first by arguing that all confirmation is differential (or that strong confirmation is, and interpreting "confirmation" in E as strong confirmation). The second step is to provide evidence that, for causal claims in clinical psychology, there generally are rival hypotheses of equal or greater plausibility to the one being tested and that experimentation (or some suitable substitute) is generally necessary to choose between them.

Some psychoanalysts who deny the need for experimentation may be encouraged by a recent paper by Kazdin (1981), who argues that uncontrolled case studies can sometimes confirm causal hypotheses. In reply (Erwin, 1988), I agree with Kazdin, but argue that such examples are exceptional and that there are specific reasons why psychoanalytic causal claims are not likely to be among the exceptions.

A psychoanalyst might concede the necessity for experimentation but still question its value: he might hold that the variables in clinical psychology are too complicated and that, consequently, experimentation is not sufficient for confirmation. If no in-principle doubt is being raised, then the proper reply is an empirical one. The evidence shows that behavior therapists have already demonstrated the value of experimentation in both confirming and disconfirming therapeutic claims (Kazdin & Wilson, 1978; Rachman & Wilson, 1980).

Someone might also raise an in-principle doubt about the possibility of experimental confirmation. For example, a general skeptic might claim that confirmation of any empirical claim is impossible. The issue that is then raised, however, does not divide psychoanalysts from behavior therapists. If confirmation is impossible, whether we rely on case studies or on experimentation, then psychoanalytic hypotheses can be no more warranted than those of the behavior therapist. A discussion of general skepticism is beyond the scope of this paper, but some brief comments might be made concerning certain challenges to confirmation posed by some behavior therapists.

Mahoney (1978), arguing from Popperian assumptions, does not deny that experimentation is generally useful in *disconfirming* clinical hypotheses. He does claim (p. 670), however, that researchers are making a serious logical error when they interpret their results as *supporting* their hypotheses. The error is that of affirming the consequent. One is guilty of this fallacy if one deduces p from "If p, then q" and q.

One problem with Mahoney's view concerns the distinction that he tries to draw concerning confirmation and disconfirmation. As critics of Popper have pointed out, most theoretical hypotheses do not by themselves entail predictions about what is observable. We need to add auxiliary assumptions and a statement of initial conditions. For example, the therapeutic hypothesis that Beck's treatment for depression is effective does not by itself imply that treated patients will score lower on a certain test for depression than untreated patients. We need the additional assumption that the test is a genuine measure of depression. If we cannot confirm that it is (because we cannot confirm any empirical assumption), then we cannot falsify the therapeutic hypothesis. The most that we can deduce is the disjunction: either the therapeutic hypothesis or the assumption that the test measures depression is false. In short, if auxillary assumptions cannot be confirmed, then scientific theories generally cannot be falsified. The Popper–Mahoney view reduces to a general, if not total, skepticism about empirical matters.

A second problem concerns Mahoney's assertion that researchers who try to confirm hypotheses invariably use the illicit argument that he attributes to them. How does he know this if empirical assertions about what researchers do have a zero degree of confirmation? It could be replied that in trying to confirm a hypothesis, one *necessarily* commits the fallacy of affirming the consequent. This reply, however, is incorrect. If a doctor infers that someone has disease D, for example, he need not reason: "If the patient has disease D, he will have symptoms S; he does have symptoms S, consequently, he has disease D." There is no reason to think that the doctor must, or is even likely to, rely on such an illicit argument. Instead, he may reason as follows: "The postulation of disease X best explains symptoms S (all other likely causes have been ruled out); the fact that this hypothesis provides the best explanation of S is some reason to think the hypothesis is true."

We need not assume, then, that attempts to confirm hypotheses necessarily involve the commission of a logical error. An alternative is to explain confirmation in terms of inference to the best explanation. (For a defense of such inferences for causal hypotheses, see Cartwright, 1983, Essay 5.)

The use of inference to the best explanation helps to answer a skeptical doubt raised by some behaviorists about the possibility of confirming cognitivist hypotheses. Rachlin (1977, p. 374) concedes that behaviorists must make inferences about past experiences, but these events, he notes, are potentially observable; cognitions are not. I question, however, whether this difference guarantees that one type of hypothesis is warrantable and the other is not. Suppose that we can warrant the inference that someone had such-and-such a history of reinforcement by pointing out that the postulation of such a history best explains the person's present behavior. If that is allowed, then we can justify the postulation of present cognitions in the same way. Which explanation will be the best in any given case will be an empirical question, but in principle either sort of postulation can be warranted. Suppose that we reject all inference to the best explanation. In that case, we will be unable to confirm hypotheses about past experiences or present cognitions. Rachlin may accept this option; he does say that both sorts of hypotheses are "speculative" (1977, p. 374). However, we then have no rational grounds to accept either sort of hypothesis: we are reduced to being skeptical about both.

Conceptual and Empirical Issues

Once relativism is rejected and the need for experimentation is demonstrated, the issues between behavior therapists and psychoanalysts become largely empirical. The key issue is not whether psychoanalysis is or ought to be a science, but whether there are grounds of any sort for accepting psychoanalytic theory or therapy. So far, the grounds appear to be unsatisfactory. Grünbaum (1984) has recently demonstrated that the support provided by the clinical evidence is "remarkably weak"; the experimental evidence is also weak (Erwin, 1986; Eysenck, 1985, Eysenck & Wilson, 1973–but see Kline, 1986), as is the evidence for therapeutic effectiveness (Erwin, 1980; Rachman & Wilson, 1980). Because of the lack of firm evidence for psychoanalysis, I will from now on focus on the behaviorist and cognitivist paradigms. Can they be reconciled? If not, are there good grounds for preferring either? Before discussing the main issues, it is necessary to characterize each paradigm.

Cognitivism and Behaviorism

The terms "behaviorism" and "cognitivism" are commonly used in clinical psychology, but not always in the same ways. To avoid misunderstanding, I will use these terms to refer to the following views. *Cognitivism* is the view that cognitivist causes must be considered in explaining human behavior. *Behaviorism* holds that (1) cognitive causes should be eliminated from a science of behavior and (2) conditioning theories should be developed instead. The second clause is needed to exclude someone who denies cognitive causation but also seriously downgrades conditioning explanations, emphasizing instead neurological and physiological causation. Paul Churchland (1981), for example, appears to hold such a position and, consequently, is not a behaviorist.

A cognitivist paradigm, then, is one that includes cognitivism (as defined above), a clinical theory that appeals to cognitive causes, and philosophical and methodological assumptions compatible with cognitivism. A behaviorist paradigm includes behaviorism, a conditioning theory of clinical phenomena, and philosophical and methodological assumptions compatible with behaviorism.

On the issue of cognitive causation, behaviorists and cognitivists hold logically incompatible positions, but on other central issues agreement may be possible. The disputes between the two camps in clinical psychology do not mirror exactly the behaviorist–cognitivist disagreements so widely discussed in philosophy and nonclinical areas of psychology. Some of the issues are the same, but some are not. It should also be stressed that the cognitivist and behaviorist categories may be of analytical use in discussing some issues, but may be very misleading in discussing others. For example, I will initially talk as if the neobehaviorist views of Wolpe and Eysenck are "behaviorist," but will question later the aptness of this classification. It is also not clear that there are very many behaviorists (in my stipulated sense) left in the field of behavior therapy. Eysenck (Chapter 4, this volume) points out that even Skinner (1974) agrees that private stimuli, such as cognitions, have to be taken into account. However, I am unclear how, in his view, this is to be done. In some of his writings, he does appear to deny that appeal should be made to cognitions as causes: "In summary, then, I am not a cognitive psychologist for several reasons. I see no evidence of an inner world of mental life relative either to an analysis of behavior as a function of environmental forces or to the physiology of the nervous system. . . . The appeal to cognitive states and processes is a diversion which could well be responsible for much of our failure to solve our problems" (Skinner, 1977, p. 10).

Other writers in the not too distant past have also questioned the need for any appeal to cognitive causes (e.g., Lacey & Rachlin, 1978; Kantor, 1978; Greenspoon & Lamal, 1978). Some may now have changed their position (however, see Rachlin, 1985), but these writers have not been alone in questioning the postulation of cognitive causes. As Wilson (1978) notes, many who accept an applied-behavior-analysis model have rejected cognitive processes as improper targets of experimental study or have relegated them to the status of epiphenomenal events. I also have doubts as to whether all neobehaviorists are willing to countenance cognitive causes. Those who use cognitive concepts only on condition that they be operationally defined in terms of observable behavior are leaving no room for cognitive causation.

I do not agree, then, that "behaviorists" (in my sense) are nonexistent in the field of behavior therapy, but I suspect that their number is relatively small. Nevertheless, the issue they raise about the explanatory role of cognitions is still of some importance.

Before we address the main issues, it might be useful to discard some pseudo-issues. Some writers see the resurgence of cognitivism as a return to dualism (Kantor, 1978, pp. 332–333; Greenspoon & Lamal, 1978, p. 346) or as a denial of determinism (Wolpe, 1978). These issues are pseudo-issues for the following reasons. First, cognitivism does not imply dualism (Erwin, 1978, pp. 72–73), and few, if any, leading behavior therapists who are cognitivists have embraced dualism. Second, cognitivism does not imply a denial of determinism (Erwin, 1978, pp. 174–178). A cognitivist can accept compatibilism (or soft determinism) and agree that all human behavior is caused *and* that there is some free choice.

I will turn now to the main conceptual and empirical issues concerning therapy and the theoretical foundations of behavior therapy.

Therapeutic Issues

Several reviews have argued for a general superiority of behavioral over cognitive techniques. I will concentrate on one such review by Latimer and Sweet (1984), but some of my comments may bear on other reviews, such as the much-discussed one by Ledwidge (1978).

Latimer and Sweet (p. 9) begin by questioning Mahoney's (1974) view that a cognitive revolution has occurred in the field of behavior therapy. They argue (p. 13) that in deciding this question, the importance or relevance of cognitions is not the issue. The real issue is whether the therapies derived from cognitive theory are more effective than behavior therapy. They argue (p. 21) that if cognitive therapies are effective only by virtue of their inclusion of existing behavioral methods, then nothing revolutionary, and perhaps nothing of value, has been added. In addressing this issue of whether cognitive components explain the success of cognitive therapies, they review two kinds of studies. The first, and the only kind they regard as definitive, compares a behavioral treatment of known efficacy to the same treatment *plus* the cognitive procedures to be evaluated. Five studies were included in this first category, and none demonstrated a clinically significant contribution for the cognitive procedures. The second and less important group included seven studies comparing cognitive therapy with other treatments. The results were mixed, but some evidence for the superiority of the behavioral techniques was found; the only study showing a superiority for a cognitive procedure lacked an attention/placebo control group. Latimer and Sweet conclude (p. 14) that the efficacy of cognitive therapy (excluding behavioral components) has not been demonstrated in clinical populations and that the available evidence suggests that the "cognitive" component of the cognitive therapies is less potent than established behavioral methods such as exposure *in vivo*.

There are several problems with Latimer and Sweet's argument. One problem that I will not discuss in detail arises for *all* general comparisons of behavior therapy and cognitive therapy: such comparisons presuppose that these are two distinct kinds of therapy. In some accounts of the nature of behavior therapy, such as my own (Erwin, 1978, pp. 38–44) and that given by the Association for the Advancement of Behavior Therapy (Erwin, 1978, pp. 35–36), that is not true. At least some cognitive techniques are forms of behavior therapy. If one accepts such an account, one cannot coherently compare behavior therapy techniques in general with cognitive techniques. That would be like trying to compare medical procedures with surgery. If cognitive procedures form a subset of behavior therapy techniques, then trying to prove the general superiority of the latter rests on a logical mistake. A reviewer could stipulate that the behavioral techniques are exactly those that are based on a certain conditioning theory, but he would then need to show that those being placed in the behavioral category *are* based on that theory. Neither Ledwidge nor Latimer and Sweet attempt to do this. One could also try to develop some other general criterion for distinguishing behavioral and cognitive techniques. Ledwidge (1978) tries to do this, but I think his attempt can be shown to have failed (Erwin, 1987), and I know of no other attempt that has succeeded.

Even if one can divide up cognitive and behavior therapy techniques in some general, nonarbitrary way, the argument of Latimer and Sweet requires a second, more refined distinction. They also need a general criterion for distinguishing cognitive and behavioral features of each type of therapy. I have tried to show elsewhere (Erwin, 1985c) that they have no such criterion and that there is no single distinction of the kind they need to draw.

Even if Latimer and Sweet were to succeed in distinguishing in a clear and general way between cognitive and behavioral components, they would still not be home free. They assume that to demonstrate the value of cognitive techniques, one must show that their cognitive ingredients account for their therapeutic effectiveness. This is why the only studies they count as definitive (p. 14) are those that compare a behavioral treatment of known efficacy to the same treatment *plus* the cognitive procedures to be evaluated. Why, however, should a cognitivist accept their criterion of success, which on the face of it is much too stringent? A cognitivist can argue that if a cognitive technique, such as Beck's treatment for depression, is more effective than a credible placebo, then it is effective. It is not necessary to claim that specific cognitive ingredients of the therapy account for its effectiveness. Eysenck, in a personal communication, points out that many cognitivists do make this claim of effectiveness of cognitive ingredients. However, at least some leading cognitivists have been more cautious. For example, Beck agrees that in using cognitive therapy he may be utilizing predominantly behavioral or emotional releasing techniques (Beck et al., 1979). One might challenge the evidence for the effectiveness of Beck's therapy, but Latimer and Sweet do not do that. Rather, they disregard the evidence (p. 13) on the grounds that Beck's technique includes behavioral procedures that could account for its success. However, they are not then entitled to conclude (p. 21) that the widespread acceptance of cognitive clinical procedures is unwarranted. The most that their argument shows is the following: the belief that cognitive ingredients account for the therapeutic effectiveness of cognitive techniques is unwarranted.

Latimer and Sweet (p. 21) anticipate the reply of the cognitivist, but counter that if cognitive therapies are effective only by virtue of their inclusion of existing behavioral methods, then nothing revolutionary, and perhaps nothing of value, has been added. This counterreply does not work. There are two issues to be separated. First, are some cognitivist techniques effective? The answer is "yes" if some are more effective than a credible placebo. The more stringent criterion of Latimer and Sweet need not be met. Second, has the cognitivist revolution produced anything of therapeutic value? The answer is again "yes" if some cognitive therapies produced by that revolution are effective for certain problems.

Even if there were no evidence that any cognitive procedure is effective, it would still not follow that the cognitivist revolution has not enhanced therapy. The change in outlook might have improved therapy in some other way than by generating effective cognitive techniques. For example, suppose that Bandura (1977) is right in his analysis of why systematic desensitization is effective: it works by enhancing self-efficacy expectations. If we then obtain empirical evidence that such expectations in certain clients, say agoraphobics, are more likely to be altered by *in vivo* methods, then we can explain why systematic desensitization is not the treatment of choice for such clients. As Bandura and other cognitivists have stressed, even if faulty cognitions are the root cause of a psychological problem, "performance methods" may be best suited for altering the cognitions and modifying the maladaptive response. Although this may appear paradoxical, the cognitive turn may have produced a therapeutic payoff by explaining why a standard behavioral technique that relies on manipulation of mental imagery, such as systematic desensitization, is not behavioral enough for certain types of clinical problems. This part of my argument depends, of course, on the correctness of Bandura's analysis; the argument fails if Eysenck's rival theory (1983) is right.

Finally, even if the cognitivist revolution had produced nothing of therapeutic value, it would still have been important. Latimer and Sweet make the therapy issue paramount because, they argue, behavior therapists had already accepted the importance of cognitions before the so-called cognitive revolution. However, at the time of publication of Mahoney's book (1974) and Bandura's Presidential Address (1974), a widely held view was that behavior therapy is based on classical and operant conditioning principles that make no mention of cognitive causes (Erwin, 1978, Chapter 3). In addition, those who accepted an applied-behavioral-analysis model rejected all cognitive causation. So, while it is true that some behavior therapists accepted cognitive causation prior to 1974, many either neglected it or repudiated it altogether. The cognitive revolution consisted mainly in altering this situation.

Is the foregoing unfair to Latimer and Sweet? Some therapists have suggested that certain so-called cognitive procedures, such as self-instruction training, can provide additional effectiveness when added to behavioral techniques. There has even been some experimental support for this proposition from analogue studies. However, in the five studies of clinical subjects cited by Latimer and Sweet, the results were disappointing. Is it not important to point this out? I think that it is, especially if some cognitivists give the impression that the irrational beliefs implicated in some serious emotional disorders can be simply talked away or eliminated by sheer logical persuasion. Thus, I am not disagreeing with Latimer and Sweet about the fairly narrow conclusion that certain so-called cognitive procedures appear not to enhance effectiveness for the disorders that were studied. What I have questioned is their argument for their more sweeping conclusions that (1) the movement to a cognitivist paradigm has produced nothing revolutionary and perhaps nothing of value and (2) the widespread adoption

of cognitive procedures is unwarranted on the basis of existing outcome data involving clinical populations. Neither conclusion is supported by their arguments, although the second might be true if it
were modified to refer to *some* cognitive procedures.

Theory

I have elsewhere argued (Erwin, 1978, Chapter 3), that conditioning
theories and principles that eschewed all cognitive causation are un-
confirmed by the extant empirical evidence, or are tautological, or are
too narrow in scope to serve as a foundation of behavior therapy.
[Other writers, such as Mahoney (1974) and Bandura (1974) had earlier reached similar conclusions.] Eysenck (1979) agrees that I have
shown the more extreme claims of some behavior therapists to be
unfounded, but, he replies, they had no business making the task of
the critic so easy. They should not have claimed to be able to explain
all behavior; it is enough that behaviorists can explain the origin of
neuroses and the workings of behavior therapy techniques. I agree
with Eysenck's point, and I think it important. The key issue is not, or
at least should not be, the mind–body problem or the general admissi-
bility of cognitions in a science of behavior, as Ledwidge (1978, p. 360)
suggests. The main issue about theory is, or should be: what sort of
theories are needed to explain *clinical* phenomena? Despite the importance of Eysenck's point, however, it does not dissolve all of the major
difficulties facing the behaviorist. Even *within* clinical psychology,
there seems to be evidence for cognitive causation, although Eysenck's
theory (1983) may be able to account for it. One line of evidence comes
from studies by Bandura and his colleagues on the role of self-efficacy
expectations (Bandura, 1982; Bandura & Cervone, 1983).

Other evidence comes from experimental studies of placebos. Rosenthal (1983) refers to a number of studies in which the placebo control
yielded outcomes as good as, or trivially weaker than, the behavior
therapy, contending that in many of these studies hypotheses explicitly drawn from conditioning theory were refuted. Eysenck and other
behaviorists however, would probably challenge Rosenthal's contention. A third line of suggestive evidence comes from experimental
studies of conditioning (Brewer, 1974; Dawson & Furedy, 1976; Dawson et al., 1982). These studies typically do not deal with clinical
subjects, but insofar as they show that awareness plays a key causal
role in the very mechanism of "conditioning" with adult humans, they
are indirectly relevant to the hypothesis that all cognitions can be
excluded from clinical psychology. There is little point, however, in
discussing the empirical evidence here in detail; behaviorists are not

unaware of it. Those who reject all cognitive causation tend to reject the evidence on methodological grounds. Another response, favored by neobehaviorists, is to argue that cognitions can be incorporated into a conditioning theory. I will consider each of these responses in turn.

Methodological Responses

Many of the methodological objections to cognitivist theories, such as those of Skinner (1963), have been answered elsewhere (e.g., Erwin, 1978, pp. 66–74) and therefore will not be discussed here. Nevertheless, even if all such objections are answered, it will still seem to many behaviorists that there is something suspicious about cognitivist explanations. Suppose that, in any given case, the evidence permitted a choice between a conditioning explanation and one that appealed to cognitions. I suspect that many psychologists, and not merely behaviorists, would agree that the conditioning explanation would be preferable. It may be an illusion, fostered by the influence of behaviorism, to think that cognitivist explanations are *prima facie* inferior, but *if* it is true, it is worth asking why. A standard answer of operant theorists is that the events postulated in conditioning explanations are at least potentially observable. For reasons discussed in the section of this chapter on "Epistemological Issues," I do not think that this answer is sufficient. The fact that cognitions are unobservable may give some edge to conditioning explanations, but not enough: as long as we can get indirect evidence that cognitions are partial causes of certain behavior, we cannot dismiss them *a priori* if we want to *explain* as well as predict and control behavior. There are other reasons that have been given, however, for being suspicious about cognitive explanations.

First, Lacey and Rachlin (1978) make some interesting suggestions in support of behaviorism. The cognitivist hopes to find regularities between cognitive variables and behavior of a certain kind. The behaviorist can reply, Lacey and Rachlin (p. 183) point out, that for each generalization relating behavior and cognitions, there will be a corresponding generalization relating the same behavior to environmental events. Thus, by ignoring cognitive variables, the behaviorist will not be overlooking the lawful involvement of any behavior. Furthermore, Lacey and Rachlin contend, the behaviorist's generalizations can at least match any of cognitive theory so far as prediction is concerned, and far surpass them from the point of view of control.

Will there always be environmental events, however, that the behaviorist can appeal to in constructing his generalizations? People who have different beliefs and motives will often respond in very diverse ways to the same external stimuli. Will citing such stimuli give us the generality we seek? Lacey and Rachlin make two additional suggestions. First, the behaviorist should deny that a cause and its effect must be temporally contiguous. Second, when nothing in the immediate environment explains someone's behavior, postulate as a cause some environmental event in the person's history of reinforcement or punishment. Roughly put, Lacey and Rachlin say (p. 184), radical behaviorism maintains that cognitive factors can be dispensed with in favor of the organism's history of environmental interaction.

I think that Lacey and Rachlin have succeeded in raising a problem for cognitivism and also in showing that behaviorism is not refuted as easily as some philosophers believe. Nevertheless, I do not think that their defense protects behaviorism from empirical criticisms. To begin with, why cannot a quirky physicist make the same initial move they recommend to the behaviorist? The orthodox quantum physicist relates observable environmental events to unobservable subatomic events, but for every such generalization, there will always be a corresponding one that relates the observable events to other observable environmental events, especially if we are permitted to postulate events that are not temporally contiguous with the events to be explained. So why not dispense not only with cognitions but also with unobservable subatomic events? The answer is fairly obvious. It is an empirical question as to whether the generalizations found at the observable level will be lawlike. In physics, the evidence is substantial that to find lawlike generalizations that will explain all of the data, the postulation of subatomic events is necessary. In psychology, the evidence is not as substantial; but, the cognitivist argues, it is weighty enough to postulate cognitive causes. The behaviorist may dispute this interpretation of the evidence, but I am not now arguing that the cognitivist is right about the evidence. I am arguing that it is an empirical question whether we will be ignoring "the lawful involvement of behaviors" (Lacey & Rachlin, 1978, p. 183) by ignoring cognitive variables. The behaviorist obtains no edge merely by pointing out that to every cognitive-behavioral generalization, there corresponds some environmental-behavioral generalization. He needs empirical evidence that the latter will always be lawful; in short, that they do explain all of the relevant data.

Second, other potential problems for cognitivist explanations stem from recent work in the philosophy of psychology. Paul Churchland (1981) has argued that in using cognitive concepts such as "belief," "expectation," "intention," and "desire," we are committed to what he calls "folk psychology." He then argues that folk psychology constitutes a theory that may well be false; if it is false, beliefs, expectations, desires, and so forth do not exist. There are, then, no cognitive causes. In a similar fashion, Stich (1983) argues that beliefs have no explanatory role to play in a cognitive science; he also questions whether there are such things as beliefs. Finally, Daniel Dennett (1978) argues for an instrumentalist interpretation of beliefs and other cognitive states: for predictive purposes, we talk *as if* organism had such states, although in fact they do not.

These proposals are quite radical, and I am not convinced that they have been backed so far by compelling arguments or evidence (see, for example, the reply of Horgan & Woodward, 1985). Nevertheless, if the new eliminative materialists (those who deny the existence of most or all mental states or processes) have raised a serious issue, then there remains a serious issue about the adequacy of cognitivist explanations. That, in turn, would mean that, contrary to what most philosophers hold, the issue of behaviorism is not totally closed. Rejecting cognitivist explanations does not automatically vindicate behaviorism: clinical phenomena might be explainable entirely by neurological and physiological variables. That is a possibility, but for an important class of clinical events, including the origin of most nonpsychotic problems and the workings of behavior therapy techniques, the only plausible theories currently available (if Freudian theory is discounted) are either cognitivist or conditioning theories.

Third, there is one additional problem with cognitivist explanations that could be more troublesome than those discussed so far. It concerns their clarity.

Consider Bandura's self-efficacy theory, the *only* non-Freudian, cognitivist theory widely discussed in the behavior therapy literature. In Bandura's view (1977), it is mainly *perceived ineffectiveness* in coping with potentially aversive events that makes the events fearsome. Given that a subject has both the competence and incentive to act in a certain sort of way, then self-efficacy expectations will be the critical determinants of performance. A successful therapy, then, will work by altering the person's self-efficacy expectations, that is, by making them more optimistic. What is a self-efficacy expectation? It is a belief that one can successfully execute a certain plan of action. If systematic desensitization is successful in treating an agoraphobic, then Bandura's theory explains this success in terms of a change in the client's belief about his or her ability to go shopping or something else of this sort without experiencing aversive consequences. Bandura and his colleagues have developed ways to measure perceived self-efficacy and have done a good deal of research that supports the theory (Bandura, 1977, 1982; Bandura & Cervone, 1983).

The issue I want to focus on is not its empirical status, but its key theoretical concept: what is a self-efficacy expectation? As I have already indicated, it is a belief about what one can do. But what is a belief? Bandura might reply: "There is no reason why I have to give an informative answer to this question, except to note that I mean by 'belief' or 'expectation' what is generally meant in the literature of psychology." However, I think it can be questioned whether this reply is satisfactory. Suppose I have a rival to Bandura's theory. In my account, subjects suffer anxiety about phobic situations when they have a bad soul. A successful therapy is one that changes the soul to eliminate this defect. I have even developed a questionnaire for determining when anxious clients have a bad soul, and current research shows that a change in soul state and the achievement of a cure are highly correlated. If you ask me what I mean by a "soul," I mean what is usually meant by religious people and theologians. Yes, but what do they mean? Analogously, what do psychologists and common folk generally mean when they postulate beliefs or expectations, or other cognitive states or events as causes of behavioral change? It is probably misguided to insist on an operational definition of such notions, but is it unreasonable to ask that *something* be said about what a belief or expectation is?

I am not suggesting that Bandura and his colleagues are committed to the existence of mysterious, nonphysical mental states or events. As noted earlier, a cognitivist need not be a dualist; in human beings, self-efficacy expectations and other kinds of beliefs, it might be said, are brain processes. However, this does not resolve the problem I am raising. One can ask what exactly it is that is being identified with a brain process. In one view, favored by some functionalists, a belief is simply that which *causes* certain sorts of behavior; it is conjectured that this something will someday be discovered to be a brain process. However, this account makes cognitive explanations rather unilluminating. Suppose I say, for example, that the cause of the client's improvement was his belief that the therapy would be effective. If a belief is nothing more than whatever causes behavioral changes of a certain sort, then I seem to be saying no more than that the change in the client's behavior was caused by whatever causes that sort of behavioral change. A functionalist might reply that what makes the explanation informative is that the belief is causally connected to *other* behavioral and cognitive changes as well. However, that is also true of a bad soul. The elimination of this spiritual defect not only causes client improvement, but in conjunction with other variables it causes other types of behavioral and cognitive change. Does pointing this out save the bad-soul theory from obscurity? As long as I talk only about the effects of a bad soul, and say nothing about what a bad soul is, then my theory is unclear. For the same reason, the functionalist account of belief that talks only about the *effects* of beliefs renders cognitivist theories unclear.

Some who favor cognitive behavior modification have managed to give more content to the concept of a belief: they identity beliefs with internal sentences, that is with sentences (or statements) that the client utters subvocally. However, this identification seems incorrect for many beliefs. I have long believed that 983 is greater than 6, that B.F. Skinner is not 8 feet tall, and that Freud is dead. Yet I have until now never expressed these beliefs either vocally, subvocally, or in writing. A client who receives rational-emotive therapy may believe that it is necessary to be approved by every other person, and yet the client may never have uttered this sentence to himself prior to the therapist's bringing it to his attention. How, then, can a belief *be* an internal sentence?

In another account, suggested by Ryle (1949), a belief is merely a disposition to behave in certain ways. There are standard objections to this account, but even if it is correct, it does not help the cognitivist. Reducing beliefs to dispositions seriously diminishes their explanatory power. Suppose I say that a client can now approach a phobic object because he believes, as a result of therapy, that no adverse consequences will follow. If the attribution of this belief means that he now has the disposition to approach the phobic object in this sort of situation, then my explanation is not very informative. The client can approach the phobic object, I say, because he now has the disposition to do so. Why not also say that he can now approach the object because his bad soul has been rectified? What is the rectification of a bad soul for this sort of client? It is the development of a disposition to approach a phobic object.

I am not suggesting that speaking of beliefs, desires, or expectations never explains anything. A newspaper reported recently that a man beat his young son to death because he believed that the child was possessed by the devil and also believed that striking the child vigorously would expel the demon. Even without an account of what a belief is, the explanation is informative. Nevertheless, some modest points may be made. First, if concepts such as "belief" and "expectation" are incorporated into a scientific theory, something should be said about what these terms refer to. Second, some standard accounts of the nature of belief either are wrong or tend to trivialize cognitivist explanations. Third, if nothing illuminating at all can be said about beliefs, cognitive maps, expectations, cognitive structures, and so forth, then conditioning explanations may, other things being equal, obtain an advantage over cognitive explanations. How large an advantage will depend on how much less clear cognitivist explanations are than those of their rivals. Such an explanatory advantage can also translate into an epistemic one. If certain cognitive states or processes are postulated only on the grounds that doing so best explains the phenomena, but a conditioning hypothesis fits the data just as well *and* provides a clearer explanation, then the balance is tipped in favor of the latter. In areas where the evidence clearly favors cognitivist explanations, the advantage I am speaking of may not matter; but in certain areas in clinical psychology, it may make a difference.

The Neobehaviorist Response

Eysenck, Wolpe, and other neobehaviorists have indicated that they accept cognitive causation. They are not "behaviorists," then, in the sense that I have been using the term. In what sense are they behaviorists? Eysenck (Chapter 4, this volume, p. 52–55) suggests that the crucial issue on which cognitive therapists may differ from traditional behavior therapists is whether cognitions are changed by changes in behavior, or vice versa. His own view is that verbal methods by themselves and without behavioral interaction do not produce good therapeutic results. I do not deny that the issue raised by Eysenck is important, but I question whether it divides behaviorists and cognitivists in general. Leading cognitivists who have stressed the importance of performance-based techniques, such as Albert Bandura, also have doubts about the effectiveness of verbal methods. Having such reservations does not suffice, therefore, to make one a behaviorist, unless some cognitivists are also behaviorists. There is another issue, however, that may be thought to separate cognitivists and neobehaviorists. The latter place much more emphasis on conditioning in explaining clinical phenomena than do those who are called "cognitivists." This emphasis suggests one final issue that I want to discuss: can neobehaviorists consistently combine their views about conditioning and cognitions?

One position on this issue is that cognitions are behaviors and are governed by the same principles governing other behavior (Latimer & Sweet, 1984, p. 13). I am not sure what purpose is served by calling cognitions "behaviors" (in some technical sense), and it has the disadvantage of giving the misleading impression that neobehaviorists are following Watson in restricting psychology to the study of behavior. The more important issue, however, concerns the exact principles being referred to. If it is principles of operant and classical conditioning, then the evidence indicates that they do not explain all behavior:

when interpreted as having universal application they are false; when proper scope restrictions are included, there is much behavior that they do not even apply to (Erwin, 1978). Perhaps the reference is to some unknown conditioning principles that will be formulated in the future. What evidence is there, however, that such principles will explain all behavior (in the ordinary sense) *and* all cognitive processes?

Another position is not that conditioning principles will explain all cognitive processes, but that they will explain a significant part of clinical phenomena *and* will incorporate cognitions. As Eysenck (Chapter 4, this volume) points out, exactly how cognitive processes will be integrated in conditioning theory is an important task for future study. Nevertheless, some kind of constraint can and should be laid down in advance; if that is not done, any theory that explains learned responses in terms of psychological factors could qualify as a "conditioning" theory. To illustrate, contrast playing a slot machine with Eysenck's example (Chapter 4, this volume, p. 58) of a scopolamine injection. In the latter case, the association of the Unconditioned Stimulus and Conditioned Stimulus presumably caused the subsequent "conditioned" responses; cognitive instruction did not affect these responses (Campbell et al. 1964). Playing a slot machine is also often thought to involve conditioning, but it need not. Consider three people who place six quarters in a slot machine; two win all six times and the third loses each time. The loser and one of the winners continue inserting additional quarters for two hours; the other winner stops playing immediately after winning six straight times. In all three cases, there is a contiguity of events; placing a quarter in the machine is paired with winning or losing. But this contiguity may not play a major role in the causation of the player's subsequent behavior. Suppose, for example, that the winner who stopped playing knows that there is no causal or even probabilistic connection between his winning six times in the past and winning in the future. He played six times because he was willing to risk some loose change and, given his beliefs, his winning does not induce him to play further. He would have stopped, however, even if he had lost; thus the juxtaposition of inserting a quarter and receiving a payoff does not explain his stopping play. Even if winning or losing was of some importance for the other two players, their peculiar beliefs might have been of even greater causal significance. Suppose that each is a victim of a variant of the gambler's fallacy. The winner believes that subsequent outcomes are not independent of earlier ones: he takes his early success to be evidence of future success. It is primarily because of this belief that he continues to play. The loser believes that a machine that fails to pay six straight times is "overdue" and likely to produce a big payoff in the near future. It is this belief that largely explains why he continues to play. These examples are different from the scopolamine case in that the beliefs of the individuals, rather than the contiguity of external events, play the more important causal role in explaining behavior.

We might, then, try the following constraint: any conditioning theory that incorporates cognitive factors must still attribute a primary causal role to the pairing of environmental events, such as a conditioned and unconditioned stimulus. This condition would be acceptable to many traditional behaviorists, but it does not fit well with the view of conditioning accepted by many current researchers. MacIntosh (1983) notes that the view of conditioning as the establishment of stimulus-response (S-R) connections has given way to the view of conditioning as the acquisition of knowledge about the relationship between events in an animal's environment. When a conditioned stimulus is regularly followed by a reinforcer, the animal learns that the CS signals the reinforcer; it learns by the establishment of some central representation of the two. Is, however, such an acquisition of knowledge really conditioning? It may be, but it may not. Consider a voter in the United States who prior to 1980 associated relatively large federal deficits with Democratic presidents. He forms the hypothesis that there is a causal connection between the election of Democrats and the increase in the national debt. Because he thinks this increase is bad, he votes for the Republicans in 1980. If he votes the way he does because of the theory he holds, why say that he was "conditioned" to vote for Republican presidents? What is important in understanding the voters' behavior is not the knowledge that he has experienced the pairing of the election of Democratic presidents and an increase in deficits, or that he has, in MacIntosh's phrase, "a central representation" of the pairing; what is important to know is what hypothesis he forms because of his experience. Someone who has had the same experience with Democratic presidents and deficits might vote differently if he believed that the correlation was accidental or that deficits were not harmful.

It appears, then, that it is too narrow to insist that the contiguity of external events plays the key causal role; we have to allow, as MacIntosh indicates, for the influence of the organisms's mental representation for the contiguity. It is also too lax, however, to count as conditioning every case in which the organism acts as a result of knowledge acquired about the relationship between events in its environment. A criterion that steers between these two extremes might be the following: a conditioning theory must attribute an important (if not primary) causal role either to the pairing of external events or to the mental representation of that pairing. At the very least, if a theory does not do that, then some explanation is required as to why it should be called a "conditioning" theory.

If the above criterion is acceptable, then cognitive factors can play some causal role in a conditioning theory. A case in which the strength of the unconditioned response "overrides conscious considerations" (Eysenck's phrase, Chapter 4, this volume, p. 58) may be a case of conditioning even though consciousness plays some causal role. For example, conditioning may explain the behavior of a man who is afraid to ride an elevator because of a traumatic experience. He believes that the next time he rides one he is unlikely to suffer harm, but the lingering effects of the pairing of elevator riding and traumatic experience override this belief.

Several things follow if the criterion I am suggesting is correct. First, the repeated finding for adult humans that awareness of the CS-UCS relationship is usually required for so-called "conditioning" to occur (Brewer, 1974; Dawson & Furedy, 1976; Dawson et al., 1982) does not by itself show that in these experiments conditioning did not take place. Some additional argument might show this, but it would have to be argued that cognitive factors other than the representation of the CS-UCS relationship played a *primary* causal role. What the finding would refute is a behavioristic conditioning view, that is, one that attributes no causal role at all to cognitive factors. Second, a theory that incorporates cognitive factors, such as Eysenck's (1983), may still be a conditioning theory. Third, neobehaviorists can characterize their position as "behavioristic" because, like earlier behaviorists, they stress conditioning explanations for an important range of clinical phenomena. If neobehaviorism is characterized in this way, however, then I doubt that there remains a paradigm dispute between cognitivists and neobehaviorists. The dispute reduces to an empirical one about the sort of theory most suitable in clinical psychology. There need not be any disagreement about the sort of theory needed in other areas, nor disagreement about methodological issues, what counts as proper science, determinism, or the mind–body problem.

Conclusion

I began by rejecting certain relativistic theses that have been advanced recently in the behavior therapy literature. I then considered certain empiricist doctrines said to lie at the foundation of behavior therapy and argued that behavior therapists were not logically compelled to accept them unless they were interpreted in a trivial (and defensible) form. By shedding these superfluous empiricist commitments, the behavior therapist's position becomes more secure against skeptical attacks. I conceded, however, that the commitment to experimental testing constituted a nontrivial empiricist commitment, one that is not acceptable to many psychoanalysts. I then argued that it could be justified without appeal to standards internal to a behavior therapy paradigm.

If relativistic and skeptical objections can be answered, then the way is opened to a rational resolution of paradigm disputes. However, several obstacles remain. There has been some apparent disagreement about determinism and the mind–body problem, but, I argued, these are based on a misunderstanding of the cognitivist position. A more serious issue concerns methodological objections to admitting cognitions into the scientific study of clinical phenomena. Almost all of these objections, I have argued, lack cogency. The exception, I believe, concerns the clarity of cognitivist hypotheses. Although this objection is potentially more serious, I think, at best, it makes cognitivist explanations inferior to conditioning or physiological explanations *other things being equal.* Other things are not equal, however, when the evidence clearly supports cognitive causation. Once the methodological objections are overcome, then the empirical evidence becomes persuasive, not necessarily for any particular cognitivist theory, but rather for the view that cognitive causes must be appealed to in explaining clinical phenomena. If most behavior therapists now agree on this issue, is there any remaining paradigm dispute between them? There remains the issue about the relative superiority of behavioral and cognitivist techniques. On this issue, I pointed out that cognitivists as a class did not affirm the superiority of cognitivist techniques. There are also issues about theory. One is whether neobehaviorists can integrate cognitive causal factors into a conditioning theory. On this issue, I agreed with Eysenck (Chapter 4, this volume) that they can. Another is whether this sort of theory is likely to suffice for the explanation of clinical phenomena. It may be misleading to characterize disagreement about this issue as a "cognitivist–behaviorist" dispute. Some who are associated with cognitive behavior modification and who are thought of as "cognitivists" may agree with Eysenck and Wolpe about the prospects for developing an adequate conditioning theory. Perhaps the terms *associationists* and *nonassociationists* (or *conditioning theorists* and *nonconditioning theorists*) better capture the disagreement between those who disagree about how cognitive causal factors are to be integrated into a clinical theory. The associationists place heavy emphasis on an associative mechanism and tend to make cognitive factors (other than the representation of contiguous events) secondary. The nonassociationists, such as Bandura, place more emphasis on beliefs and expectations that are thought to operate independently of an associative mechanism.

In sum, there remains a paradigm dispute between those who reject all cognitive causation in clinical psychology (the behaviorists) and those who do not (the cognitivists). There may be relatively few, however, who hold the former position. Within the much larger class of those who accept cognitive causation, there are disputes about theory and therapy, but these are primarily empirical disagreements. Within this same group, it is hard to discern a general split about the mind–body problem, determinism, the appeal to unobservables, or the value of experimentation. It is hard, then, to find a genuine paradigm dispute. The acceptable elements left over from the cognitivist and behaviorist positions adopted in the 1960s and 1970s can now be welded into a single behavior therapy paradigm.

References

Bandura, A. (1974). Behavior theory and the models of man. *American Psychologist, 28,* 859–869.

Bandura, A. (1977). Self-efficacy: Toward a unifying theory of behavior change. *Psychological Review, 84,* 191–215.

Bandura, A. (1982). Self-efficacy mechanisms in human agency. *American Psychologist, 37,* 122–147.

Bandura, A., & Cervone, D. (1983). Self-evaluative and self-efficacy mechanisms governing the motivational effects of goal systems. *Journal of Personality and Social Psychology, 45,* 1017–1028.

Beck, A., Rush, A., Shaw, B. & Emery, G. (1979). *Cognitive therapy of depression.* New York: Guilford.

Brewer, W. (1974). There is no convincing evidence for operant or classical conditioning in adult humans. In W. Weimer & D. Palermo (Eds.), *Cognition and the symbolic processes,* (pp. 1–42). Hillsdale, NJ: Erlbaum.

Campbell, D., Sanderson, R., & Laverty, S. (1964). Characteristics of a conditioned response in human subjects during extinction trials following a single traumatic conditioning trial. *Journal of Abnormal and Social Psychology, 68,* 627–639.

Cartwright, N. (1983). *How the laws of physics lie.* New York: Oxford University Press.

Churchland, P. (1981). Eliminative materialism and the propositional attitudes. *Journal of Philosophy, 78,* 67–90.

Davison, G., & Neale, J. (1974). *Abnormal psychology: An experimental clinical approach.* New York: Wiley.

Dawson, M., & Furedy, J. (1976). The role of awareness in human differential autonomic classical conditioning: The necessary gate hypothesis. *The Society for Psychophysiological Research, 13,* 50–53.

Dawson, M., Schell, A., Beers, J., & Kelly, A. (1982). Allocation of cognitive processing capacity during human autonomic classical conditioning, *Journal of Experimental Psychology, 111,* 273–295.

Dennett, D. (1978). *Brainstorms.* Cambridge, MA: Bradford Books.

Erwin, E. (1978). *Behavior therapy: Scientific, philosophical and moral foundations.* New York: Cambridge University Press.

Erwin, E. (1980). Psychoanalytic therapy: The Eysenck argument. *American Psychologist, 35,* 435–443.

Erwin, E. (1988). Psychoanalysis: Clinical vs. experimental evidence. In P. Clark & C. Wright (Eds.), *Psychoanalysis and the philosophy of mind.* London: Blackwell.

Erwin, E. (1986). Psychotherapy and Freudian psychology. In S. Modgil & C. Modgil (Eds.), *Hans Eysenck: A psychologist searching for a scientific basis for human behavior* (pp. 179–203). London: Falmer Press.

Erwin, E. (1987). *Comparisons of behavioral and cognitive therapy.* Unpublished manuscript.

Erwin, E., & Siegel, H. (1987). *Is confirmation differential?* Unpublished manuscript.

Eysenck, H. (1979). Behavior therapy and the philosophers. *Behavior Research and Therapy, 17,* 511–514.

Eysenck, H. (1983). Classical conditioning and extinction: The general model for the treatment of neurotic disorders. In M. Rosenbaum, C. Franks, & Y. Jaffe (Eds.), *Perspectives on behavior therapy in the eighties* (pp. 77–88). New York: Springer.

Eysenck, H. (1985). *The decline and fall of the Freudian empire.* New York: Viking.

Eysenck, H., & Wilson, G.T. (1973). *The Experimental Study of Freudian Theories.* London: Methuen.

Greenspoon, J., & Lamal, P. (1978). Cognitive behavior modification—Who needs it? *Psychological record, 28,* 343–351.

Grünbaum, A. (1984). *The foundations of psychoanalysis.* Berkeley: University of California Press.

Hall, C. (1963). Strangers in dreams: An experimental confirmation of the Oedipus complex. *Journal of Personality, 31,* 336–345.

Horgan, T., & Woodward, J. (1985). Folk psychology is here to stay. *Philosophical Review, 94,* 197–226.

Kantor, J. (1978). Cognitions as events and as psychic constructions. *Psychological Record, 28,* 329–342.

Kazdin, A. (1981). Drawing valid inferences from case studies. *Journal of Consulting and Clinical Psychology, 49,* 183–192.

Kazdin, A., & Wilson, G.T. (1978). *Evaluation of Behavior Therapy: Issues, Evidence and Research Strategies.* Cambridge, MA: Ballinger.

Kline, P. (1986). Kline replies to Erwin. In S. Modgil and C. Modgil (Eds.), *Hans Eysenck: A psychologist searching for a scientific basis for human behavior.* London: Falmer Press.

Krasner, L., & Houts, A. (1984). A study of the "value" systems of behavioral scientists. *American Psychologist, 39,* 840–850.

Kuhn, T. (1970). *The structure of scientific revolutions.* Chicago: University of Chicago Press.

Lacey, H., & Rachlin, H. (1978). Behavior, cognition and theories of choice. *Behaviorism, 6,* 177–202.

Latimer, P., & Sweet, A. (1984). Cognitive versus behavioral procedures in cognitive-behavior therapy: A critical review of the evidence. *Journal of Behavior Therapy and Experimental Psychiatry, 15,* 9–22.

Ledwidge, B. (1978). Cognitive behavior modification: A step in the wrong direction? *Psychological Bulletin, 85,* 353–373.

MacIntosh, N. (1983). *Conditioning and associative learning.* Oxford, UK: Oxford University Press.

Mahoney, M. (1974). *Cognition and behavior modification.* Cambridge, MA: Ballinger.

Mahoney, M. (1978). Experimental methods and outcome evaluation. *Journal of Consulting and Clinical Psychology, 46,* 660–673.

Rachlin, H. (1977). Review of M.J. Mahoney's *Cognition and behavior modification. Journal of Applied Behavior Analysis, 10,* 369–374.

Rachlin, H. (1985). Pain and behavior. *The Behavioral and Brain Sciences, 8,* 43–53.

Rachman, S., & Wilson, G.T. (1980). *The effects of psychological therapy.* Elmsford, NY: Pergamon.

Rosenthal, T. (1983). Outcome research: Isn't sauce for the goose sauce for the gander? *The Behavioral and Brain Sciences, 6,* 299–300.

Ryle, G. (1949). *The concept of mind.* New York: Barnes and Noble.

Salmon, W. (1982). Confirmation and relevance. In P. Achinstein (Eds.), *The concept of evidence.* (pp. 95–123). Oxford, UK: Oxford University Press.

Siegel, H. (1980). Epistemological relativism in its latest form. *Inquiry, 23,* 107–123.

Siegel, H. (1986). Relativism, truth and incoherence. *Synthese, 68,* 225–259.

Skinner, B.F. (1963). Behaviorism at fifty. *Science, 140,* 951–958.

Skinner, B.F. (1974). *About behaviorism.* New York: Knopf.

Skinner, B.F. (1977). Why I am not a cognitive psychologist. *Behaviorism, 5,* 1–10.

Stich, S. (1983). *From folk psychology to cognitive science: The case against belief.* MIT Press/Bradford.

Von Eckardt, B. (1981). On evaluating the scientific status of psychoanalysis. *Journal of Philosophy, 78,* 570–572.

Wilson, G.T. (1978). Cognitive behavior therapy: Paradigm shift or passing phase? In J. Foreyt & D. Rathjen (Eds.), *Cognitive behavior therapy: research and application.* New York: Plenum.

Wolpe, J. (1978). Cognition and causation in human behavior and its therapy. *American Psychologist, 33,* 437–446.

Woolfolk, R., & Richardson, F. (1984). Behavior therapy and the ideology of modernity. *American Psychologist, 39,* 777–786.

7

Cognitive Behavior Therapy

Philip C. Kendall
Steven F. Bacon

It is understandable why so many social scientists, especially psychologists, are attracted to Kuhn (1970a, 1970b, 1970c). In many ways he writes like a personality theorist, using scholarly yet nontechnical prose to construct arguments that are supported by many interesting examples. Some philosophers, like Feyerabend (1970), have suggested that some of Kuhn's appeal may be his ambiguity, which encourages reinterpretation of his work. For example, Kuhn comforts many insecure social scientists who see in his work support for the proposition that the social sciences are equals of the physical sciences, albeit immature equals, even though Kuhn himself questions the applicability of his work to underdeveloped sciences (Kuhn, 1970a). In addition, as with many personality theorists, we have the feeling after reading Kuhn that something brilliant and revolutionary has been said, but at the same time that something is missing. The looseness of his argument and his historical style make separating the philosophical wheat from the chaff no easy task.

There are several possible ways to evaluate Kuhn's ideas. A tack often taken by philosophers and historians of science is to analyze a writer's choice and interpretation of the historical facts used in support of his argument. Skeptics may also critique a philosophical position on logical grounds, arguing that conclusions do not follow from premises. Although these are certainly worthwhile approaches to criticism, we will not emphasize them here since we see little benefit arising from our dabbling in what the historian and philosopher can do much better. (For evaluations of Kuhn by philosophers of science, see Lakatos & Musgrave, 1970: Suppe, 1974). Our approach will be to evaluate Kuhn's ideas in terms of their usefulness to behavioral scientists. The questions posed by the editors of this volume require answers that are prescriptive, and it is our hope that a discussion of paradigms and other issues in the philosophy of science will advance our understanding of behavioral and cognitive-behavioral therapies. With this in mind we will focus on practical matters and will attempt to formulate prescriptions based on our interpretation of philosophical issues. We confess at the outset, however, that some of our suggestions may not be developed to the degree required by many philosophers. Nevertheless, we hope that our treatment proves helpful to social scientists confronting philosophical issues.

Critique of Kuhn

Although the multiple aspects of a "paradigm," as Kuhn uses the concept, cannot be clearly teased apart, our focus will be primarily on what Masterman (1970) calls "metaphysical paradigms." These comprise the shared philosophical and theoretical beliefs of a scientific community. By choosing this aspect, we are forced to abandon areas of discussion that might have proved quite interesting. However, the advantages of focusing on metaphysical paradigms far outweigh what must be abandoned. First, we feel the most important contribution of Kuhn is his emphasis on frameworks that both structure and limit perception. Second, most of the philosophical criticism brought against Kuhn is in regard to metaphysical paradigms. Finally, focusing on metaphysical paradigms allows us to discuss issues pertinent to the cognitive-behavioral perspective that are superordinate to the specific theoretical content of our perspective.

Although we find Kuhn's concept of the paradigm helpful, we question the utility of his usage of the term to mean not only *a* way of seeing but also *the* dominant way of seeing. If *paradigm* can only be applied after one way of seeing has beaten out all the others, its usage is severely restricted and its application to anything in the behavioral sciences will be nearly impossible. Puzzle solving certainly takes place in the behavioral sciences, but if *paradigm* cannot be applied to the behavioral sciences because there are several competing conceptualizations at any given time, then these activities, which so closely resemble Kuhn's normal science, must be called something else.

We also find the options that Kuhn makes available regarding a discipline's paradigmatic status limited. According to Kuhn, a field is either pre-paradigmatic, paradigmatic, or in the process of shifting its paradigm. By Kuhn's criteria, psychology in general and behavior therapy in particular are probably pre-paradigmatic. Knowing, however, that behavior therapy is pre-paradigmatic is not very informative; does this mean we lack any paradigms, that many paradigms are vying for position, or that two paradigms are competing for supremacy? Masterman (1970) recognizes that Kuhn's term, *pre-paradigmatic*, was incompletely analyzed and attempts to distinguish the three states of affairs illustrated above, calling them *nonparadigmatic* science, which occurs when investigators first start to think about some aspect of nature; *multiparadigmatic* science, when, far from a shortage of theories, there are many; and *dual-paradigmatic* science, when the number of competitors has been whittled down to two. Using Masterman's scheme, the psychotherapeutic sciences, of which behavior therapy or cognitive-behavioral therapy would be one perspective, would be considered multiparadigmatic.

In addition to the problem of an incomplete classification system, one of the reasons we hesitate to answer such questions as "is behavior therapy paradigmatic?" or "is behavior therapy's paradigm shifting?" is that doing so is more likely to cause heat than to shed light. In our discussions with colleagues we have found that a value system usually underlies such questions: to be paradigmatic is good, and suggests a mature science that is following in the path of respectable sciences like physics; to be pre-paradigmatic is bad, and implies that one's life work borders on the metaphysical, a step or two above astrology. Likewise, if a paradigm is shifting, then it is good if it is shifting toward one's pet theory and bad if it is shifting away. For example, if we could conclude that behavior therapy was paradigmatic while psychodynamic therapy was still in the Stone Age of pre-paradigmatic science, then we might have another politicophilosophical argument with which to clobber psychoanalysis. If our thesis was that behavior therapy's paradigm has shifted in the direction of cognitive behavior therapy, we would almost certainly meet with resistance, not because of lack of evidence for such a shift, but because many scientists hold more behavioral constructions of psychology and do not want to move or be left behind. We will argue shortly that the answer to the question "is a shift currently underway?" is always "with respect to what?"

Kuhn devotes little attention to the size of the scientific community that uses a paradigm. Many of his examples, like the Copernican system or Einstein's relativity, suggest that paradigms represent the commitments of a great many scientists. Nevertheless, Kuhn tells us that a community need not be so large, that it may consist of fewer than 25 members (1970c, p. 181). Kuhn recognizes that a particular scientist may belong to several different scientific communities simultaneously and that scientific communities may be hierarchically arranged, with the most global communities representing the greatest number of scientists. For example, a cognitive behaviorist would belong to the global community of all scientists. He* might also belong to the more specialized communities of psychology, clinical psychology, and behavior therapy. Finally, at Kuhn's lowest level of resolution, are scientists who attend the same conferences, exchange unpublished works, and cite each other with high frequency; this is where our researcher would reemerge as a member of cognitive-behavioral community. Although this is the lowest level recognized by Kuhn, we could continue to zoom in on even more microscopic groups. Our scientist would share more in common with a group of cognitive behaviorists working in his specialty area (e.g., cognitive-behavioral therapy for stress) than with those specializing in other areas, and more still with a handful of co-authors. If we continued to reduce the community even further we would arrive at the elementary unit of any scientific community: the individual, who shares all of his commitments with a community of one.

Individuals within the most global communities will share a few very broad commitments. For the community of all scientists some of these might include "One should test theories," "One should not fudge data," and "The physical world is real." More specialized scientific communities will be smaller, and the number and specificity of shared commitments among members will be greater.

A particular scientist may not agree with all of the commitments of his communities. He need only agree with a majority of them, or perhaps only the core. To say that a group shares a paradigm is to suggest that there is a good deal of overlap in the individual commitments of its members.

Kuhn has frequently been criticized for positing discrete periods of normal and revolutionary science. Some critics have argued that all *true science*, is revolutionary (Popper, 1970), and others that science is a constant interplay between problem-solving and discovery, without any discrete normal and revolutionary periods (Lakatos, 1970). This last view is consistent with what we have observed among individual behavioral scientists. When we look at our peers, we see some who appear to be solving the puzzles posed by the exemplary works of their field and others who are struggling to develop new models. Unfortu-

---

* For ease of reading, *he* will be used as the pronoun for the scientist. We recognize that there are valid justifications for the use of *she* as well. Sexism is not our intention in using the one pronoun.

nately, we also see many who are fixated with demonstrations of what is already known. At the same time, when we take the long view, there do appear to be periods of normal and revolutionary science. For example, when we look back on the past 20 years or so, we see the emergence of the behavioral and biological paradigms in clinical psychology and the receding of the psychodynamic and humanistic ones. How can both Kuhn and his critics be correct? Focusing on the elementary unit of a scientific community may help us with an answer.

Kuhn suggests that scientific communities of all sizes are guided by paradigms. We would extend this to include even the smallest community, the individual scientist. Individuals, like communities, are guided in their search for knowledge by frameworks that structure perception. In social-cognition research these frameworks are called *schemata*, and there is good evidence that schemata influence both the search for and interpretation of information (Nisbett & Ross. 1980). There is every reason to believe that scientists, too, are guided by schemata and will interpret data in ways that are consistent with their theories. Social-cognition research has demonstrated that even highly trained scientists are susceptible to theory-based biases. *

If individual researchers are guided by their schemata, then it seems quite likely that they would go through periods of revolutionary and normal science. In his normal science phase, the researcher solves the problems for which he has been trained in ways that are consistent with his schemata. He *assimilates* new information into preexisting cognitive structures. Since new information will not be entirely consistent with old structures, new information will be partially distorted or selectively ignored in order to make it consistent. A personal paradigm shift will occur when a researcher continues to obtain data that are inconsistent with his theory. When new data are so inconsistent with an old theory that no amount of distortion can successfully reconcile the discrepancy, then the old theory will be modified in order to fit the new data through the process of *accommodation.* The scientist who attempts to develop a new theory that will reconcile the old findings and newer anomalies is functioning in the revolutionary mode. In the revolutionary mode, instead of working on a problem *within* the theory, the scientist works on the problem *of* the theory.

If we look at the life-span development of the average scientist, we can see that he may go through several periods of normal and revolutionary science within his career. For example, many new Ph.D.'s continue for several years to work on problems related to the theories

---

* The evidence does not support Popper's contention that "if we try we can break out of our framework at any time" into one that is "better and roomier" (1970, p. 56).

of their doctoral advisors. In time and with greater exposure to competing theories, they begin to notice the discrepancies between data and theory and may attempt a modification of the theory. If the modification is slight, business continues as usual. Often, however, the modification requires new assumptions and new auxiliaries. The young scientist at this time may be said to be doing revolutionary science. As the young scientist sets off to solve the puzzles of this new conceptualization, he returns to normal science. The individual scientist thus alternates between periods of normal and revolutionary science; he sticks to problem solving as long as he can, but becomes a revolutionary when minor modifications to theory prove inadequate.

A scientific community's paradigm may be thought of as the *mean* set of assumptions or *average* framework used by the group. The community is composed of a heterogeneous collection of individuals whose individual commitments differ slightly from the mean. The larger the community, the greater the variability around the average of individual commitments. At any given point in time, most individual scientists will be engaged in normal science, that is, solving the puzzles of their personal paradigms. Some scientists, however, will be working in the revolutionary mode, altering their personal paradigms and changing their positions with respect to the paradigms of the groups to which they belong. These personal paradigm shifts will usually have little effect on a group's average paradigm, since personal shifts may be toward the mean or away from the mean in an infinite number of directions. The fluctuating commitments of individual scientists will usually cancel each other out, like random noise around a statistical mean. It is only when the personal paradigm shifts of many individual scientists are in the same direction that a shift in the group's paradigm will be observed. Anomalies that are problematic for many researchers and persuasive papers that change the schemata of many members are likely to produce this kind of movement. The paradigm shifts that Kuhn talks about appear to be the aggregate of personal paradigm shifts.

If we look at paradigm shifts in this way, then it follows that smaller, homogeneous groups will have more frequent paradigm shifts than larger, heterogeneous groups. It should also be clear that paradigm shifts need not be the dramatic, sudden changes that Kuhn suggests. In behavior therapy we do not see any rapid shifts taking place. Certainly behavior therapy has become broader as it has matured, that is, there has been increased variability around the paradigmatic mean. Rather than a sudden shift, we and others have observed what might be called "paradigm drift" toward cognitively mediated conceptions of behavior, with a gradual increase in the number of behavior therapists whose personal paradigms include an emphasis on cognition.

Viewing a scientific community's paradigm as the mean of its members' personal paradigms, we can reconcile Kuhn and his critics on the openness of science. Several critics have suggested that Kuhn, in labeling the activities of scientists engaged in solving paradigmatic puzzles as "normal," is advocating dogmatism and mob rule in settling scientific questions. Watkins (1970) succinctly offers the objection of several of Kuhn's critics when he describes Kuhn's normal science community as a "closed society of closed minds" (p. 27). Popper (1970) too, characterizes the normal scientist as a narrow-minded plebe:

> The "normal scientist," as Kuhn describes him, is a person one ought to feel sorry for . . . The "normal scientist" . . . has been badly taught. He has been taught in a dogmatic spirit: he is the victim of indoctrination. He has learned a technique which can be applied without asking for the reason why. (pp. 52–53)

In our extension of Kuhn, neither the individual scientist nor the community to which he belongs are closed-minded and dogmatic. The individual scientist adheres to his personal paradigm, not because he is compelled to do so by the community, but because it is useful. *

Most behavioral scientists cannot be neatly typed as normal or extraordinary, but, as we have earlier suggested, alternate between periods of both. Most model-testers spend some time developing new models and sometime extending old ones. Surely, as Popper (1970) suggests, there are some poorly trained scientists who can do little more than apply the techniques they learned in school. However, not all scientists working in the normal mode are a part of this group. A scientific community may include a number of bright, creative, well-trained scientists. Nevertheless, the impact of a single scientist will be minimal unless that individual's way of seeing organizes the work of many others as well. From what we have seen in the behavioral sciences, and we realize this is a somewhat limited view of all science, individuals are quite free to investigate the questions posed by their personal paradigms, without pressure from the "closed minds" of their community. In this sense, science is quite open. Communities, however, are conservative, since shifting the paradigmatic mean, especially of large, heterogeneous communities, requires a strong push. We believe that science can be open, but at the same time conservative.

---

* Research in social cognition suggests that the scientist may, in fact, hold onto a personal paradigm longer than is reasonable (Nisbett & Ross, 1980).

Kuhn's Prescriptions for the Scientist

We return now to the question of what prescriptions Kuhn has to offer the behavioral scientist. Kuhn is primarily descriptive in his account of how science works. He rarely engages in the evaluation of scientists or scientific movements. He attempts to capture the nature of the scientific enterprise without trying to improve it.

Although we find Kuhn's major prescription to be lacking, we feel that certain useful prescriptions pertaining to the individual scientist can be derived. First, Kuhn appears to imply throughout his work that revolutionary science ought not be valued over normal science. Kuhn realizes that there are an infinite number of ways to structure perception and that the framework adopted will influence one's interpretation of data. Without a framework there is chaos; one cannot solve a problem without a schema for it. Popper and others would have us believe that the true scientist ought not settle for problem solving and ought not settle into a single framework. Unlimited flexibility, however, appears not to be the nature of the scientist, and to make this his goal is to present him with an ideal that is impossible to achieve (Faust, 1984). It may be lamentable, but appears to be the nature of schemata that they both structure *and* limit perception (Nisbett & Ross, 1980).

How might the individual scientist improve himself? If the individual realizes that science consists of both puzzle solving and reconstruction of theory, he will prepare himself for these very different activities. Kuhn suggests that one learns puzzle solving by being part of a community, reading its textbooks and exemplary writings, and then adopting the metaphors, conventions, and tools of that community. In general, one learns to do normal science by becoming thoroughly familiar with a single point of view.

This thorough familiarity is necessary but not sufficient to become a productive scientist. The effective scientist must also develop a readiness for revolutionary activity, since it is quite likely that there will be times in his career when he is confronted with anomalies that cannot be reconciled with old theory. At such times the scientist who is not prepared for extraordinary science will be forced to throw up his arms in defeat and move on to something less challenging. The prepared scientist, however, will be able to draw on his familiarity with other conceptualizations and examine the applicability of new metaphors and different ways of seeing to the anomaly. It seems reasonable that one prepares himself for revolutionary activity by becoming familiar with disciplines and points of view that are different from or even unrelated to his own. Of course, a scientist can never understand and be as familiar with another school as with his own—no one can be an expert in all things—but he can certainly expose himself to other points of view. The cognitive behaviorist, then, might expose himself to not only other behaviorists but also to cognitive scientists, developmentalists, social-cognition researchers, humanists, psychodynamic theorists, and biopsychologists, as well as to works in medicine, biology, physics, and mathematics. One may never do serious work in these others areas, but familiarity with them expands the pool of metaphors from which one can draw should a personal paradigm prove inadequate.

So that we are not misunderstood, let us emphasize that we do not advocate the uncritical acceptance of all theories, nor do we see them as equally plausible. Familiarity and acceptance are quite different things. Criticism is the foundation of science, and competition between theories is to be encouraged. We do, however, see benefit coming from attempting to understand view points opposed to one's own. Even Kuhn sees the problem of incommensurability to be only partial.

In summary, we derive the following prescription for the individual scientist from Kuhn: Prepare yourself for both the expected and unexpected discovery. A scientist prepares himself for the expected discovery by working within a paradigm about which he is thoroughly knowledgeable. A scientist prepares himself for the unexpected discovery through familiarity with frameworks other than his own. Regarding the science of behavior therapy, we now turn to conceptualizations other than Kuhn's for further prescriptions.

Technology and Science in Behavior Therapy

Much of the confusion and lack of fruitful exchange between behavior therapists of different theoretical orientations has occurred because of the participants' failure to recognize that a therapeutic endeavor, such as behavior therapy, involves two aspects: the scientific and the technological. Some authors have argued that behavior therapy is science (e.g., Eysenck, Chapter 4, this volume), and others that it represents technology (e..g, London, 1972). We believe that it is both and that the two components are conceptually separable, though certainly overlapping and interacting. Both technology and science are cumulative endeavors in which knowledge increases with time, in contrast to nonprogressive fields of study like art, literature, and even some areas of psychology. There are differences, however, between the two. *Technology*, as it applies to a therapeutic endeavor, refers to the body of knowledge concerning particular techniques and their outcomes. The evaluation of technology asks the relatively atheoretical question, "does a particular procedure successfully achieve the effect it is expected to produce?" (e.g., demonstration studies). For the past hundred years or so our knowledge of aspirin has been primarily technological; we have known that it is a very effective analgesic, antipyretic, and anti-inflammatory agent—without knowing why. With regard to behavior therapy, a relevant technological question might be, "How effective is social-skills training in treating unipolar depressives?" Questions concerning how and why a technique works, and those concerning the origins and maintenance of psychopathology, are *scientific* questions. Science has as its goal the accumulation of knowledge that is more than descriptive; science attempts to explain. Its hallmark is theory testing. Psychopathological and psychotherapeutic *processes* are the focus of the science of behavior therapy.

We make no assumption here that technology necessarily follows from science, and, as will become more clear, this assumption will at times run counter to our argument. We hope to illustrate that the failure to recognize the distinction between theory testing and evaluation of technology can cloud many of the philosophical issues that are relevant to behavior therapy.

For the practitioner, technological questions are far more important than scientific ones. The therapist's duty is to provide the best available treatment to his client, given tradeoffs between efficacy and other relevant variables such as cost and side effects. Although questions regarding the process and etiology of disorder may be of intellectual interest to the scientifically minded therapist, they may contribute little to the establishment of a treatment plan. Etiology does not necessarily imply a treatment modality (Hollon & Garber, 1980), as evidenced, for example, by the success of cognitive-behavioral treatments for depressions that are also relieved by antidepressant medication (Hollon & Beck, 1978; Simons, et al. 1984). Likewise, we might ask how many behavior therapists would suspend the use of systematic desensitization with a simple phobic until an etiologically significant event had been gleaned from the client's life history? Historically, behavior therapists have championed the use of empirically validated therapeutic techniques with little regard for the elegance of the theories that inspired them. For the clinician, the measure of a technique is not its scientific lineage, but its efficacy.

Researchers in behavior therapy may be interested in both technological and scientific questions. Psychotherapy research, which has as its focus the evaluation of treatment outcomes, is mostly technological in nature. Such research attempts to determine how much of what kind of therapy is required to effect what kind of change in what kinds of patients. Theories are not tested by such research, but rather techniques are evaluated. A negative result in psychotherapy research does not kill a theory; it merely implies that a particular technique must be applied differently or perhaps that the technique should not be applied to the problem at hand. For instance, if contingency management does not work with a particular juvenile delinquent, we do not assume that a black eye has been delivered to reinforcement theories—the theory and technique are too far removed from one another. Evaluation research also differs from theory testing in that a result that would spell defeat for a theory might be an encouraging success for a technique. For example, a technique that is effective 30% of the time with a particular type of patient might be considered a breakthrough if earlier procedures had success rates of 5–10%. On the other hand, a theory that is only correct in 30% of its predictions will be found wanting, regardless of the achievement of other theories. Evaluation research must be less destructive than falsificationist theory testing, since the practitioner must be able to intervene in the presence of an incomplete scientific picture.

Researchers interested in theories of psychopathology and therapeutic processes must play by a stricter set of rules. Most contemporary philosophers of science would agree that theory testing in the sciences entails subjecting theories to the grave threat of falsification. Dogmatic falsificationists suggest that a single failure to pass an empirical test is enough to bring down a theory (see Lakatos, 1970). Although most philosophers do not require a spotless record against experimental tests, most require much more than a winning record against such tests, and there is good reason for this asymmetry between confirmation and refutation (see Lakatos, 1970; Meehl, 1978; Popper, 1968). We mention this because the history of theories within clinical and counseling psychology has not been an illustrious one, especially when compared to the better-developed sciences like physics and chemistry. Meehl (1978) suggests that this slow progress is not due to the intellectual inferiority of behavioral scientists, but rather to our methods and the intrinsic difficulties of scientizing human psychology. Meehl lists 20 such difficulties, without claiming completeness. The difficulties include slicing up raw behavior into meaningful units; dealing with individual differences; deciding between idiographic and nomothetic methods; ascertaining critical events in an individual's life history that have contributed to personality development; working with a large number of variables; teasing out cause and effect among many intercorrelated variables; making sense of behavioral feedback loops; corroborating theories when statistical relationships observed are highly context-dependent; operationalizing interesting theoretical concepts; establishing lawful relationships concerning the behaviors of beings who possess the ability to think and act intentionally and who may possess characteristics not found in other species; and being limited by ethical constraints on human research. The task before behavioral scientists is immense indeed.

Given these difficulties, it would not be surprising if the science of behavior therapy had not kept pace with the technology; in fact, this is our position regarding the science of behavior therapy. We are certainly not going to end the controversy regarding the scientific foundations of behavior therapy here (see Breger & McGaugh, 1965, 1966; Erwin, 1978; Eysenck, 1972; London, 1972; Mahoney et al. 1974; Rachman & Eysenck, 1966); given the limitations of space, about the best we can do is present our view and some of the arguments that support it.

The technology of behavior therapy has done quite well. Many reviews attest to the fact that techniques that were developed by behavior therapists work well with many kinds of patients. To the question "do behavior therapy techniques work?", even the most skeptical critics would have to admit that many of them do within a range of specific patient types.

Theorists from other schools, however, would not be forced to make the same concessions regarding the science of behavior therapy. Behavioral theories of psychopathology (e..g, Lewinsohn, 1974, on depression) have typically received the same equivocal support as the partial explanations of other theoretical approaches. S-R theories of simple phobias seem well entrenched, but even these are difficult to defend, since, supposing the problems of confirmatory bias could be eliminated, it is very hard to determine with any certainty whether or not an etiologically significant UCS-CS pairing has taken place within a patient's life; such a nonfalsifiable theory cannot be considered scientific.

It might be argued that the success of behavior therapy techniques is itself sufficient corroborating evidence for theories underlying the techniques. There are at least two problems with such an argument. First, knowing that a technique works does not imply that you know how it works, nor does it imply that you know anything about the cause of the disorder in the first place. For example, Professor Smith may have a theory that a shortage in endorphins causes depression. He reads that running increases the amount of endorphins released, and so encourages all of his depressed patients to jog. Smith finds that most of his patients improve and concludes that his theory regarding endorphins is correct. Smith's error, of course, is that he has not eliminated the multitude of other possible explanations for the same result.

In addition, it has occasionally been observed that dismantling a technique to uncover its active components may produce results that are in conflict with the underlying theory; the finding by Wilkins (1971) that neither relaxation training nor a descending hierarchy is needed for systematic desensitization to be effective illustrates this point. Finally, if researchers wish to use outcome successes as corroborating evidence for their theories, they must be willing to accept the failures, which occur frequently, as falsifications.

In general, behavior therapy has proceeded from the laboratory to the clinic—at least that is the way new techniques have been presented in the literature. A rather common assumption among behavior therapists seems to be that technology arising from a well-formulated theory is superior to technology arising from other technology or careful clinical observation. This assumption may take two separate forms. The strong form says that techniques derived from theory have a different status from techniques originating elsewhere, such that simply pointing out this difference is enough to reasonably choose the former over the latter. In such cases, one technique is preferred without recourse to empirical evaluation. The weaker form of this assumption says that techniques based on theory are more likely to prove successful; this weaker form argues for the greater efficiency of theory-based techniques.

We can dismiss the strong assumption as it applies to behavior therapy rather quickly by examining what it requires. In order for the strong form to work, one must have both a strong theory and a technology that is derivable from the theory. An example of a derivable technology might be something like this: suppose you buy a 10-foot seesaw with an adjustable fulcrum for your two children, who weight 40 pounds and 80 pounds; suppose also that you have just moved into the neighborhood, and so your children's primary playmates will be each other; finally, you realize that no one likes being stuck on the down end of a seesaw, and so you want to place the fulcrum in such a way that the ends of the seesaw are balanced when the children get on; where is the best place to put the fulcrum? This, of course, is a technological question, and if you know some physics and do some vector addition, you will put the fulcrum three and one-third feet from one of the ends. Without empirically evaluating this technological solution you can argue confidently from the laws of physics that this must be the optimal placement for the fulcrum. We believe, then, that in some instances technological solutions can be derived from scientific theories. The relevant question here, however, is whether or not behavior therapy techniques are derivable from learning theory.

If a therapeutic technique is not directly derivable from theory, then

it must be empirically evaluated and judgments regarding its value
based on its effectiveness, not its theoretical lineage. The origins of a
technique, or a scientific theory for that matter, are of little import if
the technique works. Kekule's discovery of the structure of benzene,
which some say came to him as he dreamt of a circular chain of snakes,
is a frequently cited illustration of this point in the history of science.
Similar examples of important technological discoveries may be found
in fields of study as close to behavior therapy as psychiatry.* Few
behavior therapists, even those most vehemently opposed to medical
models, would dispute the effectiveness of pharmacotherapy with depressed, bipolar, and schizophrenic patients, and yet all of the significant breakthroughs in psychiatric drug therapy were made serendipitously; none followed from a theory of psychopathology.
Chlorpromazine, the prototype of all later phenothiazines, a class of
antipsychotics, was first developed as an antihistamine to be used as a
presurgical preparation; imipramine, the granddaddy of the tricyclics,
so useful in the treatment of depression, was developed for use as an
antipsychotic with schizophrenic patients; the first MAO inhibitor,
also used with depressives, was originally tested as a treatment for
tuberculosis; finally, lithium carbonate, which has proved so useful
with manic-depressive patients, was originally used to reduce the toxic
effects of urea in guinea pigs before being administered to humans
(Wender & Klein, 1981). In addition, it is not uncommon for a technique that has been developed with a particular scientific theory in
mind to be later reexplained in terms of a different theory. Within
behavior therapy, the theorizing behind systematic desensitization is a
good illustration. Whether it is effective because of countercondition-
ing (Wolpe, 1958), extinction, or some other mechanism (Kazdin &
Wilcoxon, 1976), the evaluation research seems to show that it often
works (Paul, 1969).

   But what of the weak form of the assumption? Are theory-based
techniques superior to clinically derived techniques because they are
more efficient? Given the large number of possible techniques for
treating a behavioral problem, it makes sense to focus time and attention on those techniques with the highest probability of succeeding,
even if it means overlooking some that may also have worked. Imagine yourself as a cancer patient who knows nothing about two experimental treatments except that one is based on physiological research
on laboratory animals and the other on astrology; which treatment

---

* Many of our examples are drawn from medicine, not because we see it as the paragon
  of science-technologies, but because it is the other applied endeavor with which we,
  and probably most clinical psychologists, are most familiar.

would you choose? Although you could not say, prior to formal evaluation, which treatment, if either, would work best, most of us would choose the treatment whose rationale was supported by scientific research. In cases such as this, we believe the weak assumption has intuitive appeal.

Consider, however, the more typical case in clinical psychology. Can one make the choice as confidently, prior to evaluation, between a technique based on animal learning and one based on the therapist's clinical experience? We think the answer is "no" for the following reasons. First, the jump from the laboratory to the clinic is much smaller for the cancer-patient scenario than for the behavior therapy client. The physiology of animals and humans is probably far more similar than the psychology of animals and humans. Also, the background knowledge in physiology is far greater than that in psychology; our "laws" tend to be very general and difficult to apply to specific situations. Second, the alternate approach in our behavior therapy scenario is more plausible than astrology as an alternate approach to cancer treatment. When practitioners develop techniques for use in the clinic, they use implicit theories of interpersonal relations. Some people are able to make reasonable predictions about behavior and even advise friends who are having interpersonal difficulties without any training in the behavioral sciences. Certainly people's implicit theories are not all correct. Nevertheless, it is difficult to imagine how we could survive in our social environment if most of our implicit theories were incorrect. In summary, theory-based techniques may have a greater probability of succeeding than those based on more intuitive approaches when the theory is strong and the hunch is based on little experience; when the opposite is true, which seems typical in clinical psychology, then we suggest greater open-mindedness about clinically derived techniques.

For several years a popular formula in television programming has been the creation of spinoffs of successful programs. We think a similar formula ("treatment spin-offs") might be practical in expanding the technical armamentarium of the behavior therapist. Pharmaceutical companies have successfully used this approach for years. In the search for better medications, the chemical structure of older successful drugs is often slightly modified, without reference to any specific theory of action, and the effects of these new derivatives are then empirically tested. These newer drugs may prove generally more effective than their predecessors, more effective with certain patients, or equally effective but with fewer adverse side effects; in each of these cases there is good reason for making the new drug available. Such an approach appears to be frequently employed in behavior therapy, but infrequently acknowledged. Often a new technique, which is quite similar to a successful extant technique, is justified in its introduction to the literature by its relationship to theory rather than its similarity to other techniques. Since technology need not follow from science, we have no qualms about suggesting spinoffs as legitimate sources of new clinical techniques. The need to tie technique to theory, no matter how Procrustean the effort, may be indicative of psychologists' professional insecurity.

Some might argue that although techniques derived from the clinic may be valid, they cannot be considered techniques of behavior therapy, since by definition behavior therapy techniques are derived from learning theory. Depending on which definition of behavior therapy one chooses to apply, and there are many diverse ones (Krasner, 1982; Wilson, 1978), this may be true. There is no sin in cutting psychotherapy into territories. Keep in mind, however, that this is a classification problem, not a scientific or technological one. Knowing whether or not a technique is included within behavior therapy contributes nothing to our knowledge regarding its effectiveness.

In summary, the links between modern learning theory and the technology of behavior therapy may be looser than many of us had thought (Erwin, 1978). We acknowledge the great strides made within the technology of behavior therapy but recognize that the science of behavior therapy is limited by the same factors that make all behavioral science difficult. We believe that there are several defensible ways to develop therapeutic techniques, one of which is through the application of a well-corroborated theory. In the end, however, the value of a technique must be based on empirical evaluation, not *a priori* arguments that give extra weight to theory-derived techniques.

Why We Choose Cognitive-Behavioral Approaches

There have been many attempts to define cognitive behavior therapy and to describe how it is similar to and different from traditional behavior therapy and other approaches (e.g., Beck, 1970: Kendall, 1985: Kendall & Hollon, 1979: Mahoney, 1977: Mahoney & Arnkoff, 1978: Meichenbaum, 1977). All of these reviews have come to a similar conclusion: it may be undesirable to specify with much precision what cognitive behavior therapy is and where its boundaries lie. Cognitive behavior therapy is a general perspective that lacks a single unifying theory.

Cognitive behavior therapists share with other behavior therapists a commitment to rigorous, methodologically sound, empirical evaluation of interventions. Put more strongly, a commitment to empirical evaluation may be the only necessary (but not sufficient) condition for membership within the cognitive-behavioral or behavioral communities. We know of many different viewpoints within our subdiscipline regarding the relationship between cognition and behavior, behavior and affect, and affect and cognition, but we would have to look as long and hard among our peers to find someone lacking a commitment to empirical evaluation as a traditional behavior therapist would among that group. We believe that reason dictates a commitment to empirical evaluation, since corrective feedback is required for both scientific and technological progress; the converse is true as well, namely, that it is unreasonable not to value empirical findings.

We find no compelling reason for a similar commitment to the theoretical content areas of traditional behavior therapy. To reiterate an earlier point, we cannot deny (nor would we want to) the technological advances that have occurred within traditional behavior therapy; however, these successes say little about the science of behavior therapy. The evidence is not compelling with regard to the applicability of animal models to human psychopathology. Certainly traditional models deserve further study, but they need not be the only approaches pursued. Unlike the choice of behavioral method, which we see as an act of reason, the choice of theoretical approach, at least for the present time, is an act of faith. Since the data are equivocal, we are simply betting that pursuing mediational theories will prove at least as fruitful as continued work on nonmediational ones.

Behavior therapists never *really* thought that cognition did not exist. No one believed that the mind was truly a black box that could not be investigated. The decision to investigate only overt behavior was a methodological, not logical, one (Erwin, 1978; Eysenck, 1972). These decisions represented convenient simplifications that allowed the science of behavior to proceed. We are not, therefore, suggesting anything revolutionary in positing mediational models. We are simply recommending that it may be useful at this time to carefully reintroduce into our models some of the complexity that is known to characterize human behavior.

It has been argued that the reintroduction of mediational concepts can only harm behavior therapy. The pros and cons of these arguments have been presented in detail elsewhere (e.g., Erwin, 1978; Mahoney, 1974), and so we will not go into them here. In general, the arguments against mediational concepts have been based on a philosophical distaste for inferential variables, usually arising from an outdated attachment to operationism. Mahoney (1977) summarizes his rebuttal to the argument that scientists ought to avoid inferential (mediational) variables: "(a) science never deals with *directly* observable events, (b) all science is necessarily inferential, (3) parsimony is not a logical requirement" (p. 9). In our view, there is nothing sinful about higher-order constructs, as long as some of the relationships between variables are anchored to publicly verifiable observations (Cronbach & Meehl, 1955). Mediational concepts such as Bandura's (1977a) self-efficacy, which lead to better predictions than less inferential variables, should certainly not be ignored.

Since we view theory choice as an act of faith, we feel no compulsion to convince other behavior therapists that ours is the way to ultimate truth. In fact, we encourage others to expand behavior therapy on other frontiers. For example, few behavior therapists have attempted to integrate the findings of behavior genetics and psychobiology within a behavioral framework. This must be accomplished before claims to a complete understanding of pathological behavior can be made. The recent remarkable growth of behavioral medicine suggests that strong ties between medicine and behavior therapy are currently being made (Agras, 1982; Schwartz & Weiss, 1978; Turk et al., 1983). In addition, we predict that future work will continue to emphasize the connection between affect and behavior, perhaps introducing a new hybrid, cognitive-affective-behavior therapy. As long as these developments are grounded in rigorous theory testing and empirical evaluation, they are to be encouraged. Progressive proliferation need not await the falsification of a previous theory (Lakatos, 1970).

Kendall (1982) presents four arguments in favor of integration between behavior therapy and other psychotherapeutic schools. The same arguments, with minor modifications, can be used to partially explain why we favor including cognition in our theories of behavior.

1. *The human organism is multifaceted, and focusing on behavior alone is not enough.* People think as well as act, and the assumption of cognitive behavior therapists is that such thinking influences behavior and affect. Multiple procedures, some cognitive and some behavioral, are needed to address the multidimensional problems of our clients.

2. *The dissatisfaction with behavior therapy's less than perfect success justifies the search for additional techniques based on other approaches.* The progress traditional behavior therapy has made in the treatment of a variety of disorders has been impressive indeed (Kazdin & Wilson, 1978), but there remains a long way to go. Although lacking the breadth of empirical support of a technique like systematic desensitization, the early reports on several cognitive-behavioral approaches are quite promising. Just a few examples of problems treated

with cognitive-behavioral approaches include depression (e.g., Murphy et al., 1984; Rush et al., 1977); impulsiveness in children (Kendall & Braswell, 1982, 1985); anger (Novaco, 1978, 1979); pain (Turk et al., 1983); and anxiety (Goldfried, 1979). In addition, several authors have proposed ways in which therapists can more effectively deal with client noncompliance, a little-researched but pervasive problem, from a cognitive-behavioral perspective (Goldfried, 1981; Lazarus & Fay, 1981; Meichenbaum & Gilmore, 1981).

3. *New formulations inspire new enthusiasm.* Cognitive behavior therapy has certainly inspired enthusiasm. Loosening the old boundaries on behavior therapy has produced a surge in professional and research activity. Journals devoted to the cognitive-behavioral approaches have been created (*Cognitive Therapy and Research* is now past its tenth year), handbooks have been written (e.g., Beck et al., 1979; Kendall & Braswell, 1984; Turk et al., 1983), and many edited volumes (e.g., Kendall & Hollon, 1979; Meichenbaum & Jaremko, 1983) are available. In addition, many of the activities at psychological conventions (including AABT) and articles in mainstream clinical journal have moved squarely in the direction of cognitive-behavioral conceptions. Such a burst of activity does not prove that cognitive-behavioral approaches are the way to go—we do not subscribe to a philosophy of science that might makes right. Nevertheless, we think that such activity is an indication of the generativity of the cognitive-behavioral perspective.

4. *While acknowledging the success of traditional behavioral approaches, we can reevaluate their theoretical assumptions and perhaps improve on them.* Cognitive behavior therapists may be able to evaluate and improve on traditional techniques from a different vantage point, just as behavior therapists have done with the techniques of other psychotherapeutic schools.

Viewing cognitive behavior therapy as an *integration from within* illustrates our belief that most cognitive behavior therapists do not see themselves as a dissatisfied splinter group or "malcontents" (Wolpe, 1976) who wish to start another school of therapy. Cognitive behaviorists want the best of behavior therapy without the limiting assumptions. The arguments of some authors (Wilson, 1982; Yates, 1981) against the integration of behavior therapy with other psychotherapies are based on the conceptual, methodological, and technical incompatibilities of different theoretical approaches (e.g., psychoanalysis); cognitive behavior therapy offers the advantages of integration without this disadvantage.

It is difficult to extract the content-relevant tenets of cognitive behavior therapy from the varied approaches that are subsumed by the label. In review papers, authors have focused on themes within cognitive behavior therapy that are consistent with their own theoretical formulations (Kendall & Bemis, 1983). Only a very general list of paradigmatic assumptions will serve to adequately characterize what most cognitive behaviorists believe. Kendall and Bemis (1983) have culled from several earlier attempts (Kendall & Hollon, 1979; Mahoney, 1977; Mahoney & Arnkoff. 1978) to list six principles of cognitive behavior therapy:

1. The human organism responds primarily to cognitive representations of its environments rather than these environments per se.
2. Most human learning is cognitively mediated.
3. Thoughts, feelings, and behaviors are causally interrelated.
4. Attitudes, expectancies, attributions, and other cognitive activities are central to producing, predicting, and understanding psychopathological behavior and the effects of therapeutic interventions.
5. Cognitive processes can be cast into testable formulations that are easily integrated with behavioral paradigms, and it is possible and desirable to combine cognitive treatment strategies with enactive techniques and behavioral contingency management.
6. The task of the cognitive-behavioral therapist is to act as diagnostician, educator, and technical consultant, assessing maladaptive cognitive processes and working with the client to design learning experiences that may mediate these dysfunctional cognitions and the behavioral and affective patterns with which they correlate. (pp. 565–566)

Examining these tenets suggests both what the field is moving away from and what it is moving toward. The first three tenets suggest what cognitive-behavioral approaches are moving away from: the limitations of traditional behavior therapy. Prior to the advent of behavior therapy, listing these three assumptions as tenets would have seemed peculiar and unnecessary. Of course behavior is not based on pure sensation; of course learning entails thinking. Psychoanalysis and humanistic therapists alike would subscribe to these tenets. It is only because cognitive behavior therapy emerged from traditional behavior therapy that stating explicitly what seems so self-evident is necessary. A paradigm drift requires much clarification.

The second three tenets describe what cognitive-behavioral conceptions are moving toward. Researchers are betting that cognition and behavior will prove as good or better a predictor of behavior than overt behavior alone. As Mahoney (1977) observes, since behavior and cogni-tions influence one another, cognitive-behavioral researchers would expect a combination of cognitive and behavioral variables to prove the best predictor of behavior. Although cognitive variables are cen-tral to the origin, maintenance, and amelioration of psychopathology, the cognitive-behavioral perspective does not assign an exclusive role to cognition (Mahoney & Arnkoff, 1978; Meichenbaum and Cameron, 1982). A characteristic of our perspective, like traditional behavior therapy, has been an emphasis on performance-based interventions. To our lights, there is nothing inconsistent about positing cognitive change mechanisms while also advocating a combination of tradition-ally behavioral techniques and the newer cognitive techniques. This position has been proposed by and has received some support from Bandura (1977a), whose work seems to show that enactive procedures may be the best way to bring about cognitive changes.

There are several theoretical perspectives within psychology that are consistent with the tenets of cognitive-behavioral therapy. Al-though we have argued that the technology of behavior therapy need not be derivable from a scientific theory, there are certainly advan-tages for the researcher whose work takes place within a theoretical framework. First, it is not really a matter of choice for the individual interested in psychopathological processes, since these are scientific questions and the nature of science is theory testing. For the re-searcher interested in developing new techniques, theory is an invalu-able source of ideas. Not only does theory provide the metaphors on which new techniques may be based, but as scientific knowledge of psychopathological processes increases, the gap between what is known via our implicit theories and what is known scientifically in-creases, thereby strengthening the weak form of the argument in favor of theory-derived techniques (i.e., theory-derived techniques have a higher probability of success).

Two orientations that might serve as bases for cognitive behavioral theorizing, just as classical and operant conditioning formed the foun-dation for much of traditional behavior therapy, are social-learning theory (Bandura, 1977b; Rosenthal, 1982) and information-processing approaches (Anderson, 1980; Ingram, 1986; Lachman, et al., 1979; Neisser, 1976, 1980). We will not discuss social-learning theory here since Frederick Rotgers covers that territory in Chapter 9 of this volume.Before leaving social-learning theory, however, we wish to stress that we and others sympathetic to the cognitive-behavioral ap-proach (e.g., Mahoney & Kazdin, 1979; Meichenbaum & Cameron, 1982; Rosenthal, 1982) do not view social learning as outside the pur-view of cognitive behavior therapy, even though edited volumes sometimes separate the two (e.g., this volume; Wilson & Franks, 1982).

Experimental cognitive psychology, especially the information-processing approach, has much to offer those interested in the cognitive-behavioral perspective. Ingram and Kendall (1986) have summarized the approach in this way:

> The information processing paradigm may be broadly defined as a conceptual approach which assumes that human functioning can be productively conceptualized and understood in terms of how both environmental and internal information is processed and used. Thus, the paradigm essentially conceptualizes the person as an information processing system and focuses largely upon the structures and operations within the system and how they function in the selection, transformation, encoding, storage, retrieval, and generation of information and behavior. (p. 5)

Intelligence, memory, language, and the meaning of information are all areas of analysis within the information-processing perspective. Ingram and Kendall are careful to point out that the information-processing approach represents a broad perspective under which many specific theories are subsumed; information processing is not a theory in itself.

Ingram and Kendall (1986) discuss several of the advantages of this approach for cognitive-behavioral psychologists. First, the information-processing approach carries with it many theoretical constructs that have been developed to guide conceptualization, prediction, and empirical research on cognition. Applying these constructs to disordered cognition is just another small step. Just as a technology has been developed from broad principles of animal learning, the constructs of information processing might also be broadly adapted to the development of a new technology.

The information-processing approach would also bring an empirical methodology to cognitive behavior therapy that could be exploited. One of the major difficulties within cognitive behavior therapy is the assessment of cognition (Kendall, 1983; Kendall & Hollon, 1981; Kendall & Korgeski, 1979). The reliance on self-report measures and difficulties of measuring changes in cognition are limitations that must be confronted if cognitive-behavioral approaches are to continue progressing. The information-processing paradigm has developed ways to analyze cognition that do not rely exclusively on the self-report of subjects and that can directly assess some of the parameters of mediating cognitive variables. In addition to a number of unique theoretical constructs and methodological tactics, the information-processing approach can contribute empirical findings that may be of interest to clinical researchers (e.g., the parameters surrounding the fact that meaningful information is more likely to be recalled than nonmeaningful). It is early, but it appears that experimental cognitive psychology has much to offer the clinician.

Cognitive behavior therapists share many commitments with other behavior therapists, but do we share a paradigm? Our analysis of Kuhn suggests a mixed reply. If we answer by examining the theoretical, philosophical, and methodological commitments of small, homogeneous camps within behavior therapy, then certainly our differences will emerge. If we look to the larger, heterogeneous group of behavior therapists, the level at which comparisons are made between schools (e.g., between humanistic, psychodynamic, and biopsychiatric psychologists), then our similarities become apparent. Behavior therapists share the overarching commitment (based on reason) to empirical evaluation of interventions. We differ in the faith we hold in different theories of psychopathological process. Cognitive-behavioral therapists are betting that our faith in cognitively mediated processes will prove useful.

References

Agras, W.S. (1982). Behavioral medicine in the 1980s: Nonrandom connections. *Journal of Consulting and Clinical Psychology, 50,* 797–803.

Anderson, J.R. (1980). *Cognitive psychology and its implications.* San Francisco: W.H. Freeman.

Bandura, A. (1969). *Principles of behavior modification.* New York: Holt, Rinehart & Winston.

Bandura, A. (1977a). Self-efficacy: Toward a unifying theory of behavioral change. *Psychological Review, 84,* 191–215.

Bandura, A. (1977b). *Social learning theory.* Englewood Cliffs, NJ.: Prentice-Hall.

Beck, A.T. (1970). Cognitive therapy: Nature and relation to behavior therapy. *Behavior Therapy, 1,* 184–200.

Beck, A.T., Rush, A.J., Shaw, B.F., & Emery, G. (1979). *Cognitive therapy of depression.* New York: Guilford.

Breger, L., & McGaugh, J.L. (1965). Critique and reformulation of "learning theory" approaches to psychotherapy and neurosis. *Psychological Bulletin, 63,* 338–358.

Breger, L., & McGaugh, J.L. (1966). Learning theory and behavior therapy: A reply to Rachman and Eysenck. *Psychological Bulletin, 65,* 170–173.

Cronbach, L., & Meehl, P.E. (1955). Construct validity in psychological tests. *Psychological Bulletin, 52,* 281–302.

Erwin, E. (1978). *Behavior therapy: Scientific. philosophical, and moral foundations.* New York: Cambridge University Press.

Eysenck, H.J. (1972). Behavior therapy is behavioristic. *Behavior Therapy, 3,* 609–613.

Faust, D. (1984). *The limits of scientific reasoning.* Minneapolis: University of Minnesota Press.

Feyerabend, P.K. (1970). Consolations for the specialist. In I. Lakatos & A. Musgrave (Eds.), *Criticism and the growth of knowledge* (pp. 197–230). New York: Cambridge University Press.

Goldfried, M.R. (1979). Anxiety reduction through cognitive-behavioral intervention. In P.C. Kendall & S.D. Hollon (Eds.), *Cognitive-behavioral interventions: Theory, research, and procedures* (pp. 117–152). New York: Academic Press.

Goldfried, M.R. (1981). Resistance and clinical behavior therapy. In P.L. Wachtel (Ed.), *Resistance: Psychodynamic and behavioral approaches* (pp. 95–113). New York: Plenum.

Hollon, S.D., & Beck, A.T. (1978). Psychotherapy and drugs: Comparison and combinations. In S.L. Garfield & A.E. Bergin (Eds.), *Handbook of psychotherapy and behavior change: An empirical analysis* (2nd ed.) (pp. 437–490). New York: Wiley.

Hollon, S.D., & Garber, J. (1980). A cognitive-expectancy theory of therapy for helplessness and depression. In J. Garber & M.E.P. Seligman (Eds.), *Human helplessness: Theories and applications* (pp. 173–195). New York: Academic Press.

Ingram, R.E. (Ed.). (1986). *Information processing approaches to clinical psychology.* New York: Academic Press.

Ingram, R.E., & Kendall, P.C. (1986). Cognitive-clinical psychology: A paradigm shift without a paradigm. In R.E. Ingram (Eds.), *Information processing approaches to clinical psychology.* New York: Academic Press.

Kazdin, A.E., & Wilcoxon, L.A. (1976). Systematic desensitization and nonspecific treatment effects: A methodological evaluation. *Psychological Bulletin, 83,* 729–758.

Kazdin, A.E., & Wilson, G.T. (1978). *Evaluation of behavior therapy: Issues, evidence, and research strategies.* Cambridge, MA.: Ballinger.

Kendall, P.C. (1982). Integration: Behavior therapy and other schools of thought. *Behavior Therapy, 13,* 559–571.

Kendall, P.C. (1983). Methodology and cognitive-behavioral assessment. *Behavioral Psychotherapy, 11,* 285–301.

Kendall, P.C. (1985). Toward a cognitive-behavioral model of psychopathology and a critique of related interventions. *Journal of Abnormal Child Psychology.*

Kendall, P.C., & Bemis, K.M. (1983). Thought and action in psychotherapy: The cognitive behavioral approaches. In M. Hersen, A.E. Kazdin, & A.S. Bellak (Eds.), *The clinical psychology handbook.* Elmsford, NY.: Pergamon.

Kendall, P.C.,& Braswell, L. (1982). Cognitive-behavioral self-control therapy for children: A components analysis. *Journal of Consulting and Clinical Psychology, 50,* 672—690.

Kendall, P.C., & Braswell, L. (1985). *Cognitive-behavioral therapy for impulsive children.* New York: Guilford.

Kendall, P.C., & Hollon, S.D. (Eds.). (1979). *Cognitive-behavioral interventions: Theory, research, and procedures.* New York: Academic Press.

Kendall, P.C., & Hollon, S.D. (Eds.) (1981). *Assessment strategies for cognitive-behavioral intervention.* New York: Academic.

Kendall, P.C., & Korgeski, G.P. (1979). Assessment and cognitive-behavioral interventions. *Cognitive Therapy and Research, 3,* 1–21.

Krasner, L. (1982). Behavior therapy: On roots, contexts, and growth. In G.T. Wilson & C.M. Franks (Eds.), *Contemporary behavior therapy: Conceptual and empirical foundations* (pp. 11–62). New York: Guilford.

Kuhn, T.S. (1970a). Logic of scientific discovery or psychology of research? In I. Lakatos & A. Musgrave (Eds.), *Criticism and the growth of knowledge* (pp. 1–23). New York: Cambridge University Press.

Kuhn, T.S. (1970b). Reflections on my critics. In I. Lakatos & A. Musgrave (Eds.), *Criticism and the growth of knowledge* (pp. 231–278). New York: Cambridge University Press.

Kuhn, T.S. (1970c). *The structure of scientific revolutions* (2nd ed.). Chicago: University of Chicago Press.

Lachman, R., Lachman, J.L., & Butterfield, E.C. (1979). *Cognitive psychology and information processing: An introduction.* Hillsdale, NJ.: Erlbaum.

Lakatos, I. (1970). Falsification and the methodology of scientific research programmes. In I. Lakatos & A. Musgrave (Eds.), *Criticism and the growth of knowledge* (pp. 91–196). New York: Cambridge University Press.

Lakatos, I., & Musgrave, A. (Eds.). (1970). *Criticism and the growth of knowledge.* New York: Cambridge University Press.

Lazarus, A.A., & Fay, A. (1981). Resistance or rationalization? A cognitive-behavioral perspective. In P. Wachtel (Ed.), *Resistance: A behavioral and psychodynamic perspective* (pp. 115–132). New York: Plenum.

Lewinsohn, P.M. (1974). A behavioral approach to depression. In R.M. Friedman & M.M. Katz (Eds.), *The psychology of depression: Contemporary theory and research.* New York: Wiley.

London, P. (1972). The end of ideology in behavior modification. *American Psychologist, 27,* 913–920.

Mahoney, M.J. (1974). *Cognition and behavior modification.* Cambridge, MA: Ballinger.

Mahoney, M.J. (1977). Reflections on the cognitive-learning trend in psychotherapy. *American Psychologist, 32,* 5–13.

Mahoney, M.J., & Arnkoff, D.B. (1978). Cognitive and self-control therapies. In S.L. Garfield & A.E. Bergin (Eds.), *Handbook of psychotherapy and behavioral change: An empirical analysis* (pp. 689–722). New York: Wiley.

Mahoney, M.J., & Kazdin, A.E. (1979). Cognitive behavior modification: Misconceptions and premature evacuation. *Psychological Bulletin, 86,* 1044–1049.

Mahoney, M.J., Kazdin, A.E., & Lesswing, N.J. (1974). Behavior modification: Delusion or deliverance? In C.M. Franks & G.T. Wilson (Eds.), *Annual review of behavior therapy* (Vol. 2) (pp. 11–40). New York: Brunner/Mazel.

Masterman, M. (1970). The nature of a paradigm. In I. Lakatos & A. Musgrave (Eds.), *Criticism and the growth of knowledge.* (pp. 59–89). New York: Cambridge University Press.

Meehl, P.E. (1967). Theory testing in psychology and physics: A methodological paradox. *Philosophy of Science, 34,* 103–115.

Meehl, P.E. (1978). Theoretical risks and tabular asterisks: Sir Karl, Sir Ronald and the slow progress of soft psychology. *Journal of Consulting and Clinical Psychology, 46,* 806–834.

Meichenbaum, D. (1977). *Cognitive-behavior modification: An integrative approach.* New York: Plenum.

Meichenbaum, D., & Cameron, R. (1982). Cognitive-behavior therapy. In G.T. Wilson & C.M. Franks (Eds.), *Contemporary behavior therapy: Conceptual and empirical foundations* (p. 310–338). New York: Guilford.

Meichenbaum, D., & Gilmore, J.B. (1981). Resistance: From a cognitive-behavioral perspective. In P. Wachtel (Ed.), *Resistance: A behavioral and psychodynamic perspective* (pp. 133–156). New York: Plenum.

Meichenbaum, D., & Jaremko, M. (Eds.). (1983). *Stress management and prevention: A cognitive-behavioral perspective.* New York: Plenum.

Murphy, G.E., Simons, A.D., Wetzel, R.D., & Lustman, P.J. (1984). Cognitive therapy and pharmacotherapy, singly and together in the treatment of depression. *Archives of General Psychiatry, 41,* 33–41.

Neisser, U. (1976). *Cognition and reality.* San Francisco: W.H. Freeman.

Neisser, U. (1980). Three cognitive psychologies and their implications. In M.J. Mahoney (Ed.), *Psychotherapy process: Current issues and future directions.* New York: Plenum.

Nisbett, R., & Ross, L. (1980). *Human inference: Strategies and shortcomings of social judgment.* Englewood Cliffs, NJ.: Prentice-Hall.

Novaco, R.W. (1978). Anger and coping with stress. In J.P. Foreyt & D.P. Rathjen (Eds.), *Cognitive behavior therapy: Research and application* (pp. 135–173). New York: Plenum.

Novaco, R.W. (1979). The cognitive regulation of anger and stress. In P.C. Kendall & S.D. Hollon (Eds.), *Cognitive-behavioral interventions: Theory, research, and procedures.* (pp. 241–285). New York: Academic Press.

Paul, G.L. (1969). Outcome of systematic desensitization, II: Controlled investigations of individual treatment, technique variations, and current status. In C.M. Franks (Ed.), *Behavior therapy: Appraisal and status* (pp. 105–159). New York: McGraw-Hill.

Popper, K.R. (1968). *The logic of scientific discovery.* New York: Harper Torchbooks.

Popper, K. (1970). Normal science and its dangers. In I. Lakatos & A. Musgrave (Eds.), *Criticism and the growth of knowledge* (pp. 51–58). New York: Cambridge University Press.

Rachman, S., & Eysenck, H.J. (1966). Reply to a "critique and reformulation" of behavior therapy. *Psychological Bulletin, 65,* 165–169.

Rosenthal, T.L. (1982). Social learning theory. In G.T. Wilson & C.M. Franks

(Eds.), *Contemporary behavior therapy: Conceptual and empirical foundations* (pp. 339–363). New York: Guilford.

Rush, A.J., Beck, A.T., Kovacs M., & Hollon, S.D. (1977). Comparative efficacy of cognitive therapy and pharmacotherapy in the treatment of depressed outpatients. *Cognitive Therapy and Research, 1,* 17–37.

Schwartz, G.E., & Weiss, S.M. (1978). Yale conference on behavioral medicine: A proposed definition and statement of goals. *Journal of Behavioral Medicine, 1,* 3–12.

Simons, A.D., Garfield, S.L., & Murphy, G.E. (1984). The process of change in cognitive therapy and pharmacotherapy for depression. *Archives of General Psychiatry, 41,* 45–51.

Suppe, F. (Ed.). (1974). *The structure of scientific theories.* Urbana: University of Illinois Press.

Turk, D.C., Meichenbaum, D., & Genest, M. (1983). *Pain and behavioral medicine: A cognitive-behavioral perspective.* New York: Guilford.

Watkins, J.W.N. (1970). Against normal science. In I. Lakatos & A. Musgrave (Eds.). *Criticism and the growth of knowledge* (p. 25–37). New York: Cambridge University Press.

Wender, P.H., & Klein, D.F. (1981). *Mind, mood, and medicine: A guide to the new biopsychiatry.* New York: Meridian.

Wilkins, W. (1971). Desensitization: Social and cognitive factors underlying the effectiveness of Wolpe's procedure. *Psychological Bulletin, 76,* 311–317.

Wilson, G.T. (1978). On the much discussed nature of the term "behavior therapy." *Behavior Therapy, 9,* 89–98.

Wilson, G.T. (1982). Clinical issues and strategies in the practice of behavior therapy. In C.M. Franks, G.T. Wilson, P.C. Kendall, & K. Brownell (Eds.), *Annual review of behavior therapy* (Vol. 8) (pp. 305–346). New York: Guilford.

Wilson, G.T., & Franks, C.M. (1982). *Contemporary behavior therapy: Conceptual and empirical foundations.* New York: Guilford.

Wolpe, J. (1958). *Psychotherapy by reciprocal inhibition.* Stanford, CA: Stanford University Press.

Wolpe, J. (1976). Behavior therapy and its malcontents: II. Multimodal eclecticism, cognitive exclusivism, and "exposure" empiricism. *Journal of Behavior Therapy and Experimental Psychiatry, 7,* 109–116.

Yates, A.J. (1981). Behavior therapy: Past, present, future—Imperfect? *Clinical Psychology Review, 1,* 269–291.

8

The Self in Cognitive Behavior Therapy

Robert L. Woolfolk

In the pages that follow, I shall outline certain developments in philosophy that run parallel to shifts in the theories and metaphors that have predominated within behavior therapy. The relationship of psychological science to philosophy has been and continues to be problematic. Clearly, there has been mutual influence. The operationalism of Bridgman (1927) affected the practices of several generations of psychologists, and the speculations of Freud on unconscious mentation have challenged philosophers to expand their views of the determinants of action, to name just two examples. I intend to address the topic of personhood (selfhood) in order to bring into sharp focus issues in the domain of philosophical anthropology that are rarely touched upon or appreciated by scientific psychology.

Every psychological theory carries with it some tacit understanding of what humans are capable and, often, what goals they should seek. From a pragmatic perspective, these ideological dimensions of psychological theory are among their most important features. An examination of philosophical positions that are to an extent supportive or inimical to various developments in behavior therapy can serve more precisely to locate behavior therapy within intellectual culture as well as draw out its tacit view of human nature.

There is a dialectic operating within behavior therapy today between the thesis of low-inference, observation-bound, parsimonious, conceptual circumspection, and the antithesis of broader, deeper, clinically pertinent, interdisciplinary richness. The choice between the poles of trivial certitude and confused profundity is one between unacceptable alternatives. This writing aims at fostering further conversation and future syntheses.

Behavior therapy, in its early years, looked with great suspicion upon such private phenomena as thoughts and feelings. This position resulted from a number of factors. Early behavior therapy was closely identified with methodological behaviorism and with conditioning-based models of human behavior derived from experimental studies of animal learning. This tradition was predicated upon operationalism and a philosophy of science that required explanations to be couched in the language of observables. Behavior therapy was fashioned, to some extent, out of opposition to psychoanalysis and other insight therapies, whose lack of demonstrable efficacy was thought to provide evidence for the futility of exploring the internal realms of the psyche and whose stance was in direct contrast to the powerful effects of manipulation of environmental reinforcement.

If behavior therapy has experienced anything that would qualify as a paradigm shift (Kuhn, 1962, 1970b), it would be in the advent of cognitive behavior therapy. The move from a classical behavior therapy that relied exclusively on analogies from operant and respondent conditioning to a cognitive behavior therapy that is the dominant position today is commonly regarded as a development in which a framework possessed of anomalies and other explanatory inadequacies came to be superseded by other frames of reference better able to subsume those phenomena that proved so troublesome to its classical predecessor. This shift began with the work of Homme (1965) and Cautela (1967), who hypothesized that covert behavior (thinking) was in principle no different from overt behavior, was subject to the same laws of learning as overt behavior, and was therefore appropriate subject matter for the efforts of behavior modifiers. Empirically successful attempts to change behavior, such as the work on modeling of Bandura (1969, 1977) and the various self-control therapies (Kanfer & Karoly, 1970; Mahoney, 1974), were formulated within a cognitive-meditational framework that was both parsimonious and deemed necessary to account for the observed effects. From the clinical direction, Lazarus (1971) introduced cognitive methods into the clinical mainstream of behavior therapy and identified affinities between the behavioral clinical sensibility and such preexisting work as Beck's (1963, 1976) cognitive therapy and Ellis's (1962) rational-emotive therapy.

As Kuhn (1970a, 1970b) and other philosophers and historians of science (Burtt, 1964; Feyerabend, 1975) have noted, developments of this kind are invariably influenced by factors other than the objective explanatory adequacy of paradigms. The social psychology of the scientific community, historical and cultural factors, and economics all play a role in the development of scientific ideas.

Behavior therapy was unquestionably pulled along by the rest of psychology, which had become, as had all of society, profoundly influenced by the computer and the information-processing metaphor. A cognitive revolution had been occurring in all of psychology (Dember, 1974) that had removed behavioristic learning theory from its position of preeminence. The cognitive social-learning theory of Bandura (1977) and Mischel (1973) was of a piece with widespread trends in psychology and provided a broad set of theoretical underpinnings that not only encompassed behavior, environmental contingencies, and stimulus-response contiguities, but also perceptions, thoughts, and cognitive strategies.

By the early 1970s behavior therapy's campaign for a place in the therapeutic firmament had been successful and its polemical fervor largely dissipated. What was distinctive about early behavior therapy, as opposed to psychoanalysis, was its insistence on scientific self-scrutiny, the specification and refinement of technique, a radical egalitarian attitude toward clients, and the insistence on the achievement of measurable results as a therapeutic *sine qua non* (Woolfolk & Richardson, 1984). The ability of behavior therapy to generate direct treatments with powerful and durable results for a certain range of disorders came to be generally accepted. Increased professional security and perhaps some dissipation of its initial missionary fervor led to internal controversies and some breaking of ranks. The clinical disadvantages of S-R, nonmediational models began to be addressed in the literature. Behavioral clinicians, frustrated with the limitations of the classic techniques (e.g., Lazarus, 1971, 1973), expanded their clinical repertoires in directions that took account of human symbolic processes.

If we regard behavior therapy as somewhat broader and more complex than science, as a set of healing practices characterized by an implicit philosophy of human nature (Woolfolk & Richardson, 1984), then the transition from traditional behavior therapy models to those of cognitive behavior therapy is more than a Kuhnian paradigm shift. It represents a transformation of philosophical anthropology as well. The shift from classical behaviorism to cognitive social-learning theory represents a shift in the implicit understanding of personhood that has important implications for the way in which human action is characterized and construed. In particular it represents a form of philosophical progress that allows questions to be addressed that previously were either limited or excluded. Thus the cognitive "revolution" within behavior therapy has transformed not only the experimental and clinical practices of classical behavior therapy but also its implicit conception of selfhood.

The transition from traditional behavior therapy to contemporary cognitive behavior therapy has witnessed the newer cognitive approaches' achievement of philosophical and metatheoretical advances in their conceptualizations of personhood. This advance over previous notions of the self implicit in the S-R models of early behavior therapy, I shall suggest, has further yet to go.

I shall discuss three concepts of the self that are inherent in philosophical behaviorism, functionalism/cognitive science, and ordinary language/hermeneutic views of human action. I shall also describe the relationship that each of these views of the self bears to historical and current positions within behavior therapy and develop the implications of each of these positions for issues of valuation, emotion, and self-understanding. Some implications for clinical activity will also be explored.

Behaviorism

The behaviorist model of personhood involves us in a bit of an anomaly at the outset. The notion of a self who initiates action is foreign and antithetical to the behaviorist program. The person is a "locus, a point at which many genetic and environmental conditions come together in a joint effect" (Skinner, 1974, p. 168).

In its most extreme form it takes the view that mental events are simply imprecise descriptions of either behaviors or of behavioral tendencies. Mental descriptions are therefore reducible to behavioral descriptions. This is a self whose own phenomenology is of little importance to a scientific understanding of it or its own self-understanding. Private events (thoughts and feelings) are outside the causal chain that affects behavior. Mental events cannot be the causes of behavior.

In the ethics of such a self, values can refer to nothing other than consistent behavioral probabilities or preferences. Such that they are, values must be inferred from behavior. For example, we can state, somewhat figuratively, that a cat values one brand of cat food over another. The concept of value is tied to such notions as reinforcer effectiveness or some other form of hedonic calculus. The notion of a rational moral agent deliberating among ends or choosing on the basis of reasons cannot be captured. Freedom or moral responsibility, if preserved at all, must be characterized entirely in environment–behavior relations (e.g., "Freedom is the absence of a certain level of environmental restraint on behavior").

Behaviorism even allows for some rendering of emotion. Simple emotions such as fear can be described as coextensive with physiological arousal, behavioral avoidance, and acts within the language community (reports of fear). More complicated emotions, on the other hand, are quite difficult for the behavioristic framework to encompass. Emotions that have less clear-cut behavioral correlates, guilt, for example, are harder to give a satisfactory behaviorist account of. There are many different behavioral manifestations of guilt, including, sometimes, no distinctive motor activity at all. The emotion of guilt also seems to require some unified phenomenological representation of oneself as a social actor or moral agent that a behavioral view of the self cannot countenance.

Two venerable philosophical arguments are used to support the position that thoughts cannot be the causes of behavior.

The first is that of the category mistake first proposed by Ryle (1949) and later endorsed by the behaviorist Rachlin (1977). The category mistake is illustrated by the following quote from Ryle (1949):

> A foreigner visiting Oxford or Cambridge for the first time is shown a number of colleges, libraries, playing fields, museums, scientific departments and administrative offices. He then asks 'But where is the University? I have seen where the members of the Colleges live, where the Registrar works, where the scientists experiment and the rest. But I have not yet seen the University in which reside and work the members of your University.' It has then to be explained to him that the University is not another collateral institution, some ulterior counterpart to the colleges, laboratories and offices which he has seen. The University is just the way in which all that he has already seen is organized. When they are seen and when their co-ordination is understood, the University has been seen. His mistake lay in his innocent assumption that it was correct to speak of Christ Church, the Bodleian Library, the Ashmolean Museum *and* the University, to speak, that is, as if 'the University' stood for an extra member of the class of which these other units are members. He was mistakenly allocating the University to the same category as that to which the other institutions belong. (p. 16)

According to Ryle, the Cartesian mind–body category mistake was made when: "The differences between the physical and the mental were . . . represented as differences inside the common framework of the categories of 'thing,' 'stuff,' 'attribute,' 'state,' 'process,' 'change,' 'cause,' and 'effect'" (p. 19).

Ryle contends that thoughts and bodily movements (behavior) stand in the same relation to mental activity as do the buildings of a university to the university itself, or as the players on a cricket team do to the team *esprit de corps*. Mental events and physical events belong to two different logical categories and hence cannot be related causally.

In adapting Ryle's argument to his criticism of cognitivism, Rachlin (1977) suggests that thoughts and behavior belong to two different logical categories in that cognition refers to a set of relationships between behavior and environmental events or a description of behavioral organization.

On close examination, however, Ryle's argument appears flawed. What seems at first glance to be an adroit short-circuiting of the mind–body problem does not either rule out or, by a behavioristic reduction, explain away mental causation. The categories Ryle is concerned with are based upon the semantic properties of a natural language. Even if we grant that the linguistic anomalies illustrated in his examples are most readily explained by reference to a set of putative categories, it would not follow from this that members of different semantic categories cannot share properties or predicates. To take Ryle's example, we could praise both the university and the Bodleian Library, or either could be objects of our affection. We could, of course, not put a new roof on the university as we could on the Ashmolean Museum, but this point seems to be of little consequence with regard to the issue in question, which is whether, in principle, members of different semantic categories could be propositionally conjoined. Rachlin's adaptation fares no better, for it is revealed to be a bit of behavioristic question-begging in which a behavioristic reduction of thoughts to descriptions of environment–behavior relations is assumed prior to "demonstrating" that cognition does not causally interact in direct fashion with either behavior or environment.

The second argument against the causation of the physical by the mental is the Humean dictum found, in one or more versions, in Melden (1961) and Peters (1958), which states that relations between cause and effect must be contingent and empirical rather than necessary and *a priori*. For example, if we "explain" the efficacy of a soporific on the basis of its "dormitive powers," we have in a scientific sense explained nothing. We have merely restated the logical or semantic relation between terms that logically entail one another, or we have redescribed the event in superficially different but semantically equivalent terms. For the behaviorist, an internal state is either a statement about behavioral probabilities or an epiphenomenal event. Thus when Skinner (1953) considers the statement, "He is drinking because he is thirsty," he concludes:

> If to be thirsty means nothing more than to have a tendency to drink, this is a mere redundancy. If it means that he drinks because of a state of thirst, an inner causal event is invoked. If this state is purely inferential—if no dimensions are assigned to it which would make direct observation possible—it cannot serve as an explanation. (p. 33)

Behaviorists contend that mentalistic explanations invoke "explana-tory fictions," require stopping at "mental way stations," and inevita-bly entail a homunculus whose actions require explanation as well. Thus any internal event that is not subject to direct observation can-not serve as a causal explanation of observed behavior.

The requirement in psychology that cause and effect be given se-mantically independent descriptions imposes constraints upon expla-nation that are undesirable. For example, Fodor (1968) refers to a period in the history of genetics

> when the best that could be done by way of specifying a gene was to refer
> to the presumed causal consequences of its presence—that is, when genes
> were identified as "whatever it is that causes" the blossom to be red or
> the plant to be tall. This sort of specification of the cause by reference to
> its effect was harmless . . . because no one doubted that logically indepen-
> dent descriptions of the cause and the effect must eventually be forthcom-
> ing. (p. 36)

To use Skinner's example, the fact that "thirst" and "drinking" are semantically related does not establish that all eventual descriptions at all levels of analysis—physiological, neurochemical, and so forth—of that which we colloquially call thirst will necessarily involve *concep-tual* linkages with consumatory behavior.

In seeking to avoid a dualism in which the corporeal is influenced by the noncorporeal (Descartes's problem), philosophical behaviorism is-sues an uncategorical prohibition against the causation of the physical by the mental. Environmental contingencies or brain events (both of which are directly observable by the scientist) may serve as causes, but beliefs, thoughts, and feelings may not. Of course, if we assume that mental states are associated with phenomenological manifesta-tions of neural events, then mental events may be reliable "markers" of some as yet poorly understood biology. And if we follow Hume and assume that cause and effect are empirical correlatives rather than events that "touch" in some palpable way, causation of the physical by the mental would simply refer to consistent covariation between the two. The mental simply becomes a different level of analysis appropri-ate to a science of persons in the same way that the social is a level of analysis appropriate to sociology.

Nor is tautology inevitable in all mentalistic explanation. This is the case only if we assume, as do the logical behaviorists, that mental predicates are translatable into behavioral tendencies, therefore mak-ing mentalistic explanation redundant. In fact, the assumption of phil-osophical behaviorism that statements about the mental are translat-able into behavioral dispositions is one of its chief weaknesses. Clearly some mental processes refer to events that are neither behavioral nor dispositional. A behavioral account of mental states indicates an important and necessary component of some mental states but not a sufficient description of all of them. Let us take the example of pain. Groaning, crying out, wincing, biting one's lip, and taking aspirin are all "pain behaviors." But pains hurt. This is indeed their primary and most critical feature, one which cannot be done away with. Malcolm (1964) characterizes this error of behaviorism as an assumption that first-person psychological sentences have the same content or verification as their third-person counterparts. This is, however, an error: "I can verify that another man is excited by the trembling of his hands. But I do not verify in this way that *I* am excited. In the normal case I do not verify it at all" (p. 150).

The weaknesses of behaviorism as a philosophy of psychology and of a behavioral account of persons are to some extent addressed by the two positions that will be outlined below: (1) functionalism/cognitive science and (2) hermeneutics/ordinary language. I am using the aforementioned labels somewhat loosely to refer in the former case to the philosophy inspired by work in the cognitive sciences and represented by Fodor and Dennett, and in the latter to a loose confederation of humanistic positions seeking to retain an ordinary-language, phenomenological view of the self and drawing from both the later Wittgenstein and such continental philosophers as Heidegger and Merleau-Ponty.

Functionalism/Cognitive Science

A second version of personhood is very much in evidence in the field of cognitive science and in the functionalist philosophy of such writers as Fodor and Dennett. Much as cognitive behavior therapy arose as a response to the explanatory inadequacies in S-R behaviorism, functionalism sought to address difficulties in the philosophy of mind that remained unresolved within behaviorist and materialist positions. As Fodor (1981) puts it:

> We were driven to functionalism . . . by the suspicion that there are empirical generalizations about mental states that can't be formulated in the vocabulary of neurological or physical theories; neurology and physics don't, we supposed, provide projectible kind-predicates that subtend the domains of these generalizations. (p. 25)

Under these various functionalist formulations the phenomenology of the individual can function causally. Human beings are viewed as one category of intentional systems, along with Turing machines and some infrahumans "whose behavior can be—at least sometimes—explained and predicted by relying on ascriptions to the system of beliefs and desires (and hopes, fears, intentions, hunches, . . .)" (Dennett, 1978, p. 3).

Thoughts, especially, are seen as the proximate causes of other internal states, such as affects, or of behavior. Also, mental causes interact with and influence one another, a possibility for which behaviorism does not produce a satisfactory account.

Rather than a black box or switch board, the self is seen as an information-processing system analogous to a computer. The software, programming, and internal states of the computer are viewed as essential to a complete explanation of its activities. "Unlike behaviorism, functionalism is not a reductionist thesis; it does not envision—even in principle—the elimination of mentalistic concepts from the explanatory apparatus of psychological theories" (Fodor, 1981, p. 10).

Such internal entities as values and emotions are internal variables that reside in the software of the system and mediate the effects of environment on behavior. The individual who is afraid not only presents behavioral avoidance and physiological arousal, as in the case of the behaviorist self, but also numerous cognitive concomitants, such as "This is dangerous," "I'm in trouble," and so forth. A sense that some activity is "good" or "bad" cannot only be characterized as an internal state of the person; it can have an explicit representation within the system and can function causally. If we question such a self it may even be able to give us an articulate account of some aspects of its internal programming. We can even imagine this self involved in a rational deliberation between alternatives that are more or less valuable, moral, and so forth.

Hermeneutics/Ordinary Language

A third view of the self is that present in ordinary language (especially under the influence of the later Wittgenstein) and hermeneutic philosophy. In some respects this position is consistent with and overlaps the view of the person put forth by functionalism.

One such position in this tradition is that of Searle (1983), who offers a holistic theory of action that purports both to dissolve the mind–body problem and to demonstrate that it is inevitably in the nature of mental causation of behavior to *require* a logical connection between cause and effect, such that intentions (mental phenomena) concurrently describe and cause the same behavior. Searle's response to charges of dualism is essentially a level-of-description kind of argument. Mental states are regarded as biological phenomena that are both *caused by* and *realized in* the structure of the brain, in the same way that the liquid properties of water are both caused by and realized in a collection of H_2O molecules. At a macrolevel of analysis, mental states cause bodily movements, while at a parallel microlevel, the neuron firings that cause and realize mental states also cause the physiological changes that cause and realize bodily movements. All these processes and entities are real, biological events, but occur at different levels of description.

Searle's theory of the mental causation of behavior requires a partitioning of the concept of intention and a substitution of the term *action* for *behavior* in cases of intentional causation. Prior intentions cause actions that are made up of two parts: an *intention in action* and a body movement. Let us take the example of a student who wishes to ask a question in class. The prior intention, "I want to raise my arm to ask a question in class," would cause the action of hand-raising in order to ask a question. Both the bodily movement (hand-raising) and the intention in action (signaling in order to ask a question) are, under Searle's account, necessary to form an action. An intention in action is the accompanying motivational ground of directed behavior (action), and its propositional content (hand-raising in order to ask a question) is identical to its corresponding prior intention. The intention in action is what is removed if we use Wittgenstein's example and subtract "my hand goes up" from "raising my hand." In this scheme mental events are the *sine qua non* of most human conduct and are both fundamental and inextricably bound up in the ontology of action.

According to hermeneutic/ordinary language perspectives, persons are not simply entities who possess consciousness that can be characterized in terms of a set of cognitive elements. They also possess a kind of reflexive self-consciousness that is unique among known animals or machines. Human beings are not only aware, they are aware of their own acts of awareness. They not only evaluate, but also reflect upon and judge, their evaluative processes (Frankfurt, 1971):

> Besides wanting and choosing and being moved *to do* this or that, men may also want to have (or not to have) certain desires and motives. They are capable of wanting to be different, in their preferences and purposes, from what they are . . . No animal other than man, however, appears to have the capacity for reflective self-evaluation that is manifested in the formation of second-order desires. (p. 7)

Taylor (1976) contrasts the evaluations that an agent might make between alternatives based upon values already established (by a program in the case of a Turing device or by a social-learning history in the case of a person) and evaluations that may call into question the foundations upon which choices are made. He refers to this latter process as "strong evaluation." The sense of self is, in part, the sense of where one stands in relation to one's standards. Persons are such that, potentially, the question arises for them of what kind of beings they are going to be. The roots of this position can be found in both Heidegger and Sartre. Taylor contends that in the modern world, a world in which selfhood is not defined in relation to a meaningful cosmological order, it is increasingly "up to each of us," by processes of second-order evaluation, to engage in an ongoing process of self-definition.

This view of the self is consistent with a hermeneutic approach to the social sciences that sees qualitative differences between the natural sciences and the *Geisteswissenschaften,* the former able to rely upon "brute data" from which the human significance has been removed while the latter considers *meaning* to be the one indispensable construct within the human sciences. Our processes of consciousness not only represent reality but also serve to constitute what is real and significant to us (Taylor, 1982).

There are many philosophical advantages to this view of the self. It captures the commonsense, everyday aspect of the lived human experience and accords it a primary role in social explanation, unlike either psychoanalysis or behaviorism. The person as moral agent, in all senses thereof, so vital to both law and systems of ethics, is preserved. Complex emotions such as shame and guilt, which require both a reflexive self-awareness and a sensitivity and openness to both societal standards and self-evaluation, are rendered richly by this position.

Cognitive Behavior Therapy and the Self

The view of selfhood implicit in cognitive behavior therapy partakes of all three positions we have discussed: behaviorism, functionalism, and hermeneutics. The shift from S-R models in behavior therapy has meant that the underlying philosophy of psychology, which was once strongly behavioristic, has moved decisively in the direction of functionalism and hermeneutics.

The stronger parallels exist between cognitive behavior therapy and functionalism, and great affinities between these two approaches exist at a number of levels. At the metaphysical level both endorse mechanism, for which the root metaphor is the machine (Pepper, 1942). Explanations are couched in terms of laws that hold between the component parts of a whole. Both cognitive behavior therapy and functionalism tend to support the unity of sciences and adopt the approaches of the most successful of these, the natural sciences. Both tend to view the mind as a system for representing external reality. Thoughts and feelings are thought of as internal variables, causal atoms, or discrete entities rather than processes or patterns. The mind is viewed as analogous to a computer; its output is a joint function of its hardware (constitutional endowment) and its programming (social-learning history). The generative or creative capacities of the mind are rarely addressed and little elaborated.

In its rendering of relations among internal variables, however, cognitive behavior therapy sometimes seems closer to behaviorism than to functionalism. Whenever possible, internal variables are defined in terms of some objectively measurable index, for example, fear and physiological arousal. Cognitions were first described in the behavioral literature as "mediators," meaning that they mediated between environment and behavior. Often, however, this mediation involves one stop at only one cognitive variable. One of the chief aims of functionalism, the description of the relationships among internal states, is rarely addressed. Desires and purposes, endorsed by functionalism as internal states with causal powers, are seldom part of the cognitive-behavioral lexicon.

Although one could hardly claim that behavior therapy has moved very far in the direction of hermeneutics, there are certain indications of an attempt to broaden the concept of a person in the directions that a hermeneutic conception of the self allows.

Perhaps as some evidence of this, contemporary social-learning theory (Bandura, 1977, 1978) has come to view an adequate account of human self-determination as essential to a comprehensive theory of behavior and, consequently, has attempted to deal explicitly with the issue of human freedom. The social-learning account of human freedom can be viewed as a kind of midpoint between the libertarian portrait of the autonomous individual whose will is free and whose choices are uncaused events and the conceptualization of human action as an essentially passive response to environmental and biological forces. In this formulation the cognitive processes of the choosing individual can be viewed as one of a triad of determinants (the other two being behavior and the environment) that interact reciprocally. Thus behavior is a partial function of the environment as is the environment a partial function of behavior (Bandura, 1978):

> Because people's conceptions, their behavior, and their environments are reciprocal determinants of each other, individuals are neither powerless

objects controlled by environmental forces nor entirely free agents who can do whatever they choose. (p. 357)

Compare this to the following passage by hermeneutic phenomenologist Merleau-Ponty (1945/1962):

> What then is freedom? To be born is both to be born of the world and to be born into the world. The world is already constituted; in the first case we are acted upon, in the second we are open to an infinite number of possibilities. But this analysis is still abstract, for we exist in both ways *at once*. There is therefore, never determinism and never absolute choice, I am never a thing and never bare consciousness. (p. 453)

Bandura, despite his disclaimers, at times describes a self that is a rather static amalgam of cognitive structures that seem ultimately implanted by an environment as it functions in reciprocal interaction with person and behavior. The ordinary-language conception of moral agency and the status of ethical propositions, for example, are rendered questionable in the following:

> In the social learning analysis, considerate people perform culpable acts because of the reciprocal dynamics between personal and situational determinants of behavior rather than because of defects in their moral structures .(Bandura, 1978, p. 354)

At other times Bandura describes a more proactive self. Though ambivalent about the status of agency and the self within his theory, he specifically abjures a cybernetic view of relations among self, behavior, and environment. He suggests that the relations among these are very complicated and dynamic and that cognition involves "integrative judgments" and a "generative mechanism." He elaborates a mechanism that would allow for the development of the second-order evaluations described earlier (Bandura, 1979):

> Social learning theory assigns a prominent role to reflective and self-referent thought in human functioning. There is no great mystery about what *reflective* means. Reflective thought refers to thoughts about one's thoughts. By operating on what they know, people can derive knowledge about things that extend beyond their experiences and generate innovative courses of action . . . . An advanced cognitive capacity coupled with the remarkable flexibility of symbolization enables people to create ideas and to engage in trains of thought that transcend their sensory experiences. (pp. 439–440)

Behavior therapy, by "going cognitive," allowed the return of a conceptual exile, the lived experience of the human being, to the realm of scientific legitimacy. The self was in some very real sense rediscovered or resurrected in this shift of paradigms. The recovery of phenomenology meant a self for whom the rat was a less appropriate analog than the ape, dolphin, or computer. Along with an increase in dignity, human self-protective capabilities were avowed. The automaticity of conditioning was repudiated, and the mediating function of cognitive structures became a prophylactic against future Brave New Worlds. The behavior therapist as brainwasher was replaced by the cognitive therapist—a Socratic, rational teacher. The upgrading of stereotypes alone was worth the trip.

What continues to be lacking in cognitive behavior therapy is an adequate accounting of that which makes us human, in Sartre's terminology, the *pour-soi*, that being which is not only aware and conscious, but is also conscious of its own awareness. This kind of second-order awareness could receive no translation into behavior, as could such simple inner states as fear or thirst. A failure to encompass that self-reflection and self-understanding that constitute the significance and meaningfulness of behavior for the individual impoverished the conceptual underpinnings of early behavior therapy. And although certain recent developments in social-learning theory are beginning to allow for a rendering of that which is distinctively human, the potential for a depiction of the full range of human proclivites and capacities is as yet undeveloped.

There are a number of factors that resist a full-scale assimilation of a more comprehensive and philosophically adequate conception of the self into behavior therapy.

The first of these might be called "residual behaviorism." Although internal variables are allowed in social-learning–based accounts of conduct, these variables are often defined operationally with close ties to observed behavior. Relationships between cognitive events and behavior are mapped, but little research has investigated the relationship among different cognitive events. We are referring here, of course, to what would be behavior therapy's version of psychodynamics. Relational propositions about internal states are fundamental to cognitive science, but have been slow in coming to a discipline whose ideology has required of its concepts short steps from and strong ties to observable behavior.

The second is the continuing wish to *emulate the natural sciences*. As has been the case with much of psychology, behavior therapy has sought to emulate the procedures and methods of the natural sciences. The great successes of physics and chemistry came after teleological explanations were replaced by explanations relying on mechanisms of material and efficient causation. Any attempt to incorporate a broader view of the self requires the assimilation of a self acting on the basis of reasons, desires, beliefs, and goals—in short, to accept teleological explanation. It is one thing to model human behavior on a computer or to accept as an adequate metaphor for human selfhood a piece of hardware consisting of programmable electronic circuitry, but a much more radical departure from scientific orthodoxy is required to introduce a genuinely purposive conception of the self.

The rather narrow and constricted view of personhood of early behavior therapy had many undesirable correlates. The shift in the direction of cognitive models has remedied many, but not all, of those problems.

In an earlier work, Richardson and I (Woolfolk & Richardson, 1984) argue that behavior therapy had great difficulties in encompassing questions of value and meaning. These difficulties can now be understood in relation to behavior therapy's implicit conception of personhood. Behavior therapy emerges as a form of mixed discourse in which the person is sometimes viewed as a moral agent/second-order intentional system (during discussions and setting of therapeutic objectives) and sometimes as a quasi-mechanistic entity (during treatment). Fundamental anomalies result from this intermingling of language games. [The client is thought to be "responsible" for "choosing" therapeutic objectives but not responsible for the fact that he or she possesses low self-efficacy. Rather this low self-efficacy is seen as derivative of a social-learning history involving a series of unsalutary reciprocal interactions between personal determinants and environment.] Cognition, if seen as an aspect of the proactive, generative, self-definitional capacities of the person, promotes a conception of therapy as dialogue, as discussion. Conversely, if mental life is conceptualized as a set of relatively static, environmentally implanted cognitive structures, then cognitive restructuring becomes the analog of reprogramming a Turing device and psychotherapy is reduced to a technical task.

In order to ponder and be affected by questions related to the meaning and purpose of one's existence, or human existence at large, one must possess the rather sophisticated second-order self-reflective capacities outlined earlier. Behavior therapy has not been much interested in such concerns, at times disavowing their appropriateness to a truly "scientific" therapy (Kanfer & Saslow, 1969). Nor has behavior therapy addressed with any frequency or originality such truly worthy and fascinating problems as the so-called self disorders, such as borderline and narcissistic personality disorders (Mays, 1985). These varieties of psychopathology have many behavioral concomitants, but no set of behavioral criteria is even vaguely sufficient to define either of these disorders in the way that behavioral criteria can define phobias or substance abuse. Conceptualization of such syndromes requires relational cognitive propositions—statements that show how different aspects of mental life affect each other and interrelate.

As we have seen, by "going cognitive" behavior therapy repudiated its early behavioristic philosophical underpinnings and opened itself to a more philosophically adequate conception of personhood. Both functionalism and hermeneutic/ordinary language philosophy have grappled with the limitations of behaviorism as a philosophy of mind and have learned lessons of value to those who examine the foundations of behavior therapy and who desire to see it bring to bear its uncompromising commitment to public self-scrutiny and the practical utility of its procedures to a wider range of human miseries.

References

Bandura, A. (1969). *Principles of behavior modification.* New York: Holt, Rinehart & Winston.

Bandura, A. (1977). *Social learning theory.* Englewood Cliffs, NJ: Prentice-Hall.

Bandura, A. (1978). The self system in reciprocal determinism. *American Psychologist, 33,* 344–358.

Bandura, A. (1979). Self-referent mechanisms in social learning theory. *American Psychologist 34,* 439–441.

Beck, A.T. (1963). Thinking and depression: I. Idiosyncratic content and cognitive distortions. *Archives of General Psychiatry, 9,* 324–333.

Beck, A.T. (1976). *Cognitive therapy and the emotional disorders.* New York: International Universities Press.

Bridgman, P.W. (1927). *The logic of modern physics.* New York: Macmillan.

Burtt, E.A. (1964). *The metaphysical foundations of modern science.* London: Routledge & Kegan Paul.

Cautela, J.R. (1967). Covert sensitization. *Psychological Reports, 20,* 459–468.

Dember, W.N. (1974). Motivation and the cognitive revolution. *American Psychologist, 29,* 161–168.

Dennett, D.C. (1978). *Brainstorms,* Montgomery, VT: Bradford.

Ellis, A. (1962). *Reason and emotion in psychotherapy.* New York: Stuart.

Feyerabend, P. (1975). *Against method.* London: NLB.

Fodor, J.A. (1968). *Psychological explanation.* New York: Random House.

Fodor, J.A. (1981). *Representations.* Montgomery, VT: Bradford.

Frankfurt, H. (1971). Freedom of the will and the concept of a person. *Journal of Philosophy, 68,* 5–20.

Homme, L.E. (1965). Perspectives in psychology: XXIV. Control of coverants, the operants of the mind. *Psychological Record, 15,* 501–511.

Kanfer, F.H., & Karoly, P. (1972). Self-control: A behavioristic excursion into the lion's den. *Behavior Therapy, 3,* 398–416.

Kanfer, F.H., & Saslow, G. (1969). Behavioral diagnosis. In C.M. Franks (Ed.), *Behavior therapy: Appraisal and status* (pp. 417–444). New York: McGraw-Hill.

Kuhn, T.S. (1970a). Reflections on my critics. In I. Lakatos & A. Musgrave (Eds.), *Criticism and the growth of knowledge* (pp.). Cambridge, England: Cambridge University Press.

Kuhn, T.S. (1970b). *The structure of scientific revolutions* (2nd ed.). Chicago: University of Chicago Press.

Lazarus, A.A. (1971). *Behavior therapy and beyond.* New York: McGraw-Hill.

Lazarus, A.A. (1973). Multimodal behavior therapy: Treating the BASIC I.D. *Journal of Nervous and Mental Disease, 156,* 404–411.

Mahoney, M.J. (1974). *Cognition and behavior modification.* Cambridge, MA: Ballinger.

Malcolm, N. (1964). Behaviorism as a philosophy of psychology. In T.W. Wann (Ed.), *Behaviorism and phenomenology* (pp. 141–162). Chicago: University of Chicago Press.

Mays, D.T. (1985). Behavior therapy with borderline personality disorders: One clinician's perspective. In D.T. Mays & C.M. Franks (Eds.), *Negative outcome in psychotherapy and what to do about it* (pp. 301–311). New York: Springer.

Melden, A.I. (1961). *Free action.* London: Routledge & Kegan Paul.

Merleau-Ponty, M. (1962). *The phenomenology of perception* (C. Smith, Trans.). London: Routledge & Kegan Paul. (Original work published 1945.)

Mischel, W. (1973). Toward a cognitive social learning conceptualization of personality. *Psychological Review, 80,* 252–283.

Pepper, S.C. (1942). *World hypotheses: A study in evidence.* Berkeley: University of California Press.

Peters, R.S. (1958). *The concept of motivation.* London: Routledge & Kegan Paul.

Rachlin, H. (1977). Reinforcing and punishing thoughts. *Behavior Therapy, 8,* 659–665.

Ryle, G. (1949). *The concept of mind.* London: Hutcheson.

Searle, J.R. (1983). *Intentionality.* Cambridge, England: Cambridge University Press.

Skinner, B.F. (1953). Science and human behavior. New York: Macmillan.

Skinner, B.F. (1974). *About behaviorism.* New York: Alfred A. Knopf.

Taylor, C. (1976). Responsibility for self. In A.O. Rorty (Ed.), *The identities of persons* (pp. 281–299). Berkeley: University of California Press.

Taylor, C. (1982). Consciousness. In P. Secord (Ed.), *Explaining human behavior* (pp. 35–51). Beverly Hills, CA: Sage.

Woolfolk, R.L., & Richardson, F.C. (1984). Behavior therapy and the ideology of modernity. *American Psychologist, 39,* 777–786.

IV

Behavior Therapy Paradigms: Integrationist Approaches

9

Social-Learning Theory, Philosophy of Science, and the Identity of Behavior Therapy

Frederick Rotgers

In recent years there has been a renewed interest in the exploration of the philosophical assumptions that underpin and guide the discipline of psychology. With the centenary of the establishment of the first psychological laboratory by Wilhelm Wundt, American psychologists seem to have begun a process of philosophical soul-searching and reflection on the state of psychology as a science (Koch & Leary, 1985). Dissatisfaction among many psychologists with the behavioristic approach that ruled American psychology for much of the first half of this century has led to significant criticisms, from both within and without, of the epistemological and methodological approaches that psychologists have used (e.g., Neisser, 1967; Toulmin & Leary, 1985). In addition, there has been a renewed debate regarding the possibility of a "unified" psychology, with strong arguments voiced on both sides of the question (Koch, 1981; Staats, 1983).

Behavior therapy, probably one of the most programmatically successful branches of psychology, has not been immune to this trend toward questioning of philosophical underpinnings. Erwin (1978) was the first to demonstrate clearly that, contrary to its stated position, behavior therapy was not really behavioristic in a formal sense. Since that time, and coincidentally with the development of a growing movement toward the inclusion of cognitive variables in the behavior therapist's conceptual, research, and technical domains, there has been a significant increase in the number of articles by behavior therapists that address philosophical issues.

Kuhn (1962, 1970) has pointed to renewed philosophical debates as one sign of an impending paradigm shift, or revolution in a scientific discipline. While one can debate at length the paradigmatic status of psychology, and behavior therapy as a subfield of psychology, it seems clear that a questioning and rethinking of values, both scientific and pragmatic, is now occurring within behavior therapy. Basic questions are being asked about the ontological and epistemological stances that behavior therapists have taken and should take in the future. This chapter focuses on questions about which approach to science should be adopted, what course research in behavior therapy should take, and what the consequences are of adopting a particular approach to science and, in particular, to the study of human behavior.

Behavior therapy faces somewhat more complex issues of direction and focus than many other fields of psychology. From its beginnings, behavior therapists have attempted to adopt both a scientific and a technological identity. This has produced, among other side effects, a clear scientist–practitioner split (see Barlow, 1981; Barlow et al., 1983; Franks & Barbrack, 1983). Some writers (e.g., Franks & Barbrack, 1983) believe that this results from an inconsistency between what behavior therapists actually do and what they say they do in their writings. Others (e.g., Barlow, 1981) see this split as characteristic of clinical psychology in general and as being due, in part, to basic philosophical differences between clinicians and researchers. Attempts to reconcile the seeming art of clinical practice, with its emphasis upon therapeutic relationships and the rapid, effective treatment of the individual client's difficulties, with the experimental requirements of the logical-empiricist, laboratory approach that has characterized behavioristic approaches from early on (Zuriff, 1985) have produced a spectrum of proposals. These range from Krasner's (Chapter 3, this volume) prescription that behavior therapy should return to its original behavioristic roots, with corresponding emphasis on environmental variables and experimental methodology, to the cognitive behavior therapist's insistence that cognition and intraorganismic processes must be explored and used in producing therapeutic change (Mahoney, 1974; Meichenbaum, 1977), to Lazarus's (1981) contention that, within a strictly empiricist and critical perspective, "anything that works" should be utilized to help produce therapeutic change.

Social-learning theory is a school of behavior therapy that falls somewhere between the radical behaviorist and technically eclectic poles of the behavior therapy spectrum. The present chapter is written from the perspective of one particular version of social-learning theory, that formulated by Bandura and his students (Bandura, 1977). By adopting this perspective, I acknowledge a certain philosophical preference. That preference will become clear as the chapter progresses.

In this chapter I will pursue several goals. First, I will attempt to place Bandura's social-learning theory in the context of present-day behavior therapy by briefly outlining its distinguishing features. Selected aspects of the present philosophical debate in psychology will then be examined with a view toward identifying a suitable behavior therapy approach to science and practice, a scrutiny inevitably colored by adoption of the perspective of social-learning theory.

Philosophy of science is a prescriptive as well as descriptive endeavor, and I shall approach it as such in the final section of the chapter. Here, I will attempt to derive a prescriptive formulation for behavior therapy based upon the adoption of a particular view of science and scientific goals. In this context, I will discuss the future of behavior therapy and the possible implications of a shift in the field's acknowledged, though questioned and questionable, behavioristic preference. This is an ambitious project that could, if thoroughly done, easily fill a volume of its own. It is my hope that the present effort, unavoidably sketchy and opinionated as it is, will serve to stimulate further exploration and intellectual argument.

Social-Learning Theory in Perspective

Woodward (1982) has identified several versions of what he calls "social behaviorism." Tracing their roots back to the early psychologies of James, Freud, and others, Woodward notes that theories of behavior based upon social-learning processes have become more and more prominent in psychology in recent decades. As exemplars of this sort of theorizing, he cites the writings of Bindra, Mischel, Staats, and Bandura, among others.

Bandura's version of social behaviorism, or, as he prefers to call it, social-learning theory (Bandura, 1977), is unique in several important ways. These differences, a departure from strictly behavioristic views, imply innovative ontological and epistemological viewpoints that have clear-cut implications for the future of behavior therapy.

While other social behaviorists, particularly Staats, have attempted to account for complex human behavior within the framework of traditional learning theory (e.g., focusing on the interactions of classical and operant conditioning in the acquisition of complex behaviors), Bandura has added a third form of learning, modeling (Bandura & Walters, 1963; Bandura, 1977), to the list of processes by which people learn new behaviors. This addition of modeling, has resulted in a shift of emphasis in both behavioral research and therapy away from reinforcement and other environmental influences on behavior.

Bandura's conceptualization of learning processes has enabled behavior therapists to shift their emphasis to a more organism-focused viewpoint in which cognitive factors play an important part. Beginning with his landmark *Principles of Behavior Modification* (1969), Bandura's version of social-learning theory has been, and remains, in the forefront of the cognitive revolution in behavior therapy. However, unlike most cognitive behaviorists, Bandura has neither abandoned nor reduced the emphasis on learning principles. Rather, he has attempted to integrate traditional ideas about the acquisition of behavior with a new focus on the internal processes that, in his view, both accompany behaviors and play a causal role in their production (Bandura, 1977, 1982).

Two concepts exemplify social-learning theorists' commitment to an exploration of intraorganismic factors that, by strategic decision (Zuriff, 1985), have traditionally been ignored by psychologists working within a strictly behavioristic framework. The concept of "self-efficacy" (Bandura, 1977, 1982) forms the centerpiece of social-learning theory's attempt to integrate cognition into behavioral theory. However, Bandura has not simply postulated cognitive mechanisms; he has performed extensive research that anchors self-efficacy in observable behaviors and has demonstrated the utility of the concept in both guiding and predicting behavior change (see Bandura, 1982, for a review of this work). Thus social-learning theory has attempted to remain within an empiricist and experimentalist framework while still postulating and exploring the role of "unobservable" cognitive factors in the production of behavior.

The second key concept in social-learning theory is "reciprocal determinism." While not a new concept (Zuriff, 1985), reciprocal determinism in social-learning theory provides a means for explaining many complex human behaviors (e.g., self-control) that have been difficult for other behavioristic systems to accommodate without postulating such problematic concepts as "action at a distance" and atemporal causality that seem to violate traditional Humean notions of causality (Rachlin, Chapter 5, this volume; Zuriff, 1985). Reciprocal determinism, simply stated, means that causal influences extend both from the environment and from the organism. Organisms, particularly humans, are able, through intentional action, to construct their environments in ways that lead to anticipated consequences. In addition, the environment also influences behaviors, which, in turn, give feedback to the environment, changing it and producing new reinforcement contingencies. Thus, rather than a one-way, linear system of behavioral causality, social-learning theory implies a circular feedback system in which behavior, intraorganismic variables, and environment all influence each other.

From this conceptual framework, Bandura has constructed an empirically based theory of behavior change of demonstrated utility for guiding and predicting the outcomes of efforts to produce behavior change (Bandura, 1982). While Bandura's conceptualizations have not gone uncriticized (See Wilson, 1984), they have proven to be a fruitful spur to research on the processes involved in behavioral change, the primary interest of behavior therapists. This interest in *internal processes*, as opposed to the more limited focus on relationships among input and output variables that characterizes more traditional behavioral theories [e.g., molar behaviorism and neobehavioristic theories (Zuriff, 1985)], has substantial implications for the future of behavior therapy, as well as significant implications for a philosophy of science for behavior therapists.

In the next section, I will briefly review some of the contenders currently being discussed in the broader psychological literature for philosophies that might guide general psychology in the future. In addition, I will highlight a new philosophy of science, constructive empiricism (Van Fraassen, 1980), that seems to hold promise for behavior therapy both for promoting useful ontological and epistemological stances, and for helping to resolve the scientist–practitioner split noted above.

Philosophy of Science and Behavior Therapy

Before I review some of the major contenders for a philosophy of science to guide behavior therapy, several caveats are in order. Despite being presented as completed systems that are generally advocated by many, these philosophies of science are themselves in a state of flux and debate. While one may talk of, for example, hermeneutics as an approach to understanding, it is important to recognize that hermeneutic philosophy is not a monolithic corpus in which basic agreement has been reached about the methods to be employed in interpretation and the means to resolve problems of interpretation. Thus, one may follow Habermas, Ricoeur, Gadamer, or other hermeneutic philosophers and come to very different philosophical positions as a result. While all of these philosophers have the same basic (with apologies to Kuhn) "paradigm," they still have many important disagreements among themselves (Thompson, 1981). In the presentation that follows

I will try to distill from each of the approaches discussed those aspects that appear most relevant to behavior therapy.

It is thus important to recognize that the choice of a philosophy or paradigm is ultimately not a rational one (Bartley, 1962). Rather, it is based more on an intuitive commitment to what feels right and what one *believes* will be most productive in pursuing a given endeavor. While the choice of a philosophical position may be disputed rationally, its ultimate acceptance is based not so much on logical argument as a commitment to one's personal values (see also Van Fraassen, 1980). That values correlate rather highly with choice of theoretical and philosophical position has been shown rather convincingly by Kimble (1984) and Krasner and Houts (1984), among others.

The acknowledgment of the role of values and commitment in the selection of a set of guidelines for doing science is important in that each of the positions to be covered below assumes a different set of basic values upon which its enterprise is based. Certain aspects of phenomena may be allowed or disallowed, certain types of theoretical structure may be permitted or not, depending upon the basic values one believes science should follow.

An example of this conflict of nonsystemic values can be seen in the interchanges between logical empiricists and scientific realists, as described by Zuriff (1985) and Van Fraassen (1980). Logical empiricism, or logical positivism, aims at eliminating metaphysics from science; from this, a major set of values follows, for example, a reliance upon communally observable data, an emphasis on falsifiability (Popper, 1959) as a major criterion for scientific theories, and a focus on prediction and control rather than understanding and explanation as goals of science. Conversely, scientific realists readily admit unobservable entities to scientific theorizing because they view the main goal of science as providing an understanding and explanation of a real world that they believe exists beyond merely observable phenomena (Van Fraassen, 1980; Churchland & Hooker, 1985).

Thus, in adopting a philosophy of science one is making certain commitments and statements about what one believes science ought to be. It seems clear that certain trends in behavior therapy, characterized by social-learning theory and cognitive approaches, may demand a rethinking of some of the commitments behavior therapists hold as well as a shift in view about the nature and goals of science. It may be that behavior therapy cannot adopt a consistent philosophy of science across both research and practice at this time. The requirements of empirical research simply may not fit with values clinicians must pursue when they treat patients. While one philosophical perspective may be able to guide our formulation of treatments, it is not clear that the same philosophical commitments will be fully sufficient in both the laboratory and the clinic (cf. Woolfolk & Richardson, 1984).

Finally, when one approaches the task of defining or delineating an underlying philosophy, one must have a reasonably clear idea of what it is that one is trying to develop a philosophy for and of. This question of definition has long plagued writers in behavior therapy for reasons unnecessary to elaborate here. Definitions have ranged far and wide, with varying emphases (see Erwin's [1978] discussion for a good overview). For the sake of ease and brevity I will adopt the "official" definition of behavior therapy that has been promulgated by the Association for the Advancement of Behavior Therapy (AABT) (Franks & Wilson, 1975):

> Behavior therapy involves primarily the application of principles derived from research in experimental and social psychology for the alleviation of human suffering and the enhancement of human functioning. Behavior therapy emphasizes a systematic evaluation of the effectiveness of these applications. Behavior therapy involves environmental change and social interaction rather than the direct alteration of bodily processes by biological procedures. The aim is primarily educational. The techniques facilitate improved self-control. In the conduct of behavior therapy, a contractual agreement is negotiated, in which mutually agreeable goals and procedures are specified. Responsible practitioners using behavior approaches are guided by generally accepted principles. (pp. 1–2)

While this definition implies certain moral and ethical values that may or may not lead to paradoxical positions (Woolfolk & Richardson, 1984), it is on the technical and evaluational side of behavior therapy that one must focus when considering a philosophy of science. Such questions as how one derives the "principles" upon which practice is based, what "environmental change" and "social interaction" consist of, and what the terms *educational, self-control,* and *generally accepted principle* mean are all important ones that are not answered by this definition. This vagueness of language allows many different approaches to fit under this definition, thus making the task of prescribing or delineating a philosophical position vis à vis behavior therapy as a whole all the more difficult. Like our parent science of psychology, behavior therapy suffers from a proliferation of views that at times seem incapable of being fitted into one conceptual basket.

With these cautions in mind, let us now turn to a consideration of some of the major philosophies of science and social science that have been advanced as candidates for revitalizing psychology and moving it forward toward more effective practice (whatever one takes that to mean). Underlying each of these brief, and necessarily sketchy, presentations is the goal of evaluating that position's suitability for adoption by behavior therapists. In keeping with the editors' charge to examine Kuhn's thinking about science in relation to behavior therapy, I will start with this assignment.

Since the publication *The Structure of Scientific Revolutions* in 1962, Kuhn has perhaps been the most influential philosopher for psychologists thinking about the status of their science. Since Kuhn's basic position is well known and has been thoroughly reviewed, criticized, and somewhat revised by Kuhn himself (Kuhn, 1962, 1970, 1977; Lakatos & Musgrave, 1970), I will not set it out in detail here. However, I will point to several aspects of Kuhn's view of science that have clear implications for behavior therapy, particularly in view of its past and present allegiance to a logical-empiricist approach to science.

Kuhn views the practice of science as being constructed largely by virtue of commitments by scientists to certain ways of viewing the world, which he calls "paradigms." The role of commitment in Kuhn's view is extremely important. Once a commitment has been made by a community of scientists to follow a particular paradigm, the whole focus of that community becomes the elaboration of a worldview consistent with the paradigm. Newcomers to the community (e.g., students) are indoctrinated into the ways of viewing the world prescribed by the paradigm by virtue of their education in the profession. They learn to see the world as their mentors do, with both the elaborations and exclusions that their mentors' paradigm permits. Thus, in Kuhn's view, scientific views of the world are constructed by a community rather than being "objective" reflections of what is. Paradigms represent a filter through which the vast complexities of observed and postulated phenomena are sorted and made coherent, understandable, and manageable.

A second important aspect of Kuhn's view is his notion of scientific change. In periods of "normal science," little change occurs in the overall paradigm within which a science is conducted. Research is focused on fortifying the existing paradigm. Unfortunately for paradigms, in addition to data that fortify the existing view, normal scientific activities accumulate what Kuhn calls "anomalies," findings that seem to be inexplicable within the existing paradigm. Some anomalies become assimilated through minor modifications in the paradigm, some are simply excluded from consideration as being irrelevant (as internal processes were by radical behaviorists [Zuriff, 1985]), while others fester unexplained. At some unspecifiable point, enough of these unexplained anomalies accumulate that the paradigm has to confront them. It is not clear from Kuhn's writings when or how this critical point is reached, but he does note that it is characterized by a growing turn to philosophy to guide the progress of the science and a search by some members of the paradigm community for better alternatives. Once this process starts, a revolution is in progress and a new world view begins to appear.

Contrary to logical-positivist and logical-empiricist views of science as a progressive accumulation of new facts and a consequent revision of our theories to accommodate them, in Kuhn's view science progresses in fits and starts, with long periods of doctrinaire defense of established viewpoints. If Kuhn's view is correct (and many believe it is not; see Lakatos & Musgrave, 1970), then one might liken the behavior of the scientific community in the face of research anomalies to that of a phobic patient in the face of a phobic stimulus—avoidance of confrontation, with consequent failure to change. Thus, while Kuhn's view is consistent with the observations behavior therapists have made of their patients' resistance to change, it is not consistent with the logical-empiricist view of science. Perhaps consistency requires a reexamination of that view and behavior therapy's movement into the realm of later 20th-century philosophy of science. As Toulmin and Leary (1985) point out, philosophers of science have long since abandoned the logical-positivist and logical-empiricist positions as untenable.

The newer philosophies of science try to avoid what Toulmin and Leary (1985) call the "cult of empiricism," which places observational sensory data at the pinnacle of scientific epistemology. The empiricists attempted to follow Newton's maxim *hypotheses non fingo* to its utmost. As reflected in American psychology, this position required the elimination of theorizing about causes and process, and a focus on correlating observable data into systematic theories of behavior whose main foci were prediction and control, not understanding (Zuriff, 1985). According to this behavioristic perspective, all theoretical language must be firmly rooted in observables or otherwise be held meaningless. Nonobservable theoretical entities are to be avoided. This sort of position led the behaviorists, and positivists such as Popper (1959), to make the strategic decision to deny that there was any reason for science to consider phenomena not directly observable or somehow linkable to observables. Likewise, one was not being scientific in one's theories if the postulated theoretical terms could not be subjected to empirical test, especially through a process of falsification (Popper, 1959). One result of this position was that most early behaviorists were unwilling even to postulate the existence of anything beyond what could be fitted into an empirical framework and studied experimentally. The cognitive revolution, first in experimental psychology and later in behavior therapy, brought about a questioning of this view by many behavior therapists (Mahoney, 1974, 1980; Meichenbaum, 1977). The endorsement of a strictly empirical correspondence principle for theoretical terms (Zuriff, 1985), in which every theoretical term had to be directly linked to an observable entity, began to be questioned, if not abandoned, by most cognitive behavior therapists.

In contrast to this logical-empiricist and (in psychology) behavioristic position is that of scientific realism (Manicas & Secord, 1983; Churchland & Hooker, 1985). Realism espouses both different goals for science and admits different language in theories. In addition, while the positivists attempted to make the case that observation should be theory-independent and based strictly on sense data, realistic philosophers specifically espouse the view that all observations are, by necessity, theory-dependent (see Mahoney, 1974, 1976; Kuhn, 1962, 1970; Laudan, 1984; Guidano & Liotti, 1983). Thus realists are willing to admit as scientific theories that include speculations about underlying processes: "the realist is willing to extend belief beyond observables, the nonrealist insists on confining belief within that domain" (Churchland, 1985, p. 41). Further, from a realist philosophical perspective, scientific legitimacy does not necessarily reside in empirical verifiability. Thus,

> the meaning of a reality-statement is by no means exhausted in mere assertions of the form "Under these circumstances this particular experience will occur" . . . : the meaning, he says, in fact lies beyond this in something else, which must be referred to, say, as "independent existence," "transcendent being," or the like, and of which our principle (the verification principle) provides no account. (Schlick, cited in Hanflung, 1981, pp. 55–56)

In addition, the realist and empiricist positions represent different views of the aims of science. In this regard, Ellis (1985) maintains that "science aims to provide the best possible explanatory account of natural phenomena" (p. 51). Thus, based on a belief in a world beyond observables, the realist is interested in explanation and understanding of underlying structures and processes rather than "merely" prediction and control.

Manicas and Secord (1983) have recently argued that adoption of one form of realist philosophy of science, transcendental realism (Bhaskar, 1978), in place of psychology's traditional reliance upon some version of positivism or empiricism, makes sense in terms of the subject matter of psychology and, it follows, behavior therapy as a subset of psychology. This subject matter includes not only behaviors, but people's interpretations of the world, social contexts, and the influences the latter have upon behavior. Behavior is viewed as an open rather than closed system. Thus, to capture the complexity of human behavior, they argue, one must be willing to look inside the organism, beyond the observables, and to place the organism in its social context. Likewise, scientists themselves must recognize the influence that theories have upon both the type of data gathered and how that data is interpreted (see Scarr, 1985, for a convincing demonstration of the potential effects of this process). The main difficulty with Manicas and Secord's view emerges when their realism is extended to the question of what the "real" phenomena are that psychology should study. What is it that lies beyond the observable or measurable factors that are currently the focus of psychological thinking?

Certainly the realist perspective on science is very different from the one that has been accepted by behavior therapists for many years. However, the emergence of cognitive and social-learning points of view would seem to indicate a shift in the style of theorizing that behavior therapists are willing to undertake. While social-learning theory in particular still attempts to anchor theoretical terms in some form of observables, the nature of these observables has been shifted to systematic reports by individuals of their internal states (e.g., self-efficacy expectations), a class of observables traditionally viewed with skepticism by behaviorists (Zuriff, 1985). This may represent a step toward acknowledging the existence of unobservable processes that nonetheless can be "measured," given careful controls. Certainly the admission of theoretical concepts such as "self-efficacy" would be unheard of within a strictly logical-empiricist perspective. While behaviorists have traditionally admitted intervening variables (e.g., Tolman, 1932; Zuriff, 1985) into their theoretical discussions, Bandura's "self-efficacy" seems to contain much broader connotations than do previously admitted intervening variables, such as "drive," or "discriminative stimulus." The use of this concept almost demands some explication of the mechanisms by which self-efficacy expectations exert their influences and how they come about. Perhaps a move toward a realist philosophy of science would be useful to behavior therapy in expanding the ability of therapists and researchers to openly and consistently acknowledge such internal processes as beliefs, attitudes, and emotional states as having potentially casual significance for behavior. The key question to be answered before such a shift is contemplated is whether the behavior therapist's effectiveness with a broad range of behavioral problems would or would not be enhanced by adopting such a position. *A priori* this question is, of course, unanswerable.

The realist position advocated by Manicas and Secord is consistent with a growing trend in psychology (see Koch & Leary, 1983; Gergen, 1982, 1985a, 1985b; Faulconer & Williams, 1985; Toulmin & Leary,

1985) toward an open effort to shift its philosophical allegiance away from positivism and empiricism to a more wide ranging philosophy that, in the view of its proponents, better accommodates the sort of data that comprise human behavior. One major focus in this effort seems to arise directly from Kuhn's (1962, 1970) view that science is a sociological and communal phenomenon. The movement toward explicit acknowledgment and use of this perspective is probably best exemplified by the work of Gergen (1982, 1985a, 1985b). Calling his approach "social constructionism," Gergen has combined elements of hermeneutic and other antipositivist philosophies into what he labels a "sociorationalist" perspective. Like realism, Gergen's approach acknowledges the influence of theory on the data one gathers. He is also willing to acknowledge unobservable processes. However, Gergen goes further still and openly acknowledges the role of moral values in the practice of science, thus challenging traditional criteria for demarcating science from other disciplines of thought. He further challenges the necessity of making scientific theories beholden to observations, citing the difficulty in determining what any particular observed event really means (Gergen, 1982, 1985a, 1985b).

Stated rather simply, Gergen's approach has four main tenets (Gergen, 1985a):

1. There is a reduction in the faith placed in observation and a questioning of the "objective basis of conventional knowledge" (p. 267).
2. The terms in which people (and scientists) express their understanding of the world are seen as "social artifacts, products of historically situated interchanges among people" (p. 267).
3. Theories of the world prevail not as a result of empirical support, but depend "on the vicissitudes of social processes (e.g., communication, negotiation, conflict, rhetoric)" (p. 268).
4. The form that our theories take is itself a political and social statement that "serve[s] to sustain and support certain patterns to the exclusion of others" (p. 268), thus shaping in a reciprocal fashion how we construe our world.

Social constructionism, Gergen acknowledges, has the potential to plunge its adherents into rampant relativism. He proposes to avoid this possibility, however, by drawing on hermeneutic methods to assess the accuracy of any interpretation of behavior and/or social interaction. (The word *interpretation* is used intentionally here to indicate that what is gleaned from hermeneutic methods is neither explanation, prediction, nor control. Rather, it is understanding of the phenomena and individuals in question within a historical context.) Different hermeneutic authors have proposed various criteria for determining the correctness of interpretations (see Thompson, 1981; Skinner, 1985), all of which have been criticized by other writers. Unlike the radical behaviorists, however, Gergen does not advocate the elimination of nonempirical and metaphysical ideas from consideration because of a fear that such ideas may be misused and degenerate into speculation and skepticism (Zuriff, 1985). Rather, Gergen places faith in the power of rational persons to set the guidelines by which knowledge will be accumulated and then adhere to them. His main thrust in this endeavor (along with other philosophers such as Feyerabend [1975] and Bartley [1962]) is to acknowledge and put trust in critical rationalism as a check against metaphysical excesses. Gergen tries to keep an open mind about the adequacy of empirical and experimental methods for studying human behavior.

From the standpoint of social-learning theory, what does seem interesting to behavior therapists in Gergen's position is his explicit and heavy reliance on cognition as a determinant of human behavior. Thus, "human action is critically dependent upon cognitive processing of information, that is on the world as cognized, rather than the world as it is" (p. 269). This position is clearly parallel to the positions held by Kuhn and some scientific realists; it is certainly consistent with the writings of recent behavior therapists that focus on behavior therapy's place in modern society and how being a product of that society influences behavioral practice and values (e.g., Krasner & Houts, 1984; Woolfolk & Richardson, 1984).

By now, the reader has probably noticed a common thread that seems to run throughout the philosophical positions I have been describing. This thread might be characterized as (1) a reaction against positivist and solely empirical approaches to the study of human behavior; (2) a greater reliance on social processes in determining what is to be included within the scientific domain; (3) a correspondingly greater emphasis on cognitive processes as causal determinants of scientific knowledge and human behavior, as well as an explicit acknowledgment of unobserved processes as causal factors; and (4) a movement away from a reliance on rationalism (as exemplified by empiricism and experimental methodology) alone to provide adequate explanations of behavior, with a corresponding shift in the emphasis of science from prediction and control to explanation and understanding. In all, these positions seem to represent a movement away from those philosophical values that behaviorally oriented psychologists (Kimble, 1984; Krasner & Houts, 1984) hold dear. Nonetheless, they also seem to reflect a trend in philosophy of science that parallels the "cognitive revolution" in psychology and behavior therapy. Does this mean that behavior therapists must revise their views of the world in order to be consistent if they wish to evoke cognition as a causal process? Perhaps, but not necessarily. I will next review a recent attempt by Bas Van Fraassen (1980, 1985) to salvage an empiricist epistemology, an attempt that seems to have received little attention in the psychological and behavioral literatures but that may provide a means for retaining some of our more successful philosophical assumptions while still keeping pace with the sort of advances represented by social-learning theory.

In his major work, *The Scientific Image* (1980), and later in response to a series of challenging essays by scientific realists (Churchland & Hooker, 1985), Van Fraassen sets forth a revision of logical empiricism that he calls "constructive empiricism." Formulated mainly in response to criticisms by scientific realists of the logical-positivist and logical-empiricist approaches to science, constructive empiricism represents an attempt to salvage empiricism as a means to scientific knowledge and a revision of the concept of what scientific theories must be in order to be useful.

Three brief quotations from Van Fraassen hold the gist of constructive empiricism for behavior therapists. All appear early in *The Scientific Image.*

> Empiricism requires theories only to give a true account *of what is observable*, counting further postulated structure as a means to that end. (p. 3)

> Correlative of discussions of the relation between a theory and the world, is the question what it is to accept a scientific theory. This question has an *epistemic dimension* (how much *belief* is involved in theory acceptance?) and also a *pragmatic* one (what else is involved besides belief?). On the view that I shall develop, the belief involved in accepting a scientific theory is only that it "saves the phenomena," that is, correctly describes what is observable. (p. 4, emphasis added)

> I use the adjective "constructive" to indicate my view that scientific activity is one of construction rather than discovery; construction of models that must be adequate to the phenomena, and not discovery of truth concerning the unobservable. (p. 5)

Based on these quotations, it is possible to see Van Fraassen's position as one that is likely to evoke a sympathetic ear from behavior therapists, particularly those who are willing to acknowledge a causal role for cognition, as are social-learning theorists. Van Fraassen proposes that we admit unobservables to our thinking, but only if they are firmly tied to empirical findings. In an important step away from the realist position, Van Fraassen permits the postulation of unobservables only as a means toward building more adequate models of observable phenomena.

Van Fraassen admits the possibility of several theories being empirically adequate, yet different in content. Further testing will, accordingly to his view, reveal which theory better "saves the phenomena," thus giving us a guide for choosing which theory to adhere to and deciding which theory is most likely to lead to a productive research program (Lakatos, 1970).

Furthermore, Van Fraassen places an implicit trust in the individual theoretician to avoid postulating true or "existent" structures beyond what aids in developing better models of the observable world and beyond what can be tied in some clear, observable way to empirical facts. This position is not unlike psychological empiricism and behaviorists' reaction to intervening variables and hypothetical constructs (Zuriff, 1985). It does not demand that one believe in a theory as being a true description of some "real (but partly unobservable) world," but rather that adherence to a theoretical framework be consistent with empirical findings.

Later on in *The Scientific Image*, Van Fraassen gives an account of the role of theory acceptance in scientific enterprises that is not radically different from Gergen's social constructionism or Kuhn's (1980) view of paradigms: "Once the theory is accepted . . . it guides our language use in a certain way. The language we use at that point has a logical structure which derives from the theories we accept" (p. 199). This statement might be interpreted as implying that observation and theory provide feedback to each other, further shaping the world we observe and then contributing to our theories about that observed world. This position is quite different from the logical empiricist's view of the theory-independence of observation (Hanflung, 1981; Zuriff, 1985).

Van Fraassen further holds that acceptance of a theory involves certain commitments scientifically. The main commitment is the responsibility to confront any observable phenomena that fall within the conceptual parameters of that theory. Thus Van Fraassen would probably disagree with Kuhn's view of normal science as being in any way desirable, but rather would hold scientists to stricter values of looking for anomalies and attempting to accommodate them within one's theories. Like Feyerabend (1975), Van Fraassen does not commit the theoretician to addressing any *a priori* prescribed concepts in a theory, only to confronting anything that falls within the theory's purview. This provides both a wide latitude for acceptable theorizing and strict guidelines for both the form a theory should take and how it is to be tested.

Finally, in summing up his position, Van Fraassen makes a statement containing many points that are consistent with Gergen's (1985) social constructionist view, yet which seem to avoid Gergen's willingness to abandon empirical methods as largely fruitless (1985):

> To be an empiricist is to withhold belief in anything that goes beyond the actual, observable phenomena, and to recognize no objective modality in nature. To develop an empiricist account of science is to depict it as involving a search for truth only about the empirical world, about what is actual and observable. Since scientific activity is an enormously rich and complex cultural phenomenon, this account of science must be accompanied by auxiliary theories about scientific explanation, conceptual commitment, modal language, and much else. But it must involve throughout a resolute rejection of the demand for an explanation of the regularities in the observable course of nature, by means of truths concerning a reality beyond what is actual and observable, as a demand which plays no role in the scientific enterprise. (pp. 202–203)

It should be clear from this brief presentation of alternative philosophies of science that there is a wide range from which to choose. Which of these, if any, should behavior therapy choose to follow? Upon what criteria should behavior therapists base such a choice? What effects would a change in the philosophical underpinnings of behavior therapy be likely to have on behavior therapy's future as an identifiable entity? Can behavior therapy function with only one philosophy of science for both research and applied endeavors? I will address these questions below.

The Identity of Behavior Therapy

As noted at the beginning of this chapter, behavior therapy has been one of the most successful branches of clinical psychology in establishing the effectiveness of its techniques in changing a variety of problem behaviors (Rachman & Wilson, 1980). Nonetheless, the research evidence also suggests that, when it comes to more complex constellations of behaviors (e.g., those characterized as "personality disorders" in DSM-III), behavior therapy has not been demonstrably more effective than other treatment strategies. One of the main questions facing behavior therapy now is how the field can begin to address these more complex behavioral disorders in an effective way.

Another question facing behavior therapy, particularly in view of the AABT's definition of behavior therapy as relying upon experimental research for both treatment techniques and as a means to evaluate the effectiveness of those techniques, is the question how to address the growing experimental literature that appears to be therapeutically relevant, but theoretically antithetical to many of the basic tenets of behaviorism. For example, psychodynamically oriented theorists have begun to apply experimental methodology to the testing of psychodynamically derived hypotheses about the roles of certain nonobservable, "unconscious" processes, utilizing methodology that is apparently based on the controlled experimental method that characterizes good behavioral research. Thus, Pennebaker and his colleagues (Pennebaker & Beall, 1986; Pennebaker & O'Heeron, 1984) have examined the long-term effects of revealing inner secrets to others, while Silverman (Silverman & Weinberger, 1985) has reported on an extensive research program to assess the efficacy of psychoanalytically derived subliminal stimulation in enhancing the effects of psychotherapeutic treatments, including behavioral approaches. No matter how experimental the methodology, most behavior therapists would be reluctant to incorporate the findings of these research programs into the domain of behavior therapy. Yet here are two lines of experimental research that have produced promising, if not conclusive, results. How is behavior therapy to confront these results within its current positivistic framework?

A third question concerns how behavior therapy is to deal with therapeutic failures. While two recent works have brought this issue to the forefront (Foa & Emmelkamp, 1983; Barbrack, 1985), the behavior therapy literature (like the psychological literature in general [Mahoney, 1976, 1985]) has traditionally failed to publish negative or disconfirmatory results. While the early proponents of behavior therapy as a revolt against psychoanalytic orthodoxy (Krasner, Chapter 3, this volume) might have been justified in overstating their case for the efficacy of behavioral techniques, the field is now established. How are we to confront our failures? Can they be confronted within our existing paradigm and without threatening the identity of behavior therapy as an autonomous field within clinical psychology? Certainly, the movement toward unification of psychodynamic and behavioral approaches (e.g., Goldfried, 1982; Wachtel, 1977) suggests that many behavior therapists and psychodynamicists are reacting to their respective failures by looking for underlying bases for unification of the approaches. While many on both sides believe such unification is impossible (see Messer & Winokur, 1980; Franks, 1984), the fact that the debate has occurred at all should raise questions for behavior therapists.

Finally, there is the question of the sociopolitical forces that impinge upon behavior therapists and how we are to respond to them from our particular perspective (Fishman & Neigher, 1982; Fishman, Chapter 11, this volume). With the advent of such funding controls as Diagnosis-Related Grouping (DRGs) and the increased demand by funding sources for accountability, behavior therapists find themselves in an advantageous position with regard to their success with certain behavioral disorders, but in the same boat as other theoretical approaches with regard to others. What effects will these factors have on behavior therapy's identity as a unique approach to behavior change? These questions form the backdrop for the remainder of my discussion.

Howard (1985) notes that there exists a conflict between the values that underlie theory acceptance in theoretical, as opposed to practical, sciences. In theoretical sciences, theory acceptance is a function of the degree of empirical support that exists for a given theory and the fruitfulness of that theory in generating research. In practical sciences, in contrast, theory acceptance occurs as a function of the importance of error in application of the theory. Thus the values of utility, ease of application, and minimization of risk of negative outcomes are much more salient in the practical (read "clinical") sciences than in purely research endeavors. As behavior therapy purports to be simultaneously a theoretical and a practical science, it would seem that we need a set of philosophical assumptions that can guide us in both areas of practice.

The approaches to science outlined above would seem to meet the criterion to varying degrees. This criterion is a rather conservative one that would seem to dictate against behavior therapy's adopting a set of assumptions that encourage or promote the risk of speculation and unproven practice that could lead to errors in application. We must find a set of principles that both acknowledges the tentativeness of the theory–observation link (Gergen, 1985; Howard, 1985; Scarr, 1985) and promotes strong efforts toward developing theories that work in practice.

The philosophies outlined first in the preceding discussion (e.g., Kuhn's paradigmatic view, scientific realism, and social constructionism) all represent an acknowledgment that reality is socially constructed to some degree. They all, therefore, adopt a rather tentative view of the degree of confidence one can place in any view about human behavior. Yet these approaches all leave open the question of what sort of approach to studying human behavior is most likely to be useful and progressive in Lakatos's sense of a progressive research program (Lakatos, 1970). While prompting us to adopt a different view of how psychology should function, they are all rather vague about how this new functional stance is to be attained. The best that can be suggested seems to be a resort to some sort of hermeneutic methodology, which, as noted previously, is very much open to questions about the criteria by which one is to judge the outcome of an interpretive effort and how that effort is, in fact, to be achieved when the text one is studying in human behavior. Thus, while these approaches are clearly based upon dissatisfaction with positivistic empiricism as a means of understanding behavior, they provide little in the way of alternatives that could be construed as scientific. In fact, the thrust of these approaches is toward acknowledging what their proponents view as the bankruptcy and failure of empirical psychology, and away from the positivistic goal of developing a science of human behavior. It is not clear, however, that the latter goal is unattainable, just that we have not yet attained it using present approaches. Certainly the radical-behaviorist program of prediction and control based on utilization of principles derived from laws of behavior has not been realized. But does this means that there are no reliable laws of behavior? Does it mean that a scientific attempt to understand behavior must continue to be fruitless? It is fruitless only if we continue to accept the positivistic program unchanged.

Perhaps, as its critics have maintained, empirical behavioral science misjudged the applicability of a positivistic view of science to human behavior. If so, then perhaps what is needed is not to abandon science altogether, but to look beyond positivism and scientific method for ways of improving our discipline. It is my contention that the approaches represented by social-learning theory and constructive empiricism provide a vehicle for doing just that.

As a guiding philosophy, constructive empiricism has several advantages for behavior therapists. First, it continues the emphasis on linking theoretical terms to observable or measurable entities wherever possible. However, constructive empiricism does not require of theories that they be falsifiable or that they be subject to experimental test, only that they be consistent with observable phenomena and that they be testable in some way that is empirical. This leaves the choice of empirical methodology open to the individual researcher and allows accommodation of the variety of research entities that Fishman (Chapter 11, this volume) advocates. Further, constructive empiricism contains the explicit requirement that, when two theories appear to be equally supported by observable facts, there must be additional efforts to differentiate them, carried out by devising a variety of empirical tests that extend the theories beyond their current coverage into broader areas where empirical adequacies can be compared. Likewise, when observations that belong the set of phenomena a theory purports to describe appear anomalous, the theoretician is obliged to confront them rather than denying their existence or dismissing them as epiphenomenal. This requirement serves as a twofold safeguard against the excesses of a positivistic behaviorism. First, it prevents the promulgation of metaphysical theories based on postulated but unobserved, unobservable, and unmeasurable phenomena and processes that the positivists fear would dilute science into meaninglessness. This is accomplished, however, without excluding phenomena from consideration as long as they can be linked in some way to observables. Second, it forces the theoretician to confront phenomena that are observed and covered by the theory. Thus, self-reports of intentional states, for example, must be confronted by theories that purport to explain human behavior or behavior change. They cannot be dismissed—as has been the case with such phenomena when encountered by many behavioristic theorists. If both a behavioristic, external analysis of behavior and a cognitively based internal analysis have adequate empirical support, then constructive empiricism requires that both views be included as part of the corpus of scientific theory. However, both would then be subjected to further test, because, as Van Fraassen (1980) asserts, no two competing theories are ever completely empirically adequate. If two theories appear to be so, it is because we have not tested them enough or our measurement techniques are inadequate. This prompts further progress in terms of either more extensive testing or the development of methodology—without postulating unobservable underlying processes or abandoning the search for behavioral regularities and laws.

Construed according to the preceding framework, social-learning theory seems to conform well to the tenets of constructive empiricism. By constructing a theory in which unobservable events (e.g., cognitive judgments of self-efficacy) were postulated as causal of behavioral performance, and then developing an observable way of assessing these events and tying them to observable behaviors, Bandura has produced a significant advance in our understanding of the process of behavior change and a means for predicting behavioral performances.

In practical or applied settings, constructive empiricism also provides a reasonable set of guiding assumptions. By keeping our thinking about the process of behavior change tied to observables, but not totally prohibiting consideration of the role of nonobservable intraorganismic events in producing behavior, constructive empiricism allows for the possible accommodation of such findings as Silverman's and Weinberger's (1985), providing we can discern a clear link with measurable observable phenomena. By adopting constructive empiricism as a guide, behavior therapists could remain theoretically and philosophically consistent, while gaining the flexibility to explore and use new therapeutic techniques, that, while not specifically behavioral in origin, have been demonstrated to be empirically adequate and effective. This is exactly what Lazarus (1981) has advocated, but with a much less clearly stated philosophical and theoretical basis than that provided by constructive empiricism.

The flexibility of constructive empiricism, combined with its rigorous requirements for theoretical testing and modification in the face of anomalies, would address the questions raised at the beginning of this chapter in a much more consistent fashion. In fact, constructive empiricism would mandate that these questions be addressed. Failures represent anomalies that fall within the purview of our theories. We would have to address them not haphazardly, as has been the case until recently, but systematically and in such a way that our thinking about the process of behavior change would be enhanced.

Finally, behavior therapy would preserve the major defining characteristic that separates it from other approaches—its clear demand that techniques and theoretical views be rigorously and empirically tested and evaluated. In constructive-empiricist terms, a technique's level of success can be construed as representing its empirical adequacy. Behavior therapy would be able to preserve the rigor of its science while not arbitrarily excluding potentially useful phenomena from consideration. The demands upon adherents to behavior therapy would be great (we would have to begin consideration of a much broader range of literature), but the prospects for growth in our ability to treat a variety of behavior problems and to pursue a continued scientific effort to evaluate our techniques and understand what makes them work, or not work, would seem to be endless.

References

Bandura, A. (1969). *Principles of behavior modification.* New York: Holt, Rinehart & Winston.

Bandura, A. (1977). *Social learning theory.* Englewood Cliffs, NJ: Prentice-Hall.

Bandura, A. (1982). Self mechanism in human agency. *American Psychologist, 37,* 122–147.

Bandura, A., & Walters, R.H. (1963). *Social learning and personality development.* New York: Holt, Rinehart & Winston.

Barbrack, C.R. (1985). Negative outcome in behavior therapy. In D.T. Mays & C.M. Franks (Eds.), *Negative outcome in psychotherapy and what to do about it* (pp. 76–105). New York: Springer.

Barlow, D.H. (1981). On the relationship of clinical research to clinical practice: Current issues, new directions. *Journal of Consulting and Clinical Psychology, 49*, 147–155.

Barlow, D.H., Hayes, S., & Nelson, R.M. (1983). *The empirical clinician.* New York: Pergamon.

Bartley, W.W. (1962). *The retreat to commitment.* New York: Knopf.

Bhaskar, R. (1978). *The possibility of naturalism.* Brighton: Harvester Press.

Churchland, P.M. (1985). The ontological status of observables: In praise of the superempirical virtues. In P.M. Churchland & C.A. Hooker (Eds.), *Images of Science* (pp. 35–47). Chicago: University of Chicago Press.

Churchland, P.M., & Hooker, C.A. (Eds.). *Images of science* (pp. 35–47). Chicago: University of Chicago Press.

Ellis, B. (1985). What science aims to do. In P.M. Churchland & C.A. Hooker (Eds.), *Images of science* (pp. 48–74). Chicago: University of Chicago Press.

Erwin, E. (1978). *Behavior therapy: Scientific, philosophical and moral foundations.* New York: Cambridge University Press.

Faulconer, J.E., & Williams, R.N. (1985). Temporality in human action: An alternative to positivism and historicism. *American Psychologist, 40*, 1179–1188.

Feyerabend, P. (1975). *Against method: Outline of an anarchistic theory of knowledge.* London: Verso.

Fishman, D.B., & Neigher, W.D. (1982). American psychology in the eighties: Who will buy? *American Psychologist, 37*, 533–546.

Foa, E., & Emmelkamp, P.M.G. (Eds.). (1983). *Failures in behavior therapy.* New York: Wiley.

Franks, C.M. (1984). On conceptual and technical integrity in psychoanalysis and behavior therapy, two fundamentally incompatible systems. In H. Arkowitz & S. Messer (Eds.), *Psychoanalysis and behavior therapy: Are they compatible?* (pp. 223–247). New York: Plenum.

Franks, C.M., & Barbrack, C.R. (1983). Behavior therapy with adults: An integrative perspective. In M. Hersen, A.E. Kazdin, & A.S. Bellack (Eds.), *The clinical psychology handbook* (pp. 507–524). New York: Pergamon.

Franks, C.M., & Wilson, G.T. (1975). *Annual review of behavior therapy* (Vol. 3). New York: Brunner/Mazel.

Gergen, K.J. (1982). *Toward transformation in social knowledge.* New York: Springer-Verlag.

Gergen, K.J. (1985a). The social constructionist movement in modern psychology. *American Psychologist, 40*, 266–275.

Gergen, K.J. (1985b). Social psychology and the phoenix of unreality. In S. Koch & D.E. Leary (Eds.), *A century of psychology as science* (pp. 528–557). New York: McGraw-Hill.

Goldfried, M.R. (Ed.). (1982). *Converging themes in psychotherapy.* New York: Springer.

Guidano, V.F., & Liotti, G. (1983). *Cognitive processes and emotional disorders.* New York: Guilford.

Hanflung, O. (1981). *Logical positivism.* New York: Columbia University Press.

Howard, G.S. (1985). The role of values in the science of psychology. *American Psychologist, 40*, 255–265.

Kimble, G.A. (1984). Psychology's two cultures. *American Psychologist, 39*, 833–839.

Koch, S. (1981). The nature and limits of psychological knowledge: Lessons of a century qua "science." *American Psychologist, 36*, 257–269.

Koch, S., & Leary, D.E. (Eds.). (1985). *A century of psychology as a science.* New York: McGraw-Hill.

Krasner, L. (1983). Behavior therapy: On roots, contexts and growth. In G.T. Wilson & C.M. Franks (Eds.), *Contemporary behavior therapy: Conceptual and empirical foundstions* (pp. 11–64). New York: Guilford.

Krasner, L., & Houts, A.C. (1984). A study of the "value" systems of behavioral scientists. *American Psychologist, 39*, 840–850.

Kuhn, T.S. (1962). *The structure of scientific revolutions.* Chicago: University of Chicago Press.

Kuhn, T.S. (1970). *The structure of scientific revolutions* (2nd ed.). Chicago: University of Chicago Press.

Kuhn, T.S. (1977). *The esential tension: Selected studies in scientific tradition and change.* Chicago: University of Chicago Press.

Lakatos, I. (1970). Falsification and the methodology of scientific research programmes. In I. Lakatos & A. Musgrave (Eds.), *Criticism and the growth of knowledge* (pp. 91–196). New York: Cambridge University Press.

Lakatos, I., & Musgrave, A. (1970). *Criticism and the growth of knowledge.* New York: Cambridge University Press.

Laudan, L. (1984). *Science and values: The aims of science and their role in scientific debate.* Berkeley: University of California Press.

Lazarus, A.A. (1981). *The practice of multimodal therapy.* New York: McGraw-Hill.

Mahoney, M.J. (1974). *Cognition and behavior modification.* Cambridge, MA: Ballinger.

Mahoney, M.J. (1976). *Scientist as subject: The psychological imperative.* Cambridge, MA: Ballinger.

Mahoney, M.J. (Ed.). (1980). *Psychotherapy process: Current issues and future directions.* New York: Plenum.

Mahoney, M.J. (1985). Open exchange and epistemic progress. *American Psychologist, 40*, 29–39.

Manicas, P.T., & Secord, P.F. (1983). Implications for psychology of the new philosophy of science. *American Psychologist, 38*, 399–413.

Meichenbaum, D. (1977). *Cognitive-behavior modification: An integrative approach.* New York: Plenum.

Messer, S.B., & Winokur, M. (1980). Some limits to the integration of psychoanalytic and behavior therapy. *American Psychologist, 35*, 818–827.

Neisser, U. (1967). *Cognitive psychology.* New York: Appleton-Century-Crofts.

Pennebaker, J.W., & Beall, S.K. (1986). Confronting a traumatic event: Towards an understanding of inhibition and disease. *Journal of Abnormal Psychology, 95*, 274–281.

Pennebaker, J.W., & O'Heeron, R.C. (1984). Confiding in others and illness rates among spouses of suicide and accidental death victims. *Journal of Abnormal Psychology, 93*, 473–476.

Popper, K.R. (1959). *The logic of scientific discovery.* New York: Harper & Row.

Rachman, S.R., & Wilson, G.T. (1980). *The effects of psychological therapy.* New York: Pergamon.

Scarr, S. (1985). Constructing psychology: Making facts and fables for our times. *American Psychologist, 40*, 499–512.

Silverman, L.H., & Weinberger, J. (1985). Mommy and I are one: Implications for psychotherapy. *American Psychologist, 40*, 1296–1308.

Skinner, Q. (Ed.). (1985). *The return of grand theory in the human sciences.* New York: Cambridge University Press.

Staats, A.W. (1983). *Psychology's crisis of disunity: Philosophy and method for a unified science.* New York: Praeger.

Thompson, J.B. (1981). *Critical hermeneutics: A study in the thought of Paul Ricoeur and Jürgen Habermas.* New York: Cambridge University Press.

Tolman, E.C. (1932). *Purposive behavior in animals and men.* New York: Century.

Toulmin, S., & Leary, D.E. (1985). The cult of empiricism in psychology, and beyond. In S. Koch & D.E. Leary (Eds.), *A century of psychology as a science.* New York: McGraw-Hill.

Van Fraassen, B.C. (1980). *The scientific image.* Oxford, England: Clarendon Press.

Van Fraassen, B.C. (1985). Empiricism in the philosophy of science. In P.M. Churchland & C.A. Hooker (Eds.), *Images of science* (pp. 245–308). Chicago: University of Chicago Press.

Wachtel. P. (1977). *Psychoanalysis and behavior therapy.* New York: Basic Books.

Wilson, G.T. (1984). Fear reduction and the treatment of anxiety disorders. In C.M. Franks, G.T. Wilson, P.C. Kendall, & K.D. Brownell, *Annual review of behavior therapy* (Vol. 10). New York: Guilford.

Woodward, W.R. (1982). The "discovery" of social behaviorism, and social learning theory, 1870–1980. *American Psychologist, 37*, 396–410.

Woolfolk, R.L., & Richardson, F.C. (1984). Behavior therapy and the ideology of modernity. *American Psychologist, 39*, 777–786.

Zuriff, G.E. (1985). *Behaviorism: A conceptual reconstruction.* New York: Columbia University Press.

10

Paradigmatic Behaviorism, Unified Positivism, and Paradigmatic Behavior Therapy

Arthur W. Staats

Psychology, looking always at the natural sciences as its model, has never understood itself or what it needs to make of itself a compact, organized, consensual, generally meaningful—in a word, *unified*—science and profession. I cannot deal here with all that is involved, but I will begin with one point. Works that have a local, specialized foundation can contribute only local, specialized perspectives. Consensuality, general meaningfulness, and unity of knowledge can come only from very broadly based theory. In my view, with respect to behavior therapy, a paradigm (a constellation of theory, findings, general methodology, and technology—which includes instrumentation, tests, and therapy techniques) must involve several levels of development if it is to be able to relate to, draw upon, and contribute to the rich knowledge of psychology. First, the paradigm must have a philosophy of science that provides the foundation for the development of the theory. Second, within that philosophy, a general theory must be constructed that deals with the major fields of psychology. Finally, the behavior therapy approach must be constructed within that theory, in a closely linked manner so the approach is capable of accessing new developments in the general theory and contributing its own new developments in return. Without that type of construction, the field of behavior therapy is doomed to be composed of local efforts—separated, inconsistent, competitive, with narrow limits for growth.

It is my purpose in this chapter to indicate something about these three components of the approach I have been working on for more than three decades. The philosophy has been set forth in greater detail (Staats, 1983a, 1986b, 1987), as has the general theory (Staats, 1963, 1968a, 1971a, 1975, 1981) and the behavior therapy (Evans & Eifert, in press; Leduc, 1984; Staats, 1963, Chapter 11, 1975, Chapters 8 & 9, 1986a, in press; Staats & Fernandez-Ballesteros, in press; Staats & Heiby, 1985).

Developmental Problems of Behavior Therapy

Let me say, in setting a context for this analysis, that psychology has the characteristic of developing new movements of varying generality (Staats, 1983a). They arise in a burst of confidence and they generate great activity in research, organizational matters, and so forth. Ordinarily, they are based upon some conceptual framework, a research or application methodology, and a set of problems in a subarea of psychology. These constituents facilitate the creation of new findings, a capability that constitutes the *raison d'être* for the movement. Such movements in the past, however, have been of a finite nature. Their theories have been local, not general, and have not had the ability to confront the various problems of psychology, even in their field, in a progressively advancing way. Their limitations guarantee that a point is reached where simply repeating the same type of study ceases to be inspiring but, lacking theoretical connection to psychology's other problems, no new directions are provided. At this point, questioning of the basis of the approach begins and interest in advancing the frontiers of the movement dies. Those who remain in its fold do so in a workmanlike way, no longer buoyed by the vision of establishing the general answer to psychology's search for a general paradigm. Psychoanalytic theory has had time to go through these various stages. Contemporary cognitive psychology is still in the stage of heady growth. Behavior therapy (and behavioral psychology in general) has arrived at the point where our first advance has been accomplished, where we have created a vast number of works under the inspiration of our launching framework, but where the present framework provides few new directions. Presently there are signs of stultification and the problems that stultification engenders.

Although there have been questions regarding its definition, historically, behavior therapy was an outgrowth of behaviorism. The first-generation behaviorists before 1930, especially Thorndike and Watson, were interested in conditioning principles in part for their ability to explain human behavior. The second-generation behaviorists after 1930, such as Hull and Skinner, became immersed in their contest to establish *the* dominant animal-learning theory. While each also considered the conditioning principles to apply to human behavior, they were primarily animal-learning psychologists. Although the particulars of historical development might be seen differently from different personal perspectives, it is clear that those of us who launched the new behavioral psychology of the 1950s were all behaviorists. Thus when we explore the nature of behavior therapy, we need to consider its relationship to behaviorism, and this requires an understanding of what behaviorism is.

First, it should be understood that behaviorism is the name of the genre. There have been and are various behaviorisms, produced by different individuals. Hull's (1943) theory was a behaviorism, as was Skinner's (1938), Watson's (1930), Bandura's (1968) early social-learning theory, Staats's (1963, 1975), and so on. They have traditionally been considered to be different theories. What is not so readily understood, in the competitive nature of psychology, is that in central features they are very much alike. In Skinner and Hull's generation they all had the same philosophical basis, that of logical positivism and operationism (although they emphasized different features of this philosophy). They all drew upon the same conditioning principles and the research that established those principles. They all had the same general methodology. For example, they all agreed that principles could be established with animals that applied to humans and that work in the field should be based upon experimentation. Moreover, they all had the same goals, for example, that of creating a general theory that would apply to the behavior of animals and humans. Pavlov, Thorndike, Watson, Skinner, Guthrie, Hull, and Tolman provided the clearest statements of these views. Dollard and Miller, Mowrer, Keller and Schoenfeld, and Osgood projected the second-generation behavioristic structure into additional conceptual analyses. Those various works were available in the early 1950s, and they constituted the knowledge from which some of us in my generation constructed the field of applied human behavioral psychology. It is important to realize that most of the work in behavior therapy derives from and supports each of the past and present behaviorisms—because the work uses only the basic principles, which are common to all. The theories are different, however, as shown by the different types of research and practice they have suggested and the new directions they presently suggest.

Thus the grand old behaviorisms constituted the framework theories that provided specific principles, an experimental orientation, and prototypical procedures that were elaborated and applied by some of us in the 1950s to deal with problems of functional human behavior. But let us realize what was involved; that is, the application of a few behavior principles to a number of specific problems of behavior, with the aim of changing the behavior. This is actually a very restricted framework. There is a limit to the number of studies that can be conducted on behaviors that are, on the one hand, significant, and on the other hand, clearly stipulable and changeable through elementary reinforcement or classical conditioning principles. We have to remember that some of the significance of our first studies that manipulated conditioning variables came not from the importance of the behavior itself, but from the miracle of showing that functional human behavior was learned and was subject to alteration according to laboratory-established principles. In the 1950s this had not been well shown, was in doubt, and had to be proven (see Staats, 1957). After this demonstration has been gained from hundreds of studies, however, it ceases to be significant. The only importance then must come from the significance of the behavior involved and from the efficacy of one's ability to deal with that behavior. While not unimportant, these are very applied problems. As a consequence, contemporary behavioral psychology has changed in its thrust from being a new frontier of scientific development to that of application and applied research. This has brought additional changes, one being the loss of the field's "explanatory" value. Its works no longer deepen our knowledge of human behavior, but only extend the samples of behavior with which we can usefully deal. As part of giving up the goal of explanation, the field has become less closely linked to basic-science endeavors. Thus although behavior therapy sprang from basic-science developments in behaviorism, once the basic principles, procedures, and experimental orientation had been "skimmed off" there appeared to be no need to return to the basic level for fundamental knowledge. This, too, has hastened the shift toward strictly applied concerns and professionalism.

An applied field, even though it has roots in the basic field, loses its appeal to members of the basic field when the applications no longer connect to the contemporary interests of the basic field and vice versa. As the field loses its promise as a general explanatory system and as it centers on application to specific problems and techniques, the field loses the ability to indicate the direction to take in recouping its fundamental quality.

Problems of Adulthood

The developmental approach that has been described implies that the field involved will experience problems in its mature stage. What has been outlined above describes the growing rift that can appear in a field between its basic researchers and applied practitioners. We have much evidence that this has occurred already in the behavioral movement, both in the Association for Advancement of Behavior Therapy (AABT) and in the Association for Behavior Analysis (ABA).

The same is true in terms of theoretical orientation. When the human behavioral movement began in its contemporary form in the 1950s, one of its features was a generic use of behaviorism. In part, this was a rebellion against the theoretical battles of the 1930s and 1940s. While some of us took a Hullian view (see Wolpe, 1958), and others took a Skinnerian view (see Williams, 1959), the partisanship was not strong. Moreover, some efforts purposefully used reinforcement and classical conditioning principles generically (Staats, 1957, 1961, 1963). But that unification dissipated as the behavioral movement became popular. This was fostered by the formation of the ABA and Division 25 of the American Psychological Association. Another tradition became that of social-learning theory and its variations. A less well known orientation, one that has continued to have a unifying goal, has been that of paradigmatic (or social) behaviorism. Additional variations appeared, such as cognitive behavior modification, or were incorporated into the general field, such as rational-emotive therapy. There are now numerous variations, large and small, and many behavior therapists have adopted an eclectic approach in applied behavioral psychology.

Having reached adulthood, the field shows various signs of exhaustion, aimlessness, and stultification. New studies seem to be little more than variations upon those already conducted. There is much seeking of identity and definition, and there is a loss of forward momentum. Many wonder in what direction the field should move. Moreover, the field no longer appears to be making progress in unifying itself with psychology in general. Nonbehavioral psychologists are aware of the value of a behavioral approach in the applied fields. But there is a strong voice that considers the heyday of behaviorism to be over, replaced by what is called cognitive science (for example, Baars, 1984).

Problem Solutions?

Although the malaise has not been systematically studied, I think we could obtain strong consensual agreement that there is trouble of the type that has been described. In response to this malaise, different solutions are being proposed. The next section analyzes some of contemporary psychology's solutions to the types of problems described.

Retreat to Second-Generation Behaviorism

Dissatisfaction with the state of the field can be clearly seen in developments within the radical-behaviorist group. Many feel that their organization (ABA) must separate itself from psychology (Epstein, 1984; Fraley & Vargas, 1986; Leigland, 1984). Fraley and Vargas explicitly indicate that radical behaviorism has failed in its goal of making psychology behavioral and that radical behaviorists cannot hold their own in interaction with "majority" psychologists. The separatist movement represents admission of an inability to deal with most of the knowledge of the field of psychology and the need to withdraw to the protected atmosphere of its own organization (Staats, 1986b). But no solution to the problems of behaviorism or psychology is to be found in retreat and separation.

Retreat to Traditional Psychology and Eclecticism

In the past decade we have also seen the return of a number of behavioral psychologists to the tradition of cognitive psychology. Like the retreat of separation from psychology, this represents a surrender of the formerly held belief that the behavioral approach could deal with the problems of general psychology. As an example, various behavior therapists who once attempted to deal with problems of human behavior within a behavioral framework have since included strictly cognitive principles in their work (see Bandura, 1977, 1978; Mahoney, 1977; Meichenbaum, 1977). Much of this effort utilizes a cognitive methodological approach without behavioral definition and explicitness. Moreover, the cognitive concepts are not closely related to or derived from behavioral principles. Since this movement does not involve the unification of the cognitive concepts with the behavioral principles, the result is an eclecticism. These theories are actually neither fish nor fowl, since they do not really tie into and use the knowledge of cognitive psychology. They gain some popularity by using a popular terminology, but, lacking good, fundamental theory construction, the approach does not provide a solution.

Retreat to Philosophy

In Watson's (1930) original statement of the premises of behaviorism, he rejected the goal of studying ineffable processes of the mind in favor of studying that which was observable, stimuli and responses. This was in harmony with a parallel development in philosophy. The latter, logical positivism, aimed to clear the same questionable conjecturing from philosophy in favor of studying the actual characteristics of science. Early behaviorism had an influence upon the development of logical positivism (Mackenzie, 1977), but by the time of the second generation of behaviorism, it was logical positivism (and the closely related operationism) that exerted strong influence upon behavioristic formulations. Logical positivism focused upon the analysis of science, which was said to consist of (1) the formal realm, having to do with theory, and (2) the empirical realm, having to do with observational matters, especially the observational definition of terms employed in theory. It was said that scientific theory has only one form, that of axiomatic statement. If a theory was to be scientific, it had to be capable of axiomatization, with the logical-mathematical derivation of experimental hypotheses (Suppe, 1977, p. 64). This requires a science that is capable of precise, mathematically ordered observations.

As the theories of the second-generation behaviorists demonstrate, this philosophy has had and does have profound effect upon psychology. For example, Tolman (1932) and Hull (1943) were concerned with the problems of the definition of empirical terms, especially when the events involved were not open to direct observation. Parallels were seen between the definition of electrons in physics and cognitive maps or habit strength in psychology. Spence (1944) was also concerned with the types of empirical definition of terms, as was Skinner, who advocated a methodology of employing only terms that were susceptible to direct observation. Although Skinner's first general work (1938) was stated in the form of the types of propositions demanded by logical positivism, he later rejected concern with the formal (theoretical) realm of study in favor of a simple inductive method (Sidman, 1960; Skinner, 1950). In contrast, at that time Hull (1943) brought the directives of logical positivism to their highest development in behaviorism by the construction of a theory that had the axiomatic-mathematical-deductive form demanded by that philosophy of science.

Thus there was a close use of the developments in the philosophy of science by psychologists during the era of the second-generation behaviorism. But there was little continued development of that philosophical analysis. There was not much to develop, for logical positivism—entranced by the natural sciences—did not illuminate psychology's extensive tasks of theory construction (as will be indicated below). Nevertheless, the body of behavioral psychologists has remained within that philosophy of science, notwithstanding that this philosophy came to be criticized and rejected in its own field.

Alternatively, in recent years other psychologists have attempted to relate their field to nonpositivistic developments in the philosophy of science. For example, Gergen (1973, 1985) and van Hoorn (1972) both reject the influence of logical positivism by contending that psychology is not a natural science, but rather a historical or interpretive science.

A related nonpositivistic position is the view that there are incompatible (incommensurable) theories in science, all of which may be valuable (Feyerabend, 1963, 1970; Kuhn, 1962). Koch (1981) has used such arguments to reject the goal of attempting to construct large-scale theories in psychology, stating that the failure of the behaviorists' theories has proven the futility of the goal.

Interest in applying the philosophy of science to psychology has also developed around the work of Kuhn (1962). Kuhn describes the process of science as the development of paradigms and the clashes between competitive paradigms. Because I have used the terms *paradigmatic* and *pre-paradigmatic* in describing unified and disunified sciences, some have assumed that unified positivism is generally harmonious with Kuhn's analysis. This is not the case. Unified positivism is not relativistic, it does not accept incommensurability as a natural state of scientific knowledge, it does not interpret scientific progress as a series of paradigm clashes, and it does not consider Kuhn's works to provide a general philosophy for psychology. In my view, Kuhn's important contribution was in providing descriptions of the early state of the natural sciences. For unified positivism sees the early natural sciences to have had the same characteristics of disunity that psychology displays today. As I will indicate, such descriptions of early natural science (see also Shapere, 1979; Toulmin, 1972) were very valuable to me, providing one foundation for my concept that all sciences face the task of advancing along a dimension of disunity–unity.

In general, unified positivism takes the position that none of the philosophies of science has fulfilled psychology's needs. As will be indicated, it is necessary to construct a tenable, productive positivistic philosophy stating that behavior can be studied using the general—not the specific—methods of science. Further, however, it is necessary to formulate a philosophy of science that deals with what psychology is, what it should become, and what tasks it must complete to make that transition. Unified positivism asks that the science and profession of psychology be studied from within, directly confronting its problems and generating solutions that are tailored to those problems rather than to those of the natural sciences. The task of constituting a philosophy for psychology is a hands-on job, to be done by those whose work has brought them into contact with a broad sample of psychology. None of the indigenous or adopted philosophies of science that has been applied to psychology fulfill these characteristics. Let us look more specifically at some of the questions raised by these statements.

Unified Positivism: Additional Elements of the Philosophy of Paradigmatic Behaviorism

The Light That Failed

The second-generation behaviorisms of Hull, Skinner, and others were planned as general theories that would apply to all of the problems of psychology. The preface of Hull's 1943 book, for example, says this clearly. Psychology was very taken by the promise of these behaviorists, especially Hull. But the promise was never fulfilled, and disillusion took its place (see Koch, 1981, for a vivid description of this disappointment). The consequence of that disillusion for much of psychology was the rejection of everything that was involved in that behavioristic period—the specific theories, their approach of establishing general theory by studying animal learning and extrapolating the principles, and the philosophical underpinnings of the approach, that is, logical positivism and operationism.

Moreover, parallel to this occurrence, logical positivism came under critical review within the philosophy of science. Logical positivism, during its heyday considered the "received view," was criticized, called into question, and then rejected by influential philosophers, as were theories that were based upon logical positivism and operationism (Suppe, 1977):

> It seems to be characteristic, but unfortunate, of science to continue holding philosophical positions long after they are discredited. Thus. for example, Skinner's radical behaviorism, which insists on operational definition, came into prominence and dominated behavioral psychology well after most philosophers had abandoned the doctrine of operational or explicit definition. (p. 19)

It is not possible to present a detailed critique of logical positivism and operationism here (see Staats, 1983a), but some of the points of criticism will be referred to in the process of describing the present philosophy of unified positivism.

Objective Observations: Ultimate Truth or the Progressive Principle?

Logical positivism is based upon two major assumptions: "(1) there is an external world independent of human experience, and (2) objective knowledge about this world can be obtained through direct sense experience" (Fishman, 1985, p. 5). For logical positivism, observations are the ultimate truths upon which scientists can come to agreement because observations are objective. However, this sacrosanct nature of observations has been challenged. "It became clear that facts are not even facts, at least as the final anchoring bastion of authority, uncontaminated by theory influences (Feyerabend, 1970; Hanson, 1969; Kuhn, 1962; Lakatos, 1970; Popper, 1963)" (Staats, 1983a, p. 28). Lakatos's example (1970, p. 98) is that of Galileo's telescope: why accept its observations without having a theory of optics? Lacking such theory, why would we give a telescope more authority than a kaleidoscope? The observations made by the scientist are selective and guided by theory, thus not simply objective. We can see that what one psychologist takes as truth-revealing observations are considered unimportant by another, with each position being determined by theoretical orientation. Competitive approaches in psychology are distinguished by their realms of observation, and this is a theory-directed, not an empirically derived, difference.

The criticism of logical positivism's view that "pure" observation yields the ultimate truth has had various byproducts. Most importantly, the criticism has had the effect in psychology of undermining the credibility of observation as the basic method of science. Couple this with the failure of the behavioristic theories, based upon logical positivism, to provide a continuing avenue of development for psychology, and what has emerged has been a rejection of the natural science model (Weimer, 1979). Van Hoorn (1972), for example, has said that psychology is not a natural science but an interpretive science in the hermaneutic mold. Gergen (1973) considers psychology to be a historical science rather than a natural science. The social-constructionist position is that different viewers see different things (Scarr, 1985, pp. 499–500) and that the basis of scientific views is an "artifact of communal interchange" (Gergen, 1985, p. 266). (The weakness of behaviorism's philosophical foundation has been one of the reasons our approach has been rejected and cognitivism has become ascendant.)

In contrast, the present unified-positivist view is that such philosophical positions are detrimental in that they constitute a wholesale rejection of the view that psychology should be an experimental science. What is needed instead is a philosophy that serves as a basis for improving the nature of the observations we make in psychology, not one that will turn us away from this avenue of advancement or that will disillusion us with the observational basis of science. The progressive aspect of unified positivism recognizes that observations are on the one hand basic to gaining scientific knowledge but, on the other, are not the ultimate truths, uncontaminated by nonobjective factors. Unified positivism formulates a principle of progressivism in this and other cases (Staats, 1983a):

In the present view, we do not have to assume that the empirical world is capable of being known objectively, without taint by one's conception, in a certain and pure manner, before we can take an empirical position and recognize observations as a fundamentally important source of knowledge. The present conception of the growth of scientific knowledge admits the interaction of theory and observation always. Moreover, it states that this is the basic form of knowledge acquisition. . . . [T]he present view is that humans began their knowledge quest with poor conceptions and made poor observations. But added experience led to the rejection of some aspects of the conception and the support of others. Through this conceptual improvement it was possible to make better observations. The two realms are in continuous, progressive interaction in producing a progressively refined fund of knowledge—a fund that is not without error, that contains distortion, that is idealized, and that is never a perfect knowledge mirror of the world. (p. 35)

This analysis leaves psychology squarely in the position of being just like the natural sciences with respect to the empirical basis of knowledge. No support is given here for a return to the subjectivist philosophies and psychologies of old (Koch, 1981; van Hoorn, 1972; Weimer, 1979). Moreover, there is no justification here for a rejection of experimentation as a fundamental aspect of psychological science, in the manner of some of the new philosophical positions in our field (Gergen, 1973). Experimentation by itself is not sufficient, and experimentation as an end rather than a means, to the exclusion of nonexperimental concerns, is stultifying. But experimentation is essential (Staats, 1983a).

Theory: Axiomatic Dichotomization or Progressivism?

One of the central characteristics of logical positivism is its view of scientific theory: "if a theory does not admit of a canonical [axiomatized] reformulation, . . . it is not a genuine scientific theory" (Suppe, 1977, p. 64). That was the view that shaped psychology's (and the other behavioral sciences') understanding of theory. That was what underlay Hull's attempt to construct an axiomatic theory, elegant in mathematics and replete with interacting intervening variables, stipulated in a quantified manner. And it was this view of theory that led to Skinner's rejection of theory in psychology (1950).

The present position is that the logical-positivist characterization of theory construction, as applied to psychology, established a wrong path. The central problems of psychology (or the other behavioral sciences) will not be resolved by seeking axiomatic theory, certainly not at this stage of development. On the other hand, Skinnerian rejection of theory is nihilistic with respect to one of the fundamental activities of science, theory construction. Skinner has never provided a useful methodological framework for theory construction, and he himself has followed a methodology that is inadequate, as has been the case with those employing his approach (see Staats, 1983a). But logical positivism did not provide a framework either with which to guide the study of theory in psychology or to project lines of needed theory development. In dividing theory into two categories—axiomatic on the one hand and nonscientific on the other—logical positivism does not lay a basis for the analysis of psychology's theory needs or provide theory-construction methods by which to fulfill those needs.

My view was and still is that science involves a progression, from early primitive beginnings in inquiry to those that pertain today. Unified positivism considers the individual's language to constitute a theory thereby providing a basis for introducing a progressive concept. Theory is not restricted to that which is axiomatic and mathematical. Theory is that which functions in the role of theory. Theory is on a continuous developmental dimension, beginning with common language statements that claim to relate to events of the world in a manner expressing some knowledge of those events and progressing to sophisticated scientific theories. This conception provides a basis for considering all types of theory and for concern with advancing the quality of all types of theory.

Some of the major theoretic needs in psychology require an understanding of theory that was not broached at all in logical positivism and its elaborations in psychology, or indeed in the contemporary philosophies of science that have emerged in the behavioral or the natural sciences. As will be indicated further on, psychology's theory needs can only be seen using a philosophy of the science that accurately characterizes the science's nature, that understands what theory is in a generic sense, and that adapts that understanding to psychology's subject matter (Staats, 1983a). The unified-positivist position is that scientists learn—individually and over generations—how to conduct science. All of the features of science, some of them now considered to be basic methodological assumptions, were learned through the experience of trying to formulate knowledge about the world (Staats, 1983a, pp.40–45). Science is a building, advancing endeavor and must be recognized as such.

Logic and Fact: The Whole of Science?

From the perspective of logical positivism, science has two aspects: that having to do with theory and that having to do with empirical events and observation. There is no systematic recognition of the social factors that affect science—for example, that personal and group interests can determine the paths that science takes and the outcomes it achieves. With the assumption of objectivity goes a personification of the scientist as a selfless, disinterested party, guided only by the logical and empirical nature of the subject matter. Sociologists of science (Merton, 1973) and philosophers of science (Toulmin, 1972) have disabused us of such idealized notions. Moreover, Kuhn (1962) and others of the *weltanschauung* school of philosophy have asserted that the background conceptions and worldviews of scientists affect their conduct of science. The concept, which is very similar to that of Boring's (1950) *zeitgeist*, serves to widen our view of what science is about in ways that are important to consider.

The Unity Dimension: A Fundamental Principle of Science Development

A new thesis has been presented within the present philosophy of unified positivism. The thesis is that essential features in the development of a science include (1) the unification of knowledge that was once considered diverse; (2) the accumulation of a large amount of knowledge upon which there is consensual agreement; (3) the development of a philosophy of science that emphasizes unification; and (4) the creation of methods of study and organizational means by which to attain unification of knowledge.

The thesis is that early in the development of scientific inquiry there is chaos of diversity, of theory, of methods, of phenomena studied, of results accepted, and so on. Each scientist works in a small part of the total field and sees the world only through the special knowledge of that part and the conceptual–observational position created in that part—denying the importance of the other parts and trying to convince others that the other parts are wrong or inconsequential. The competition is to establish the ascendant position. The proponents of each position create their own idiosyncratic theory language, idiosyncratic organizations, and publication media. The result is a scientific babel.

Unified positivism considers disunity to be the central problem of a developing science and considers the science's essential tasks to be those of establishing connections between its diverse and competing parts, of translating the idiosyncratic languages into common idioms, of creating groups of cooperating scientists out of competitive cliques, of developing common goals and problems, of developing a conceptual methodology that rationalizes and relates the different methods used in the different positions, of creating a philosophy that features the goal of establishing unified knowledge, and, finally, of creating via these means a large body of unified fact and theory and method that is consensually held in the science and profession. This is a very brief description of very fundamental matters.

Logical positivism does not have (1) a well-formed rationale for examining what unification is in science and how unification is established in a disunified science through long-term, progressive processes; (2) a good grasp of the importance of unification and the search for unity in a science; or (3) a conceptualization of how sciences differ in the extent to which they have attained unity. With regard to this last point, the present theme is that the different groups of sciences have attained different degrees of advancement along the dimension of disunity–unity. While the natural sciences are quite advanced on the dimension, the behavioral sciences have not yet begun their climb toward the enlightenment of unification. Moreover, the thesis is that the disunified behavioral sciences cannot progress, except in the establishment of local, specialized, and conflicting knowledge, until they begin to work on their unification. Thus, a philosophy of science that is to be valuable to the behavioral sciences must deal with the unification dimension of scientific progress. Logical positivism does not offer the needed framework. With its fixation on axiomatic theory, its only guidance is in how a less general axiomatic theory can be *reduced* to a more general axiomatic theory that pertains to the same realm of events. Logical positivism addresses itself only to the unified science, and this is one of its central weaknesses. Unified positivism makes the problems of unification central and states this is necessary in any general philosophy of science (Staats, 1983a). (As will be indicated, moreover, none of the other behaviorisms—with their foundations in philosophies of the natural sciences—have dealt with psychology's problem of unification.)

The Revolution to Unity

To understand the importance of the unification aspect of unified positivism it is necessary to understand the history of science. In the natural sciences, advancement to the state of unification took place at the same time as did advancements in the various other aspects of science. It should be noted that early in the development of the natural sciences there were few scientists, no means of publication other than by personal declaration and writing, no agreed-upon methods of objective observation, and disputed separation from religious influence. Science was advancing in various features at the same time that its unification of knowledge, of method, and of philosophy took place. A dramatic revolution based upon work toward unification did not occur, and the change went unnoticed, at least as far as systematic study is concerned. That is why we have had no clear-cut understanding of how unification is achieved in science, or why it is so central a development for the behavioral sciences.

We must realize that the behavioral sciences came into being when the basic characteristics of the natural sciences had already been established. Thus, in a brief period of time psychology became a field of study with a large number of scientists who had inherited the other methods of science by which to churn out a large number of works. Now, about 100 years after the birth of the field, there are in excess of 60,000 psychologists in the United States alone, as well as many journals, books, and other publications to disseminate the multitudes of elements of psychological knowledge that are produced. Psychology is drowning in its scientific productivity long before it has had a chance to develop skills by which to weave its chaotic diversity together into unified knowledge. I have called psychology a modern disunified science because its problems of disunity are much greater than were those of the natural sciences. Moreover, since unification took place quietly in the natural sciences, the philosophy of science—which takes the natural sciences as the model—has had nothing to say about how to deal with the new problem of disunity in the behavioral sciences. Because of the enormity of the problem, a revolutionary change is required. Moreover, psychology must make this revolution, to develop the characteristics of the unified science, on its own. Among these characteristics, which themselves require systematic consideration and study, are the following.

The Sociological Revolution

There are social characteristics that should be considered a substantive part of science because they affect the conduct of the science and hence its products. We can use the "reward system," a concept of the sociology of science (see Merton, 1973), to exemplify how social forces may affect the nature of the science's unity. As Merton describes, the reward system in science consists of recognition for the originality of one's work. This is true of all science. But it is the thesis of unified positivism that there are important differences between the unified and disunified sciences in what originality is considered to be. In the disunified science, originality is considered to be something that is new or appears to be new. Pristine newness is certainly part of scientific creativity. However, in the unified science it is also recognized that showing relationships between already known elements of knowledge—the unification and simplification of knowledge—is also of central value. Without the goal of unification and simplification, the goal of creating the new and different goes out of control. That is the circumstance today in psychology (Staats, 1983a). For example, there are many organizations and journals given to specialization and to producing local knowledge. Without a countering effort at interrelating and simplifying the chaos that is produced, the sociological character of the science and profession works against the science's knowledge elements being interrelated or considered within a common language, with mutual relevance.

Thus an important part of the revolution to unity must consist of examining and changing the sociology of psychology. For example, psychology must examine its reward system and change it to be appropriate to the task of unifying its chaotic diversity. It must devote a portion of its resources to works of unification. Journals must give space to such endeavors. Journals must be created solely for the purpose of dealing with the many facets of unification. An organization (See Staats, 1985c) or organizations must be created whose purpose is to study and produce unification.* These developments call for a philosophy of science that recognizes the importance of unification as focal.

The Philosophical Revolution

It is necessary for the progress of the disunified sciences to begin to study their nature in a way that has not occurred before. We need historical studies of the way that unified knowledge was developed in the natural sciences. We need studies to compare the differences in operation of the disunified and unified sciences. We need studies of the importance of unification accomplishments in the advancement of science. We know enough about axiomatic theory. We need to study theory of a lesser sort, to analyze the manner in which theory can be improved throughout its levels of advancement. We need sociological, historical, and philosophical works that begin to study what is actually done in the disunified science and what the actual problems of the science are, rather than accepting the contemporary natural sciences as the model.

---

* An organization, called the Society for Studying Unity Issues in Psychology, was founded within the American Psychological Association, during the 1986 convention. Also Division I of the APA inaugurated in 1986 the annual William James Award for a work that has contributed importantly to psychology's unification.

The Methodological and Theoretical Revolution

It has not been recognized that there are many implicit methodological characteristics in science. The *weltanschauungen* philosophies have indicated that there are more elements to science than logic and fact, such as a scientist's background concepts. It is also important to recognize that there are central methodological factors that are associated with the characteristics of the disunified science. For example, the emphasis on producing the new, the novel, and the different—equating these features with originality—sets the framework for producing certain methodological developments. Because of this emphasis on newness, the psychological scientist follows methodological procedures by which to make his or her work as distinctive and different as possible. There are various means by which this can be accomplished, some of which are not constructive for the science. As an example, rather than showing how their own work relates to that of others, scientists may change terminology and theoretical statement to get as much differentiation, and hence uniqueness, as possible. Such methodological practices produce artificial diversity—and psychology is replete with such diversity.

It is necessary that we begin studying the practices by which artificial diversity is produced and to develop standards by which to decrease such practices. This is a methodological problem as important as any that exists in science, especially for the disunified science. Moreover, there are various theory tasks to be performed in the construction of unified knowledge in psychology. Essentially, these tasks lie along a dimension of difficulty. There are varying degrees of difficulty in detecting commonality in underlying principles despite superficial differences. At one end of the dimension is simply the recognition of conceptual terms that are literally the same, even though they have been given different names. Hull's "concept formation" (1920) is the same as Skinner's "abstraction" (1953), for example. The Hullian concept of secondary reinforcement is the same as the Skinnerian concept of conditioned reinforcement, yet two separate research areas formed around the two concepts (see Staats, 1983a, for more examples). There are many elements in psychology of this kind, and a host of works are needed to cross-reference and interrelate the elements. Because psychology has so many different methods, areas of study, subjects, apparatus, theoretical languages, and so on, there also exist a multitude of theories that have an intimate relationship with one another but whose superficial differences hide that fact. For example, the principles in cognitive-dissonance theory are closely related to principles in psychoanalytic theory in a manner that has gone unrecognized (see Hishinuma, 1987). We need many theoretical analyses whose aim is to simplify psychology by relating its theories. Moving further out on the difficulty dimension, we must realize that one of the central tasks of a science is to search for relationships in underlying principles between phenomena that appear to be quite different. Shapere (1977, pp. 519–521) describes how scientists spent much effort and many years in finding the relationships between electricity and magnetism, between electricity and chemical phenomena, and between electricity and light. Should we not look for common principles that might underlie the many phenomena that are investigated within psychology? There is also the need for the many theoretical works that can show the complementary relationships between the different and sometimes opposing methods of investigation of psychology and that can unify the various schisms in psychology, such as the nature–nurture schism.

These few words can only hint at the many tasks of unification that psychology needs (see Staats, 1983a, for additional discussion). There is a mixture of methodological and theoretical concerns here. What is involved in many of the tasks is a methodology of theory construction that aims to establish unification in the disunified science. In the next section, I further discuss broader, more general theory construction for unification.

The Theory Revolution: Conceptual Unification

Philosophies such as logical positivism, based primarily on the study of the natural sciences, have never confronted the problems of constructing unified theory of the type relevant to the behavioral sciences. While recognizing that generality is important in science, in its fixation on the advanced, axiomatic theories, logical positivism recognized only one method of establishing generality and unity—reductionism. This occurs where the principles and statements of one axiomatic theory can be derived in formal logic fully from another, more general axiomatic theory (Suppe, 1977, pp. 54–56). In a sense, the more general theory swallows the less general theory. A common view is that the same process can apply to whole sciences (Popper, 1972, pp. 290–294), for example, that biology and physiology would reduce to physics; and psychology to biology and physiology, and hence to physics.

Many scientists, however, are alienated by reductionism. Some have rejected the idea that the social sciences would disappear into psychology (see Durkheim, 1927, pp. 124–125; Mandelbaum, 1955), or that psychology would disappear into the biological sciences (see Skinner, 1950). Nevertheless, with no philosophy of science to follow, psychologists have generally borrowed the reductionistic concept when constructing grand, unified theories. "Reductionism" was the explicit or implicit theory-construction methodology of the second-generation behaviorists, including Skinner. Their methodology was to formulate a basic theory of animal learning derived from laboratory experimentation with good experimental and theoretical methodology. The theorists considered that this type of theory construction was the heart of the task, that all the other interests of psychology could be derived from (reduced to) the basic animal-learning theories. What was not readily reducible was considered to be worthless. Basically, this was a methodology of rejecting most of psychology's knowledge. Skinner's theory, and behaviorism generally, epitomizes this approach, but the same methodology is employed in all grand theories, for example, psychoanalytic theory and cognitive theory (see Baars, 1984; Staats, 1985a, 1985b).

Because it alienates all types of psychologists who are not of the particular orientation, the methodology of reductionism (actually "rejectionism") has not been able to generate any consensus, only conflict and separatism. It is important in the third generation of behaviorism to develop a theory-construction methodology that utilizes rather than rejects the broad knowledge of psychology and that brings both the human and animal levels of study into intimate relationship in the *basic* theory-construction task. An explicit demand is that any theory that claims generality must systematically consider the existing knowledge in psychology's purview, not just reject blocks of that knowledge by simple fiat.

Paradigmatic behaviorism incorporates these principles. It aims to construct a framework that has conditioning as its basic principles but that utilizes and unifies knowledge from the other areas of psychology throughout the range of its theory construction. This is not done in an eclectic way, but in a closely reasoned way. Eclectic combinations do not theoretically connect disparate concepts; they only lump them together. Paradigmatic behaviorism's philosophy of unified positivism requires precision of statement, parsimony, internal consistency, closely reasoned unification, explicitness in an empirical sense, detail, and breadth of coverage throughout its purview. First and foremost, it requires that its theoretical unifications produce heuristic, theoretical, empirical, applied, and methodological products.

Part of the methodology of large-scale theory in psychology has to deal with the problem of unifying disparate elements. There are in our science different fields of study, different theoretical structures, different methods, different phenomena, and different studies of the same phenomena. Unified theory construction requires the mutual influence of disparate elements in forming a theoretical structure that can bridge the separations. The paradigmatic behavioristic method of theory construction, by which to bridge separate knowledge elements, has been called "interlevel theory" (see, especially, Staats, 1975, Chapter 16; 1983a, Chapters 8 & 9) and, more recently, "bridging theory" (Staats, in press b). It is significant that two philosophers of science, Darden and Maull (1977), have described in the biochemical sciences a very similar analysis of bridging theory, calling it "interfield theory." These independent methodological analyses, across different science areas, suggest that an important generality, pertaining to various science areas (see Staats, 1983a), is involved. Paradigmatic behaviorism, moreover, elaborates the methodology of bridging theory construction and develops the methodology of the multilevel theory, created to address the fact that there are multiple fields in psychology whose knowledge elements must be unified with one another. Multilevel theory-construction methods represent a more advanced methodology especially relevant to the problems of the behavioral sciences.

Multilevel Theory Construction

Paradigmatic behaviorism is the theory derived within and simultaneously affecting the unified-positivist philosophy. In constructing that theory, following a strategy of advancing from simple to more complex phenomena, it became clear that the various fields of psychology fall into a roughly ordered *hierarchy* of levels, with one field basic to the next field and it to another. Since each level of study was historically developed independently of the others, there could be many unrecognized cases of elements in one level of study that are closely related to elements in one or more of the other levels of study. The unified theory thus has the task of constructing a framework that weaves the levels together. This does not mean the more advanced levels are reduced to the principles of the more basic levels; it only means that the basic principles constitute the potential foundation for resolving the tasks of unification. However, those elementary principles must be elaborated and joined with other principles in the advancing theoretical effort, level by level, in such a manner as to bridge the lacunae and antagonisms among the various levels. This is a real theory-construction task that demands contact with knowledge of the various levels so that major principles and phenomena may be unified. It should be understood that the second-generation behaviorists did not see the task in this way. Thus, they did not attempt to deal with the various levels of psychology in a manner by which to construct a true unified theory. Skinner's work may be used as an example here, since it contains almost no reference to the knowledge to be found in the various fields (levels) of study of psychology. There is no indication in his theory-construction methodology that there might be valuable knowledge elements in the other parts of psychology, in study other than his own type. Actually, his most influential treatise on theory explicitly says not to cross levels of study (Skinner, 1950), and radical behaviorism is characterized by its "rejectionism," a methodology quite opposite that of paradigmatic behaviorism. The field of behavior therapy needs to compare the several behaviorisms on this and other characteristics, as a means of establishing heuristic worth (see Minke, in press b).

To continue, the theory-construction task involves more than simply relating the levels of psychology in a loose, descriptive way. It is easy to say that learning theory is basic to child development, child development to personality, personality to personality measurement and abnormal personality, and abnormal personality to clinical psychology. Much more is necessary, however. For example, none of the individual levels of study has been constructed in order to be related to the others. Thus, each level or field contains much that has no relevance for constructing a unified theory that is in concert with *all* levels. Each level contains much that is erroneous or not useful, so each level requires that the theorist abstract from it those parts that are important, valid, and relevant to the task. The theory must then be constructed to include those elements in such a way that they can be linked to the others. The task is not simply one of selection and abstraction, however. It is a true theory-construction task. New conceptual materials need to be formulated in a theory language that is consistent across the levels and phenomena. The goal is to produce a theory structure in each case that will be valuable to both the specialized area and to the larger theory unifying the various areas. These things have never been accomplished in the traditional theories that have claimed generality in psychology. They have never systematically addressed the knowledge in the various levels of study with the objective of formulating an overarching theory that is unified and heuristic within and between the levels. Moreover, they have not had or followed a systematic method and program for developing grand, unified theory.

It is not possible here to do justice to the theory-construction methodology involved in formulating multilevel theory, and there are methodological developments yet to be made. However, the methodology has been developed in the work of the long-term theory program that paradigmatic behaviorism constitutes (see Burns, 1980, in press; Evans & Eifert, in press; Eifert, in press; Leduc, 1984; Minke, in press a, in press b; as well as the works of the author listed in the References). There is a prototypical multilevel theory in paradigmatic behaviorism (see Staats, 1975, 1981, in press b; Staats & Fernandez-Bellesteros, in press), and the methodology has been set forth with the idea that it is general, to be used by others in the construction of other large-scale, unified theories (see Staats, 1981, 1983a, 1983b). The next section summarizes the theory itself.

Paradigmatic Behaviorism's Multilevel Theory: A Paradigm for Psychology

Paradigmatic behaviorism is a framework theory in the sense that while it extends to a wide range of psychology's knowledge, with its characteristics established in extensive, systematic work, it is the first psychology theory to recognize that every grand theory must be incomplete, constructed in detail only in selected areas. Full construction for all grand theories cannot be a one-person job; additional major theorists and researchers are needed. As with classic theories, paradigmatic behaviorism principles have been formulated (1) to bridge and unify diverse elements of knowledge, (2) within a closely reasoned and consistent set of principles, (3) in a manner that is theoretically and empirically heuristic. Its basic principles are behavioral, but they have been elaborated and concepts have been added that enable the theory to incorporate nonbehavioral knowledge from various areas (levels) of psychology—for example, psycholinguistics, child development, personality theory, psychometrics, psychopathology, and social psychology. The original name was changed from "social behaviorism" to "paradigmatic behaviorism" to emphasize the revolutionary potential of a framework theory such as this to organize the chaotic knowledge elements of contemporary psychology generally, as well as of behavioral psychology particularly (Staats, 1981), and to do so with the heuristic properties of classic theories.

In the brief space available here, the outline of the structure of paradigmatic behaviorism is best be illustrated by Table 10.1.* The areas to which the theory is addressed are presented in the left column. These areas generally follow a hierarchical relationship, starting with basic and moving to more complex principles and phe-

---

* I wish to thank Daniel Fishman for editorial contributions and for suggesting the use of a table, including the form, to illustrate more succinctly the levels of the theory and their manner of unification.

TABLE 10.1 The Multilevel Theory of Paradigmatic Behaviorism

Levels (and content-area examples)	Principles, concepts, and purposes
1. Biological mechanisms of learning a. Sensory psychology b. Brain and central nervous system c. Response systems d. Evolution of learning mechanisms	*The neurophysiology of learning:* The central purpose of this level of theory is to unify the biological study of organisms with their behavioral study, making the two mutually heuristic, and removing the schism that separates so much of psychology along "nature-nurture" lines. The basic bridge relates the biological concepts of sensory, response, and association organs with the behavioral concepts of stimuli, responses, and learning.
2. Basic-learning theory a. Elementary study: conditioning principles b. Generalizing study: types of stimuli, responses, and species to which principles apply c. Motivation principles	*Three-function learning theory:* Stimuli that elicit an emotional response will because of this be reinforcing stimuli. Both functions (emotional elicitation and reinforcement) are transferred in classical conditioning. Moreover, organisms generally learn to approach positive emotional (and reinforcing) stimuli and to avoid negative emotional (and punishing) stimuli. As a consequence, emotional stimuli direct (are incentives for) behavior. This learning theory makes the study of the various forms of the classical conditioning of emotions to be a central concern in explaining behavior, giving new directions for animal and human research.
3. Human-learning principles a. Complex stimulus-response learning (e.g., response sequences, response hierarchies, and multiple controlling stimuli) b. Response repertoires c. Cumulative-hierarchical learning principles and others unique to humans	*Complex stimulus-response mechanisms, internal responses and stimuli, response repertoires, and cumulative-hierarchical learning:* The basic learning theory states the behavioral principles in elemental simplicity. Human skills and general characteristics are composed of exceedingly complex combinations of the basic principles. The field of human learning must study such complex combinations and the manner in which complex, interrelated sets of responses (repertoires) are learned. Centrally, complex human skills are complex repertoires that can only be acquired if the individual has already learned necessary prior repertoires (e.g., reading can only be learned after prior language repertoires are learned). These principles of cumulative-hierarchical learning require systematic, basic study.

cont.

TABLE 10.1 *(continued)*

Level (and content-area examples)	Principles, concepts, and purposes
4. Personality a. Personality concept b. The three personality systems: language-cognitive, emotional-motivational, and sensory-motor c. Personality and environment interaction	*Personality is composed of basic behavioral repertoires:* From birth the child begins to learn complex systems of "skills" in the three general areas. These are learned in advancing complexity. There are subrepertoires that additional learning combines together (as language is composed of separately learned subrepertoires), and there are repertoires that are basic to the later learning of more advanced repertoires (as algebra skills rest on the prior learning of arithmetic operations). The three repertoires constitute personality. In interaction with the environment they determine the individual's experience, learning, and behavior. This theory makes many conceptual unifications possible in psychology and opens many new avenues of research.
5. Child development a. Language-cognitive development b. Sensory-motor development, including modeling skills c. Emotional-motivational development	*Cumulative-hierarchical learning and development:* Traditional developmental psychologists have studied many aspects of the child's development. But there has been little analysis of this development in terms of its complex learning. Paradigmatic behaviorism calls for this systematic analysis, provides exemplary theoretical–empirical analyses of language-cognitive, emotional-motivational, and sensory-motor development through learning, and calls for various new types of theory and research.
6. The social-personality level of study a. Attitudes and social cognition b. Interpersonal relations and group processes c. Personality processes, individual and group differences, and cross-cultural psychology	*Interactions among individuals and groups:* The three-function learning principles are basic. Attitudes are emotional responses to social stimuli. Thus, such stimuli have reinforcing and incentive (directive) power, depending on their emotion elicitation. Social phenomena such as group cohesion, attraction, persuasion, prejudice, and intergroup relations function by these principles. In addition to the emotional response individuals have for each other, the language-cognitive and sensory-motor personality repertoires of interactors are determinants of their social behavior. Group character and social role phenomena also operate according to the basic principles and personality principles.

TABLE 10.1 *(continued)*

Level (and content-area examples)	Principles, concepts, and purposes
7. *Personality measurement* a. Theory relating behavior principles, the concept of personality, and personality measurement and behavioral assessment b. Application of theory to tests and their uses (clinical, etc.) c. Applications to test construction and assessment	*Unifying theory for a behavioral psychometrics:* The personality theory provides a conceptual framework within which the personality concepts, methods, and instruments of the traditional field of psychometrics can be analyzed in a manner compatible with behaviorism. Personality tests measure aspects of the basic behavioral repertoires, which accounts for their ability to predict behavior. For example, intelligence tests heavily measure language repertoires and sensory-motor skills, and interest tests measure aspects of the emotional-motivational repertoire. The theory explains why verbal tests provide knowledge of nonverbal behavior and emotional states—because the three personality repertoires are interconnected and covary—helping resolve the behaviorism/psychometrics schism. The theory is heuristic for basic research and test construction (Staats, 1986a; Staats & Fernandez-Ballesteros, 1987).
8. *Abnormal psychology* a. The personality repertoires as basic determinants of abnormal behavior b. Diagnostic categories as deficient and inappropriate personality repertoires c. Personality and environment interaction in abnormal behavior	*Paradigmatic behaviorism's theory of abnormal behavior:* The individual learns personality repertoires that interact with his life situation in determining his behavior. The personality repertoires may be rich and adaptive, or sparse and inappropriate. In the latter case the individual's behavior will be abnormal in certain situations. Life situations that are not normal may also produce abnormal behavior. Biological conditions can directly affect the personality repertoires and produce abnormal behavior. Using this theory, a unified analysis can be made of the various diagnostic categories. For example, schizophrenia involves disturbances especially in the language-cognitive and emotional-motivational repertoires, phobias involve only a part of the latter repertoire, and the various subtypes of depression differ in the repertoires, life events, or biological conditions involved.

cont.

TABLE 10.1 *(continued)*

Level (and content-area examples)	Principles, concepts, and purposes
9. Clinical psychology a. Behavior modification of simple problems, behavior therapy, and the psychodynamics/conditioning schism b. Paradigmatic behaviorism c. Personality change and personality measurement d. Language-cognitive methods of treatment	*Paradigmatic behavior therapy:* The various levels of paradigmatic behaviorism are applied to clinical problems involving various methods of treatment. The basic learning principles can be employed to directly treat simple problems. Sometimes personality or social-environmental problems are involved and assessment instruments and personality measurement may be needed, as well as complex social-environmental changes and learning programs. The language-cognitive level of theory indicates how behavior and personality can be changed by various verbal methods of therapy. Paradigmatic behaviorism's clinical psychology has been in development since, the 1950s, has yielded seminal contributions to behavior therapy, and now projects, new avenues for development.
10. Educational psychology a. Paradigmatic behaviorism's theories of school subjects b. Intelligence, learning readiness, retardation, and learning disability c. Treating problems of school learning	*Education and paradigmatic behaviorism:* Reading (like writing and number-concept skills) is explicated in theory and research; considered in specific terms as complex language-cognitive repertoires, learned in a cumulative-hierarchical manner, based on earlier-acquired language repertoires. Theory and research yield a conception of intelligence as composed of learned and trainable repertoires. Learning readiness, retardation, and learning disability, which are typically inferred to result from biological conditions can be better explained within a unified learning-biological theory that stipulates the repertoires involved, with directives for problem resolution. The approach provides new ways for treating and researching educational problems (Staats, 1973).

TABLE 10.1 *(continued)*

Level (and content-area examples)	Principles, concepts, and purposes
11. Organizational psychology a. Personnel selection b. Motivation in organizational settings c. Behavioral analysis of jobs d. Organizational conditions and problems	*Applying paradigmatic behaviorism to tasks in organizations:* Paradigmatic behaviorism's various levels of theory provide a richer conceptual framework than usual for analysis of organizations and their characteristics and problems. For example, the emotional-motivational theory specifies that individuals *and* institutions have "emotional-motivational systems" and that individual-institutional adjustment depends on harmony between the two. Because of the personality and psychological measurement levels of theory the approach can link more harmoniously with traditional knowledge in such areas as personnel selection, job analysis, and job training.

nomena. The right-hand column characterizes the principles, concepts, and purposes of each level. Each level requires a subtheory framework that joins with the others to yield the grand theory. The task is (1) to confront the knowledge elements of the level being treated, using a tentative theory framework derived from the parent body as the "template" with which to guide the selection, rejection, and reformulation of the elements within the level; (2) to adapt the principles of the level-theory in accord with the empirical and theoretical knowledge of the level itself; (3) to utilize the level-theory in theoretical and empirical analyses that extend and test it; (4) to project new lines of development; (5) to deal progressively in these ways with additional concerns at that level of study; and (6) to interweave these developments with the other level-theory developments in a manner that will insure a tightly woven theoretical-empirical-methodological-philosophical fabric overall.

Such goals have not been understood in other behaviorisms. They have been reached in different degrees in the various levels of study of paradigmatic behaviorism. The utility of a theory, other things equal, is a function of its detail and empirical–theoretical specification. Paradigmatic behaviorism has been in construction for over three decades and has had time to develop a good deal of detail, at least at points of concentration, in comparison to new unified theories that are now being announced (see Ardila, 1983; Gilgen, 1987). Radical behaviorism has begun to admit the failure of its mission to become a general

psychology (Fraley & Vargas, 1986; Staats, 1986b). Paradigmatic behaviorism, by contrast, has been constructed to enable behavioral psychology to undertake that huge task. It contains full theories in such
areas as language, intelligence, attitudes, verbal psychotherapy, images, emotions and motivation, reading, depression, psychopathology,
and psychological measurement. It also includes less encompassing
analyses of such areas of behavior as toilet training, communication,
social interaction, number-concept acquisition, problem solving, and
self-concept. Paradigmatic behaviorism makes a heuristic call for co-
workers to perform the extensive theoretical, methodological, and basic and applied empirical works needed in the huge task involved, as
will be exemplified. The nature of the task, once stipulated, indicates
that constructing a grand, unified theory is not a one-person job, but
must be an organized group effort.

Basic-Learning Theory

The basic-learning theory in Skinner's operant behaviorism, although
very generally accepted in behavioral psychology, has serious disadvantages. These include its separation of instrumental and classical
conditioning, its lack of study of the latter, and its consequent inability
to accept or deal with the manner in which emotions determine behavior. For example, the approach is not able to shed understanding on
various clinical methods, such as systematic desensitization, that
treat behavior problems by changing emotional responding (Staats,
1979b). Paradigmatic behaviorism, in contrast, has formulated the
interrelationships among the emotion-eliciting, reinforcing, and incentive (directive or discriminative) functions of stimuli. By so doing it
provides a theoretical basis for new studies of animal learning, for
researching and treating the effects of emotions on human behavior
(Staats & Burns, 1982; Staats, et al., 1973), and for the study of the
emotional characteristics of personality (see Burns, in press; Staats,
1986a; Staats & Fernandez-Ballesteros, 1987; Staats & Heiby, 1985).
The basic-learning theory, as yet stated only in summary form, provides multiple avenues for experimental-theoretical development in
the animal and human laboratory (see Harms & Staats, 1978; Staats
& Hammond, 1972; Staats & Warren, 1974; Staats, 1968a, 1968b,
1970, 1975).

Human-Learning Theory

The field of human learning has elaborated a few complex stimulus-
response mechanisms, but there has been no realization that we need.

full, systematic knowledge in this general area. According to paradigmatic behaviorism, conditioning principles are basic to all learning. There are not different basic forms of learning as some approaches (e.g., Bandura & Walters, 1963; Gagne, 1965) assume. The problem giving rise to that assumption is that the basic conditioning principles have been stipulated in simple stimulus-response situations and do not seem relevant to real-life situations involving very complex stimulus-response events. Thus the manner in which complex stimulus-response combinations are learned must be clearly conceptualized to serve as basic tools in analyzing complex human behavior. Behavior therapists who know only the few basic conditioning principles are limited in their ability to analyze complex problems in behavioral terms and thus are forced to introduce nonlearning (cognitive) concepts into their analyses.

Human behavior acquisition is complex. It occurs in a cumulative fashion, with more and more complex stimulus-response structures (repertoires) being formed, each one built upon the preceding. The idea that only the basic principles of learning are central, the assumption of the traditional behaviorists, is bankrupt. We need a specific field whose purpose is to study complex human learning. Without this level of theory development, basic-learning theory does not contain heuristic elements for those who wish to study complex behavior (such as cognitive psychologists). Perhaps for this reason, Skinner's (1957) analysis of verbal behavior produced no research on the complex mechanisms involved (McPherson, et al., 1984). Contrast this with research generated by paradigmatic behaviorism in the area of language (e.g., Eifert, 1983; Hekmat, 1972; Harms & Staats, 1978; Leduc, 1984; Rondal, 1985; Staats, 1963, 1964, 1968a, 1971b, 1974; Staats & Hammond, 1972; Staats & Warren, 1974), and with that which is called for (e.g., Staats, 1968a, 1972, 1986a; Staats & Burns, 1981, 1982).

Personality Theory

One of the deepest schisms between traditional and behavioral psychology involves the question of whether personality is a causal process that determines behavior. Traditional psychology accepts that view, while traditional behaviorism (including social learning theory, see Staats, 1980) vehemently rejects it. Paradigmatic behaviorism resolves this schism with a tightly reasoned, experimentally based theory that derives from conditioning and human-learning principles, while also introducing new conceptual elements. Personality is viewed as composed of repertoires (very complex stimulus-response structures) of the type studied in human-learning theory. In human-learning theory the concern is with investigating the abstract principles. In personality theory, those abstract principles are used to analyze how people actually learn their personal repertoires, how differences in learned repertoires determine an individual's distinctive behavioral characteristics, and how those repertoires can conceptually explain traditional personality concepts, such as introversion–extraversion, self-concept, intelligence, interests, and other "traits" (Burns, 1980; Leduc, 1984, 1986; Staats, 1971a, 1975, 1986a; Staats & Fernandez-Ballesteros, 1987; Staats & Burns, 1981, 1982; Staats et al., 1973; Staats & Heiby, 1985).

More specifically, the view is that humans learn very complex repertoires of behavior cumulatively. For example, the infant begins to acquire the subrepertoires of language. These progressively grow into a full language-cognitive repertoire, aspects of which are referred to traditionally with such concepts as beliefs, attitudes, values, self-concept, intelligence, aptitudes, worldview, and cognitive style. For example, it has been shown that a child's concept-recognition skills, evidenced by sorting objects conceptually and identifying concept classes, depends upon having learned a repertoire of verbal names for objects and for classes of objects (Staats & Burns, 1981). These object and class names constitute a language repertoire that will help determine the individual's cognitive performance in various tasks, in ways that are used to define personality traits such as intelligence. Paradigmatic behaviorism, as one example, calls for the study of the language-cognitive (personality) repertoires that determine the individual's behavior, experience, and further learning.

There are three general personality repertoires, the others being the emotional-motivational and the sensory-motor repertoires (Leduc, 1984; Staats, 1975). The theory of personality thus far established in framework form provides a foundation for unification with traditional knowledge and for new directions of systematic research in various areas of personality. An additional avenue of unification comes from paradigmatic behaviorism's conception that biological conditions can directly effect the personality repertoires, either during original learning, or later, after the repertoires have already been acquired (Staats & Heiby, 1985).

Child-Development Theory

Although there are studies extending conditioning principles to children as subjects, there has not been a systematic program for the study of child development that utilizes the many elements of knowledge of traditional child-developmental study in conjunction with behavioral methods and principles. Paradigmatic behaviorism's character makes this unified theory possible. The goals of paradigmatic behaviorism's child-development theory are (1) to establish the generalizability of elementary conditioning principles for children, using basic laboratory procedures and simple responses; (2) to use basic principles to analyze simple, but developmentally important, behaviors, such as beginning eye–hand coordination, walking, swimming, and first-word production and reception; (3) to use the principles to solve problems of child training, such as bedwetting, temper tantrums, trouble going to bed willingly, and improper eating habits; (4) to analyze more complex repertoires, such as moral behavior, honesty, socialization, and cooperative play; and (5) to create a detailed theoretical–empirical analysis of the development of the three personality repertoires in children. This last goal is basic to the fields of personality, personality measurement, social-personality psychology, abnormal psychology, and the applied areas of clinical, educational, and organizational psychology. The personality repertoires should be studied in a developmental way for various reasons. One is that, when the repertoires are still simple, they are easier to study. Even more importantly, since human learning is cumulative-hierarchical in nature, it will only be understood when developmental studies have analyzed this cumulative process in detail. Paradigmatic behaviorism has begun to investigate the development of the language-cognitive and sensory-motor repertoires (see Leduc, 1984, 1986; Staats, 1963, 1968a, 1971a, 1975; Staats et al. 1970; Staats & Burns, 1981). Again, in doing so it has produced the framework of an approach to be employed in constructing the many specialized works that are necessary.

Abnormal-Psychology Theory

Standard behaviorist approaches to the field of psychopathology have primarily involved behavior modification and behavior therapy treatments of certain kinds of problems. Paradigmatic behaviorism contributed to the origins of this work and considers it valuable but also states that the work does not link with traditional knowledge of abnormal personality, does not provide an integrated view of the various psychopathologies, and does not indicate new types of research. Paradigmatic behaviorism presented the first analysis of a behavioral abnormal psychology (Staats, 1963, Chapter 11). Paradigmatic behaviorism's further development of the theory of personality establishes an outline for a heuristic theory of psychopathology (Staats, 1975, Chapter 8). Briefly, the theory states that the individual learns his personality repertoires, the "normality" of which, in interaction with the life environment, determines the normality of the individual's behavior. Understanding of abnormal behavior requires an understanding of an individual's personality repertoires, not simply of reinforcement contingencies. The diagnostic categories can be analyzed in terms of deficits in and inappropriate aspects of the three personality repertoires (which can be biologically caused) as well as of the life situation. This enables the theory to draw upon traditional knowledge in abnormal psychology as well as the experimental knowledge of the basic behavioral repertoires, creating a unifying theory with extensive directions for theoretical–empirical development (see also Burns & Farina, 1987; Leduc & Dumais, in press), as has been shown with the new theory of depression that has been developed in the framework (Staats & Heiby, 1985) and the new research being conducted within that framework (Gordon & Staats, 1987; Heiby, 1985).

Paradigmatic Behavior Therapy

In setting the stage for this brief treatment of paradigmatic behavior therapy, let me indicate that paradigmatic social behaviorism was involved in the inception of and has made seminal contributions to behavior therapy (defined to include behavior modification/analysis/assessment). In illustration, an early analysis of an abnormal behavior in terms of reinforcement principles (Staats, 1957) was instrumental in one of the first behavior modification applications in the United States (Ayllon & Michael, 1959). The 1958 introduction of the token-reinforcer system and its dissemination (Staats & Butterfield, 1965; Staats et al., 1964b) provided a foundation for later token economy developments. Moreover, its demonstration with children's reading problems, along with the suggestion that the methods be used widely (Staats et al., 1964a, 1982), was followed by studies that developed those uses (Barnard et al., 1974; O'Leary et al., 1969; O'Leary & Drabman, 1971; Sulzer-Asaroff & Mayer, 1985, Chapter 15; Wolf et al., 1964). Paradigmatic behaviorism (see Staats, 1963) was one of the first conceptual treatments that underlay the development of the field and its unification of behavioral and cognitive concerns (Staats, 1968a), its legitimization of verbal psychotherapy (Staats, 1972), and its criticism of the operant approach (see Tryon, 1974) for its resistance to such developments (see Staats, 1963, 1968a, 1970, 1971b, 1972) contributed to the *zeitgeist* for developing contemporary cognitive–behavioral approaches (Eifert, 1987).

The above specific contributions have been incorporated easily into behavior therapy. But the underlying paradigm, different as it is from radical behaviorism, has not been so easily recognized and adopted for use. Nevertheless, behavioral psychologists in increasing numbers have begun developing their creative works within this framework. A book edited by Ian Evans and Georg Eifert (in press) will present collected readings of paradigmatic behaviorism applications. Aimee Leduc (1984) has already published another collection, which samples the work of the members of the Quebec Association for the Advancement of Paradigmatic Behaviorism. Ian Evans has invented the name *paradigmatic behavior therapy* with which to designate the applied parts of the broader paradigm.

As is the case with the other fields described in Table 10.1, much work is called for in the development of paradigmatic behavior therapy—but that represents the promise as well as the challenge. Let me just mention some of the ways that the approach can serve the behavior therapist. Paradigmatic behaviorism provides theories that will allow therapists to tap into findings in various fields of psychology in a manner not provided by the other behavioral approaches. Researchers interested in particular problems of human behavior can find in paradigmatic behaviorism full or preliminary theories that can serve as the foundations for research. The usefulness of paradigmatic behavioristic theories is enhanced by the specificity the approach demands. In addition, there are a number of methods of research and treatment included in the works of this approach. Paradigmatic behaviorism also provides an understanding of cognitive characteristics that is valuable in treatment and in projecting research, but in a way that connects the cognitive concepts to basic behavioral principles. Paradigmatic behaviorism provides also new theories of abnormal classifications, like depression, that can serve as the basis for specific research studies or programs of research. Moreover, these specialized theories, along with paradigmatic behaviorism's more general framework theory of abnormal psychology, provide models for the development of additional theories of psychopathologies. The psychological assessment theory of the approach provides the basis for new directions in research as well as for test construction. Limitations of space preclude indicating the various additional new directions that can be derived from the paradigm, but there are many. As with any overarching heuristic theory, the more expert one becomes in the elements of the approach, the more one is able to exploit its heuristic value.

Framework Theory and Its Functions

Logical positivism, as developed in psychology, offers a very restricted view of theory (Staats, 1983a, 1987). Skinner (1950; Sidman, 1960), for example, was led to reject theory, without realizing that his most significant works constituted a theory, albeit not a systematically constructed one. In aiming their theories to be general to psychology, behaviorists actually formulated "framework" theories, as did nonbehavioral theorists such as Freud and Piaget, without having a methodology of what a framework theory should be or how one should be constructed. Part of paradigmatic behaviorism's theory-construction methodology centers on the concept of the framework theory, and we must begin to understand what such a theory is and what its functions are (see Staats, in press). The concept is related to the concept of the paradigm in a general way. But how to construct a framework theory or paradigm in psychology calls for systematic study. One approach, now being actively developed, is that of multilevel theory construction. It is relevant to add here a few words concerning the functions of a framework theory.

Interpretation, Meaning, and Analysis

The philosophy of unified positivism has already characterized psychology as a buzzing confusion of knowledge elements (Staats, 1983a). Most of us would agree that understanding the knowledge of areas such as child development, personality, social psychology, educational problems, communication, motivation, and learning would be important to the researcher or clinician. But knowledge in such fields is generally inaccessible because too many different languages are used. There are antagonistic viewpoints, and it is impossible to separate the important and useful from the irrelevant and erroneous. One of the important functions of a framework theory is to guide us in the task of interpreting the various findings of psychology and of making them meaningful in a related way. We must compare and evaluate such framework theories as Skinner's behaviorism, paradigmatic behaviorism, social-learning theory, and cognitive-behavioral theory with regard to the extent to which they provide foundations for utilizing the knowledge of the different areas of psychology.

Other Heuristic Products of Framework Theories

It should be understood that there are various ways that a theory can be heuristic. A theory can serve as a source from which hypotheses can be derived in an axiomatic manner for experimental test. In addition, a framework theory can offer concepts, principles, and methods of analysis by which psychology's phenomena can be analyzed. This is especially important for the clinician, but it is also important for any researcher concerned with the analysis of behavior. A framework theory also can be heuristic in projecting empirical discovery in various ways. The theory, for example, may provide a general but well-supported statement that shows areas where empirical research and applications are needed. To illustrate, radical behaviorism's rejection of the concept of personality as mentalistic provides no basis for the study of individual differences, called "personality," as determinants of behavior. Paradigmatic behaviorism's personality level of study, in contrast, provides a basis for projecting, explicitly, new areas of such study, to unify psychometric and behavioral research (see Staats, 1986a). As another example, paradigmatic behaviorism's analyses established one of the central foundations for the development of the field of behavioral assessment, as Goldfried and Sprafkin (1974) indicated in referring to paradigmatic behaviorism's taxonomy of abnormal behavior (Staats, 1963, chapter 11), as described by Bandura (1968). The following, a part of the paradigmatic behavioral analysis of psychopathology, illustrates this function in making, seemingly, the first call for a field of behavioral assessment (Staats, 1963):

> Perhaps a rationale for learning psychotherapy will also have to include some method for the assessment of behavior. In order to discover the behavioral deficiencies, the required changes in the reinforcing system, the circumstances in which stimulus control is absent, and so on, evaluational techniques in these respects may have to be devised. Certainly, no two individuals will be alike in these various characteristics, and it may be necessary to determine such facts for the individual prior to beginning the learning program of treatment. Such assessment might take a form similar to some of the psychological tests already in use. It is possible, however, that [this] general learning rationale for behavior disorders and treatment will itself suggest techniques of assessment. (pp. 508–509)

Neither social-learning theorists (Bandura & Walters, 1963) nor operant behaviorists (Skinner, 1953, 1957) of this period provided a conceptual foundation from which to launch the field of behavioral assessment, although the operant language was employed when the field was launched. This is not said for proprietal purposes. Rather, it is to indicate that the track record is there, much more than is known, and the works of paradigmatic behaviorism should be examined for other new directions for development of our field. In general, this framework theory has instigated broad new developments as well as specific theoretical formulations and empirical research and clinical works, and such theories must be compared and evaluated for their ability to do these things, along with their other heuristic potentialities. This has not been done, for the last consideration of behavioral theories involved the disputes of the 1930s, 40s, and 50s rather than the comparative evaluations that are needed (see Minke, in press a).

Conclusion

If behavior therapy is not to become merely an applied field, limited in generating new developments, it cannot settle down to workaday science and practice—on the implicit assumption that the basic development of the behavioral approach has occurred and all that remains is application and perhaps some eclectic elaboration. The contemporary behavioral framework that is most generally held is of the last generation. However, it is the next generation framework that must be established among today's researchers. This must include the three major developments: a new philosophy of science, a new general behaviorism theory, and a new framework for behavior therapy (applications). The field must now devote central efforts to selecting what its framework is to be.

We are at a crossroads, much as the field was in the 1950s. As one of those involved at that time in initiating the field of behavioral analysis, I was moved then to exhort psychologists that learning theory should "no longer be ignored" (Staats, 1957, p. 269). At that time psychodynamic psychology had the attention and resources of those interested in human problems, and the potentialities of behavioral analysis were not being considered. Yet psychodynamic psychology was stultified with respect to providing vital new directions for theory, research, and applied development; a new framework was needed.

I am moved to convey the same message today. Central to the concept of the framework theory is its need to be exploited in opening new directions of development. The more potential the framework has, the greater the number of people who can work creatively, with general meaning, within its structure. Thus far Skinner's works have been the most widely accepted behavioral framework theory, the only one generally employed that makes a serious attempt to address basic principles as well as human applications. It has drawn off the overwhelming number of people working within behavioral psychology, making it the only such approach whose heuristic potential has had a chance to be exhausted. Notwithstanding its unique opportunity, there are already influential admissions that the behaviorism based on this theory cannot succeed in becoming a general approach in psychology (Epstein, 1984; Fraley & Vargas, 1986). An argument has been mounted that this behaviorism is now stultified, that it has not been giving impetus to new developments for some time (Staats, 1986b). The message is that the field of behavioral psychology should now give other framework theories, intended for the purpose, the resources and opportunity to exhibit their heuristic potentialities.

I have herein attempted to particularize this message; that is, the philosophy, general behaviorism, and the specialized behavior therapy of the present approach have been in the process of progressive elaboration during the more than 30 years of its continuing growth. During that time its analyses and other developments repeatedly have preceded new areas of creative work that have become part of behavioral psychology. None of its elements have led to wasted research efforts (consider in this light the hundreds of studies of reinforcement schedules inspired by Skinner's theory) or have been set aside as disproved. Paradigmatic behaviorism's growth has been cumulative, along the same path, toward an ever more comprehensive, detailed, penetrating, and unified framework theory and body of research. There has been an accelerating development of the framework by others in original theoretical, research, and applied works (see, for example, Evans & Eifert, in press; Leduc, 1984). It is not an easy paradigm to incorporate, because of its wide range and its systematic, analytic, closely reasoned character. However, because of its value as a framework for making psychology's chaotic diversity generally meaningful, and because of its value as a framework with many new heuristic directions, it is time to say this paradigm should no longer be ignored.

References

Ardila, R. (1983, April). La sintesis experimental del comportamiento. *Interamerican Psychologists,* no. 58, 4–8.

Ayllon, T., & Michael, J. (1959). The psychiatric nurse as a behavioral engineer. *Journal of the Experimental Analysis of Behavior,* 2, 323–334.

Baars, B.J. (1984). View from a road not taken. *Contemporary Psychology, 29,* 804–805.

Bandura, A. (1968). A social learning interpretation of psychological dysfunctions. In P. London & D. Rosenhan (Eds.), *Foundations of abnormal psychology* (pp. 293–344). New York: Holt, Rinehart & Winston.

Bandura, A. (1977). *Social learning theory.* Englewood Cliffs, NJ: Prentice-Hall.

Bandura, A. (1978). The self-system in reciprocal determinism. *American Psychologist, 33,* 344–358.

Bandura, A., & Walters, R. (1959). *Adolescent aggression.* New York: Ronald.

Bandura, A., & Walters, R. (1963). *Social learning and personality.* New York: Holt, Rinehart & Winston.

Barnard, J.D., Christopherson, E.R., & Wolf, M.M. (1974). Supervising paraprofessional tutors in a remedial reading program. *Journal of Applied Behavior Analysis, 7,* 481.

Boring, E.G. (1950). *A history of experimental psychology* (2nd ed.). New York: Appleton.

Burns, G.L. (1980). Indirect measurement and behavioral assessment: A case for social behaviorism psychometrics. *Behavioral Assessment, 2,* 197–206.

Burns, G.L. (in press). Affective-cognitive-behavioral assessment: The integration of personality and behavior assessment. In I.M. Evans & G.H. Eifert (Eds.), *Unifying behavior therapy: contributions of paradigmatic behaviorism.* New York: Springer.

Burns, G.L. & Farina, A. (1987). Physical attractiveness and self perception of mental disorders. *Journal of Abnormal Psychology, 96,* 161–163.

Darden, L., & Maull, N. (1977). Interfield theories. *Philosophy of Science, 44,* 43–64.

Durkheim, E. (1927). *Les regles de la metode sociologique* (8th ed.). Paris: Alcan.

Eifert, G.H. (1983). Test of social behaviorism's conceptualization of self verbalizations. An analogue treatment of phobias. *International Newsletter of Social Behaviorism, 2,* 2–19.

Eifert, G.H. (1987). Language conditioning: Clinical issues and applications in behavior therapy. In H.J. Eysenck & I.M. Martin (Eds.), *Theoretical issues in behavior therapy.* London: Pergamon.

Epstein, R. (1984). The case for praxics. *The Behavior Analyst, 7,* 101–119.

Evans, I.M., & Eifert, G. (Eds.). (in press). *Unifying behavior therapy: contributions of paradigmatic behaviorism.* New York: Springer.

Feyerabend, P.K. (1963). How to be a good empiricist—A plea for tolerance in matters epistemological. In B. Baumrin (Ed.), *Philosophy of science. The Delaware Seminar* (Vol. I). (pp. 3–40). New York: Wiley.

Feyerabend, P.K. (1970). Against method: Outline of an anarchistic theory of knowledge. In M. Radner & S. Winokur (Eds.), *Minnesota studies in the philosophy of science* (Vol. 4) (pp. 3–16). Minneapolis: University of Minnesota Press.

Fishman, D.B. (1986). Where the underlying boundaries are: Organizing psychology by paradigm analysis. *International Newsletter of Uninomic Psychology, 2,* 4–9.

Fraley, L.E., & Vargas, E.A. (1986). Separate disciplines: The study of behavior and the study of the psyche. *The Behavior Analyst, 9,* 47–59.

Gagne, R. (1965). *The conditions of learning.* New York: Holt, Rinehart & Winston.

Gergen, K.J. (1973). Social psychology as history. *Journal of Personality and Social Psychology, 26,* 309–320.

Gergen, K.J. (1985). The social constructionist movement in modern psychology. *American Psychologist, 40,* 266–275.

Gilgen, A.R. (1987). The psychological level of organization in nature and the interdependencies among major psychological concepts. In A.W. Staats &

L.P. Mos (Eds.), *Annals of theoretical psychology: Vol. 5.* New York: Plenum.

Goldfried, M.R., & Sprafkin, J. (1974). *Behavioral personality assessment.* Morristown, NJ: General Learning Press.

Gordon, G.D., & Staats, A.W. (1987). Depression and the frequency and strength of pleasant events: Exploration of the Staats-Heiby theory. Unpublished manuscript.

Hanson, N.R. (1969). *Perception and discovery: An introduction to scientific inquiry.* San Francisco: Freeman, Cooper and Company.

Harms, J.Y., & Staats, A.W. (1978). Food deprivation and conditioned reinforcing value of food words: Interaction of Pavlovian and instrumental conditioning. *Bulletin of the Psychonomic Society, 12*(4), 294–296.

Heiby, E.M. (1985, May), *Depression: Radical vs. paradigmatic behaviorism.* Paper presented at the Association for Behavior Analysis, Columbus, OH.

Hekmat, H. (1972). The role of imagination in semantic desensitization. *Behavior Therapy, 3*, 223–231.

Hishinuma, E.S. (1987). Psychoanalytic and cognitive dissonance theory: Producing unity through the unifying theory review. In A.W. Staats & L.P. Mos (Eds.), *Annals of theoretical psychology: Vol. 5* (pp. 157–177). New York: Plenum.

Hull, C.L. (1920). Quantitative aspects of the evolution of concepts. *Psychological Monographs, 28*, No. 123.

Hull, C.L. (1943). *Principles of behavior.* New York: Appleton-Century-Crofts.

Koch, S. (1981). The nature and limits of psychological knowledge: Lessons of a century qua "science." *American Psychologist, 36*, 257–269.

Kuhn, T.S. (1962). *The structure of scientific revolutions.* Chicago: University of Chicago Press.

Lakatos, I. (1970). Falsification and the methodology of scientific research programmes. In I. Lakatos & A. Musgrave (Eds.), *Criticism and the growth of knowledge* (pp. 91–196). London: Cambridge University Press.

Leduc, A. (1984). *Recherches sur le behaviorisme paradigmatique ou social.* Quebec: Behaviora.

Leduc, A. (1986). Dominique aprende á de nombrer les objects. *Apprentissage et Socialisation, 9*, 115–124.

Leduc, A., & Dumais, A. (in press). Applications of social behaviorism in psychiatric institutional settings. In I.M. Evans & G.H. Eifert (Ed.), *Unifying behavior therapy: Contributions of Paradigmatic Behaviorism.* New York: Springer.

Leigland, S. (1984). Praxics and the case for radical behaviorism. *The Behavior Analyst, 8*, 127–128.

MacKenzie, B.D. (1977). *Behaviorism and the limits of scientific method.* Atlantic Highlands, NJ: Humanities Press.

Mahoney, M.J. (1977). Reflections on the cognitive-learning trend in psychotherapy. *American Psychologist, 32*, 5–13.

Mandelbaum, M. (1955). Societal facts. *British Journal of Sociology, 6*, 305–317.

McPherson, A., Bonem, M., Green, G., & Osborne, J.G. (1984). A citation analysis of the influence on research of Skinner's *Verbal Behavior: The Behavior Analyst, 7,* 157–168.

Meichenbaum, D. (1977). *Cognitive behavior modification.* New York: Plenum.

Merton, R.K. (Norman W. Storer, Ed.). (1973). *The sociology of science.* Chicago, IL: University of Chicago Press.

Minke, K.A. (in press a). A comparative analysis of modern behaviorism's general theories: Unification through generational advance. In A.W. Staats & L.P. Mos (Eds.), *Annals of theoretical psychology: Vol. 5* (pp.315–343). New York: Plenum.

Minke, K.A. (in press b). Research foundations of a developing paradigm: Implications for behavioral engineering. In I.M. Evans & G.H. Eifert (Eds.), *Unifying behavior therapy: contributions of paradigmatic behaviorism.* New York: Springer.

O'Leary, K.D., Becker, W.C., Evans, M.B., & Saudargas, R.A. (1969). A token reinforcement program in a public school: A replication and systematic analysis. *Applied Behavior Analysis, 2,* 3–13.

O'Leary, K.D., & Drabman, R. (1971). Token reinforcement programs in the classroom: A review. *Psychological Bulletin, 75,* 379–398.

Popper, K.R. (1963). *Conjectures and refutations.* New York: Harper & Row.

Popper, K.R. (1972). *Objective knowledge.* Oxford, England: Clarendon Press.

Rondal, J.A. (1985). *Adult-child interaction and the process of language acquisition.* New York: Praeger.

Scarr, S. (1985). Constructing psychology: Making facts and fables for our times. *American Psychologist, 40,* 499–512.

Shapere, D. (1977). Scientific theories and their domains. In F. Suppe (Ed.), *The structure of scientific theories* (2nd ed.) (pp. 518–565). Urbana: University of Illinois Press.

Shapere, D. (1979). The character of scientific change. Unpublished manuscript.

Sidman, M. (1960). *Tactics of scientific research.* New York: Basic Books.

Skinner, B.F. (1938). *The behavior or organisms.* New York: Appleton.

Skinner, B.F. (1950). Are theories of learning necessary? *Psychological Review, 57,* 193–196.

Skinner, B.F. (1953). *Science and human behavior.* New York: Macmillan.

Skinner, B.F. (1957). *Verbal behavior.* New York: Appleton-Century-Crofts.

Spence, K.W. (1944). The nature of theory construction in contemporary psychology. *Psychological Review, 51,* 47–68.

Staats, A.W. (1957). Learning theory and "opposite speech." *Journal of Abnormal and Social Psychology, 55,* 268–269.

Staats, A.W. (1961). Verbal habit families, concepts, and the operant conditioning of word classes. *Psychological Review, 68,* 190–204.

Staats, A.W. (with contributions by C.K. Staats). (1963). *Complex human behavior.* New York: Holt, Rinehart & Winston.

Staats, A.W. (Ed.). (1964). *Human learning.* New York: Holt, Rinehart & Winston.

Staats, A.W. (1965). A case in and a strategy for the extension of learning principles to complex human behavior. In L. Krasner & L.P. Ullmann (Eds.), *Research in behavior modification* (pp. 27–55). New York: Holt, Rinehart & Winston.

Staats, A.W. (1968a). *Learning, language, and cognition.* New York: Holt, Rinehart & Winston.

Staats, A.W. (1968b). Social behaviorism and human motivation: Principles of the attitude-reinforcer-discriminative system. In A.G. Greenwald, T.C. Brock, & T.M. Ostrom (Eds.), *Psychological foundations of attitudes* (pp. 33–66). New York: Academic Press.

Staats, A.W. (1970). A learning-behavior theory: A basis for unity in behavioral-social science. In A.R. Gilgen (Ed.), *Contemporary scientific psychology* (pp. 183–239). New York: Academic Press.

Staats, A.W. (1971a). *Child learning, intelligence and personality.* New York: Harper & Row.

Staats, A.W. (1971b). Linguistic-mentalistic theory versus an explanatory S-R learning theory of language development. In D.I. Slobin (Ed.), *The ontogenesis of grammar* (pp. 103–152). New York: Academic Press.

Staats, A.W. (1972). Language behavior therapy: A derivative of social behaviorism. *Behavior Therapy, 3*, 165–192.

Staats, A.W. (1973). Behavior analysis and token reinforcement in educational behavior modification and curriculum research. In D.E. Thoresen (Ed.), *Behavior modification in education: 72nd yearbook of the National Society for the Study of Education* (pp. 195–229). Chicago: University of Chicago Press.

Staats, A.W. (1974). Behaviorism and cognitive theory in the study of language: A neopsycholinguistics. In R.L. Schiefelbusch & L.L. Lloyd (Eds.), *Language perspectives: Acquisition, retardation, and intervention* (pp. 615–646). Baltimore, MD: University Park Press.

Staats, A.W. (1975). *Social behaviorism.* Homewood, IL: Dorsey Press.

Staats, A.W. (1978). *About social behaviorism and social learning theory.* Unpublished manuscript (mimeographed).

Staats, A.W. (1979b). The three-function learning theory of social behaviorism: A third-generation, unified theory. *Learning and Behavior, 2*, 13–38.

Staats, A.W. (1980). "Behavioral interaction" and "interactional psychology" theories of personality: Similarities, differences, and the need for unification. *British Journal of Psychology, 71*, 205–220.

Staats, A.W. (1981). Paradigmatic behaviorism, unified theory, unified theory construction methods, and the zeitgeist of separatism. *American Psychologist, 36*, 240–256.

Staats, A.W. (1983a). *Psychology's crisis of disunity: Philosophy and method for a unified science.* New York: Praeger.

Staats, A.W. (1983b). Paradigmatic behaviorism: Unified theory for social-personality psychology. In L. Berkowitz (Ed.), *Advances in experimental social psychology: Vol. 16. Theorizing in social psychology: Theoretical perspectives* (pp. 126–179). New York: Academic Press.

Staats, A.W. (1985a). Disunity's prisoner, blind to a new approach to unification. *Contemporary Psychology, 30,* 339–340.

Staats, A.W. (1985b). Toward unity: A cognitive *pax romana*? Or a general philosophy and methodology? *Contemporary Psychology, 30,* 420–421.

Staats, A.W. (1985c). Editorial: Projection for paradigmatic psychology. *International Newsletter of Paradigmatic Psychology, 1,* 1–5.

Staats, A.W. (1986a). Behaviorism with a personality: The paradigmatic behavioral assessment approach. In R.O. Nelson & S.C. Hayes (Eds.), *Conceptual foundations of behavioral assessment* (pp. 244–296). New York: Guilford.

Staats, A.W. (1986b). Left and right paths for behaviorism's development. *The Behavior Analyst, 9,* 231–237.

Staats, A.W. (1987). Unified positivism: Philosophy for the revolution to unity. In A.W. Staats & L.P. Mos (Eds.), *Annals of theoretical psychology: Vol 5. On unification.* New York: Plenum.

Staats, A.W. (in press). Paradigmatic behavior therapy: A unified framework for theory, research, and practice. In I.M. Evans & G.H. Eifert (Ed.), *Unifying behavior therapy: Contributions of Paradigmatic Behaviorism.* New York: Springer.

Staats, A.W., Brewer, B.A., & Gross, M.C. (1970). Learning and cognitive development: Representative samples, cumulative-hierarchical learning, and experimental-longitudinal methods. *Monographs of the Society for Research in Child Development, 35* (8, Whole No. 141).

Staats, A.W., & Burns, G.L. (1981). Intelligence and child development: What intelligence is and how it is learned and functions. *Genetic Psychology Monographs, 104,* 237–301.

Staats, A.W., & Burns, G.L. (1982). Emotional personality repertoire as cause of behavior: Personality specification and interaction theory. *Journal of Personality and Social Psychology, 43,* 873–881.

Staats, A.W., & Butterfield, W.H. (1965). Treatment of nonreading in a culturally-deprived juvenile delinquent: An application of reinforcement principles. *Child Development, 26,* 925–942.

Staats, A.W., & Fernandez-Ballesteros, R. (1987). The self-report in personality measurement: A paradigmatic behaviorism approach to psychodiagnostics. *Evaluacion Psicologica/Psychological Assessment.*

Staats, A.W., Finley, J.R., Minke, K.A., & Wolf, M.M. (1964a). Reinforcement variables in the control of unit reading responses. *Journal of the Experimental Analysis of Behavior, 7,* 139–149.

Staats, A.W., Gross, M.C., Guay, P.F., & Carlson, C.C. (1973). Personality and social systems and attitude-reinforcer-discriminative theory: Interest (attitude) formation, function, and measurement. *Journal of Personality and Social Psychology, 26,* 251–261.

Staats, A.W., & Hammond, W.W. (1972). Natural words as physiological conditioned stimuli: Food-word elicited salivation and deprivation effects. *Journal of Experimental Psychology, 96,* 206–208.

Staats, A.W., & Heiby, E.M. (1985). The paradigmatic behaviorism theory of depression. In S. Reiss & R. Bootzin (Eds.), *Theoretical issues in behavior therapy.* (pp. 279–330). New York: Academic Press.

Staats, A.W., Minke, K.A., Finley, J.R., Wolf, M.M., & Brooks. L.O. (1964b). A reinforcer system and experimental procedure for the laboratory study of reading acquisition. *Child Development, 35,* 209–231.

Staats, A.W., Staats, C.K., Schutz, R.E., & Wolf, M.M. (1962). The conditioning of reading responses using "extrinsic" reinforcers. *Journal of the Experimental Analysis of Behavior, 5,* 33–40.

Staats, A.W., & Warren, D.R. (1974). Motivation and three-function learning: Deprivation-satiation and approach-avoidance to food words. *Journal of Experimental Psychology, 103,* 1191–1199.

Sulzer-Azeroff, B., & Mayer, R.G. (1985). *Achieving educational excellence.* New York: Holt, Rinehart & Winston.

Suppe, F. (1977). *The structure of scientific theories.* Urbana: University of Illinois Press.

Tolman, E.C. (1932). *Purposive behavior in animals and men.* New York: Appleton-Century.

Toulmin, S. (1972). *Human understanding.* Princeton, NJ: Princeton University Press.

Tryon, W.W. (1974). A reply to Staats' language behavior therapy: A derivative of social behaviorism. *Behavior Therapy, 5,* 273–276.

van Hoorn, W. (1972). *As images unwind.* Amsterdam: University Press of Amsterdam.

Watson, J.B. (1930). *Behaviorism* (rev. ed.). Chicago: University of Chicago Press.

Weimer, W.B. (1979). *Notes on the methodology of scientific research.* Hillsdale, NJ: Erlbaum.

Williams, C.D. (1959). The elimination of tantrum behavior by extinction procedures. *Journal of Abnormal and Social Psychology, 59,* 269.

Wolf, M.M., Risley, T., & Mees, H. (1964). Applications of operant conditioning procedures to the behaviour problems of an autistic child. *Behaviour Research and Therapy, 1,* 305–312.

Wolpe, J. (1958). *Psychotherapy by reciprocal inhibition.* Standord, CA: Stanford University Press.

11

Pragmatic Behaviorism: Saving and Nurturing the Baby

Daniel B. Fishman

Introduction: Of Paradigms and "Social Constructionism"

As noted in Chapter 2, Kuhn's (1970) concept of "paradigm" refers to the explicit and implicit assumptions—epistemological, theoretical, methodological, technological, ethical, sociopolitical, and historical—to which a scientific discipline adheres. Gergen's (1982, 1985) "social constructionism" argues for the importance of the paradigm concept by emphasizing that a science's disciplinary assumptions are subjective, culturally and historically embedded, and logically and scientifically unprovable. Scientific knowledge is a linguistic human construction rather than a direct representation of nature. Because this is so, there is no one-to-one correspondence between scientific theories and the mind-and-discourse-independent "real" world that absolutely necessitates acceptance. Rather, scientific paradigms—shared sets of assumptions among a group of scientists—occur when the individual members of the group become persuaded, through communal dialogue, of the merits of those assumptions and committed to them in their work. Thus, in the end:

> Science, in its various functions as a mode of inquiry into and explanation of phenomena, is a rhetorical transaction. The "logic" of scientific inference, the nature of theoretical understanding and explanation, even problems of theory choice and paradigm allegiance are intrinsically rhetorical if one abandons the traditional justificationist conception of rhetoric as a

"second rate" art which pales by comparison to logic and dialectic. (Weimer, 1977, p. 1)

In studying the growth and change within the natural sciences, Kuhn found that their development has not been a continuous, linear progression, in which knowledge is slowly and steadily accumulated. Rather, progress has often been sudden, with abrupt changes that sweep away the foundation of existing theory, for example, the scientific "revolutions" of Copernican astronomy, Darwinian evolution, and Einsteinian physics. This is very understandable within the context of social constructionism. The "soft," flexible link between scientific concepts and external reality allows for the interplay of political and social dynamics among scientists as they struggle for and negotiate consensus about paradigmatic assumptions.

In advocating the usefulness of Kuhn's paradigm concept, I am not necessarily passing judgment on his specific theory about the nature of scientific development and the incommensurability of successive paradigms within a science. [There is a sizable literature of controversy that has developed on these topics. For an excellent summary, see Gholson and Barker (1985)]. Rather, I am supporting the notion that a scientific discipline consists of a group of individuals who share a body of explicit and implicit assumptions about epistemology, theory, technology, ethics, and sociopolitical organization. (To be more precise, a group's "sharing" of assumptions is a quantitative concept. Within any designated scientific group, the extent of agreement on the total relevant assumptions can vary from zero to 100%. Moreover, some assumptions might be weighted more highly than others. Thus, it is feasible to characterize quantitatively the "weighted" extent to which a group does share a consensus and to understand the process and products of that group in part as a function of the degree of consensus.)

With the above as a prologue, the present chapter will argue the following five propositions:

1. From 1879 until about 1945, psychology generally and the theories of learning underlying behavior therapy specifically were conducted within a single "experimental" paradigm.

2. Since 1945, two additional, partially conflicting paradigms have emerged—the "technological" paradigm and the "hermeneutic" (or interpretive) paradigm.

3. In behavior therapy, the technological paradigm can be concretized into a paradigm first proposed by Erwin (1978), called "pragmatic behaviorism."

4. One of the great strengths of pragmatic behaviorism is its abil-

ity to provide a rational justification for those accepted practices of behavior therapists that conflict with the experimental paradigm. In other words, the pragmatic behaviorism paradigm prevents us from throwing out the proverbial "baby" of effective behavior therapy practice with the "bathwater" of oversimplistic, overmechanized, incompetently delivered, or otherwise unsuccessful behavior intervention activities.

5. It follows from the above that, while complete commitment to a single paradigm is not warranted at this time, the technological paradigm, as embodied in pragmatic behaviorism, looks particularly promising for the future and should receive at least its fair share of scientific and professional resources from the field.

Scientific Psychology and Behavior Therapy Until 1945: Agreement on the Experimental Paradigm

In 1879, Wundt established the world's first psychological laboratory for the application of quantification, statistics, and the experimental method to phenomena of human behavior and experience. This event is usually identified as the point at which psychology broke away from philosophy and declared itself an independent discipline (Lamb, 1983; Staats, 1983). The justification for this separation was the belief that psychology could employ the empirical, laboratory-based methods developed in the natural sciences that had been so dramatically successful in those fields. Thus psychology could develop a truly scientific approach to the understanding, control, and prediction of human behavior and experience.

Also at this time, a development taking place within philosophy itself supported psychology's "Declaration of Independence." This development was the evolution of Comte's philosophy of positivism. This system spawned the logical-positivism movement of the Vienna Circle, which was particularly dominant and productive between the two World Wars.

In broad terms, logical positivism contends that there is an external world independent of human experience and that objective knowledge about this world can be obtained through direct sense experience, as interpreted within the framework of the experimental scientific method. The core of this method is the theory-embedded laboratory experiment, which, in psychology, should meet the following criteria: (1) the experiment is derived from a theory in which at least some of the concepts are tied to operational variables (Mahoney, 1974); (2) the experiment tests one or more hypotheses that are logically related to the samples of subjects, experimental situations, and measures of independent and dependent variables employed (Epstein, 1980); Rosenthal, 1976); (3) the experiment adequately controls "artifactual" variables that could interact with those under study, such as demand characteristics (Orne, 1962), response sets, and situation-specific contextual variables; (4) the experiment is replicated with similar results (Epstein, 1980); and (5) the results are generalizable to a large variety of settings (Mahoney, 1974), such that they provide verification or falsification of the general laws implied in the hypotheses.

Until World War II, there was a fair degree of consensus within organized psychology upon this experimental paradigm (Staats, 1983). Specifically, there was consensus upon two assumptions: (1) that the theory-based experiment, as practiced primarily by academic researchers, would yield a cumulative body of context-free, universal laws about significant aspects of human behavior; and (2) that these general laws could be applied to help solve significant psychological and social problems in a unique, scientifically based manner.

With the publication in 1913 of Watson's "Psychology as the Behaviorist Views It," behaviorism and its closely associated learning theories and experiments came increasingly to dominate psychology until 1945. During this time, especially the period from 1930 to 1945, the following assumptions predominated: the epistemology that should underlie psychology is logical positivism; the theoretical goal of psychology is to discover universal psychological principles for predicting and controlling acquired and new behaviors; and the best method for discovering such laws is to conduct theoretically important experiments in the laboratory by using genetically, historically, and environmentally controlled animals as subjects. The basic "normal science" (Kuhn, 1970) that took place within this paradigm was the search for the particular psychological principles that best seemed to predict the behavior of laboratory animals.

Breakdown of Consensus on the Experimental Paradigm

Lack of Substantive Results

Since World War II, for at least four reasons, there has been a growing breakdown of consensus on the experimental paradigm. First, as numerous well-known psychologists have discussed, consistent, coherent, and relevant substantive results have failed to emerge from all the experiments (e.g., Cronbach, 1975; Epstein, 1980; Gergen, 1982; Greenwald, 1976; Koch, 1959; Levine, 1974; Staats, 1983; Wachtel,

1980). For example, in 1959, Koch, editor of a seven-volume study focusing on the state of psychological learning theory, concluded as follows:

> Consider the hundreds of theoretical formulations, rational equations and mathematical models of the learning process that we have accrued; the thousands of research studies. And *now* consider that there is still no wide agreement, even at the crassest descriptive level, on the empirical conditions under which learning takes place. (p. 731)

As another example, in 1982 Gergen summarized the situation thus:

> Dismay over the accumulation of knowledge in psychology is hardly difficult to locate. . . . In the field of personality psychology, Lee Sechrest (1976) has compared the major issues of study over a ten-year period and asked: "Now why have the themes changed? If it were because issues have been resolved, because important phenomena are now so well understood that they no longer merit attention, it would be cause for encouragement—rejoicing perhaps. Alas, one cannot escape the conclusion that investigators ran out of steam, that issues were abandoned, and the problems were never resolved" (p. 26). Similarly, in reviewing the nearly three hundred studies on individual versus group risk-taking, Dorwin Cartwright (1973) concludes: "After 10 years of research the original problem remains unresolved. We still do not know how the risk-taking behavior of 'real-life' groups compares with that of individuals" (p. 3). In cognitive psychology, Allen Newell (1973) has commented on the "ever increasing pile of issues in cognitive psychology which we weary of or become diverted from but never settle" (p. 289). . . . And Clara Mayo (1977) has said of contemporary social psychology, "Few theoretical formulations of any power have emerged and few of the empirical findings have proved replicable or generalizable beyond the college sophomore for whom they were developed." (Gergen, 1982, p. 4)

In Staats's (1984) words,

> In the face of all of [theory-based research] psychology's efforts, its thousands of studies conducted with scientific finesse, its hundreds of theories, its hundreds of tests, experimental designs, apparatuses, data analysis methods, and so on, those who systematically study sciences are of the opinion that psychology is a "would-be" science, a pretender to science. (p. 3)

A confirmatory negative picture of psychology's substantive, theory-based research accomplishments emerges from a special section in the 15th anniversary issue of *Psychology Today* (Nessel, 1982). Eleven distinguished psychologists, "the best minds in the field," were asked to describe what each considered to be "the most significant work in psychology over the past decade and a half." Their resulting answers to this question were summarized in a *New York Times* editorial (Wade, 1982):

> The results are astonishing: it would seem that there has been none [i.e., no significant work]. "Significant work" implies work generally agreed to be important, but the 11 Best Minds in psychology agree on hardly anything. Stanley Milgrim of the City University of New York hails the teaching of sign language to apes as an enduring recent achievement. But another contributor, Ulric Neisser of Cornell, cites as important the evident *failure* to teach sign language to apes.
>
> B.F. Skinner, alleging himself not well informed of recent progress in other fields of psychology, recounts the advances in behavioral psychology, which he pioneered. But two other sages, Jerome Brunner of the New School for Social Research and Richard Lazarus of Berkeley, laud the escape from Skinnerian psychology as the most significant accomplishment.
>
> Almost the only recent achievement hailed by more than one contributor is the discovery of endorphins. . . . This is certainly an interesting development, but the credit belongs to pharmacologists and physiologists; psychology had little to do with it.
>
> Perhaps because of the apparent difficulty of naming significant work, two of the Best Minds [Bernice Neugarten and Philip Zimbardo] make no effort to do so.
>
> The failure of the 11 psychologists to agree on almost anything evinces a serious problem in their academic discipline. Physicists or biologists asked the same question would not concur on everything but there would be a substantial commonality in their answers. Can psychology be taken seriously as science if even its leading practitioners cannot agree on its recent advances? . . . Mature science [should] possess a certain level of agreement as to what has been accomplished and what constitutes a fruitful research program. (p. 28)

The results of such a survey of psychology's "best minds" perhaps justifies some legislators' view of "psychology as an intellectual boondoggle undeserving of the research appropriations given other scientific fields" (Hill, 1981, p. 18E); or, in the more flamboyant words Ohio Congressman John Ashbrook: the social and behavior sciences constitute "the foolish fringe folly of researchers who use tax money like the dilettante squanders his inheritance!" (cited in Hill, 1981, p. 18E).

Sociopolitical Factors Undermining the Experimental Paradigm

A second reason for the breakdown in consensus has come from a realization that the present functioning of the mechanism for accumulating systematic knowledge in psychology, publication in journals and books, discourages research that meets the experimental paradigm outlined above in at least six ways (Fishman & Neigher, 1982; Neigher & Fishman, 1985). These discouraging factors include: (1)

negative incentives for replication (Epstein, 1980; Smith, 1970); (2) bias against studies that support the null hypothesis (Greenwald, 1975; Mahoney, 1977); (3) a publication decision-making process that is unreliable and biased (Mahoney, 1977; Peters & Ceci, 1980; Scott, 1974); (4) valuation of methodology over substance (Hogan, 1979); (5) little encouragement of data that have ecological relevance (Bronfenbrenner, 1977; Gibbs, 1979; Neisser, 1976; Jenkins, 1974); and (6) discouragement of detailed description of data-collection procedures and of sharing raw data with other investigators, thereby increasing the chance for inadvertent or deliberate bias and error (Burstein et al. 1985; Ceci & Walker, 1983).

The Unlinking of Practice from Experimental Research

A third reason for the breakdown in consensus comes from the experiences of psychologists in the applied sector. These professionals have discovered that they can sell their services without having to show a tight link between their practices and the experimental literature. For example, projective testing continues to be widely used and accepted today despite its dismal record when subjected to experimental validation (Lubin, et al., 1985; Zubin et al., 1965). As Marshall (1982) pointed out, this same dynamic appears true of behavior therapy:

> During the first full decade of the widespread deployment of behavior therapy (the 1960s), claims were make (Eysenck, 1964) for strong ties with general theories in basic psychology (particularly [experimentally-based] learning theories). The historical value of this general position was to give our arguments and our proposals for treatment a cloak of scientific respectibility (London, 1972). Such was the success of behavior therapists that during the past decade they no longer needed this cloak. (p. 57)

It is not surprising that behavior therapy, like other fields of applied psychology, separated itself from experimentally based theory once that theory was no longer politically necessary. As stated above, in psychology generally there exists little theory upon which there is scientific consensus. In the area of behavior therapy specifically, Erwin (1978) analyzed the learning-theory literature and concluded that: "There is no known theory or law of any kind that is of sufficient scope to serve as a foundation [for behavior therapy] and that has also been empirically confirmed" (p. 128). In a similar vein, Barlow, Hayes, and Nelson (1984) analyzed the relevant literature and concluded that for most practitioners, both behavioral and nonbehavioral, "research has little effect on practice" (p. 31). Rather, practitioners typically obtain their strategies and procedures from "intuitive eclecticism," a process involving an idiosyncratic choice of therapeutic approach based on the individual practitioner's trial-and-error experience and on the persuasiveness of other clinicians whom the practitioner encounters in therapy workshops and informal conversations.

Loss of Support for Logical Positivism

The fourth reason for the breakdown in consensus has been the loss of support for logical positivism, both within the philosophical community and within the disciplines of the history of science and the sociology of science. Such well-known post-positivistic philosophers as Austin, Goodman, Kuhn, Putnam, Ryle, and Wittgenstein have rejected the validity of a philosophy that posits a direct relationship between sense data and the real world (Campbell, 1984; Gergen, 1982; Putnam, 1984). Rather, in the view of these philosophers, human experience of and knowledge about the world is inextricably mediated by language, and it is the relationship between language and the world—that is, how words "hook into" the world—that is *"the* problem for analytic philosophy in the twentieth century" (Putnam, 1984). In the words of Kuhn (1974), who is describing areas in which he and Popper agree:

> [We are] in opposition to a number of classical positivism's most characteristic theses. We both emphasize, for example, the intimate and inevitable entanglement of scientific observation with scientific theory; we are correspondingly skeptical of efforts to produce any neutral observation language. (p. 2)

This loss of support has carried over into psychology. For example, in a recent two-year period, five major articles in the *American Psychologist* attacked logical positivism's view that science is value-free and that observation provides unassailable knowledge of "facts" and "raw data" (Kimble, 1984; Krasner & Houts, 1984; Gergen, 1985; Scarr, 1985; Woolfolk & Richardson, 1984). All these articles set forth the alternative view labeled by Gergen as "social constructionism."

Here are three illustrative quotes from these articles. First, from Krasner and Houts (1984):

> It is neither physically nor philosophically possible to obtain knowledge without first choosing some assumptive framework. This framework is undetermined by observations; rather it constitutes the hermeneutic [or interpretive] context for generating "facts" and giving meaning to observations. (pp. 840–841)

Next, from Gergen (1985):

> Social Constructionism views discourse about the world not as a reflec-

tion or map of the world [as in logical positivism], but as an artifact of communal interchange. . . . How can theoretical categories be induced or derived from observation . . . if the process of identifying observational attributes itself relies on one's possessing categories? How can theoretical categories map or reflect the world if each definition used to link category and observation itself requires a definition? How can words map reality when the major constraints over word usage are furnished by linguistic context? (pp. 266–267)

Finally, from Scarr (1985):

All the world's a stage, but the script is not *As You Like It,* it is *Rasho-mon.* Each of us has our own reality of which we try to persuade others. Facts do not have an independent existence. Rather, facts guide the selection of observations and the invention of reality. . . .
   [The] Constructionist position on epistemology [contends that] knowledge of all kinds, including scientific knowledge, is a construction of the human mind. Sensory data are filtered through the knowing apparatus of the human senses and made into perceptions and cognitions. The human mind is also constructed in a social context, and its knowledge is in part created by the social and cultural context in which it comes to know the world. . . .
   [In short], we do not discover scientific facts; we invent them. Their usefulness to us depends both on shared perceptions of the "facts" (concensual validation) and on whether they work for various purposes, some practical and some theoretical. (pp. 499–500)

A related quote comes from a recent chapter by the well-known research methodologist Campbell (1984), who had the following to say about the embeddedness of scientific knowledge:

We are inevitably encapsulated in some paradigm of presuppositions, implicit or explicit. Historically, we can look back and see how provincially we were embedded. We cannot do without presuppositions. We cannot pull each presupposition out individually and prove them one at a time . . . [We are enmeshed in] presuppositions about the nature of the world that are built into our retinas, the nerve wiring of our brains, our language, and our own research tradition. (p. 28)

A final quote of this type is from the renowned theoretical physicist Wheeler (cited in Bernstein, 1985):

Where is the barrier between solipsism and objective reality in a physical theory? . . . There is not a word we utter, a concept we use, an idea we form, that does not directly or indirectly depend on the larger community for its existence. "Meaning"—and what else is "objective reality" if it is not meaning?—is the joint product of those who communicate. (pp. 28–29)

The Technological and Hermeneutic Alternatives to the Experimental Paradigm

Social constructionism as an epistemology is closely related to James's concepts of contextualism and pragmatism (Lilienfeld, 1978; Pepper, 1942). Contextualism is an ontological view in which:

> The world is seen as an unlimited complex of change and novelty, order and disorder. Out of this total flux we select certain contexts; these contexts serve as organizing gestalts or patterns that give meaning and scope to the vast array of details that, without the organizing pattern, would be meaningless or invisible . . . .
> Truth is "the successful working out of an idea" (Pepper, 1942, p. 271) within a specific (and always limited) context. The contextualist hesitates to extend a theory beyond the limits of specific working contexts; all experiences are fragmentary, limited, partial, and occur within the limits of contexts beyond which is only an infinite universe of indeterminancy . . . .
> The contextualist uses . . . integrating structures (contexts) to explain experience, but denies to these integrating structures any reality. (Lilienfeld, 1978, pp. 9–11)

Because the mind-independent world is "an unlimited complex of change and novelty, order and disorder," it is not possible to attain a "true," "objective" picture of this world. Rather, the "truth" of a concept is a function of its pragmatic usefulness in particular contexts. In William James's (1955) words:

> Any idea that will carry us prosperously from any one part of our experience to any other part, linking things satisfactorily, working securely, saving labor, is true for just so much, true in so far forth, true *instrumentally.* The true . . . is only the expedient in the way of thinking. (p. 58)

Social constructionism has spawned two new types of epistemological models, each of which is associated with a psychology paradigm alternative to the experimental paradigm. The more radical is a "hermeneutic" paradigm that emphasizes qualitative interpretation and experimental meaning and feeling. This model views the goals and proper methods of psychology as similar to those of history, literary criticism, and investigative reporting (Gergen, 1982; Messer & Winokur, 1984; Packer, 1985).

The hermeneutic paradigm assumes that psychological knowledge should be idiographic—that is, such knowledge should emphasize the multidimensional complexities of the context of any particular behavior. This contrasts with logical positivism's emphasis on abstraction through quantification.

The alternative approach spawned by social constructionism is the technological paradigm. While still using quantitative methods, as in the experimental paradigm, the technological paradigm eschews the theory-based laboratory experiment and the search for general psychological laws. Rather, this model focuses on the action-oriented approaches from engineering and the field of research and development (Azrin, 1977; Broskowski, 1971; Fishman & Neigher, 1982; Gilbert, 1978; Morell, 1979; Price & Cherniss, 1977).

In the technological-paradigm model, a conceptually coherent program is designed to address a significant social or psychological problem within a naturalistic, real-world setting, in a manner that is feasible, effective, and efficient. Quantification is used to develop performance indicators of a system's functioning. The system is then monitored in terms of both baselines and changes due to identified interventions. Also, in the historical and cultural context of the particular individual, group, or organizational case, single-case experimental designs can be employed to assess causal relationships that appear true for that individual case (Barlow et al., 1984).

Following the principles of pragmatism and contextualism, the technological paradigm focuses on getting projects and programs to "work" within a particular real-world setting. The degree to which the program or project is generalizable from that particular contextual setting is an empirical one. Just because a program will not work in another setting does not diminish the program's relevance and validity in the original setting. The lack of success in the second setting is attributed to contextual differences between the two settings. These contextual differences are always present, and frequently they functionally interact with the program in question.

Table 11.1 lists a variety of contrasts among the three different paradigms—experimental, technological, and hermeneutic. Included in these comparisons are six items that Kimble (1984) found to differentiate empirically between the "scientific" and "humanistic" cultures in psychology. With one exception, these cultures are perfectly aligned with the experimental and the hermeneutic paradigms, respectively. The exception is item 9, in which the humanistic pole involves an emphasis upon "improving the human condition" rather than upon the "scholarly understanding" of the hermeneutic paradigm.

Table 11.2 analyzes the first eleven items in Table 11.1 to summarize how the technological paradigm is a hybrid, incorporating components of the other two paradigms along with possessing some of its own unique characteristics.

TABLE 11.1 Illustrative Differences Among Epistemological Paradigms

Paradigm characteristic	Experimental paradigm	Technological paradigm	Hermeneutic paradigm
1. Underlying epistemology	Logical positivism	Social constructionism	Social constructionism
2. Primary mode of research[a]	Nomothetic	Idiographic	Idiographic
3. Primary goal of research	Derivation of theory-based, general psychological laws through laboratory experiments	Solution of context-specific, practical psychological problems	Qualitative understanding of context-specific psychological events and processes
4. Primary site of research[a]	Specially created settings: laboratories, college classrooms	Natural settings	Natural settings
5. Primary type of data employed	Quantitative	Quantitative	Qualitative
6. Primary level of analysis[a]	Elemental, molecular	Elemental, molecular	Holistic, molar
7. Primary source of knowledge[a]	Observation	Observation	Intuition
8. View of how predictable and determined behavior is[a]	Emphasis on behavior as determined and predictable	Emphasis on behavior as determined and predictable	A balance between behavior as predictable vs. unpredictable, determined vs. indeterminate
9. Primary use of empirical or experimental information generated: scientific/scholarly understanding vs. improving the human condition[a]	Scientific theory development	Improving social programs by assistance to decision-makers in those programs	Scholarly addition to a cumulative body of commentary about human experience and behavior
10. Primary modes of communication	Publication in esoteric, highly technical journals	Written reports to lay decision-makers concerning their programs and policies	Publication in both academic journals and "intellectual" media like the *New York Times Magazine*

cont.

TABLE 11.1 (continued)

Paradigm characteristic	Experimental paradigm	Technological paradigm	Hermeneutic paradigm
11. Need for complex, quantitative management information systems	Low need: experiments generate relatively small amounts of quantitative data	High need: performance indicators about complex, real-world settings generate large amounts of quantitative data	No need: quantitative data are not relevant within the paradigm
12. Exemplars in psychology	Animal experiments to test Hullian learning theory; correlational studies to test personality trait theory	Market research; standardized educational tests, such as the "SATs"; behavior therapy token economies	Qualitative interpretation of the Rorschach; interpretation in psychoanalytic therapy; psychohistory
13. Exemplars outside of psychology	Natural sciences (physics, chemistry, and biology)	National economic indicators; U.S. Census; financial accounting data; sports statistics	Investigative reporting; interpretive history; literary criticism

[a]Note: Kimble (1984) found these six items to define the "scientific" versus the "humanistic" cultures in psychology on his "Epistemic Differential" scale. With the exception of item 9, the experimental paradigm embodies all the characteristics of the scientific culture, and the hermeneutic paradigm, all those of the humanistic culture, p. 266.

Pragmatic Behaviorism: Applying the Technological Paradigm to Behavior Therapy

The term behavior therapy has a diversity of meanings (e.g., see Farkas, 1980; Kazdin & Wilson, 1978; Wilson, 1978; Wilson, 1982). In fact, Wilson likened behavior therapy to Supreme Court Justice Potter Stewart's comment about pornography: "it's impossible to define but you know it when you see it" (1982, p. 292).

This definitional dilemma appears to result from the fact that behavior therapy, like many other areas in the social sciences, consists of a series of overlapping domains. These can be represented in a "Venn" diagram, as shown in Figure 11.1. Circle 1 in the diagram, "Learning Theory-Derived Behavior Therapy," includes those behavioral approaches that are derived from the major learning theories, including operant conditioning, respondent conditioning, and social-learning theory. Circle 1 is completely contained within Circle 2, Experimental

TABLE 11.2 The Hybrid Nature of the Technological Paradigm: Comparison with the Other Two Approaches[a]

Characteristics shared by the hermeneutic and technological paradigms	Characteristics shared by the experimental and technological paradigms	Characteristics unique to the technological paradigm
1. Commitment to an epistemology of social constructionism (vs. logical positivism)	5. Primary type of data employed are quantitative (vs. qualitative)	9. Emphasis upon decision-oriented, "human focused" knowledge (vs. scholarly or science-focused knowledge)
2. Emphasis on idiographic research (vs. nomothetic research)	6. Primary level of analysis is elemental (vs. holistic)	10. Reports are frequently written for lay decision-makers (vs. primarily for academic journals)
3. Exphasis on context-specific knowledge (vs. general laws)	7. A major source of knowledge is observation (vs. primary reliance on intuition)	11. High need for complex, quantitative information systems (vs. low need or no need)
4. Main site of research is the natural setting (vs. the laboratory)	8. Emphasis upon behavior as determined and predictable (vs. indeterminate and unpredictable)	

[a]Note: The item numbers are the same as in Table 11.1. Items 2, 4, 6, 7, 8, and 9 are from Kimble, 1984 (see footnote in Table 11.1).

Psychology–Derived Behavior Therapy. Circle 2 consists of behavioral approaches that are derived from any experimentally based psychological principles. These include the many approaches within cognitive behavior therapy that are based on experimental cognitive principles not associated with traditional learning theories.

Circle 3, Technique-Derived Behavior Therapy, consists of those behavioral approaches that are rooted in certain accepted techniques of behavioral assessment and change. Some of these techniques, like shaping, are clearly deducible from the experimental principles associated with Circles 1 and 2, while some, like desensitization, are not (Wilson & O'Leary, 1980, pp. 162-164). Thus Circle 3 overlaps with but is not completely included in these other two circles.

Circle 4, Psychotherapy-Derived Behavior Therapy, consists of behavioral approaches that are grounded in the psychotherapy literature and tradition. While some of these approaches clearly overlap with traditional behavioral techniques (Circle 3) and experimentally

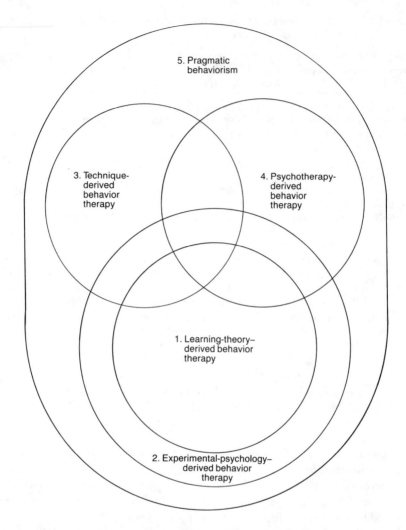

FIGURE 11.1 The overlapping domains of the behavioral movement.

based psychological principles (Circle 2), other approaches in Circle 4
do not. Examples are the extensive use made by behavior therapists of
relationship-enhancement methods, taken from Rogers's client-cen-
tered therapy (Swann & MacDonald, 1978), and of procedures for restructuring irrational beliefs, taken from Ellis's rational-emotive therapy.

What, then, justifies all of these domains being included under the
rubric "behavior therapy"? As shown in Figure 11.1, I am proposing

that are all contained within the umbrella of Circle 5, Pragmatic Behaviorism. To appreciate this concept, it is helpful to review the role of the general concept of "behaviorism" within the history of behavior therapy.

Behaviorism is the thesis that psychology is the study of behavior rather than inner mental life. Historically, three different concepts of what might be called "ideological behaviorism" have developed (Eysenck, 1972; Erwin, 1978):

> 1. *Metaphysical (or, radical) behaviorism,* . . . the view that minds (or mental events or states) do not exist.
> 2. *Analytical (or, logical) behaviorism,* . . . the view that all statements ostensibly about the mental can be translated into statements about behavior or behavioral dispositions.
> 3. *Methodological behaviorism,* . . . the view that psychologists should, for methodological reasons, abjure completely the use of mentalistic explanations. (Erwin, 1978, p. 51)

All three versions of ideological behaviorism are grounded in a logical-positivist view of science and the assumption that behavior can be objectively observed as "brute data." In the context of post-1945 critiques of logical positivism and the continuing controversies among learning theorists, Erwin (1978) uses the tools of analytical philosophy to argue that each of the three types of ideological behaviorism is untenable if considered literally. The underlying theme of his arguments is that our means of experiencing and communicating about the world is language, and language is just too intertwined with mentalistic concepts and too logically complicated to accommodate these views of behaviorism.

In the spirit of social constructionism and the technological paradigm (see Table 11.1), Erwin (1978) proposes a new version of behaviorism that he calls "pragmatic behaviorism." This, he argues, avoids the logical problems of the earlier views of ideological behaviorism while retaining the essence of what behavior therapists actually believe and do. Erwin (1978) describes pragmatic behaviorism as:

> the philosophical assumption that *clinical problems should generally be analyzed in behavioral terms.* . . . In treating a client, behavioral counterparts should generally be sought that correlate with (but are not equivalent to) any relevant problematic mental state. *The treatment should focus primarily on behavior, not because the mind is behavior, but for practical reasons.* (p. 80, emphasis added)

Erwin (1978) provides the following two examples of the pragmatic-behaviorism concept:

It is often easy to establish a base rate and to assess therapeutic change in comparison to that rate if behavior is the focus of study and treatment. It may be of some use to learn, for example, that an obese patient has a *craving for food,* but it is even more useful to learn how many eating responses are engaged in each day and under exactly what conditions. . . .

Consider a patient who claims to be suffering from existential despair . . . . A behavior therapist can begin by determining how the despair expressed itself in behavior. The therapist can then break this behavior down into smaller components and try to replace each component by behavior patterns that are not conducive to the maintenance of a despairing attitude. . . . It is likely that at least some of these behaviors would play some causal role in maintaining (not necessarily originating) the despair; by changing them the despair may well be diminished. This is not to suggest that a patient cannot justifiably feel despair, . . . nor is it to suggest that just any deeply rooted feeling of despair can be so easily diminished or eliminated. The point, rather, is that by getting the patient to discuss his problems in behavioral terms, the therapist can often deal with a situation that might otherwise prove intractable.

There is a pragmatic sense, then, in which behavior therapy is behavioristic. (pp. 80–81)

Pragmatic behaviorism can be stated as the doctrine that (1) clinical and social problems, and human action in general, should be viewed, as much as is feasible, in terms of overt behavior; and that (2) when cognitive and affective concepts seem relevant, these should be employed in a manner emphasizing characteristics identified by the behavioristic tradition, such as emphasis upon operational definition, specificity, and quantification. Pragmatic behaviorism, then, can be seen as the result of transforming ideological behaviorism from a logical positivist to a constructionist epistemology.

I have found it useful to describe pragmatic behaviorism in terms of ten methodological principles for the conduct of behavior therapy. Table 11.3 presents a summary of these as working procedural guidelines for practicing behavior therapists. Additional context for each of the principles is presented below.

The first two principles, empiricism and macrodeterminism, are closely interconnected within pragmatic behaviorism (Erwin, 1978).

1. Empiricism

Erwin (1978) describes empiricism, as it applies to pragmatic behaviorism, as the view "that observational evidence is required for choosing between most or all nontautological competing hypotheses" (p. 77). In line with the scientific tradition associated with empiricism, "observational evidence" implies information that is based upon intersubjectively reliable sensory experiences, as opposed to intuition or other

TABLE 11.3 Principles of Pragmatic Behaviorism

Principle	Description
1. Empiricism	A significant amount of the substantive information employed in behavior therapy should be based upon systematically recorded, objectively reliable observation, as opposed to intuition and other subjective modes of knowing.
2. Macrodeterminism	Every macroevent addressed in behavior therapy is assumed to have causes, although not necessarily simple ones; and thus changes in human behavior are susceptible to causal explanation.
3. Operational definition	A very important factor in selecting client, therapist, and therapy variables in behavior therapy is to choose those that are as open as possible to operational definition; i.e., those that are as objective, reliable, specific, and concrete as possible.
4. Analyzability	Complex problems addressed in behavior therapy should be structured and framed in such a manner that they can analyzed into smaller and simpler components, each of which can be dealt with one at a time.
5. Quantification	In conducting behavior therapy, significant effort should be made to record quantitatively, in a systematic fashion, relevant client, therapist, and therapy variables.
6. Value-neutrality	In line with the principle of item 3, operational definition, the behavior therapist attempts to avoid substantive value judgements about behavior being "normal" or "abnormal," "healthy" or "sick." Thus, in behavior therapy the goals of the therapy are set primarily by the client.
7. Behaviors as person samples	In behavior therapy, overt behaviors are considered as samples of what a person does in a particular situation, rather than as signs of what a person has. Thus, overt behaviors are viewed as important in and of themselves.
8. Functional analysis	The behavior therapist pays careful attention to the functional link between individual responses (overt behavior and behavior-linked cognition and affect) and the environment. Specifically, the therapist assesses antecedent environmental events in terms of their capacity to facilitate a target response, and consequent environmental events in terms of their capacity to reinforce the response, i.e., to increase the rate of the response's occurrence in the future under similar antecedent conditions.
9. Single-case experimental method	Ideally, where clinically and ethically feasible, the treatment plan of the individual case is constructed so as to include an experimental design for performing functional analyses between specific treatment procedures and behavioral change in the client. Such a design helps to determine whether "the behavior change [that does occur] in

cont.

TABLE 11.3 *(continued)*

Principle	Description
	the individual client is the result of specific treatment interventions and not simply due to the passage of time, placebo reaction, or some other uncontrolled event" (Wilson & O'Leary, 1980, p. 60).
10. Behavior-linked cognition and affect	Cognitive and affective variables are appropriate in behavior therapy provided: (1) these variables are used in a manner emphasizing items 1–9 above; and (2) these variables are linked in a substantial way to overt behavioral and environmental referents.

particularly subjective modes of knowing. For the behavior therapist, this information should derive from controlled experimentation within the individual case (Barlow et al., 1984; Barlow & Hersen, 1984).

2. Macrodeterminism

Erwin (1978) describes macrodeterminism as a "high-level working hypothesis" that "every macroevent [as opposed to events in quantum physics] has a cause . . . [so] that changes in human behavior are susceptible to causal explanation" (p. 9). This does not necessarily mean that all human behavior falls under relatively simple causal laws, because if this were implied by macrodeterminism,

> then it is doubtful that it is supported by current empirical evidence. It is doubtful that there are very many (if any) known laws of human behavior. The so-called laws sometimes cited by some behavior therapists, such as the law of effect or various principles of conditioning, generally turn out to be tautological, false, or too restrictive in scope to qualify as laws. (pp. 79–80)

However, macrodeterminism is assumed by behavior therapists in part "because it is useful to act as if the assumption were true; it would be hard to justify much current behavior therapy research if we did not assume that behavioral changes are causally explainable, although that need not be true of every such change" (p. 80).

A literature has developed on the practice of behavior therapy, including authors such as Goldfried and Davison (1976), Komaki and colleagues (1980), Nelson (1983), Ross (1981), Walker and colleagues (1981), and Wilson and O'Leary (1980). In a manner consistent with pragmatic behaviorism, these authors propose that behavior therapy's essence consists of a perspective on social action that comes from an orientation toward and emphasis on overt behavior, although not an exclusive focus on it. Thus these authors present behavior therapy as an approach to the total range of human experience (including thoughts and feelings) that emphasizes certain methodological principles. These principles are particularly applicable to the assessment and analysis of overt behavior, and they were historically derived by an exclusive focus upon overt behavior. Eight of these constitute the remaining principles defining pragmatic behaviorism.

3. Operational Definition, Objectivity, and Reliability in Assessment

It is generally easier to develop operational definitions and reliability among assessments of overt behaviors, which are publicly visible, than among assessments of mental and emotional processes, which must be inferred and tend to be open to multiple interpretations. As Komaki and colleagues (1980) point out:

> A particularly important benefit of behavioral measures is that they yield information that is less subject to distortion than the information generated by more traditional methods such as questionnaires and ratings. . . . Behavioral measures minimize the influence of judgment of the rater by providing operational definitions of performance. (p. 106)

In the words of Goldfried and Davison (1976):

> Behavior therapists . . . are operational in their use of concepts. High level abstractions such as anxiety or depression are always operationalized in specific terms, such as a particular score on a behavioral assessment device, or a concrete description of behavior. (p. 4)

4. Analysis of Complex Problems by Breakdown into Smaller and Simpler Components

Because overt behavior is concrete and publicly recordable, it is particularly accessible to analysis. Walker and colleagues (1981) describe the rationale for analysis by breakdown into simpler components:

> Behavior therapists attempt to specify in very precise terms the exact nature of the problem. When possible, they prefer to reduce the problem to specific stimuli and specific connected responses and to work with the situation at this reductionistic level. The behavior therapist assumes that complex situations can be analyzed in terms of the basic components involved and that [by] dealing with the components one at a time it is possible to effectively change behavior. (p. 7)

5. Quantification

It follows from 3 and 4 above that overt behavior, and the cognitive and affective variables that are closely linked with overt behavior, are particularly amenable to reliable counting and charting.

6. Value-Neutrality

Pragmatic behaviorism attempts to avoid substantive value judgments about "normal" and "abnormal," "good" and "bad," or "healthy" and "sick" functioning. In the words of Wilson and O'Leary (1980):

> There is no qualitative distinction between "healthy" and "sick" people; these are labels that do not reflect differences intrinsic in behavior as much as they represent the social value judgments made by mental health professionals about whether the behavior of any given person is appropriate at the given time and place. (p. 19)

From the above perspective, behavior therapists reason that the goals of therapy are value judgments about the best ways in which a client should change, and thus they should be left primarily up to the client. Again, in the words of Wilson and O'Leary (1980):

> As an applied science, behavior therapy is simply a collection of principles and techniques about how to change behavior; it says nothing about who should modify what behavior, why, or when. It is the client, and not the therapist, who ultimately should decide the goal of therapy. (p. 285)

In its emphasis upon value-neutrality and client-generated goals, behavior therapy is in contrast to all other major types of therapy, such as psychoanalysis, humanistic therapy, and family-systems therapy, which assert, *based upon their theories per se,* what behavior and personality patterns are "normal," "healthy," and "desirable."

7. Behaviors as Person Samples

It follows from the above principles that, in approaching the understanding and modification of social action, overt behaviors should be viewed as important and significant in and of themselves, "as samples of what a person does in a particular situation, rather than as signs of what a person has" (Nelson, 1983, p. 200). One implication of this view is that "behavior-dependent" measures are a necessary, although not always a sufficient, means of assessing therapy outcome. Moreover, while outcome measures do not have to monitor overt behaviors exclusively, these measures should be as closely and clearly linked to overt behaviors as feasible.

8. Functional Analysis

White (1971) defines the "functional analysis of behavior" as "the identification and statement of the functional relationships which obtain between an organism and its environment" (p. 7). These relationships involve both antecedent environmental events, which "set the stage" for a particular response to occur, and consequent events, which reinforce the response by increasing its probability of occurring in similar situations in the future. The origin of functional analysis in behaviorism comes specifically from Skinnerian learning theory (see Circle 1 in Figure 11.1). More generally, the emphasis upon environment comes from behaviorism's focus upon what is externally observable with regard to an individual's functioning.

9. Single-Case Experimental Method

An important concept from Skinnerian operant learning theory is the experimental analysis of behavior. White (1971) defines this concept as "a special case of the 'functional analysis of behavior' in which previously identified environmental events are systematically manipulated for the purpose of determining (experimentally) their functional relationship to the behavior in question" (p. 7).

The clinical application of the experimental analysis of behavior concepts involves the incorporation of experimental methods into the treatment plans of individual cases. Specifically, in Wilson and O'Leary's (1980) words:

> The clinical adaptation of operant own-control designs in which therapeutic change is evaluated relative to the individual's own performance demonstrates that behavior change in an individual client is the result of specific treatment interventions and not simply due to the passage of time, placebo reaction, or some other uncontrolled event. (p. 60)

10. Behavior-Linked Cognition and Affect

Over the last 10 years there has been a tremendous growth of "cognitive behavior therapy" (e.g., Wilson, 1982) and, more recently, the incorporation of affective variables into behavior therapy (Meichenbaum, 1983; Bowers, 1980; Lang, 1979). While at first the phrases *cognitive behavior therapy* or *affective behavior therapy* appear to be oxymorons, a review of work in this field shows its consistency with pragmatic behaviorism. For example, cognitive behavior therapists

approach cognitions and cognitive processes in a manner that emphasizes methodological principles 1–9 above, exemplified by the analysis
of overt behavior. Thus in discussing the use of cognitive variables in
behavior therapy, Goldfried and Davison (1976) state: "We do not es-
chew the use of inferred concepts, provided that we anchor internal
mediators to observable stimuli or responses" (p. 8). In similar vein,
Wilson and O'Leary (1980 point out:

> Expectations, imagery, symbolic self-regulatory processes, self-monitor-
> ing, and self-evaluation . . . [are] all fundamental features of the analysis
> and treatment of . . . clinical problems. . . . [However,] there is a funda-
> mental difference between the way they are conceptualized and the nat-
> ure of unobservable psychodynamic constructs. Psychodynamic con-
> structs like castration anxiety and the Oedipus complex are never tied
> directly to observable antecedent and consequent events; they function
> largely as autonomous psychic forces, divorced from the immediate influ-
> ence of external contingencies. They are not easily amenable to experi-
> mental testing and cannot be falsified. By contrast, cognitive concepts in
> social learning theory are firmly anchored to observable events; they are
> directly activated and influenced by specifiable behavioral procedures;
> and they can be unambiguously tested because they are defined in a
> precise manner. (pp. 26–27)

Thus pragmatic behaviorism can be described as the doctrine that
clinical and social problems, like human action in general, should be
viewed, as much as feasible, in terms of overt behavior and its environmental determinants. When cognitive and affective concepts seem relevant, these should be employed in a manner emphasizing (1) objectivity, operational definition, specification, analysis into relatively
simple components, and quantification, and (2) linkage of these concepts to overt behavioral and environmental referents. This is not to
deny that there are, at times, sharp differences within the behavioral
community as to the degree of relative emphasis on the "outer/envi-
ronmental behavior" perspective as opposed to the "cognitive-behavioral" perspective (e.g., Krasner, 1985). However, from the point of
view of pragmatic behaviorism, these differences are viewed as disagreements over degree of emphasis in a general behavioral model,
rather than as disagreements over the basic value of the "outer/envi-
ronmental behavior" perspective per se.

Krasner and Houts (1984) recently completed a study providing empirical support for the proposition that historically, relative to other
mental health professionals, behaviorists have been distinctive in
their commitment to the 10 principles in Table 11.3. Krasner and
Houts distributed questionnaires assessing various scientific values to
two groups of psychologists: "a behavioral group composed of those

behavioral scientists who launched the 'behavior modification' [behavior therapy] movement in the 30-year period following the Second World War," and "a randomly selected comparison group of nonbehavioral psychologists from the same period" (p. 840). Their data revealed that relative to the comparison group, the behaviorists had higher value scores on scales reflecting the principles listed in Table 11.3. For example, the behaviorists had higher scores on "factual (vs. theoretical) orientation"; "empiricism"; "impersonal causality (vs. personal will)"; "objectivism (vs. subjectivism)"; "inductivism"; "physicalism"; "elementarism (vs. holism)"; "quantitative (vs. qualitative) orientation"; "behavioral (vs. experiential) content emphasis"; and "environmental determinism."

Constructionist Versus Positivist Perspectives on Behavior therapy

Historically, the ten principles listed in Table 11.2 were derived by employing the logical positivist perspective within psychology and the other social sciences (Krasner, 1982; Staats, 1983; Woolfolk & Richardson, 1984). The result was the development of a variety of forms of ideological behaviorism and laboratory-based learning theories within the experimental paradigm (see Table 11.1). As described above, pragmatic behaviorism removes these principles from a positivist epistemology, which argues for their justification based on the theoretical nature of science, to a constructionist/technological epistemology, which argues for their justification based on their pragmatic usefulness in therapeutic, behavior-change practice (see the contrast between the experimental and technological paradigms in Table 11.1, item 3). In this regard, the reader is reminded of Reichenbach's (1951) distinction between the context of discovery and the context of justification. Thus, regardless of their historical origins, a constructionist reinterpretation of behavioristic principles should be judged on its own merits, regardless of its historical origins.

A number of clinical theorists have explicitly pointed to the technological paradigm as a framework for behavior therapy. For example, in discussing behavioral assessment, Nelson (1983) highlights the context-specific nature of human behavior and the subsequent need to adopt an idiographic perspective (see Table 11.1, item 2):

[Nomothetic] psychometric criteria . . . are antithetical to behavior theory. . . . Given the assumption that behavior is modifiable, test-retest reliability should not be expected. Given the assumption that behavior is situation-specific, concurrent validity across different assessment situations should not be predicted. Given the assumption that behavior frequently varies across response systems, concurrent validity across different assessment methods should not be expected. . . . For each client, an assessment process must be delineated that takes into account his or her unique problematic situations and response systems. (pp. 199, 201)

Nelson (1983) also emphasizes that the assumptions underlying behavioral assessment are oriented to the pragmatic solutions of problems rather than the derivation of general laws (see Table 11.1, item 3):

The philosophical underpinning [of behavioral assessment] is functional rather than structural. . . . Behavioral assessment techniques can serve a variety of [practical] purposes, such as screening, classification, [and] selection of target behaviors for individual clients. . . . In a functional evaluation, the question is whether or not the assessment strategy fulfills the intended purpose. (pp. 199, 202)

In line with the constructionist view of reality as being largely a social creation rather than an externally discoverable entity, Nelson (1983) points out the improbability of "discovering" universal, standardized behavioral dimensions of human functioning. For example, she shows how easy it is to generate almost infinite numbers of separate behavioral assessment techniques. Thus, simply combining Cone's (1978) three response systems (cognitive, physiological, motor) and five assessment methods (interviews, self-reports, ratings by others, self-observation, direct observation) with 192 *DSM-III* diagnostic categories of abnormal behavior to be assessed yields 2,880 separate techniques!

Goldfried and Davison (1976) discuss the problems of the positivistic assumption that behavior therapy involves the straightforward application of general psychological laws derived from experimental studies:

In all instances, a behavior therapist might be guided by a general principle, but he has to rely on his inventiveness as demanded by the clinical situation in order to translate that principle into clinical practice. (p. 9)

In fact, as Goldfried and Davison point out, this constructionist creativity is characteristic of experimental psychology in general, and they cite the following quote from the respected *Handbook of Social Psychology:*

In any experiment, the investigator chooses a procedure which he intuitively feels is an empirical realization of his conceptual variable. All experimental procedures are "contrived" in the sense that they are invented. Indeed, it can be said that the art of experimentation rests primarily on the skill of the investigator to judge the procedure which is the most accurate realization of his conceptual variable and has the greatest impact and the most credibility for the subject. (Aronson & Carlsmith, 1968, p. 25)

In a broader context, Gergen (1982) has also written on the constructionist process in the application of general psychological principles:

> *The theorist furnishes the practitioner with a set of abstractions for which there are no unambiguous particulars.* . . . In applying the theory, then, the practitioner is fitting the abstract theory to personal knowledge that he or she already possesses. The theory does not in this case furnish new knowledge; it primarily furnishes intelligibility to what is already known. (p. 77)

As an illustration, Gergen (1982) discusses an industrial psychologist in a manufacturing concern who is applying equity theory (Walster et al., 1978) for the purpose of increasing worker performance:

> [Equity] theory maintains that by increasing worker rewards over what they believe to be equitable, they might increase their performance in order to achieve equity. How is this abstract theory to be realized within the factory setting? What constitutes an inequitable "over-reward" in this situation? The theoretical term itself stands mute . . . .
>
> [Suppose] the psychologist consults the workers themselves on the matter. They should be able to specify what "over-reward" means in this context. However, ... in order to answer the question, the workers must know what the psychologist means by over-reward . . . . [However,] the term can only be defined . . . by virtue of its use within the theory. Over-reward is that which causes one to increase performance to achieve equity. In effect, the worker is then asked what could he or she be given by management that would increase productivity. At this level we see that the general theory has not served as an instrument for prediction and control, but as a device for motivating the practitioner to activate the forms of knowledge that are already possessed. (p. 78)

Implications of Pragmatic Behaviorism for Research and Practice

If the behavioral field replaces ideological behaviorism with pragmatic behaviorism, then the field exchanges its experimental paradigm for a technological paradigm. This has major implications both for the deployment of our research resources in the behavioral movement and for the nature of behavioral practice.

The experimental paradigm, being based on a positivist epistemology, dictates that the research resources of the behavioral movement be put into funding laboratory-controlled studies for discovering general laws of behavior (see Table 11.1, items 1 and 3). Dissemination of these laws to practitioners then provides a "database" for grounding practice in science.

In contrast, for two reasons, the technological paradigm does not value the laboratory-rooted process of testing theoretical hypotheses and searching for general psychological laws. First, the constructionist epistemology underlying the technological paradigm emphasizes the cultural and historical contextuality of human behavior, making the search for general transcultural and transhistorical laws futile. Also, information learned in the artificial and specific context of the laboratory is viewed as having limited relevance for behavior practice in the real world. Second, as alluded to above in the writings of Goldfried and Davison, Aronson and Carlsmith, and Gergen, the abstract format and nature of psychological laws is such that, even if they are in some way "true," at best they provide only partial guidance to the practitioner. If a good portion of behavioral practice must therefore involve components that are not, in principle, deducible from laboratory-based general laws and theories, the practice of behavior therapy cannot accrue scientific credibility simply by citing experimental studies that are conceptually linked to its procedures.

Pragmatic Behaviorism's Scientific Credibility: Moving Science from the Research Laboratory to the Therapy Office

How, then, can behavior therapy as practiced within the technological paradigm of pragmatic behaviorism accrue scientific credibility? One way is by transferring the scientific processes of empiricism, experimentation, and so forth from the laboratories of a relatively few researchers to the offices of behavioral practitioners. In other words, the principles of pragmatic behaviorism as outlined in Table 11.3 should be applied and documented within each individual case. Ideally, such documentation should be viewed as an intrinsic component of behavior therapy, as part of what one would point to in deciding whether or not to call a particular program or a particular case "behavior therapy." In accord with this ideal, Barlow and colleagues (1984) point to promising trends within health insurance companies to search for methods of insuring cost-effective services. They predict that "accountability, . . . which will be required of all behavior change agents in the near future, will necessitate, at the very least, demonstration of efficacy on every client or group of clients for whom reimbursement is sought" (p. 69).

Pragmatic Behaviorism's Scientific Credibility: The Cumulative Database of Technologically Focused Case Studies

Another way in which behavior therapy as practiced within the technological paradigm can accrue scientific credibility is by accumulating a database of systematic, quantitative, technologically focused case studies (Barlow et al., 1984; Yin, 1984). Within the technological paradigm, case studies make up the scientific database because the paradigm assumes that behavior is historically, culturally, and idiographically contingent, and thus that there are no general, nomothetic laws among a relatively few variables. The technological case study involves the design, implementation, evaluation, and documentation of the single case using the 10 principles outlined in Table 11.3 and discussed above—empiricism, operational definition, quantification, experimentation, and so forth.

Within the technological paradigm, as case studies accumulate, they should be used in two different ways. On one hand, the individual practitioner designing a particular intervention program should identify and utilize in the design those case studies that have the most likelihood of generalizing to his or her situation. On the other hand, the applied researcher working to develop a more general technology should analyze the case studies for commonalities and contrasts, looking for variables and variable clusters that are empirically associated with similar patterns and results across different case studies. Each of these usages will be discussed in more detail below.

Use of the case-study database, by practitioner or researcher, is facilitated when the database is organized in a standardized, easily accessible manner. One possible overall format is to view each case as a potential article in an empirical social science journal and to develop computerized abstract services for the cases that are similar to those now available for such articles. In such a case-study abstract service, each study would be categorized along a number of dimensions. Likely dimensions to be included are the organizational and sociocultural context of the case, the nature of the presenting problem, the techniques by which the presenting problem are operationalized and measured, the nature of the therapeutic relationship between the practitioner and the client, the types of intervention procedures employed, the type of experimental design used, and the degree of successful outcome (case failures, when properly documented, can often be as informative as case successes).

The case-study focus in the technological paradigm highlights the fact that each intervention program with a client—be it an individual, group, or organization—consists of an interactional process over time

between the client and the behavior change agent. This process involves a series of sequential, interdependent steps that can be outlined
as a flowchart (Figure 11.2). As seen from this flowchart, there is a
wide variety of ways for complex variations to evolve as different
patterns of choices and decisions occur. However, the structure of the
flowchart would seem to be a general one and might well serve as a
very helpful generic format for documenting each case study in the
database.

Implications for the Practitioner's Role

As implied above, adoption of pragmatic behaviorism, with its technological paradigm, has two major consequences for the practitioner's
role. First, since the practitioner's scientific credibility is no longer
justified by reference to laboratory-derived general theory, it becomes
incumbent upon the practitioner to conduct and document each case in
accordance with the principles in Table 11.3. Thus the practitioner has
a role to play in the development of the cumulative database of technologically focused case studies. Second, as this database is established,
it becomes incumbent upon the practitioner to consult this database in
developing assessment and intervention strategies and procedures in
order to document (1) the ways in which the practitioner's approach is
consistent with present practice; and (2) the ways in which it is not
consistent, as well as the rationale for such deviation from present
practice.

Lately, there appears to be a renewed interest in the case study. This
trend is illustrated in individual and family behavior therapy by two
recent case books (Hersen & Last, 1985; Lazarus, 1985) and by two
case-oriented handbooks (Barlow, 1985; Hersen & Bellack, 1985). In
the area of behavioral approaches to organizations, this trend is illustrated by two case-oriented handbooks (Frederiksen, 1982; O'Brien et
al., 1982) and by a recent issue of the *Journal of Organizational Management* devoted in part to case studies (Fishman, 1984).

The technological paradigm directs the individual practitioner to
published case studies for guidance in planning and conducting a
particular case. Consistent with this model, Barlow and colleagues
(1984) present a method to aid the individual practitioner in effectively "consuming" published case studies. Specifically, as shown in
Table 11.4, these authors have developed a checklist for the practitioner with a particular ongoing case. The checklist helps the practitioner to select as models those published case studies that, in terms of
both content, relevance and methodological strength, have the most
chance of generalizing to his or her particular case.

TABLE 11.4 A Checklist of Important Dimensions for Practitioners to Consider[a]

In all cases, a *yes* indicates greater likelihood of generalization to your situation:

 1. Are the clients described in detail? Does your client seem similar to those in the [case study or] series [of case series] in most or all important respects?

 2. Are the procedures used described in detail sufficient for you to do what was done in all important respects?

 3. Does the [case study or] series [of case studies] specify the conditions (therapist, therapy environment) under which intervention was applied? Are they similar to your own? Are there therapist effects?

 4. Are measures taken repeatedly across time so that an adequate individual sample is obtained?

 5. Are several different measures taken if there is not one universally accepted measure?

 6. Are individual characteristics identified that are related to treatment outcome? Do your clients share the favorable characteristics?

 7. If the results are reported in group form, is the percentage of individuals showing the effect reported? Is it high? Are individual data shown?

 8. Have the results been replicated? Several times? By others?

 9. Are the effects (and differences between effects) strong and clinically meaningful?

10. Does the study experimentally test factors that account for success or failure? If so, are the favorable conditions present in your situation?

11. Have you tried the procedures with your clients? Did you achieve similar results?

[a]From Barlow, Hayes, & Nelson (1984), p. 318. Copyright © 1984, Pergamon Press. Reprinted by permission.

Implications for the Researcher's Role

The technological paradigm directs the researcher away from theory-derived hypothesis testing in the laboratory to systematic case studies in the field. Specifically, researchers are needed to set standards for, plan, implement, and publish systematic, experimentally designed, and quantitative case studies. While an important number of the published case studies are likely to be conducted by practitioners, the researcher's priorities and incentives are much more amenable to investing large amounts of resources in the conduct, documentation, and interpretation of a small number of model cases. In addition, researchers have the option of joining practitioners to produce case-study reports as a team, with the former primarily involved in planning, eval-

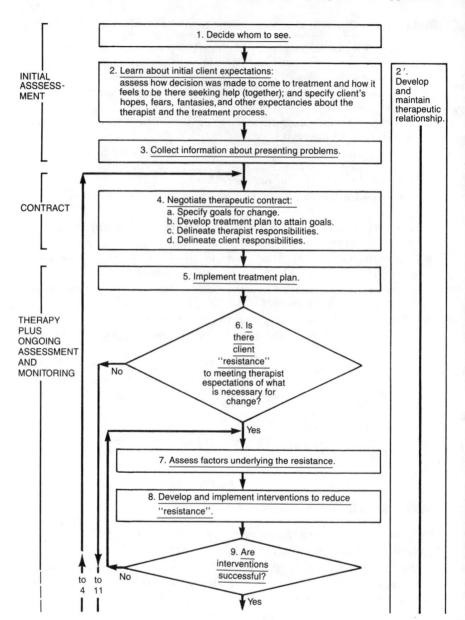

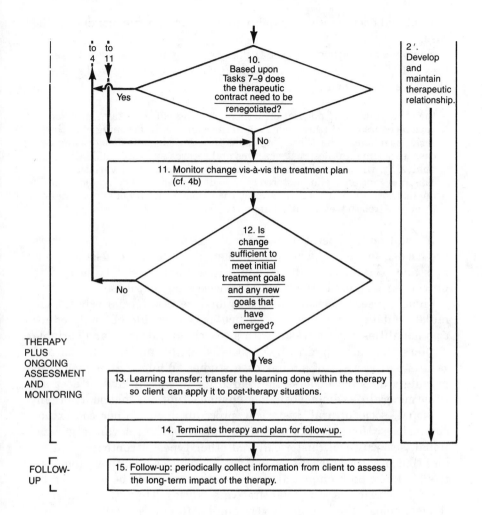

FIGURE 11.2 Flowchart of behavior therapy.

Adapted from "A Flow Chart of Psychotherapy" in Gottman and Leiblum (1974, p. 4).

uation, and documentation, and the latter in the actual conduct of the case.

Barlow and colleagues (1984) describe a type of case-study series they call "clinical replication," which seems particularly well suited to the researcher. Such research involves

> the accumulation of a series of cases presenting with the same problem, such as depression or headache. . . . In the course of intervening with this series of clients, the therapist, using time-series methodology [single-case, experimental designs], observes and records successes and failures, analyzing, where possible, the reasons for this individual variation. . . . The intervention is administered as it would normally be delivered in the applied setting in order to determine the generalizability of effectiveness from research to treatment settings. (p. 290)

In addition to generating individual case-study reports, researchers are needed to develop, edit, and manage the relevant case-study journals and to coordinate the computerized abstract service needed to provide easy access to the cumulative case-study database.

Finally, researchers are needed to analyze in a formal way the cumulative database. Cases of a particular type should be analyzed for commonalities and contrasts, with a search for variables and variable clusters that are empirically associated with similar patterns and results across a set of similar case studies. While the technological paradigm does not endorse the search for universal laws, it does assume generalities among behavior-change situations that share organizational, sociocultural, historical, procedural, and other contextual similarities. However, the particular nature of the relevant organizational, sociocultural, historical, and other types of contextual variables that predict generalities, and the degree to which those generalities hold, are both empirical questions that can only be answered by careful, descriptive, and quantitative analyses. Thus, the position of the technological paradigm is very similar to Paul's (1969) often-cited recommendation for specificity. The "ultimate question" for clinical research, he contends, is to investigate empirically "what treatment, by whom, is most effective for this individual with that specific problem, under what set of circumstances, and how does it come about?" (Paul, 1969, p. 44).

Summary

In its "Declaration of Independence" from philosophy in the late nineteenth century, psychology adopted the methods of natural science and the related epistemology of logical positivism to create an experimental paradigm for the study of human behavior and experience. Pursuit of this paradigm led to the development of laboratory-based learning theories and their accompanying principles of ideological behaviorism. When these theories were subsequently applied to the clinical dysfunction problems typically addressed in psychotherapy, behavior therapy was born. Later, the model of ideological behaviorism was used with applied problems in a variety of other areas, for example, physical health (behavioral medicine), management and organizational psychology (organizational behavior management), and community psychology (behavioral community psychology).

Since 1945, there has been a growing breakdown of consensus on the experimental paradigm for at least five reasons: (1) the lack of consistent, coherent, and relevant substantive results that have emerged from all the experiments; (2) the emergence of sociopolitical factors in the publication process that undermine adherence to the experimental paradigm; (3) the discovery by therapy practitioners—both behavioral and nonbehavioral—that they can sell their services without having to show a tight link between their practices and the experimental literature; (4) the fact that, in actuality, research has little effect on practice, with therapists typically obtaining their strategies and procedures from "intuitive eclecticism" (Barlow et al., 1984); and (5) the loss of support, both within philosophy and within the history and sociology of science, for logical positivism, the epistemological foundation of the experimental paradigm.

This breakdown of the experimental paradigm has frequently led to one of two reactions by behaviorists. Some reassert the old verities and return to pre-1945 thinking, while others reject behavior therapy in principle because of its roots in ideological behaviorism. In this chapter I have argued that both of these reactions amount to throwing the baby out with the bathwater. I have instead proposed a third alternative: retain the basic concepts and methods of behaviorism, but reframe them in a doctrine of pragmatic behaviorism that is embedded in a technological paradigm.

This technological alternative involves a twofold commitment to the principles outlined in Table 11.3. First, since within the technological paradigm the practitioner's scientific credibility is no longer justified by reference to laboratory-derived general theory, it becomes incumbent upon the practitioner to conduct and document each case in strict accordance with these principles. In other words, there must be a transfer of the scientific processes of empiricism, operational definition, quantification, functional analysis, experimentation, and so forth from the laboratories of a relatively few researchers to the offices of all behavioral practitioners. Second, the technological alternative directs the research community to set standards for, plan, implement, and document case studies that are systematic, experimentally designed, and quantitative. This documentation includes the ongoing accumulation of these studies into an organized, computerized database that is easily accessible to practitioners and researchers alike.

In conclusion, I have argued that there are compelling reasons for replacing logical positivism, along with its associated commitments to the experimental paradigm and ideological behaviorism, with social constructionism, along with its associated commitments to the technological paradigm and pragmatic behaviorism. A less radical version of the argument proposes adding social constructionism side by side with logical positivism as a competing epistemology that one segment of the behavioral field would pursue. This more conservative proposal would structure the field as a type of free market of underlying epistemological models. There would then follow a period of productive competition, so that the comparative theoretical and practical results of following each of the two models could later be systematically assessed. Thus, while a complete shift to the technological paradigm might not be warranted at this time, this paradigm, as embodied in pragmatic behaviorism, looks particularly promising for the future and deserves at least its fair share of scientific and professional resources from the field.

References

Aronson, E., & Carlsmith, J.M. (1968). Experimentation in social psychology. In G. Lindzey & E. Aronson (Eds.), *The handbook of social psychology: Vol. 2. Research methods (pp. 1–79).* Reading, MA: Addison Wesley.

Azrin, N.H. (1977). A strategy for applied research: Learning based but outcome oriented. *American Psychologist, 30,* 469–485.

Barlow, D.H. (Ed.). (1985). *Clinical handbook of psychological disorders.* New York: Guilford.

Barlow, D.H., Hayes, S.C., & Nelson, R.O. (1984). *The scientist practitioner: Research and accountability in clinical and educational settings.* Elmsford, NY: Pergamon.

Barlow, D.H., & Hersen, M. (1984). *Single case experimental designs: Strategies for studying behavior change* (2nd ed.). New York: Pergamon.

Bernstein, J. (1985, October 9). "Retarded learner": At 74, John Archibald Wheeler is still grappling with the universe. *Princeton Alumni Weekly, 85,* pp. 28–31, 38–42.

Bowers, K.S. (1980). "De-controlling" cognition and cognitive control. In M.J. Mahoney (Ed.), *Psychotherapy process: Current issues and future directions* (pp. 181–184). New York: Plenum.

Bronfenbrenner, U. (1977). An experimental ecology of human development. *American Psychologist, 32,* 513–531.

Broskowski, A. (1971). Clinical psychology: A research and development model. *Professional Psychology: 2,* 235–242.

Burstein, L., Freeman, H.F., & Rossi, P.H. (Eds.). (1985). *Collecting evaluation data: Problems and solutions.* Beverly Hills, CA: Sage.

Campbell, D.T. (1984). Can we be scientific in applied social science? In R.F. Conner, D.G. Altman, & C. Jackson (Eds.), *Evaluation studies review annual (Vol. 9)* (pp. 26–48). Beverly Hills, CA: Sage.

Cartwright, D. (1973). Determinants of scientific progress: The case of research on the risky shift. *American Psychologist, 28,* 222–231.

Ceci, S.J., & Walker, E. (1983). Private archives and public needs. *American Psychologist, 38,* 414–423.

Cone, J.D. (1978). The Behavioral Assessment Grid (BAG): A conceptual framework and a taxonomy. *Behavioral Therapy, 9,* 882–888.

Cronbach, L.J. (1975). Beyond the two disciplines of scientific psychology. *American Psychologist, 30,* 116–127.

Epstein, S. (1980). The stability of behavior: II. Implications for psychological research. *American Psychologist, 35,* 790–806.

Erwin, E. (1978). *Behavior therapy: Scientific, philosophical, and moral foundations.* New York: Cambridge University Press.

Eysenck, H.J. (1972). Behavior therapy is behavioristic. *Behavior Therapy, 3,* 609–613.

Farkas, G.M. (1980). An ontological analysis of behavior therapy. *American Psychologist, 35,* 364–374.

Fishman, D.B. (Ed.). (1984). Coping with organizational realities in program implementation. *Journal of Organizational Behavior Management, 6,* 3–52.

Fishman, D.B., & Neigher, W.D. (1982). American psychology in the eighties: Who will buy? *American Psychologist, 37,* 533–546.

Frederiksen, L.W. (Ed.). (1982). *Handbook of organizational behavior management.* New York: Wiley.

Gergen, K.J. (1982). *Towards transformation in social knowledge.* New York: Springer-Verlag.

Gergen, K.J. (1985). The social constructionist movement in modern psychology. *American Psychologist, 40,* 266–275.

Gholson, B., & Barker, P. (1985). Kuhn, Lakatos, and Laudan: Applications in the history of physics and psychology. *American Psychologist, 40,* 755–769.

Gibbs, J.C. (1979). The meaning of ecologically oriented inquiry in contemporary psychology. *American Psychologist, 34,* 127–140.

Gilbert, T.F. (1978). *Human competence: Engineering worthy performance.* New York: McGraw-Hill.

Goldfried, M.R., & Davison, G.C. (1976). *Clinical behavior therapy.* New York: Holt, Rinehart & Winston.

Gottman, J.M., & Leiblum, S.R. (1974). *How to do psychotherapy and how to evaluate it.* New York: Holt, Rinehart, & Winston.

Greenwald A.G. (1975). Consequences of prejudice against the null hypothesis. *Psychological Bulletin, 82,* 1–20.

Greenwald, A.G. (1976). An editorial. *Journal of Personality and Social Psychology, 33,* 1–7.

Hersen, M., & Bellack, A.S. (1985). *Handbook of clinical behavior therapy with adults.* New York: Guilford.

Hersen, M., & Last, C. (1985). *Behavior therapy casebook.* New York: Springer Publishing Co.

Hill, G. (1981, August 30). Of mice and men and now computers. *New York Times,* p. 18E.

Hogan, R. (1979, April). An interview with Robert Hogan. *APA Monitor, 10,*4–6.

James, W. (1955). *Pragmatism and four essays from "The Meaning of Truth."* New York: Meridan Books.

Jenkins, J.J. (1974). Remember that old theory of memory? Well, forget it! *American Psychologist, 29,* 785–795.

Kazdin, A.E., & Wilson, G.T. (1978). *Evaluation of behavior therapy.* Cambridge, MA: Ballinger.

Kimble, G.A. (1984). Psychology's two cultures. *American Psychologist, 39,* 833–839.

Koch, S. (1959). Epilogue. In S. Koch (Ed.), *Psychology: A study of a science* (Vol. 3) (pp. 729–788). New York: McGraw-Hill.

Komaki, J., Collins, R.L., & Thoene, T. (1980). Behavioral measurement in business, industry, and government. *Behavioral Assessment, 2,* 103–124.

Krasner, L. (1982). Behavior therapy: On roots, contexts, and growth. In G.T. Wilson & C.M. Franks (Eds.), *Contemporary behavior therapy: Conceptual and empirical foundations* (pp. 11–62). New York: Guilford.

Krasner, L. (1985). All aboard the train to cognition. [Review of *Annual review of behavior therapy: Vol. 9. Theory and practice].* *Contemporary Psychology, 30,* 773–774.

Krasner, L., & Houts, A.C. (1984). A study of the "value" systems of behavioral scientists. *American Psychologist, 39,* 840–850.

Kuhn, T.S. (1970). *The structure of scientific revolutions* (2nd ed.). Chicago: University of Chicago Press.

Kuhn, T.S. (1974). Logic of discovery or psychology of research? In I. Lakatos & A. Musgrave (Eds.), *Criticism and the growth of knowledge* (pp. 1–23). New York: Cambridge University Press.

Lamb, R. (1983). History of psychology. In R. Harre & R. Lamb (Eds.), *The Encyclopedic Dictionary of Psychology* (pp. 275–277). Cambridge, MA: MIT Press.

Lang, P.J. (1979). A bio-informational theory of emotional imagery. *Psychophysiology, 16,* 495–512.

Lazarus, A.A. (1981). *The practice of multi-modal therapy.* New York: McGraw-Hill.

Lazarus, A.A. (Ed.). (1985). *Casebook of multimodal therapy.* New York: Guilford.

Levine, M. (1974). Scientific method and the adversary model: Some preliminary thoughts. *American Psychologist, 29,* 661–677.

Lilienfeld, R. (1978). *The rise of systems theory: An ideological analysis.* New York: Wiley.

London, P. (1972). The end of ideology in behavior modification. *American Psychologist, 27,* 913–920.

Lubin, B., Larsen, R.M., Matarazzo, J.D., & Seever, M. (1985). Psychological test usage patterns in five professional settings. *American Psychologist, 40,* 857–861.

Mahoney, M.J. (1974). *Cognition and behavior modification.* Cambridge, MA.: Ballinger.

Mahoney, M.J. (1977). Publication prejudices: An experimental study of confirmatory bias in the peer review system. *Cognitive Therapy and Research, 1,* 161–175.

Marshall, W.L. (1982). A model of dysfunctional behavior. In A.S. Bellack, M. Hersen, & A.E. Kazdin (Eds.), *International Handbook of Behavior Modification and Therapy* (pp. 57–76). New York: Plenum.

Mayo, C. (1977, November). *Toward an applicable social psychology.* Presidential address to the New England Psychological Association, Worcester, MA.

Meichenbaum, D.H. (Chair). (1983, December). *The relationship between cognition, emotion, and behavior: Implications for treatment.* Panel Discussion presented at the meeting of the Association for Advancement of Behavior Therapy, Washington, D.C.

Messer, S.B., & Winokur, M. (1984). Ways of knowing and visions of reality. In H. Arkowitz & S.B. Messer (Eds.), *Psychoanalytic therapy and behavior therapy: Is integration possible?* (pp. 63–100). New York: Plenum.

Morell, J.A. (1979). *Program evaluation in social research.* Elmsford, NY: Pergamon.

Neigher, W.D., & Fishman, D.B. (1985). From science to technology: Reducing problems in mental health evaluation by paradigm shift. In L. Burnstein, H.F. Freeman, & P.H. Rossi (Eds.), *Collecting evaluation data: Problems and solutions* (pp. 263–298). Beverly Hills, CA: Sage.

Neisser, U. (1976). *Cognition and reality: Principles and implications of cognitive psychology.* San Francisco: W.H. Freeman.

Nelson, R.O. (1983). Behavioral assessment: Past, present, and future. *Behavioral Assessment, 5,* 195–206.

Nessel, J. (1982). Understanding psychological man: A state-of-the-science report. *Psychology Today, 16,* 40–59.

Newell, A. (1973). You can play 20 questions with nature and win. In W.G. Chase (Ed.), *Visual information processing* (pp. 283–310). New York: Academic Press.

O'Brien, R.M., Dickinson, A.M., & Rosow, M.P. (Eds.). (1982). *Industrial behavior modification: A management handbook.* New York: Pergamon.

Orne, M. (1962). On the social psychology of the psychological experiment: With particular reference to demand characteristics and their implication. *American Psychologist, 17,* 776–783.

Packer, M.J. (1985). Hermeneutic inquiry in the study of human conduct. *American Psychologist, 40,* 1081–1093.

Paul, G.L. (1969). Behavior modification research: Design and tactics. In C.M. Franks (Ed.), *Behavior therapy: Appraisal and status* (pp. 29–62). New York: McGrawHill.

Pepper, S.C. (1942). *World hypotheses: A study in evidence.* Los Angeles: University of California Press.

Peters, A., & Ceci, B.A. (1980). A manuscript masquerade. *The Sciences, 20,* 1–5.

Price, R.H., & Cherniss, C. (1977). Training for a new profession: Research as social action. *Professional Psychology, 8,* 222–231.

Putnam, H. (1984). After Ayer, after empiricism. *Partisan Review, 51,* 265–275.

Reichenbach, H. (1951). *The rise of scientific philosophy.* Berkeley: University of California Press.

Rosenthal, R. (1976). *Experimental effects in behavioral research.* New York: Irvington.

Ross, A.O. (1981). *Child behavior therapy: Principles, procedures, and empirical bases.* New York: Wiley.

Scarr, S. (1985). Construing psychology: Making facts and fables for our times. *American Psychologist, 40,* 499–512.

Scott, W.A. (1974). Interreferee agreement on some characteristics of manuscripts submitted to the *Journal of Personality and Social Psychology. American Psychologist, 29,* 698–702.

Sechrest, L. (1976). Personality. In M.R. Rosenzweig & L.W. Porter (Eds.), *Annual Review of Psychology* (pp. 1–28). Palo Alto, CA: Annual Reviews.

Smith, N.C., Jr. (1970). Replication studies: A neglected aspect of psychologist research. *American Psychologist, 25,* 970–975.

Staats, A.W. (1983). *Psychology's crisis of disunity: Philosophy and method for a unified science.* New York: Praeger.

Staats, A.W. (1984, August). *Scientific chaos is not a science: A proposal to solve psychology's disunity.* Invited address to the American Psychological Association, Toronto, Ontario, Canada.

Swan, G.E., & MacDonald, M.L. (1978). Behavior therapy in practice: A national survey of behavior therapists. *Behavior Therapy, 9,* 799–807.

Wachtel, P.L. (1980). Investigation and its discontents: Some constraints on progress in psychological research. *American Psychologist, 35,* 399–408.

Wade, N. (1982, April 30). Smart apes, or dumb? *New York Times,* p. 28.

Walker, C.E., Hedberg, A., Clement, P.W., & Wright, L. (1981). *Clinical procedures for behavior therapy.* Englewood Cliffs, NJ: Prentice-Hall.

Walster, E., Walster, G.W., & Berscheid, E. (1978). *Equity, theory and research.* Boston: Allyn & Bacon.

Watson, J.B. (1913). Psychology as the behaviorist views it. *Psychological Review, 20,* 158–17.

Weimer, W.B. (1977). Science as a rhetorical transaction: Toward a nonjustificational conception of rhetoric. *Philosophy and Rhetoric, 10,* 1–29.

White, O.R. (1971). *A glossary of behavioral terminology.* Champaign, IL: Research Press.

Wilson, G.T. (1978). On the much-discussed nature of the term "behavior therapy." *Behavior Therapy, 9,* 89–98.

Wilson, G.T. (1982). Psychotherapy process and procedure: The behavioral mandate. *Behavior Therapy, 13,* 291–312.

Wilson, G.T., & O'Leary, K.D. (1980). *Principles of behavior therapy.* Englewood Cliffs, NJ: Prentice-Hall.

Woolfolk, R.L., & Richardson, F.C. (1984). Behavior therapy and the ideology of modernity. *American Psychologist, 39,* 777–786.

Yin, R.K. (1984). *Case study research: Design and methods.* Beverly Hills, CA: Sage.

Zubin, J., Eron, L.D., & Schumer, F. (1965). *An experimental approach to projective techniques.* New York: Wiley.

12

From Behavior Therapy to Cognitive Behavior Therapy to Systems Therapy: Toward an Integrative Health Science

Gary E. Schwartz

Foreword: The Purple Hat Effect

Imagine that while visiting the Chicago Art Institute you chance upon a painting containing an array of colorful red and blue dots: thousands of red and blue dots painted adjacent to each other in no apparent order. You move closer to the canvas to get a better look. You discover that as the dots get bigger you can see the precise marks of brush strokes on each dot.

You then move away from the canvas. As the dots become smaller, you begin to see that the red and blue dots are surrounded by orange dots, yellow dots, and dots of other colors. You count the number of different colored dots and discover that the painting consists of 11 different colored dots.

As you study the red and blue dots further, you begin to notice that the collection of dots seems to have a shape. You do not recognize the shape at first. However, as you continue to move farther away from the canvas, you discover that the dots are arranged in the shape of a hat worn by a young woman. At this distance you can no longer see the individual red and blue dots. Instead, what you see is a hat, and the hat is purple, a twelfth new color!

Surprised, you continue to move farther away from the canvas. You discover that the canvas contains numerous shapes of women and men, girls and boys, dogs and trees, boats and baby carriages. Furthermore, you discover that viewed from this distance the painting appears to contain hundreds of different colors. You realize that you have been looking at the pointillist masterpiece, *Sunday on the Isle of the Grande-Jatte,* a highly organized collection of dots of only 11 colors painted by Georges Seurat over a two-year period and completed in 1884.

As you move away from the painting to look at other paintings in the Art Institute, you notice that at a certain distance the purple hat, the young women, the trees, the dogs, and all the other recognized shapes start to look curiously like hundreds of different colored "dots." The purple hat is now a purple dot.

From thousands of red and blue dots, to a purple hat, to a purple dot. Is the qualitative shift from red and blue dots to the emergence of a purple hat, what we can call the "Purple Hat Effect," a rare and isolated phenomenon? Or is the Purple Hat Effect an illustration of a general principle that has broad, integrative value? Can this principle function as a conceptual tool to help us organize and integrate information as we learn to see systems from different distances, that is, from different levels?

Can this idea, termed the "emergent property principle" in general-systems theory, be applied systematically to the diagnosis and treatment of patients? Can we gain not only more complete information, but also more focused and unified information, about our patients, by (1) discovering integrative information-processing tools, such as the emergent-property principle, and (2) developing the cognitive/emotional/behavioral skills to use these integrative information-processing tools effectively?

Introduction

The purpose of this chapter is to consider the implications of general-systems theory (von Bertalanffy, 1968; Miller, 1978; deRosnay, 1979) for the evolution of behavior therapy and therapy in general, be the therapy biological, psychological, or social in nature. The concepts of "behavior" and "therapy" take on deeper meanings when viewed from the perspective of systems theory.

As various writers have discussed (e.g. Boulding, 1978; Schwartz, 1984, 1987), systems theory is more appropriately described as a "metatheory." A metatheory is a metacognitive framework for viewing discipline per se. Systems theory (i.e., metatheory) represents a broad and far-reaching shift in human perception and conception. As such, it meets all the criteria for reflecting a prototypic shift in paradigm, using Kuhn's (1962) generic meaning of the term *paradigm* (i.e. metatheoretical).

As will become evident as the chapter unfolds, the implications of systems theory for therapy extend beyond behavior therapy per se. The recent evolution of behavior medicine and the development of the biopsychosocial model (e.g. Engel, 1977; Leigh & Reiser, 1980; Schwartz, 1982b, 1984) represent important examples of this emerging paradigm shift in modern science and society. In fact, the implications of systems theory apply to all levels of science relevant to the diagnosis, treatment, and prevention of disease—from quantum physics and modern mathematics (microlevels) to economics and ecology (macrolevels) (reviewed in Schwartz, 1984, 1987).

The chapter is organized into four main sections. It begins with an introduction to Pepper's (1942) four "world hypotheses," which are offered as an integrated set of conceptual tools for perceiving the evolution of behavior therapy and therapy in general. Five unifying concepts from systems theory are then discussed in the context of behavior therapy and therapy in general. Next, an illustrative case study is presented that integrates the world hypotheses and systems concepts and shows how they can be applied to clinical practice. Finally, a summary section expresses the need to develop integrative concepts to facilitate the evolution of integrated health science.

Pepper's "World Hypotheses"

The philosopher of science Pepper (1942) developed a particularly useful conceptual tool for viewing the distinction between various personal theories about nature, which he terms "world hypotheses." Pepper proposed that there are four basic types of these, which he terms: "formistic," "mechanistic," "contextual," and "organismic." Formistic thinking reflects categorical thinking, the most fundamental form of thinking. The formistic hypothesis is that matter, energy, and information each exist as categories and, therefore, can be placed in discrete either/or categories. For example, things are either fruit or vegetables (there can not be "fruitables"). Things are either black or white, good or bad, sick or well, and so forth.

The capacity to perceive and create categories requires the skillful use of a fundamental conceptual implement (formistic thinking) that is a *prerequisite* to being able to use the other fundamental conceptual implements (mechanistic, contextual, and organismic thinking). Certain disciplines (e.g., personality theory in psychology, botany and zoology in biology, and pathology in medicine) have developed the art of skillfully using formistic implements to achieve a high level of complexity in organizing knowledge. The reader should note that Pepper's theory itself is couched in terms of a simple formistic framework (i.e., that there are four basic categories of world hypotheses).

However, the formistic world hypothesis has proven to be limited as a sole or single unifying conceptual implement. The hypothesis that things exist solely in either/or categories in nature has been questioned on various philosophical, empirical, and practical grounds. This is particularly evident in modern quantum physics (for example, the question of whether light is a wave or a particle begins with the implicit hypothesis that things exist in solely either/or categories).

In behavior therapy per se, in the discipline of psychology, and in numerous other disciplines, the following hypotheses are typically made: (1) that cognitions exist fundamentally as separate categories from emotions (though these categories can have cause-and-effect relationships, which is Pepper's second world hypothesis, described below), (2) that thoughts and feelings exist fundamentally as separate categories from the brain and biological organs, and (3) that social, psychological, and biological processes exist fundamentally as separate categories from each other.

A second implement used by behavior therapy and therapy in general is what Pepper refers to as the mechanistic hypothesis. This world hypothesis essentially posits that specific causes (which reflect specific categories; i.e., formistic thinking) produce specific effects (which also reflect specific categories), and that this mechanism operates in a single cause/single manner (in other words, an "either/or" manner). Complex cause-and-effect chains can occur (e.g., *A* causes *B,* then *B* causes *C,* then *C* causes *D,* and so forth—the billiard ball hypothesis of nature). Again, certain subdisciplines and disciplines as a whole have developed the skill to use the mechanistic implement to model complex chains of cause-and-effect relationships. Traditional behavior therapy implicitly adopted this generic framework (specific stimuli elicit specific responses). So did traditional medicine (specific germs or agents elicit specific diseases).

Great strides in the behavioral and biological sciences have been made using the mechanistic hypothesis. However, if the single-cause/single-effect hypothesis of nature were correct, knowing *the* single cause would successfully account for *all* the variance in predicting the single effect. However, it is now recognized that this conclusion is inaccurate in describing *numerous* if not *all* phenomena occurring at inaccurate in describing *numerous* if not *all* phenomena occurring at all levels across all disciplines (Engel, 1977; Leigh & Reiser, 1980).

Two additional world hypotheses provide conceptual implements that, when used skillfully, help us move from single category/single cause models to multiple-category/multiple-cause models. The first is what Pepper terms the contextual hypothesis. It essentially states that our perception is always relatively limited and context-dependent. If we learn the skill for viewing matter, energy, and information from various perspectives, we will draw different conclusions relative to each other, all of which are partially "true." Traditionally, the contextual hypothesis has tended to be adopted more by artists; certain Western cultures such as Native Americans; and Eastern philosophies relating mind, matter, and religion.

For example, whereas a traditional Western behavior therapist would hypothesize that a phobic response was triggered by the sight of a particular stimulus (e.g., a bridge in the case of a person suffering from a driving phobia), a contextual behavior therapist (or an Eastern yogi) would hypothesize that depending on the way we look at it, we can conclude that either the stimulus, the person, or both caused the phobic response. Modern cognitive behavior therapy can be seen as reflecting a developmental shift from the use of simple mechanistic implements per se to the addition of contextual implements in diagnosis, treatment, and prevention.

The contextual approach is particularly evident in modern physics, as exemplified by Einstein's theory of general relativity (where time perception as well as the actuality of time depends on the context of the measurement), Heisenberg's uncertainty principle (where the accurate measurement of position vis-á-vis momentum depends on the context of the measurement), or the complementary principle of light (where the accurate measurement of the wave vis-á-vis the particle behavior of light depends on the context of the measurement) (see Pagels, 1982). The challenge facing us is to combine effectively the skills required for using formistic, mechanistic, *and* contextual implements in such a way as to provide a new means of organizing the information so obtained. This turns out to be the challenge in Pepper's fourth world hypothesis, organismic thinking. Today we view organismic thinking as a subset of general-systems thinking.

According to Pepper, the organismic hypothesis is that nature consists of organized units, each of which is composed of organized parts (or subunits). Moreover, the subunits interact with each other in predictable ways so as to generate unique properties (behaviors) of the unit as a whole in the context of the unit's interacting with its environment (which turns out to be a larger unit of which the given unit is itself a subunit). The hypothesis that subunits can interact with each other in such a way as to form an organized unit that functions as a predictable whole stimulated the development of organismic tools that became the foundation of systems fields such as engineering and computer science. Also, modern biology and neuroscience are becoming increasingly organismic as the complexity of structure reveals a parallel complexity of function. The complexity of structure and function necessitates the measurement of interacting multiple processes in order to describe and predict the functioning of a biological unit as a whole.

It is essential to understand that persons educated and trained to approach the world in a primarily formistic and/or mechanistic manner tend to view systems theory as just one more theory (i.e., as just another category of theory) to be evaluated in terms of its ability to generate and predict categorical and/or single-cause/single-effect relationships. Not only does this restricted view of systems theory fail to include contextual and organismic processing of information in the theory; it also is likely to occur in individuals educated and trained primarily in formistic and mechanistic perceptions of information. Understanding systems theory requires more than just recognizing the specific categories of systems concepts. It requires practicing the cognitive skills necessary to use successfully systemic tools to integrate information. Learning this skill takes substantial time.

Learning to think in systems is like learning to think in a second language. There is more to learning how to think in a second language than merely learning the words and their meanings. The connections between words and meanings across the two languages must be practiced over and over again until the translation process becomes relatively automatic and effortless, occurring as an integrated, whole process.

The major difference between thinking in systems terms and thinking in a foreign language is that systems terms are abstract and generic. The systems language is applicable to any process occurring at any level (including the learning of language itself!). Moreover, within the organismic/systems approach, formistic, mechanistic, and contextual perspectives can be productively used for certain purposes.

A question often raised about systems theory is, What can you do with it (i.e., can it function as a useful tool)? Translated into systems language, this question becomes, What are the fundamental concepts and methods that comprise systems theory, and if these conceptual tools are used skillfully, how can they improve our ability to describe, understand, predict, and modify the specific processes with which we are concerned? What follows is a discussion of a few key concepts and these concepts can be fruitfully applied to behavior therapy and to therapy in general.

Unifying Concepts from Systems Theory

Concept 1: Discovering Wholes and Parts

All systems are, by definition, semi-closed "loops," such that the behavior of each component or subsystem directly or indirectly influences the behavior of every other subcomponent. In systems theory, we ultimately must begin with the concept of a system, and this requires that we understand what it means to be whole. However, the order in which we approach these concepts is somewhat arbitrary (just as the order of *the* cause and *the* effect in a feedback loop is ultimately somewhat arbitrary). Thinking back and forth between wholes and parts contextually and shifting our thinking from part to part contextually to obtain a sense of the whole are skills that take substantial practice before becoming relatively effortless and effective.

Learning how to perform therapy can be likened to learning how to perform jazz. The skilled jazz musician learns how to shift attention from the whole of the basic rhythms, chord progression, and melody of a given musical selection to the constantly changing interactions of the various parts (e.g., instruments) as these parts creatively improvise around the agreed-upon theme (rhythm, chord progression, and melody). It takes substantial practice to reach the point where the shifting of one's thinking between the whole and the parts becomes so effortless that the process of creating new theme (general) melodies in the context of the music selected emerges and flows in a more or less continuous manner.

The abstract, artistic, and scientific challenge confronting the jazz musician is therefore (1) to understand the whole of the musical theme prior to improving on it, (2) to follow the whole of the musical performance in real time as it evolves from the generic theme to the creative modification of theme by the group as a whole (a direct parallel to words having both a generic theme and a more specific expression), and (3) to shift attention serially within and across levels in real time while maintaining parallel processing so as to interpret and respond to the group and the music as a whole (sometimes listening quietly, sometimes backing up another soloist, and sometimes taking a solo oneself). Viewing the process of performing jazz in systems terms is a useful framework for illustrating how a systems approach can be applied innovatively to behavior therapy and therapy in general.

plied innovatively to behavior therapy and therapy in general.

A systems approach to behavior therapy encourages a blending of "classical" and "improvisational" information processing and behavior on the part of the therapist. The systems-oriented behavior therapist would develop *skills* (1) in the basic "techniques" of performing therapy (just as a musician develops skills in the basic techniques of music as performed on his or her instrument), and (2) in perceiving the patient's behavior in real time as an organized "whole" comprised of a complex set of interacting "parts" as the whole interacts with the larger whole (including the therapist and her/his office environment). Furthermore, the systems-oriented behavior therapist would develop skills (3) in shifting biopsychosocial levels as the personal themes emerge, and (4) in responding to the patient with a combination of classical and improvisational techniques in a creative yet cautious fashion.

The clinical goal for the systems-oriented behavior therapist is not only to help patients solve their personal problems (be these problems biological, psychological, and/or social in level), but also to help patients learn *how* to use a general-systems—oriented improvisional approach, as modeled by the therapist, in facing life's challenges after therapy has been completed. The systems therapist models a research-oriented, improvisational approach (improvisation conducted in a systematic, experimental fashion) designed to discover which strategies work best to resolve a given problem in a given context. In other words, the systems-oriented behavior therapist implicitly encourages the patient to adopt a contextual and systemic approach to life's challenges.

Concept 2: Discovering Microlevels/Macrolevels: A "Biopsychosocial" Perspective

How does systems theory function to help the behavior therapist creatively perceive a patient as a whole comprised of interacting parts as the whole interacts with his or her environment? Using the systems tool of micro-to-macrolevels, it is possible to construct a tridimensional framework that not only organizes the discipline of psychology, but also reveals how the biological sciences at the more microlevels and the social sciences at the more macrolevels relate to the person improvisationally as a unique, whole personality (see Figure 12.1).

The first dimension (the *y*-axis) organizes processes hierarchically from the more microlevels (psychochemistry) to the more macrolevels (international psychology). Since this dimension includes phenomena at the biological, psychological, and social levels, it is called a biopsy-

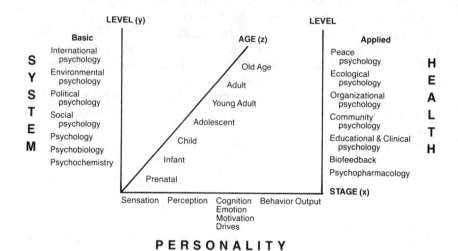

PERSONALITY

FIGURE 12.1 A tri-dimensional framework for organizing the discipline of psychology.

Source: From Schwartz (1982b). Reprinted by permission.

on the left, and associated applied-science specialities, on the right.

The second dimension (the *x*-axis) organizes the momentary temporal processes that cut across all the microlevels to macrolevels (*y*-axis), moving from input (stimulus), through information processing (organism), to output (response) along the dimension of time. The relationship between cognition, emotion, motivation, and drives is illustrated as a subdimension within the temporal dimension. The specific organization of this subdimension can be debated (and will be returned to in a later part of this chapter). Only illustrative information-processing and output processes are listed. The systems tool of level can be employed to insert additional areas, such as psychophysics, memory, decision making, and motor skills.

The third dimension (the *z*-axis) organizes processes along the continuum of age (a second dimension of time) from prenatal through adulthood to old age. The range of this dimension includes early childhood development and extends to geriatric psychology. The psychology of conception, birth, and death therefore falls on this dimension.

It should be appreciated that Figure 12.1 does *not* list *specific content areas* such as anxiety, addiction, and repression. The reader should be able to insert specific content within and across the various dimensions, using the systems concepts described thus far. This exercise is useful because it helps point out that *every content area exists along each of the three major dimensions; no content area exists along only one dimension.*

It should also be appreciated that Figure 12.1 does not explicitly depict a dimension comparing different species (the evolutionary/comparative perspective). Implicit in the z-axis, however, is a longer time frame, which can be expanded to include the evolutionary perspective. If age (of a person) is replaced with age (of life on earth), the diagram becomes complete on an evolutionary scale.

It follows that behavior at the psychological, organismic level can reflect processes occurring at the biological and social levels. As behavior therapy evolves from focusing on overt behaviors at the psychological level to becoming more cognitive and more inclusive of the biological and social levels (see below), developing tools for charting multiple behaviors occurring at multiple levels becomes essential. The Patient Evaluation Grid, or PEG (Leigh & Reisar, 1980), is an example of a systems implement designed to facilitate this process.

Figure 12.2 displays a sample evaluation PEG form, and Figure 12.3 displays a sample diagnosis and treatment plan PEG form. In the Yale Behavioral Medicine Clinic, patient data are collected across the biological, psychological, and social levels, and the data are integrated using the PEG as a unifying conceptual tool. All staff members learn to fill in PEGs and use this information to organize the complexity of biobehavioral interactions that can occur in individual patients. I will return to the PEG in the last section.

One reason why a systems tool such as the PEG is valuable is that it helps the therapist learn how to move back and forth across levels and time between the "whole" of the patient's life (including the social environment as a relevant suprasystem) and the "parts." This kind of tool also helps the therapist learn what information he or she may have forgotten to obtain (or did not realize was needed) in order to make a comprehensive evaluation. In systems terms, *in order to see the "holes" we must have a sense of the "whole."*

There is clearly a need for research to determine whether the use of conceptual tools such as the PEG improve the process of diagnosis, treatment, and prevention. Since hypotheses can be made quite specific as a function of particular contexts (e.g., disease categories, treatment types, and so forth), the practical value of the general conceptual tool can be determined.

In sum, the systems perspective proposes that a therapist's (a scientist's, or any person's) degrees of freedom for discovering novel applications can increase as that individual's scope of knowledge about whole/

DIMENSIONS	CONTEXTS		
	CURRENT (Current States)	RECENT (Recent Events and Changes)	BACKGROUND (Culture, Traits, Constitution)
BIOLOGICAL	Symptoms Physical examination Vital signs Status of related organs Medications Disease	Age Recent bodily changes Injuries, operations Disease Drugs	Heredity Early nutrition Constitution Predisposition Early disease

PERSONAL	Chief complaint
	Mental status
	Expectations about illness
	    and treatment
		Recent illness, occurrence
		    of symptoms
		Personality change
		Mood, thinking, behavior
		
		Adaptation, defenses
			Developmental factors
			Early experience
			Personality type
			
			Attitude to illness

ENVIRON-MENTAL	Immediate physical and
	    interpersonal environment
	Supportive figure, next of kin
	Effect of help-seeking
		Recent physical and
		    interpersonal environment
		Life changes
		Family, work, others
		Contact with ill persons
		Contact with doctor or
		    hospital
			Early physical
			    environment
			Cultural and family
			    environment
			Early relations
			Cultural sick role expectation

FIGURE 12.2 Patient evaluation grid (PEG)—management form.

Source: From Leigh & Reiser (1980). Copyright © 1980, Plenum Publishing. Reprinted by permission.

part and microlevel/macrolevel relationships in his or her particular area increases. Later on in the chapter, a case example is presented of therapeutic improvisations in behavior therapy and biobehavioral therapy that were stimulated by this approach.

Once one has mastered the ability to dissect whole/part and levels relationships, it is virtually impossible to perceive the world in the same way again. This inherent occupational risk is a reflection of the fact that systems theory stimulates a general paradigm shift in human perception and thought. The next three sections illustrate how significant these perceptual changes can be.

Concept 3: Discovering Levels of Linguistic Meaning

Like all phenomena in nature, words reflect combinations of levels, from the most general meanings (unifying) to the most specific. The

| DIMENSIONS | DIAGNOSIS | THERAPY PLANS | |
		SHORT TERM	LONG TERM
BIOLOGICAL			
PERSONAL			
ENVIRONMENTAL			

FIGURE 12.3 Patient evaluation grid.

Source: From Leigh & Reiser (1980). Copyright © 1980, Plenum Publishing. Reprinted by permission.

originators of behaviorism and the originators of systems theory were aware of this fundamental distinction. Where they differed was the path they took (and the tools they developed) to approach this issue.

The parallels between B.F. Skinner and James G. Miller (1978) in the 1940s and 1950s are instructive to consider as prototypes of the contrasting development of behaviorism and systems theory. Both were at Harvard (Skinner as a professor, Miller as an M.D./Ph.D. student—his Ph.D. was in psychology—and as a Junior Fellow). Both had a strong interest in philosophy. Both received training in biology and psychology. Both were aware of Whitehead's teaching and writings on the concept of "organism" in nature (Whitehead was also at Harvard at that time). Both were empirically oriented.

On the surface, it might appear that Skinner and Miller represent two extremes in terms of levels of meaning of the word *behavior.* As shown in Table 12.1 (adapted from Schwartz, 1982a), the word *behavior* varies in the specificity versus generality of its use and how it is implemented in theory, research, and practice. The use of the word *behavior* in "behavioral" medicine is also included to illustrate the power that different paradigmatic views can have on the course of tool development and tool usage in science.

Skinner saw behavior as the overt functioning of organisms, which

TABLE 12.1 Four Definitions of *behavior*, Using Behavioral Medicine as an Example, Moving up Levels of Generality and Inclusiveness

Level	Definition
Level I: Behavioral psychology	"Behavior" here refers to the study of the overt behavior of organisms, emphasizing learning without reference to cognition, emotion, and so forth. Here "behavioral psychology," a subfield within the discipline of psychology, would be defined as the "behavioral science." "Behavioral medicine" would be defined here as the application of behavioral psychology theory and techniques to health and illness
Level II: Psychology	"Behavior" here refers to the study of the behavior of organisms, broadly defined, and encompasses the complete discipline of psychology. Psychology would be classified as *the* behavioral science. "Behavioral medicine" would be defined here as the application of the discipline of psychology to health and illness (the American Psychological Association's definition of "health psychology")
Level III: Social science	"Behavior" here refers to the study of living organisms, very broadly defined. Disciplines classified here as "behavioral sciences" would include not only psychology, but anthropology, sociology, political science, and economics (i.e., social sciences). "Behavioral medicine" would be defined here as the application of the behavioral/social sciences to health and illness (Schwartz & Weiss, 1978)
Level IV: System theory	"Behavior" here refers to the study of behavior of all systems at all levels. Every scientific discipline from physics through psychology to astronomy, would be viewed as behavioral in their approach and would be classified as "behavioral sciences." "Behavioral medicine" here would be defined as the application of systems concepts toward the integration of all disciplines to health and illness

SOURCE: Adapted from Schwartz (1982a). Copyright © 1982, The Guilford Press. Used by permission.

by definition is a subset of the discipline of psychology (see Table 12.1, Level I definition). As a result, "behavior therapy" to Skinner became the application of behavioristic techniques to changing overt behavior. In this context, behavioral medicine became the application of behavioristic tools to changing overt behavior and underlying physiological behavior.

However, the word *behavior* has been used more broadly to refer not only to overt behavior, but also to inferred covert behavior (e.g., cognitions and emotions). This is shown as a Level II definition. Here, "behavior therapy" means psychological treatment in general. It follows that behavioral medicine at this level is identical to psychological medicine (now called "health psychology"—psychology as a discipline's contributions to health and illness). The evolution from strict behaviorism to cognitive behavior therapy can be viewed as a level shift from Level I to Level II.

The Level III definition of *behavior* goes one step further. Here behavior is viewed not solely in terms of the individual, but in terms of groups, organizations, and institutions as well. This use of the term "behavior" includes not only the discipline of psychology, but also sociology, anthropology, political science, and economics. "Behavior" therapy in this context would include not only behavioristic tools and broader psychological tools, but also tools drawn from sociology, political science, economics, anthropology, and so forth.

According to systems theory, all systems at all levels can be viewed as having structure or form (ultimately an abstract concept) and function (which, ultimately, is also an abstract concept). Different disciplines, or fields within disciplines, tend to focus their attention more on structure (e.g., anatomy) or more on function (e.g., physiology). However, according to systems theory, ultimately the concepts of structure and function are intimately related (contextually, they can be viewed as two qualities of the system as a whole, just as waves and particles can be viewed as two qualities of light as a whole). When viewed in terms of its most general (and essential) meaning, the word *behavior* refers to the characteristic ways in which a system *functions* in response to various stimuli. According to systems theory, what all scientists ultimately measure is the functioning, that is, the behavior, of systems (whether the system is at the level of a proton, a primate, or a planet). The idea that all systems behave, and behave in characteristic manners (i.e., express a systemic personality), can serve as a conceptual bridge that links the microlevel of subatomic physics with psychobiology, ecology, and the macrolevel of astronomy.

All disciplines involve the measurement of behavior (functioning), and they attempt to infer underlying processes to explain the patterns of behavior observed. When the word *cognition* is used in its most general meaning as information processing, it becomes clear that modern elementary-particle physicists and infant-developmental psychologists share the same conceptual problem: they both *infer* strategies of information processing at their respective levels from the *behavior* of the system they can measure (be it the behavior of patterns of bubbles in a bubble chamber or the behavior of patterns of babbling in a baby's chamber!).

Skinner and Miller can be viewed as having shared this vision in common. Where they differ is in their *comfort in drawing inferences* about underlying information processing from overt behavior observed. Skinner concluded that psychology needed to focus its attention primarily on overt behavior, while Miller concluded that the study of behavior was only meaningful to the extent that useful inferences about underlying information processing were made. Miller reasoned that to the extent that certain qualities of behavior could be observed to occur across levels, it would be possible to hypothesize the existence of common underlying information processing.

From a systems perspective, the use of the combined terms, "systems behaviorism" or "systems behavior therapy," is redundant, since all systems behave. The idea that all systems behave applies even in death, where the breakdown of body tissues and cells is found to follow a general, orderly sequence over time. Since therapists vary in their abilities to extract implicit meanings in the use of specific terms, a concept that a systems therapist can learn to use routinely is always to begin with the hypothesis that the levels to which a patient is referring at any given moment are unknown (see the clinical example below). The therapist's goals, therefore, are (1) to observe and record carefully the patient's verbal and nonverbal behavior with minimal inference (regulation) and (2) to generate specific predictions that can allow better understanding about what level or levels the patient is referring to at a given moment.

Concept 4: Discovering Levels of Emergent Behavior

A system, by definition, consists of an organized set of parts (the subsystem level) that *interact* with each other in such a way as to generate *unique properties* ("emergents") expressed at the level of the whole (the system level) as the system interacts with its environment (the suprasystem level). In other words, systems generate unique behaviors that emerge out of a complex set of subsystem/system/suprasystem interactions.

Emergent properties are ubiquitous in nature (Miller, 1978). The classic example of emergent properties concerns the individual properties of hydrogen and oxygen as atoms versus the unique properties that emerge when hydrogen and oxygen unite and become the molecular system called water. The unique properties of water expressed as a liquid at room temperature cannot be predicted by studying the behavior of hydrogen and oxygen independently (i.e., un-united) as separate gases at room temperature. The unique behaviors of water only emerge when hydrogen and oxygen interact in such a way as to become a unified, organized chemical system.

This is not to say that the relationship between water and its components, hydrogen and oxygen, cannot be studied empirically. On the contrary, the conclusion that should be drawn is that the properties that are unique to water can be revealed (i.e., discovered) when the *particular components* are *allowed* to *interact* as a *unique, integrated system*. It is worth pondering the empirical fact that no other combination of molecules produces the identical set of properties observed to emerge when hydrogen and oxygen join forces, unite, and form the system we term water.

What happens when the emergent-property concept is applied as a unifying idea in behavior therapy and therapy in general? One immediate implication concerns our strategy for conducting research and performing therapy using combinations of psychological techniques. The mechanistic hypothesis encourages us to look for "independent" effects in nature (so-called main effects in analysis-of-variance terms) and to attempt to avoid "interdependent" effects (interactions, in analysis-of-variance terms). Our statistics are based on the formistic premise that events in nature can be treated as if they functioned independently (which is a condition necessary to generate a random table of numbers). Similarly, in factor analysis, we are taught to search for "orthogonal" factors that are independent of each other. However, from a systems perspective, the independent-variable approach becomes questionable. Clearly, to the extent that nature consists of levels of systems that operate interactively, interactions should be the rule rather than the exception in nature. It follows that combinations of treatments may achieve certain *emergent* effects *only when they are allowed to combine in particular ways in particular individuals within particular contexts*. The strategy of pulling components apart, reductionistically producing a state of disunity, will by definition remove the systemic nature of the components that occurs when the components are allowed to unite and interact over time.

I have proposed that general-systems theory is of particular value in behavioral medicine as a tool for understanding how biological, psychological, and social treatments combine in comprehensive biopsychosocial therapy (Schwartz, 1981). Psychological and pharmacologic effects may not be simply additive but may interact synergistically, producing emergent effects that neither can produce alone. For example, when family history, salt intake, and stress are found to interact in producing high blood pressure, biologists may choose to view the salt as the "cause" and the stress as a "moderator" variable, while psychologists may choose to view the stress as the "cause" and the salt as a "moderator" variable. In contrast, systems theory views the high blood pressure as an emergent result of the family history, salt intake, and stress.

As another example, consider biofeedback. It is known (1) that biofeedback can have selective physiological feedback effects (called 'specificity effects'), (2) that it can lead subjects to select certain cognitive strategies, and (3) that it can lead to changes in self-concept through enhanced self-efficacy. From the systems perspective, neither the feedback specificity, imagery, nor self-concept is labeled as the main effect of biofeedback. Rather, all are interacting, emergent results from the biofeedback.

It is of value for patients and therapists to take an emergent approach to analyzing the unique patterns of effects that different individual treatments can have. For example, diuretics and progressive muscle relaxation can both achieve decreases in blood pressure. However, it is known that relaxation techniques have other side effects (such as reductions in a wide range of physiological responses to stress) that would have greater total benefit for the patient than diuretics (which do not have these other effects).

Concept 5: Discovering Levels of Self-Regulation and "Disregulation"

Another concept inherent in the notion of a system is self-regulation and its opposite process, which I call "disregulation." If parts unite and interact to create a whole, thereby allowing emergent behaviors to be expressed, then it follows that each part of the system must, to varying degrees, play some role in the regulation of the system as a whole.

If the parts are appropriately connected, the system can regulate itself (engage in self-regulation). Moreover, the system *must* engage in self-regulation if the parts are connected (e.g., if a thermostat and furnace are appropriately connected and the components are each in good working order, the resulting heating system must engage in automatic self-regulation). To connect parts in a unified fashion (i.e., to interconnect parts in an organized fashion) is to initiate self-regulation of one kind or another. Simply stated, to connect is to self-regulate.

The concept of feedback is well known in behavior therapy and medicine. The nature of the self-regulation that emerges when parts are united depends on how the information conveyed in the feedback between the parts is interpreted by the parts in the system. If the feedback is interpreted as a signal to decrease, or counteract, a behavior (negative feedback), the self-regulation that emerges will be of the homeostatic type (regression to the mean or setpoint—returning home, so to speak). If the feedback is interpreted as a signal to increase or amplify a behavior (positive feedback), the self-regulation that emerges will be of the antihomeostatic type ("progression to the extreme," away from the setpoint—going away from home).

Both types of information processing, negative feedback and positive feedback, involve self-regulation and are essential if a system is to engage in flexible and adaptive behavior.

How do we determine which particular component process is serving as a regulator in a system? The answer is conceptually simple, but deceptively so. Since self-regulation requires the components to be connected, then if the components are disconnected, the self-regulation should disappear. Unity implies connection, which in turn implies integration. If disconnection occurs, then disunity should occur and the system should disintegrate, which means disintegration (or disunite). If the system disintegrates, then the emergent properties must disappear.

In a similar vein, the essence of the scientific method can be viewed as hinging on the complementary relationship between regulation and disregulation. The ultimate proof that *A* regulates *B* is to remove ("dis") *A* and show that *B* changes accordingly (certain behaviors "dis" appear).

An important application of the concept of self-regulation in behavior therapy is that of self-monitoring. This procedure can be considered as both a measurement and a treatment process. If patients are requested to self-monitor their behavior without any instructions to alter it, their behavior will frequently change in some fashion, depending on how they interpret the feedback of their behavior and the context of the self-monitoring.

Systems-oriented therapists appreciate that to measure is to connect and therefore to regulate. The therapist and patient can become a powerful therapeutic system, for example, when a patient develops strong feelings toward his or her therapist and responds to nonverbal and verbal feedback provided by the therapist. It follows that when a therapist asks a patient a question and directs the patient's attention inward (toward bodily sensations, feelings, and/or thoughts) or outward (toward behavior, social interactions, the setting, and so forth), this will set up a feedback loop that will change the state of the patient's internal regulation and the patient/therapist regulation as a system as well. The systems therapist begins with the hypothesis that self-attention always has potential self-regulatory consequences. Since the nature and degree of the self-regulation can vary, its clinical significance in any specific instance will vary accordingly.

When we translate cognition into information-processing terms and apply these concepts across levels from the psychological through the neurological down to the peripheral endocrine, immunological, and physiological levels, a unified picture of a united psychoneurobiological system emerges in which the capability to integrate self-regulatory processes becomes not only feasible but is required. So-called placebo effects and drug/personality/belief interactions are therefore viewed in a new light and become open to new empirical tools for testing specific biobehavioral hypotheses (White et al., 1985).

In some individuals, it has been documented that participation in relaxation procedures leads to *increased* anxiety. This phenomenon of relaxation-induced anxiety (Borkovec, 1976) takes on new meaning when viewed from this perspective. If disregulated persons achieve low anxiety through motivated and effortful self-disattention, then when attention is focused inward in an attempt at relaxation, this will counteract the disattentive process, thereby increasing the person's awareness of negative emotions and physical pain. If these patients can be taught to relabel such experiences as evidence that they are moving toward health rather than as a sign that they are moving toward disease, the avoidance behavior of "repression" (including noncompliance) can be transformed into approach behavior and adaptive self-regulation can be fostered.

From Behavior Therapy to Systems Therapy: The Case of the Peach Lady

Nine basic conceptual tools of a systems-oriented approach to behavior therapy ("systems therapy") have been discussed. Included are Pepper's four world hypotheses, which involve (1) categorical, (2) cause-and-effect, (3) relativistic, and (4) relational modes of thinking. Also included are the five concepts discussed above: (1) whole/part relationships, (2) microlevels/macrolevels, (3) levels of linguistic meaning, (4) emergent behaviors and levels of emergents, and (5) self-regulation and disregulation, and levels of regulation. The following case of Martha, the "Peach Lady," illustrates how the application of these concepts within behavior therapy expands and integrates diagnostic and treatment information.

Martha was recently referred to the Yale Behavioral Medicine Clinic. Her presenting complaint was that she was terribly sensitive to odors and had had a series of reactions that severely limited her activities. Her goal was to learn behavioral techniques to lessen her reactions and to learn new coping strategies.

Employing categorical thinking, the approach would be to (1) diagnose her condition by placing her disorder in a category, (2) discover the category (or categories) of her reactions, and (3) discover the categories of odors that triggered these reactions. The behavior therapist might diagnose her condition as a learned hypersensitivity, possibly with secondary gain. It turned out that the class of reactions included rage attacks, mild epileptic seizures, catalepsy, and narcolepsy. Her methods of coping involved holding her nose (for example, when going to a public bathroom), screaming at people to stop smoking, and avoiding or fleeing situations she perceived as dangerous. Classes of odors were complex, including cigarette smoke, bathroom smells, carbon monoxide, and various cleaning supplies and perfumes.

Employing cause-and-effect thinking, the approach would be to determine more precisely which stimuli (odors) triggered which reactions. The patient would typically be asked to keep a diary and record all reactions and the odors that preceded them. Based on these findings, techniques would be designed to alter these cause-and-effect relationships. Techniques might include systematic desensitization, relaxation training, and techniques of preventive avoidance.

Employing contextual thinking, the approach would be to add to the categories and cause-and-effect relationships observed moderating variables that modulated the cause-and-effect relationships. For example, was the strength of a reaction always determined by the strength of the odor, or did the odor/reaction relationship vary as a function of certain conditions (e.g., social settings, state of mind, amount of sleep, nutritional status, phase of her menstrual period, drug status, and so forth). It turned out, for example, that her reactions seemed worse when she was irritable, when she felt lonely and needed attention, and when she was hungry (she therefore carried small snacks around with her to help raise the threshold for her reactions).

Employing relational thinking, the approach would again be to add specifiable relationships among the various stimuli, moderators, and reactions. For example, a systems approach would encourage the combination and integration of this information with other information not yet collected in order to specify more fully the whole of her condition. For example, it was important to know that she was taking Dilantin for her seizures and that her threshold for odor/reaction effects was moderated by the levels of her Dilantin.

Also applicable in analyzing Martha's case are the five systems concepts discussed above. Concept 1 indicates that whole/part relationships need to be considered in some depth. We would ask in what sense her rage reaction or her narcolepsy is a whole in that it represents a specific combination of interacting variables (parts). Moreover, we would ask in what sense her personality and behavior as a whole represent a specific combination of interacting variables, including her medical history and her sense of self? To examine her "whole," a comprehensive evaluation was made in the Yale Behavioral Medicine Clinic.

Important historical and interacting variables include the following: (1) she had had a protracted birth; (2) she was diagnosed as brain damaged early on, having shown selective deficits in memory for specific objects localized in space; (3) her parents had provided her with little love, seeing her as a "freak" of sorts; (4) she had developed her neurological symptoms relatively early and had gone from doctor to doctor for diagnoses and treatment; (5) she was very short (4'9") and looked a bit "funny," further contributing to her poor self-concept. She was led to believe that she was stupid, that she was severely damaged, and that she could do little (constrained so by her reaction to odors).

She had married a man who provided her with very selective love (and little money). Their marriage had been rocky, with poor communication. They had adopted a son, who showed clear signs of impulsivity and hyperactivity. She was chronically frightened about her condition (e.g., she feared falling asleep on the floor in a supermarket); chronically angry at doctors, her parents, her husband, and herself; and chronically depressed about her future. She took a combination of drugs for her various neurologic conditions whose interactions were neither well examined nor well managed. Against this background, the specific odor/reaction relationship becomes more complex, more interactive, and more in need of organized, multifactoral analysis and treatment.

The material in Martha's case can be organized in terms of Concept 2, the microlevel/macrolevel perspective. Thus the case data can be arranged from the genetic and early biochemical levels, to the biological level (her various neural conditions), to the psychological level (her poor self-esteem, her anger), to the social level (such as her learned reactions for either seeking attention or avoiding stressful situations).

An important addition to clinical diagnosis and treatment is Concept 3, which deals with levels of linguistic meaning. Persons vary in the levels of meaning they use for particular words, and the levels of meaning they use may vary from context to context. With this principle in mind, it becomes prudent not merely to ask a patient what he or she means by a concept, but also to locate this meaning in terms of level as well as content. When I asked the Peach Lady what she meant by terms such as *anxiety, depression, freedom,* and *love,* the level of her meanings was remarkably high and abstract. When she was stressed, or when she had a rage attack, the level of her meanings decreased; but when she was calm and involved, her analyses were not only extremely high, they were remarkably intelligent. Her description of the Bahai faith, for example, was especially insightful. We came to the conclusion that actually she was exceptionally intelligent, despite her poor memory for locations. This discrepancy caused her, her parents, her husband, and her friends tremendous confusion, if not conflict. Once she realized the level of her mental functioning, her self-concept changed. It was clear that she did not seek simple formistic/mechanistic solutions to her problems. She required a complex contextual, systemic, and, as we will see, integrated analysis of her problems. This realization altered the course of her therapy accordingly.

The concept of emergent behaviors and levels of emergent behaviors (Concept 4) allows the therapist and patient to recognize how specific parts at one level can be expressed as unique events at a higher level. In the case of the Peach Lady, an effort was made to examine levels of causes and effects and see if a solution could be found that operated on multiple levels. The hypothesis was that if a fragrance could be found that operated on multiple levels, from the chemical to the sensory to the perceptual to the affective to the cognitive to the social, and the effects were synergistic within and across levels, that some of her reactions might be reduced (the threshold would be raised). In this context, I asked Martha whether she remembered ever having smelled a fragrance that she particularly liked. A vibrant smile came over her face, and she recounted how the smell of fresh peach as a child (from peach orchards and peach pies) was very pleasant and associated with vacations.

Through the research division of the International Flavors and Fragrances Corporation (IFF), I was able to obtain a bottle of a truly luscious peach aroma. The effect on Martha was remarkable. If she was having a rage attack, the rage would virtually vanish with a brief smell of the fragrance. If she was having a small epileptic seizure, smelling the fragrance aborted the seizure. If she fell to the floor in a cataleptic state, bringing the bottle of peach to her nose enabled her to move again. And if she fell to the floor in a narcoleptic stupor, a few sniffs of the peach would revive her. Armed with aroma of peach, Martha was able not only to abort reactions, but to prevent them as well: by smelling the fragrance before she entered a restroom or before she reached a toll booth reeking of carbon monoxide. Her reactions decreased about 70%. The dramatic nature of these effects can be explained by a variety of levels of effects that may be interactive and therefore emergent. There may be some chemicals in peaches that are particularly effective in reducing seizures. There may be something primarily sensory about the strong scent of peach, or any strong fragrance, that acts as a distractor (attention splitter). The hedonics of peach, very pleasant for Martha, may act on positive emotions, which in turn may regulate attention and shift awareness. The prior learning, memories, and images could all serve to take her attention (and neural firing) away from the aversive present to the more pleasant past. Higher-order expectancy (so called placebo effects) may have acted as a catalyst for some of these effects. Finally, the social effects of wearing fragrance, being noticed, and receiving social support may also have operated here. Rather than thinking in single-cause/single-effect terms, it is possible that multiple-cause/multiple-effect processes were at work here.

This leads to Concept 5, self-regulation and disregulation, as well as levels of regulation and disregulation. When Martha could take control of her seizures, reduce them, abort them, and prevent them, her sense of self-efficacy dramatically improved. Her fear, anger, and depression were reduced as the levels of regulation, aided by the fragrance, increased.

We likened the use of the peach fragrance to a neural defibrilator. The cardiac defibrilator provides very strong electric current to stop the disregulated firing of the cardiac muscles so that, when the electric shock stops, the muscles can become coordinated (synchronized, integrated) again, forming the emergent behavior of a healthy ventricular beat. The hypothesis is that peach may be to the disregulated neurons as electric shock is to the disregulated cardiac muscles. The very strong, very positive, and very historically important effects of olfactory stimulation may "shock" the limbic system, reticular system, and frontal system, allowing them to re-regulate following the stimulus. The levels-of-regulation concept encourages us to take a more complete and organized approach to analyzing self-regulation and disregulation. And, of course, the regulation all occurs in the context of other factors, such as current medications.

Armed with this new technique, Martha realized that she has a tool that could help integrate and unify her various problems. She came to realize that the fragrance was necessary but not sufficient. Learning how to use the fragrance in appropriate contexts improved her ability to regulate her symptoms. With the change in her self-control came a more integrated view of herself. The fragrance became a unifying implement of sorts for her.

More broadly, we need to develop generic unifying implements that will facilitate our organizing the within-and-between levels of biological, psychological, and social information necessary to produce a more complete, meaningful, and responsible approach to diagnostics and treatment. Most systems concepts have the potential to function as unifying implements. However, we need to develop more specific concepts that facilitate the difficult task of integrating all the information relative to the functioning of a person's "behavior" in the broadest, multilevel meaning of this term.

Martha left therapy with a number of changes. She divorced her husband. She decided that she wanted to live in a climate and environment that would be more friendly to her physical, intellectual, and emotional qualities. For her, this linked with her religious views (she believed in the Bahai faith, which possesses a particularly integrated set of religious views). She drove to Arizona by herself (a feat that was quite impossible before the "behavioral aroma" treatment) and settled in Tucson. She was by no means "cured," and with the loss of the support of the Yale Behavioral Medicine Clinic, some of her gains declined. However, she was aware of the kind of supportive environment that she needed in order to function in a more integrated, healthy fashion.

Summary

The overreaching goal of this chapter has been to provide a framework for understanding (1) the evolution and current status of behavior therapy from the perspective of the evolution and current status of general systems theory, and (2) the application of systems principles to clinical research and practice. This framework has been based upon the general concept of an *integrative tool*. An integrative tool, by definition, is a tool developed for the purpose of functioning as a *unifying implement*. I believe that the development of a conceptual "toolbox" of unifying implements and the skills needed to use these integrative tools effectively is a prerequisite for developing a genuinely *integrative health science* approach to disease and health.

It follows that in the same way that we can have kitchen tools, garden tools, woodworking tools, and electronic tools, it is also possible to have cognitive tools, emotional tools, social tools, and even (most abstractly and generally) paradigmatic tools. In this context words themselves become tools. Similarly, the creation of theories and the development of the scientific method itself become tools of the mind, generic tools for achieving discovery, description, and prediction in nature.

This perspective suggests a number of potentially paradigmatic conclusions and hypotheses. One conclusion is that scientific theories are less *descriptions* of the "truth" about nature than they are *creations* of the mind designed to serve as "implements" of description, discovery, and prediction. If a better theoretical implement comes along, the earlier theory will eventually be replaced or incorporated by the new one. The hypothesis that theories are really tools of the mind rather than truths about nature per se has the potential value of encouraging scientists and practitioners to become more humble, more open-minded, and more creative about the development of conceptual implements for appreciating nature and its potential for novel change and evalution.

Are there classes of unifying implements that are sufficiently general yet sufficiently precise to foster more specific tools at all levels of nature? The grand hypothesis of general-systems theory is that there exists a set of unifying principles that apply to all systems at all levels in nature, from the extremely microscopic, subatomic level to the extremely macroscopic, cosmological level.

Afterword

A particularly vivid example of the use of integrative tools in the arts was illustrated at the beginning of this chapter by the pointillist paintings of Georges Seurat. As the Purple Hat Effect illustrates, the brain does not merely process sensory stimuli. The brain combines (integrates) this information into higher-order patterns of neural processes, resulting in new (emergent) experiences and properties (Powers, 1973; Luria, 1973). As our perceptions move from micro (close distance) to macro (far distance) analyses, our perceptions change qualitatively as well as quantitatively.

Had we looked at Seurat's painting only from a close distance, we would have concluded that the canvas was covered with a chaotic array of 11 different-colored dots; from a moderate distance, we would have concluded that the canvas contained hundreds of forms and colors; and from afar, we would have concluded that the canvas was splattered with painted dots of many different shapes and colors.

The emergent experience of purple at a moderate distance is the rule rather than the exception in nature. In systems theory, analyses occurring at different levels reveal different relationships and emergents. To obtain a comprehensive understanding of a system (such as a patient), it is essential for us to be able to view the system (e.g., the patient) from different levels and to integrate these views.

I believe that systems theory can most easily be understood, and most effectively be applied to research and practice, when the theory is viewed as an organized collection of *integrative conceptual tools* that can be used to build any specific theory designed to describe and predict within levels as well as between levels. As an integrative tool, general systems theory can be thought of as a collection of unifying tools for building transdisciplinary theories and applications not only in behavior therapy but in all modes of therapy, cutting across physical, biological, psychological and social levels of intervention.

References

Borkovec, T.D. (1976). Physiological and cognitive processes in the regulation of anxiety. In G.E. Schwartz & D. Shapiro (Eds.), *Consciousness and self-regulation* (pp. 216–312). New York: Plenum.

Boulding, K.E. (1978). *Ecodynamics.* Beverly Hills, CA: Sage.

deRosnay, J. (1979). *The macroscope.* New York: Harper & Row.

Engel, G.L. (1977). The need for a new medical model. A challenge for biomedicine. *Science, 196,* 129–136.

Kuhn, T.S. (1962). *The structure of scientific revolutions.* Chicago: University of Chicago Press.

Leigh, H., & Reiser, M.F. (1980). *The patient.* New York: Plenum.

Luria, A.R. (1973). *The working brain.* New York: Basic Books.

Miller, J.G. (1978). *Living systems.* McGraw-Hill.

Pagels, H.R. (1982). *The cosmic code.* New York: Simon & Schuster.

Pepper, S.C. (1942). *World hypotheses.* Berkeley: University of California Press.

Powers, W.T. (1973). *Behavior, the control of perception.* Chicago: Aldine.

Schwartz, G.E. (1981). A systems analysis of psychobiology and behavior theory: Implications for behavioral medicine. *Psychotherapy and Psychosomatics, 36,* 159–184.

Schwartz, G.E. (1982a). Integrating psychobiology and behavior therapy: A systems perspective. In G.T. Wilson & C.M. Franks (Eds.), *Contemporary behavior therapy: Conceptual and empirical foundations* (pp. 119–141). New York: Guilford.

Schwartz, G.E. (1982b). Testing the biopsychosocial model: The ultimate challenge facing behavioral medicine? *Journal of Consulting and Clinical Psychology, 50,* 1043–1053.

Schwartz, G.E. (1984). Psychobiology of health: A new synthesis. In B.L. Hammonds & C.J. Scheirer (Eds.), *Psychology and health: The Master Lecture Series (Vol. 3)* (pp. 145–193). Washington, DC: American Psychological Association.

Schwartz, G.E. (1987). Personality and the unification of psychology and modern physics: A systems approach. In J. Aronoff, A.I. Rabin, & R.Z. Zucker (Eds.), *The emergence of personality.* New York: Springer Publishing Co.

Schwartz, G.E., & Weiss, S.M. (1978). Yale conference on behavioral medicine: A proposed definition and statement of goals. *Journal of Behavioral Medicine, 1,* 3–12.

von Bertalanffy, L. (1968). *General systems theory.* New York: Braziller.

White, L., Tursky, B., & Schwartz, G.E. (Eds.), (1985). *Placebo theory, research and mechanisms.* New York: Guilford.

V
Overview and Commentary

13

Paradigmatic Decision Making in Behavior Therapy: A Provisional Roadmap

Daniel B. Fishman
Frederick Rotgers
Cyril M. Franks

In Chapters 3 through 12 a group of prominent scholars with diverse perspectives about behavior therapy responded to certain questions and issues concerning the present and future paradigmatic status of behavior therapy. These issues and questions were described in Chapter 2 and further outlined in Figure 2.1. These issues are exemplified in three major ways of viewing behavior therapy:

1. Kuhn's model of the development of paradigms in scientific fields
2. The epistemological, scientific/theoretical, technological, ethical, and sociological/political/historical arenas of a scientific paradigm
3. The contrast between paradigms that presently exist in the field and those that might or should come into being in the future

Contributors were also asked to give thought to related issues and encouraged to decide for themselves which were the most important issues to focus upon. Thus the pattern of emphasis in this volume reflects the more important, or at least the more controversial, issues in the field as currently seen by the contributors.

In keeping with our initial organization, this final chapter is structured around the three dimensions outlined in Figure 2.1. We will start with the various "arenas" (epistemological, scientific, technological, and so forth), since these comprise the basic components of a full paradigm. We will then put these components together and consider the extent to which behavior therapy functions as a Kuhnian paradigm. Finally, we will explore implications for the future of behavior therapy.

The Paradigmatic Arenas of Behavior Therapy

The Epistemological Arena

Krasner and Houts (1984) studied the epistemological value systems of a group of behavioral psychologists who had helped launch the behavior-modification movement from which behavior therapy developed in the 30-year period following the Second World War. These values are contrasted with those of a randomly selected comparison group of non-behavioral psychologists from the same period. The behavioral group was found to be significantly higher on scales reflecting a factual (vs. theoretical) orientation; a belief in impersonal causality (vs. free will); a behavioral (vs. experiential) content emphasis; elementalism (vs. holism); environmental determinism; physicalism; a quantitative (vs. qualitative) orientation; and objectivism (vs. subjectivism).

While only three of the eleven contributors to the present volume fall into the historical role of a "launcher" of behavior modification (Eysenck, Krasner, and Staats), all, with one exception (Woolfolk), appear to identify generally with these values. Thus there seems to be continuity in behavior therapy at a very general epistemological level. Woolfolk, it should be noted, does not take the position that present behavior therapists assume a different set of epistemological values. In fact, Woolfolk agrees that behavior therapy's position is consistent with these values; his goal is to present this position's limitations vis-a-vis the epistemological assumptions of functionalism and hermeneutic, ordinary-language philosophy.

Despite this commonality, however, there are diverse views about the extent to which behavior therapy should be based on an epistemology of logical positivism as opposed to social constructionism. This diversity is related to another dimension along which this book's contributors vary: the extent to which the scope of behavior therapy should be limited to conditioning principles that deal only with observable, overt behaviors as contrasted with unobservable, covert, cognitive/mental states and processes. The positions of the various authors on these two dimensions are shown in Figure 13.1.

There is an overall correlation between the two dimensions, such that a primary or exclusive emphasis on a positivistic view is associated with more behavioristic, conditioning principles, whereas a primary or exclusive emphasis on a constructionistic position is associated with cognitive principles (Figure 13.1). The cognitivist's acknowledgment that an individual's behavior is in part a function of how he or she cognitively filters external reality leads logically to the conclusion that "reality" is, to some extent, a construct of the individual concerned. Consistent with this formulation, there is no author in the upper right or lower left corner of Figure 13.1. However, the correlation is not perfect and the area encompassed by the various positions quite broad. For example, one can believe, as does Krasner, that knowledge of the world is primarily cognitively constructed rather than positivistically discovered but that, for pragmatic reasons, it is more effective to use primarily conditioning models for behavior change. The positivism–constructionism dimension is discussed below within the epistemological arena, leaving the conditioning–cognitive dimension to the theoretical modality.

Logical Positivism vs. Social Constructionism

One method of conceptualizing the differences between logical positivism and social constructionism is outlined in Figure 13.2. The figure consists essentially of three rows. The first, Box, 1, portrays the external reality of a particular psychological situation X. The second, Boxes 2 and 2 ', illustrates the logical-positivist view that, under the conditions of natural science—such as operational definitions of measurement procedures and laboratory controls for contaminating variables like experimenter bias—psychologists A and B can directly observe situation X and derive a very similar, "objective" picture of it. Thus it follows that the two can achieve a high reliability that is independent of the cultural and historical contexts of the observations.

The third row, Boxes 3 through 6 ', outlines the social-constructionist view that an external reality, such as situation X, can never be directly known. Rather, external reality impinges upon an individual, such as psychologist A or B, and is then filtered, transformed, and, in effect, constructed on the basis of at least the following five major, interacting variables.

1. *The individual's personal constructs* (3a and 3 'a). These include all the individual's present, personal, "private" constructs of the

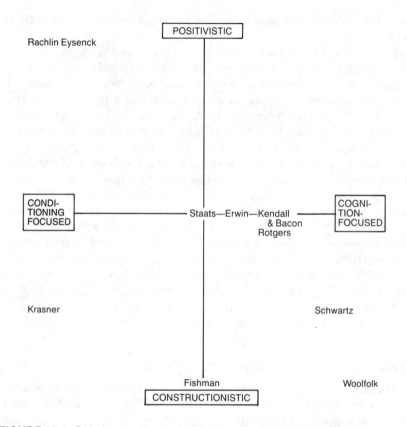

FIGURE 13.1 Relative positions of authors on two dimensions: Positivism versus constructionism, and focus on conditioning versus cognition.

world, built upon past experience just prior to exposure to situation X.

2. *Characteristics of the individual's language* (3b and 3′b). Instead of holding the logical-positivist premise of a direct relationship between sense data and the real world, social constructionists view human experience of and knowledge about the world as inextricably mediated by language. And language, as a changing human artifact, is intrinsically full of arbitrary conventions, ambiguity, vagueness, and special characteristics determined by the nature of grammar and linguistic style rather than by the structure of the external world.

3. *Social input from others* (3c and 3′c). While an individual's process of constructing reality is ultimately a private event, much input from and interaction with others takes place, thereby making it a social one.

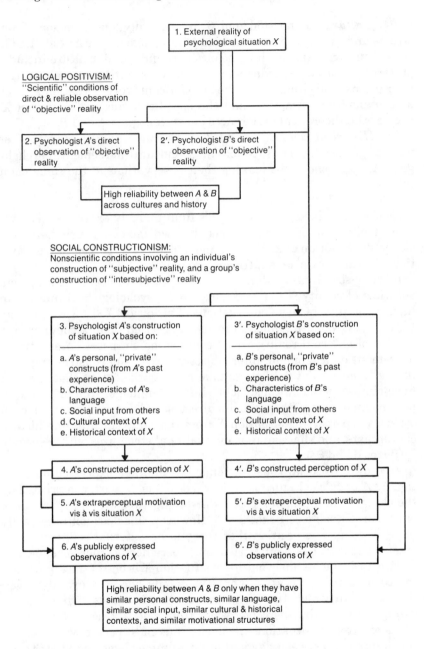

FIGURE 13.2 Contrasting epistemological assumptions of logical positivism and social constructionism.

4. *Cultural context* (3d and 3'd). An individual's personal constructs and the nature and meaning of language are intimately tied to the cultural context in which he or she is embedded. Culture includes patterns of social behavior such as customs, attitudes, values, role perceptions, and rituals, both the broader contexts of situation *X*, such as contemporary America, and the specific contexts of situation *X*, such as the theoretical preferences of psychologists *A* and *B*.

5. *Historical context* (3e and 3'e). Culture changes over time as well as geography. Thus, to maximize cultural agreement, psychologists *A* and *B* should be making their observations at the same point in time.

As shown in Boxes 4–6', *A* or *B*'s final publicly expressed observation of situation *X* is determined by two factors: a privately constructed perception of *X* (Boxes 4 and 4') and extraperceptual, motivational variables vis-a-vis *X* (Boxes 5 and 5').

In their social interactions, individuals tend to negotiate a consensus view of reality. Thus, in Figure 13.2, psychologists *A* and *B* can have reliability in their observations of situation *X*. However, unlike logical positivism, in which agreement is based upon a common perception of external reality, social consructionism bases observational agreement on a common, intersubjective process of constructing reality. Such agreement is likely to take place to the extent that *A* and *B* have similar personal constructs, similar language, similar social input (particularly if they are in direct social interaction with each other), are perceiving situation *X* from the same cultural and historical contexts, and share similar motivational structures with respect to *X* (Boxes 6 and 6').

According to social constructionism, a publicly expressed observation by *A* or *B* (see Figure 13.2, Box 6 or 6') is, in part, constructed by the observer in a complex process involving variables independent of situation *X* itself (see Boxes 3–5'). However, this does not necessarily imply a solipsistic position that there is no external reality or that external reality has no impact upon experience. Rather, as shown in Figure 13.2, the intrinsic nature of situation *X* is one of the inputs into the construction process—although it is only one of many. Moreover, the extent to which the construction process causes individuals to diverge in what they perceive varies tremendously, depending on the kinds of external situations involved. Thus most people will agree on the differences between day and night, summer heat and winter cold, and changes in color in a chemical experiment. But when it comes to such areas as pornography, insanity, and love, intersubjective consensus drops precipitously.

In the context of Figures 13.1 and 13.2, "pure" logical positivism and "pure" social constructionism are viewed as endpoints on a continuum. The former's emphasis on direct, "objective observation" of reality is at one end, and the latter's indirect, "subjective construction" of reality is at the other. Epistemological models located in the middle of the continuum involve varying degrees of "observer effects" on the perception of external reality, and thus varying assumptions about the possibility of psychologists' "discovering" general laws of behavior. In terms of Figure 13.2, the extent of these observer effects can be quantitatively framed as the statistical extent to which psychologist A and B's publicly expressed observations of situation X (see Boxes 6 and 6 ') are functions of the nature of X per se (see Box 1), as opposed to other, "non-X" factors. These non -X factors include the observers' personal constructs, their social interaction with others, the nature of their language, and the cultural and historical context of situation X (see Boxes 3 and 3 ').

In Figure 13.1, an author's placement on the positivism–constructionism continuum can be viewed as a reflection of the extent to which he emphasizes "observer effects" in an individual's perception of "reality." In behavior therapy, these observer effects apply to both client and therapist perceptions. As shown in Figure 13.1, the contributors to this volume cluster into four different positions. At the positivistic extreme, Rachlin and Eysenck hold that, under carefully designed conditions involving overt behaviors, "observer effects" are minimal or nonexistent.

The second group consists of Staats, Erwin, Kendall and Bacon, and Rotgers. All these authors generally adhere to a view that positivistic laws about human behavior can be derived through the traditional scientific method. At the same time, they all acknowledge the significant impacts of the cognitive, linguistic, social, cultural, and historical variables listed in Boxes 3a–3e in Figure 13.2; and thus all of them propose a revised version of positivism as the epistemological base of contemporary behavior therapy. For example, calling his revised version "unified positivism," Staats quotes himself to describe it as follows:

> We do not have to assume that the empirical world is capable of being known objectively, without taint by one's conception, in a certain and pure manner, before we can take an empirical position and recognize observations as a fundamentally important source of knowledge. The present conception of the growth of scientific knowledge admits the interaction of theory and observation always . . . Humans began their knowledge quest with poor conceptions and made poor observations. But added experience led to the rejection of some aspects of the conception and the

support of others. Through this conceptual improvement it was possible to make better observations. The two realms are in continuous, progressive interaction in producing a progressively refined fund of knowledge—a fund that is not without error, that contains distortion, that is idealized, and that is never a perfect knowledge mirror of the world. (p. 221, *this vol.*)

In a similar vein, while Erwin agrees with the various critiques of positivism (e.g., Erwin, 1978, pp. 56–60), he also argues that a constructionist alternative leads to the problem of relativism. To make his point, Erwin sets out five propositions:

1. Observation of raw data is both prior to and independent of theory.
2. Scientific observation provides us with hard data independent of our subjective desires, wishes, and biases.
3. The form and content of scientific knowledge are strongly influenced by sociopolitical factors as well as those related to the attitudes and sensibilities of the community of scientists.
4. There can be no neutral observation language. (p. 114, *this vol.*)

In evaluating these propositions, Erwin concludes that:

Behavior therapists . . . need not accept the distinctive epistemological views of logical empiricism; they are not compelled to accept (1) or (2) unless each is interpreted so as to make it defensible but relatively trivial; and they need not reject (3) or (4) unless each is interpreted to state an extreme doctrine that is indefensible. (p. 117, *this vol.*)

Erwin then proceeds to argue for a principle that might be termed "refined empiricism." He states the principle as follows:

5. Experimental testing is generally necessary for the confirmation of theoretical and therapeutic *causal* claims in clinical psychology (unless some suitable substitute is used). (p. 117, *this vol.*)

While not explicitly addressing the issue of positivism vs. constructionism, Kendall and Bacon's discussion implies a similar view. On the one hand, they imply a constructionist perspective by contending that "the human organism responds primarily to cognitive representations of its environments rather than these environments per se" (p. 160). On the other hand, this perspective is balanced by an emphasis on empiricism as a basis for deriving general psychological laws. Thus, while arguing for the importance of the cognitive filtering of reality, they also take the position that "cognitive processes can be cast into testable formulations that are easily integrated with behavioral [conditioning] paradigms" (p. 160, *this vol.*)

Finally, Rotgers argues for the need to assume a middle position between positivism and constructionism "to salvage an empiricist epistemology" (p. 200, *this vol.*). To meet this need, Rotgers proposes a position developed by Van Fraassen, appropriately called "constructive empiricism." Van Fraassen is committed to the principle that relatively unbiased observations of phenomena like human behavior can be made (the "empiricism" in his position). At the same time, he emphasizes the constructionistic nature of scientific theories:

> I use the adjective "constructive" to indicate my view that scientific activity is one of construction rather than discovery; construction of models that must be adequate to the phenomena, and not discovery of truth concerning the unobservable. (Van Fraassen, cited by Rotgers, p. 200, *this vol.*)

The third group for authors to hold a roughly similar position on the positivism–constructionism dimension includes Krasner and Schwartz (Figure 13.1). Although neither explicitly states a constructionistic position, both emphasize the limits of positivism and discuss the importance of contextual variables in determining the truth of statements about behavior. Thus both take an epistemological position that is somewhat more constructionist than that of Staats, Erwin, Kendall and Bacon, or Rotgers.

In terms of Pepper's (1942) "world hypotheses," Schwartz views the positivism associated with traditional behaviorism as primarily "formistic" and "mechanistic," seeing nature in terms of single causes and single effects. As a conceptualizer working within general-systems theory, Schwartz primarily adopts instead the "contextual" and "organismic" world hypotheses. These he describes as follows:

> The contextual hypothesis ... essentially states that our perception is always relatively limited and context-dependent ... The organismic hypothesis is that nature consists of organized units, each of which is composed of organized parts (or subunits). Moreover, the subunits interact with each other in predictable ways so as to generate unique properties (behaviors) of the unit as a whole in the context of the unit's interacting with its environment. (p. 298, *this vol.*)

Moreover, Schwartz describes scientific theories as

> less *descriptions* of the "truth" about nature than they are *creations* of the mind designed to serve as "implements" of description, discovery, and prediction ... The hypothesis that theories are really tools of the mind rather than truths about nature per se has the potential value of encouraging scientists and practitioners to become more humble, more open-minded, and more creative about the development of conceptual implements for appreciating nature and its potential for novel change and evaluation. (p. 318, *this vol.*)

Nevertheless, we categorize Schwartz as only moderately constructionist because he does believe in the possibility of discovering general laws in psychology, as in all natural phenomena. He describes this belief as the hypothesis that "there exists a set of unifying principles that apply to all systems at all levels in nature, from the extremely microscopic subatomic level to the extremely macroscopic cosmological level" (p. 318).

Krasner adopts an interpretive, constructionistic perspective for describing the historical development of behavior therapy in terms of cultural, political, and sociological forces. By Krasner's own admission, his approach as an historian is in agreement with that of Marx in certain focal respects:

> I view history as a creative projective enterprise ... The historian of psychology is not a passive observer or collector, but a very active participant in the creation of the history of his discipline ... The myth of disinterested science or of objective social science is no longer tenable. (Marx, cited in Krasner, p. 25, *this vol.*)

In his own words, Krasner's perspective as a historian emphasizes

> those creating behavior therapy and those reacting to the creations. My view posits a process of continuous creation as the core of behavioral science. Talented, brilliant, and creative individuals are continually inventing new ideas, models, hypotheses, experiments, ways of observing and conceptualizing human behavior. The act of observing is also the act of influencing and participating. We are all participant-observers. (p. 25, *this vol.*)

Of course, there is a paradoxical quality to Krasner's position, since the behavior therapy paradigm for which he argues is the behavioristic "outer, environmental, social-change" model of human behavior. Like that of Eysenck and Rachlin, this paradigm has traditionally been associated with a positivistic philosophy of science. However, a closer reading reveals that Krasner's main interest in the "outer" model is for pragmatic–technological and ethical rather than epistemological reasons. Krasner argues for a commitment to the "outer model" because of its utopian potential. Thus, by assuming that behavior is determined by social variables outside the individual, the "outer" model is more optimistic and progressive about improving individual and collective functioning and hence the quality of community life. This is in contrast to the more conservative "inner" model, which views personality and disease processes as the main determinants of human functioning. These variables are harder to assess and more resistant to alteration.

Fishman and Woolfolk are substantially more constructionistic. Both hold to a position that the impacts of language, culture, history, and individual cognitions are so powerful as to make the discovery of any general law in psychology highly unlikely. However, these two authors differ in the extent to which they draw upon the concepts and methods of positivism and behaviorism.

Specifically, their differences can be viewed in terms of the three contrasting epistemological paradigms—the experimental, technological, and hermeneutic—that Fishman discusses and summarizes in Table 11.1. The experimental paradigm, associated with positivism, is rejected by both Fishman and Woolfolk in favor of one of the other two positions, both of which are based on social constructionism.

Fishman adopts the technological paradigm. Although based on constructionism, it rests on the quantitative and experimental methods of scientific research. Because these methods are applied within a constructionist epistemology, their major purpose is to develop programs that include practical information to help control and predict behavior and solve problems in particular settings having a relatively homogeneous culture and historical context. The degree to which a program is generalizable from one setting to another is a matter for empirical resolution. The fact that a program does not work in another setting does not necessarily diminish its relevance and validity in the original setting. Unlike the experimental paradigm, the technological paradigm does not have as an expectation the discovery of general laws. The lack of success in the second setting is attributed to the contextual differences between the two settings.

Applying the technological paradigm to behavior therapy, Fishman builds an argument based on earlier work by Erwin (1978) positing that the methods and concepts developed within behavior therapy are useful and viable primarily for practical rather than theoretical or ideological purposes per se. For this reason, Fishman's "pragmatic behaviorism" (Table 11.3) is similar to Krasner's position—the rationale for adopting the behavioral perspective is not that it is the "truest" description of human functioning but, rather, that it is the most practically effective in facilitating desired change.

In contrast to Fishman, Woolfolk's chapter adopts a hermeneutic epistemological position. It is important to note, however, that Woolfolk's difference with Fishman is in part a difference in purpose. Fishman presents pragmatic behaviorism as a desirable paradigm for behavior therapy. Woolfolk's goal is different. His objective is to raise questions about behavior therapy as a philosophy of mind when viewed in contrast to the positions of functionalism and hermeneutic, ordinary-language philosophy. For example, Woolfolk discusses the problems of (1) behavior therapy's overly passive and mechanistic image of the individual person, disregarding the basic, existential realities of "the lived human experience"; (2) behavior therapy's insensitivity to the complexities of language; (3) behavior therapy's inability to address adequately the areas of value and meaning; and (4) the conflict in behavior therapy between the individual as a voluntary agent (in goal setting) and the individual as a pawn of the environment and his or her learning history (in treatment).

As discussed in more detail below, for most major differences among the various authors, there are trade-offs in accepting one position as opposed to another. And so it is for Woolfolk's criticisms of behavior therapy. From a different perspective, the limitations of behavior therapy that he is criticizing also comprise its strengths. For example, the inability of behavior therapy to deal with "the lived experience" and to incorporate directly into its position such concepts as "agency," "intentionality," "personhood," and "self" comes from the commitment to developing cognitive concepts that involve a low level of inference and are linked in a substantial way to overt behavioral and environmental referents. Through this commitment, behavior therapy stays in touch with phenomena that can be observed in a relatively reliable manner. (We say "relatively reliable" because even phenomena involving low levels of inference are embedded in particular cultural and historical contexts [see Chapter 11]). However, if one adopts Woolfolk's hermeneutic perspective, which does deal directly with concepts like "intentionality" and "self," the link to observables is easily broken and one embarks upon a "slippery slope" of highly inferential, autonomous psychic variables and processes that are separated from any kind of observable, concrete experience.

The Scientific/Theoretical Arena

A major focus in the various discussions of the theoretical arena is the degree to which behavior therapy should "go cognitive." The positions of the various volume contributors on this dimension are summarized by their placement on the horizontal axis in Figure 13.1. This dimension reflects the extent to which an author advocates a theoretical position that focuses exclusively on noncognitive, conditioning principles that deal with directly and exclusively observable, overt behaviors as opposed to nondirectly observable, inferential, covert, cognitive/mental states and processes. The authors range across this entire dimension, from Krasner, Eysenck, and Rachlin at the extreme conditioning end, to Woolfolk at the extreme cognitive end.

However, the differences on the conditioning–cognitive dimension are not as great as might appear at first inspection. No one actually rejects conditioning models in favor of cognitive ones. Rather, the disagreement is with respect to the extent to which conditioning models should be the exclusive ones in behavior therapy and, if cognitive variables are to be employed, the permissible levels of inferentiality. Thus the relationships among the authors on this dimension can be conceptualized as a series of concentric circles (see Figure 13.3). The innermost circle of the figure, which includes Krasner and Rachlin, emphasizes the use of pure conditioning models only. The next circle, which contains Eysenck, includes both the innermost circle and also the use of cognitive processes in explaining conditioning phenomena, such as Pavlov's concept that words can function as conditioned stimuli and conditioned responses. Similarly, each of the subsequent circles extends the domain of acceptable cognitive phenomena while, at the same time, embracing all the cognitive and conditioning processes included in the inner circles.

In the third circle, Staats and Fishman accept cognitive phenomena as explanatory processes, but do not emphasize them relative to conditioning ones. In the fourth circle, Erwin discusses in detail the validity and importance of cognitive factors. Arguing from a purely logical, philosophical perspective, Erwin comes to the conclusion that, once experimentation is accepted as the sole rational basis for assessing the adequacy of theoretical claims, there is no need to exclude cognitive events from consideration, provided that assertions about them can be assessed experimentally. He also attempts to defeat the behavioristic claim that addressing cognitive factors in therapy adds little or even nothing to therapeutic efficacy and is thus unwarranted.

In the fifth circle, Kendall and Bacon and Rotgers are more enthusiastic about cognition. Kendall and Bacon declare a type of "cognitive manifesto": "the human organism responds primarily to cognitive representations of its environments rather than these environments per se," "most human learning is cognitively mediated," "thoughts, feelings, and behaviors are causally interrelated," and so forth. In discussing Bandura's social-learning theory, Rotgers stresses the explanatory strengths of such cognitive constructs as "self-efficacy." Both Kendall and Bacon and Rotgers also underline the importance of combining cognitive approaches with conditioning-based techniques by pointing out, for example, that, in the former's words, "enactive procedures may be the best way to bring about cognitive changes."

Schwartz is placed in the sixth circle because his contextual, organismic perspective utilizes complex cognitive processes in the determination of behavior. For example, he draws a parallel between learning

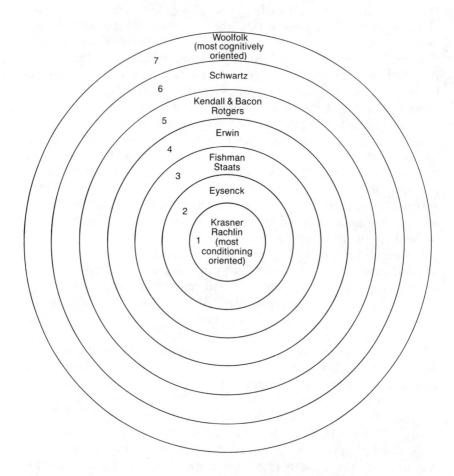

FIGURE 13.3 Relationships among authors on the conditioning–cognitive dimension.

how to approach the practice of behavior therapy in systems terms and learning how to perform jazz:

> The skilled jazz musician learns how to shift attention from the whole of the basic rhythms, chord progression, and melody of a given musical selection to the constantly changing interactions of the various parts (e.g., instruments) as these parts creatively improvise around the agreed-upon theme . . . It takes substantial practice to reach the point where the shifting of one's thinking between the whole and the parts becomes so

effortless that the process of creating new theme (general) melodies . . . emerges and flows in a more or less continuous manner . . . A systems approach to behavior therapy encourages a blending of "classical" and "improvisional" information processing and behavior on the part of the therapist. (pp. 300–301, *this vol.*)

Finally, Woolfolk is placed in the last circle. As do the others, Woolfolk endorses the conditioning models associated with the inner circles. However, he raises objections to the inner circles as a model of the way people actually experience and behave and argues for the need to expand the outermost circle to accommodate an adequate conception of personhood, the self, moral decision making, and so forth. In his words:

There is a dialectic operating within behavior therapy today between the thesis of low-inference, observation-bound, parsimonious, conceptual circumspection, and the antithesis of broader, deeper, clinically pertinent, interdisciplinary richness. (p. 168, *this vol.*)

Exactly how the outer circle can be so expanded without cutting it loose from the inner circles is an issue Woolfolk does not address. Rather, as stated earlier, his major purpose is to raise questions and to point out the limitations of accepting only the domains contained in the inner circles.

In addition to the issue of conditioning versus cognition, a second major theme that emerges across chapters in the theoretical arena is that of the type of "model of the person" behavioral theory should embrace. The various authors cluster into three main groups: those who advocate a model closely associated with the traditional, animal-learning-theory, S-R background of behavior therapy (Rachlin, Eysenck, and Krasner); those who advocate linking behavioral theory closely with contemporary, mainstream, empirically based general psychology, with its cognitivist emphasis (Erwin, Kendall and Bacon, Rotgers, and Staats); and those who reject in various ways the assumptions of the mainstream psychology models of the first two groups (Fishman, Woolfolk, and Schwartz). Specifically, Fishman rejects the assumption of experimental testing of hypotheses in the search for general laws; Woolfolk rejects the limitations imposed by an operational, quantitative approach to psychological phenomena; and Schwartz rejects the focus on testing linear relationships that involve only a few variables (in his words, the focus on formistic and mechanistic, as opposed to contextual and organismic ways of thinking).

In the first, "learning-theory" group, Rachlin adopts a classic logical-positivist position in the axiomatic, quantitative, "grand-theory" tradition of Hullian learning theory. As an exemplar of this approach,

Rachlin presents Baum's generalized version of Herrnstein's "matching law." In related vein, Eysenck highlights the continuity between
animal-learning research, with its associated formalistic and quantitative theories, and effective behavior therapy treatment techniques,
such as response prevention. Behavior therapy, argues Eysenck,
should focus on the treatment of certain kinds of "symptomatic" disorders and not be concerned about its adequacy as an overall theory of
human experience. Finally, Krasner argues against traditional emphasis upon such "inner" concepts and metaphors as "disease, pathology, traits, personality, mind, cognitions, and mind–body or health–
illness dichotomies." Instead, his "outer" model focuses "on the
environmental social consequences, on a social-learning emphasis, and
on a 'utopian' stream—the planning of social environments to elicit
and maintain the best of human behavior" (pp. 27–28).

The second group for authors link behavior theory to mainstream
psychology in a variety of ways. Erwin defends the viability of the
cognitivist position on rational, scientific grounds, while Kendall and
Bacon spell out some of the substantive assumptions of this position,
as discussed above, and Rotgers argues for Bandura's social-learning
theory, with its links both to mainstream cognitive psychology
through the concept of self-efficacy and to mainstream social psychology through the concept of reciprocal determinism. Reciprocal determinism is viewed by Rotgers as an attempt to bridge the intraorganismic and environmental determinants of behavior that frequently
compete against each other in general psychology. Finally, Staats espouses the feasibility of integrating behavioral theory with the findings and concepts of general psychology. Thus, Staats explicitly links
his behavioral approach ("social behaviorism," or, to use his latest
term, "paradigmatic behaviorism") to such concepts as child development, personality, intelligence, emotion, motivation, attitude, group
process, and cross-cultural psychology.

Within Fishman's typology of the experimental, technological, and
hermeneutic paradigms of epistemology in psychology (Table 11.1), the
first two groups of authors generally adopt the experimental paradigm. In contrast, Fishman adopts a technological paradigm. While
not stating a substantive model of the person, Fishman emphasizes
the constructionistic nature of any such model and thus the need to
judge such a model against its usefulness and relevance within particular individual, social, and cultural contexts. In contrast to a single
model of human behavior, different models are constructed for different purposes in different social, historical, and cultural contexts.

Adopting a hermeneutic paradigm, Woolfolk views the issues associated with a psychological theory's model of the person, or what he calls

"philosophical anthropology," as crucial: "Every psychological theory carries with it some tacit understanding of what humans are capable of and, often, what goals they should seek" (p. 168). He discusses "the shift from classical behaviorism to cognitive social-learning theory" as "a shift in the implicit understanding of personhood," which represents "philosophical progress" in that it "allows questions to be addressed that previously were either limited or excluded." However, he argues that there is still a need for "a more philosophically adequate conception of personhood" in behavior therapy and suggests looking for ideas about such a conception outside traditional behavioral theory. In so doing, he turns to the views of functionalism and hermeneutic, ordinary-language philosophy. Thus he calls for ways to incorporate such notions as "personhood," "phenomenology," "rational moral agent," "freedom," "self-consciousness," and "the lived experience of the human being" into the behavioral model. Bandura's concept of reciprocal determinism is viewed as "a kind of midpoint between the libertarian portrait of the autonomous individual whose will is free and whose choices are uncaused events and the conceptualization of human action as an essentially passive response to environmental and biological forces" (p. 179).

Finally, Schwartz presents a systems model of the person that emphasizes Pepper's contextual and organismic hypotheses. For Schwartz, the systems model is a qualitatively and distinctively different way of thinking about all individual and social phenomena. Behavior theory, declares Schwartz, should become encompassed within this model. In his words, "the concepts of 'behavior' and 'therapy' take on deeper and broader meanings when viewed from the perspective of systems theory" (p. 295).

Taking a constructionistic perspective similar to Fishman's, Schwartz's systems approach views a particular naturally occurring behavioral phenomenon in multiply ways: in terms of different systems levels (biological, individual, social, and environmental); different perspectives on parts and wholes; and different perspectives with respect to individual components versus emergent patterns that arise through interaction among the components. It might be noted that Fishman's constructionistic perspective also stresses alternative ways to look at the same behavioral phenomena.

The Technological Arena

A number of analysts of values implicit in behavior therapy point to the emphasis on scientific theory in developing and packaging specific intervention technologies for behavior change (e.g., Woolfolk & Richardson, 1984; Messer & Winokur, 1980; Spiegler, 1983). Stemming from the empiricist tradition of behavior therapy, a related emphasis has been on the development of measurement technologies for assessing the cost-efficiency and effectiveness of their techniques (e.g., Paul & Lenz, 1978; Paul, 1979).

In spite of the epistemological and theoretical differences, this practical, technological bent is strong and consistent across virtually all chapters. Thus, Krasner emphasizes that throughout the history of the behavioral approach there has been "a utopian stream" that involves:

> an ethical concern for the social implications of behavior control as well as offering blueprints for a better life, such as Skinner's (1948) *Walden Two*. This stream can be traced from Plato's *Republic* to the setting up of a token economy on a psychiatric ward or in a community setting. (p. 32, *this vol.*)

The "outer" behavior theoretical model is advantageous, argues Krasner, because of its technological power:

> Implicit in the "outer" model is, of course, the notion that change in human behavior is possible, even desirable, since human nature is plastic, not fixed and immutable. It is appropriate that each of the two most influential "outer"-model behaviorists of this century, Watson (1929) and Skinner (1948), has offered his own version of a "utopian" society. (p. 28, *this vol.*)

Eysenck begins by justifying a behavioral approach as an alternative to psychoanalytic therapy because the latter "simply did not work." It fails to produce behavior change. This point is boldly argued in Eysenck's classic 1952 outcome evaluation of psychoanalysis. Eysenck's starting point is that any alternative to psychoanalysis, such as behavior therapy, must be justified by its superior ability to impact positively on psychological problems. Eysenck's primary concern throughout is with what variant of learning theory leads to the best therapy outcome.

Rachlin conceptualizes the technological emphasis in behavior therapy in terms of the difference between an Aristotelian view of theory, which is to mirror and understand the world, "not to control things, not to make them different from what they are," and a Platonic view of theory, which is to control and aid in seeking the good life. Identifying the behavioral tradition with the Platonic view, Rachlin agues that the criterion for judging his theory should not be whether it adds to understanding Woolfolk's "lived experience" but, rather, whether it helps predict, change, and control behavior.

In his already noted 1978 book on the conceptual foundations of behavior therapy (see Chapter 1), Erwin analyzes the philosophical and ideological basis of behaviorism and concludes that while "behavior therapy is not behavioristic" from an ideological point of view, adopting a behavioristic perspective is justified from a pragmatic point of view—namely, that it does facilitate our ability to implement and evaluate techniques to resolve positively psychological difficulties. In the present volume, Erwin expands this argument by pointing to the technological benefits of adding cognitive concepts and methods to the behavioral armamentarium in a manner consistent with the empirical, experimental tradition of the behavioral field.

For Kendall and Bacon, the science and technology components of behavior therapy "are conceptually separable, though certainly overlapping and interacting." They continue:

> *Technology*, as it applies to a therapeutic endeavor, refers to the body of knowledge concerning particular techniques and their outcomes . . . Questions concerning how and why a technique works, and those concerning the origins and maintenance of psychopathology, are *scientific* questions. (pp. 149–150, *this vol.*)

While scientific theory can be helpful in generating cost-effective technologies, such theory is not necessary. To make their point, Kendall and Bacon use examples from pharmacology (aspirin) and psychopharmacology (chlorpromazine and lithium carbonate) of effective technologies that have been found serendipitously and whose scientific explanation of why they work is not known. Historically:

> behavior therapists have championed the use of empirically validated therapeutic techniques with little regard for the elegance of the theories that inspired them. For the clinician, the measure of a technique is not its scientific lineage, but its efficacy. (p. 150, *this vol.*)

Kendall and Bacon review various ways in which theory, particularly contemporary learning theory, can aid in the development of behavioral technology. For example, "given the large number of possible techniques for treating a behavioral problem, it makes sense to focus time and attention on those techniques with the highest probability of succeeding, even if it means overlooking some that may also have worked" (p. 154). In an area such as choosing between two experimental cancer treatments, one based on laboratory animal research and one on astrology, the *a priori* probability of success would seem higher for the research-based technique. However, does the same reasoning apply in behavior therapy in choosing between a technique based on animal learning and one based on the therapist's clinical experience? Kendall and Bacon maintain that the answer to this question is less clear:

> First, the jump from the laboratory to the clinic is much smaller for the cancer-patient scenario than for the behavior therapy client. The physiology of animals and humans is probably far more similar than the psychology of animals and humans Also, the background knowledge in physiology is far greater than that in psychology; our "laws" tend to be very general and difficult to apply to specific situations. Second, the alternative approach in our behavior therapy scenario is more plausible than astrology as an alternate approach to cancer treatment. When practitioners develop techniques for use in the clinic, they use implicit theories of interpersonal relations. Some people are able to make reasonable predictions about behavior and even advise friends who are having interpersonal difficulties without any training in the behavioral sciences. Certainly people's implicit theories are not all correct. Nevertheless, it is difficult to imagine how we could survive in our social environment if most of our implicit theories were incorrect. In summary, theory-based techniques may have a greater probability of succeeding than those based on more intuitive approaches when the theory is strong and the hunch is based on little experience; when the opposite is true, which seems typical in clinical psychology, then we suggest greater open-mindedness about clinically derived techniques. (p. 155, *this vol.*)

Understandably, Kendall and Bacon conclude that, while there are several defensible ways to develop therapeutic techniques, one of which is through the application of a well-corroborated theory, ultimately the value of a technique must be based on empirical evaluation rather than *a priori* arguments.

As an alternative to deriving new behavioral technology from experimentally derived theory, Kendall and Bacon suggest the method of the "spinoff." For example, in the search for new and better medications, pharmaceutical companies slightly alter the chemical structure of successful older drugs without reference to any specific theory of action, and then proceed to test empirically the effects of these new derivatives. As noted, this strategy is frequently employed in behavior therapy, but infrequently acknowledged. A new technique, similar to a successful extant technique, is justified by its relationship to theory rather than its similarity with other techniques. Kendall and Bacon further make the important point that, since technology need not follow from science, spinoffs can be legitimate sources of new clinical techniques. The need to tie technique to theory may be more indicative of professional insecurity than anything else.

Woolfolk points to the early technological focus in behavior therapy: "what was distinctive about early behavior therapy, as opposed to psychoanalysis, was its insistence on . . . the achievement of measurable results as a therapeutic *sine qua non*" (p. 170). He also attributes the "cognitive revolution" in behavior therapy in part to its technological origins. After initial successes with certain types of behavioral problems, behavior therapists began to find their conditioning, nonmediational models too limited. In response to these limitations, "behavioral clinicians . . . (e.g., Lazarus, 1971, 1973) expanded their clinical repertoires in directions that took account of human symbolic processes" (p. 170). Woolfolk contends that the present nature of cognitive behavior therapy still has technological limitations, such as its inability to cope adequately with "the so called 'self disorders,' (e.g., borderline and narcissistic personality disorders)." To address these limitations, following the directions of the functionalist/cognitive science and hermeneutics/ordinary language models, Woolfolk suggests that the discipline requires even further cognitive "liberalizing," with the explicit development of "relational cognitive propositions—statements that show how different aspects of mental life affect each other and interrelate" (pp. 182–183).

Rotgers also points to contemporary behavior therapy's technological limitations in dealing with the complexities of so-called personality disorders. In addition, he calls attention to the growing awareness of technological limitations as researchers formally examine behavior therapy's negative outcomes (e.g., Barbrack, 1985; Foa & Emmelkamp, 1983). In response to these limitations, Rotgers advocates Van Fraassen's "constructive empiricism" as an epistemology that can encompass a broader range of technological possibilities than the field's traditional positivism, while retaining the field's basic adherence to empiricism and experimental method.

In his chapter, Staats primarily focuses on the need to develop a unifying conceptual framework, such as his "paradigmatic behaviorism," to integrate the various fragmented elements in behavioral theory specifically and psychological theory generally. As shown in Table 10.1, Staats's approach accomplishes integration by hierarchically organizing the various areas of general psychology and linking them with behavioral theory. The hierarchy begins with basic neuropsychology and learning theory and builds to more and more complex human behaviors. At the end of the hierarchy is the technological "payoff" of the earlier theory: the theory is applied to solving practical problems by deriving better techniques for addressing such areas as clinical psychopathology, child development, learning disabilities, group prejudice, and personnel selection.

Fishman's grounding of theory within what he calls the "technological paradigm" (Table 11.1) is similar to Kendall and Bacon's position with respect to the link between theory and technology. Acceptance of

Fishman's constructionistic epistemology offers an added rationale for caution in deriving technology from experimentally derived theory. No matter how experimentally and laboratory rooted, if a theory is simply one of a number of alternate constructions of psychological reality, then the primary justification for the theory, other than the intellectual and scholarly exercise involved, would seem to be its technological benefits.

Moreover, based on a constructionistic view, which emphasizes the individual, social, cultural, and historical contexts of a particular problem behavior, Fishman argues that theories developed in the laboratory or other controlled environments are frequently off the mark because of the contextual differences between these and naturalistic settings. As a possibly more effective approach to developing cost-effective technology, Fishman proposes the documentation and systematic collation of detailed, experimental (as feasible) case studies. The resulting case-study database would then be used according to Kendall and Bacon's spinoff model. Thus the database is designed for use in general technology development (1) by researchers looking for commonalities and contrasts among the cases, and (2) by individual practitioners developing specific treatment plans for a present case through finding exemplars of successful approaches with similar cases in the past.

Finally, Schwartz introduces the notion of systems theory as a body of "unifying implements," that is, as a group of concepts that can be used as tools for pragmatic purposes. Schwartz illustrates these concepts in his "Peach Lady" case, showing how a "toolbox" of such "unifying implements" as "organismic thinking," "microlevels/macrolevels" "emergent behavior," and "self-regulation and disregulation" led to more effective treatment.

The Ethical Arena

By taking a strong position on the importance of technology per se and the related position that theory development and technological benefit must be closely linked, all the contributors espouse an ethical commitment to helping others and improving their lives, as opposed to a primary interest in the pursuit of knowledge for its own sake. Moreover, all the contributors present views that are essentially consistent with the values of twentieth-century modernism as mentioned in Chapter 2: collaborative rationality for solving interpersonal conflict, individual freedom, self-development, self-determination, social tolerance, social equality, and belief in the essential goodness of human nature and its capacity for positive change.

In response to the question of the relationship of ethical values to the other paradigmatic arenas of behavior therapy, it is clear that social constructionism views ethical values as inseparable from attempts to develop "objective" views of reality. In other words, taking evaluative positions is an intrinsic component of reality construction, whether by a single individual or a group of individuals (see steps 3a and 3d in Figure 13.2). This is in contrast to the positivistic position that facts and values can be separated.

One author, Woolfolk, concentrates on the ethical arena and, in so doing, raises important questions for the field. He cites the tradition of philosophical behaviorism in which mental events are viewed as simply imprecise descriptions of either behavior per se or behavioral tendencies. Private events (thoughts and feelings) are outside the causal chain that affects behavior. The result is a conception of the self in which:

> [ethical] values can refer to nothing other than consistent behavioral probabilities or preferences . . . The concept of value is tied to such notions as reinforcer effectiveness or some other form of hedonic calculus. The notion of a rational moral agent deliberating among ends or choosing on the basis of reason cannot be captured. Freedom or moral responsibility, if preserved at all, must be characterized entirely in environment–behavior relations (e.g., "freedom is the absence of a certain level of environmental restraint on behavior"). (p. 171, *this vol.*)

Woolfolk points out that, while most cognitive behavior therapists recognize thoughts as potentially causal, they generally retain the deterministic, mechanistic tradition of conditioning models. When cognitive behavior therapists actually practice, they inevitably engage in rational dialogue with their clients as part of the relationship and goal-setting process. This produces a contradication in that behavior therapy emerges as a form of mixed discourse in which the person is sometimes viewed as a moral agent/second-order intentional system (during discussions and setting of therapeutic objectives) and sometimes as a quasi-mechanistic entity (during treatment).

Fundamental anomalies result from this intermingling of language games. The client is thought to be "responsible" for "choosing" therapeutic objectives but not for his or her low sense of self-efficacy, which is seen as derivative of a social-learning history and a series of unsalutary reciprocal interactions with persons and the environment. If seen as an aspect of the proactive, generative, self-definitional capacities of the person, cognition promotes a conception of therapy as dialogue and discussion. Conversely, if mental life is conceptualized as a set of relatively static, environmentally implanted cognitive structures, then cognitive restructuring becomes the analogue of reprogramming a computer.

While Woolfolk's arguments are cogent, the question still remains as to how behavior therapists' scientific commitment to determinism can be reconciled with the humanistic, nonscientific tradition of free will and moral choice. Woolfolk and Rotgers both cite Bandura's concept of "reciprocal determinism" as one attempt toward this reconciliation.

The Sociological/Political/Historical Arena

Krasner and Staats both review the historical development of behavior therapy. The field's origins include Comte's positivism and the operationalism of the Vienna Circle; the early behavioristic theories of Watson; the early ground-breaking work of Pavlov; the "grand theories" of such animal-learning researchers as Skinner, Hull, Tolman, and Guthrie; and rebellion against the pre-1950 dominance in mental health services of a nonscientific theory and method, psychoanalysis.

Behavior therapy per se is viewed as having been born in the 1950s with a coming together of the work of three groups of researchers: Lindsey, Skinner, and Solomon's application of operant conditioning to the deviant behaviors of hospitalized psychotics; Wolpe and Lazarus's use of reciprocal inhibition techniques with neurotic patients; and Eysenck's application of what he termed "modern learning theory" to neurotic patients. The nature of the field at that time, as conceptualized by Eysenck, is illustrated in his 1959 comparison of behavior therapy and Freudian psychotherapy (see Table 4.1).

Behavior therapy grew very quickly as an applied discipline in the 1960s and early 1970s, developing the types of institutions Kuhn associates with the sociological aspect of paradigms. Thus, 1966 saw the birth of the Association for Advancement of Behavior Therapy (AABT), and 1974, the Association for Behavior Analysis (ABA). By 1970, four journals exclusively devoted to behavior therapy had been initiated, and by 1981 this number had grown to 18 (Spiegler, 1983). The count in 1987 has reached well into the twenties.

During the 1970s, behavior therapy grew in two directions. First, it widened its scope of application to new target areas, such as behavioral medicine; behavior-analytic instructional technologies in education; token economies in residential settings with psychotic, retarded, autistic, and correctional populations; behavioral community psychology; and organizational behavior management. Second, the field expanded epistemologically and theoretically, moving from its origins in positivism and conditioning theory to new domains of constructionism and cognitivism (Franks & Rosenbaum, 1983). This growth is graphically depicted in Figure 13.1 by expansion from the upper left quadrant to the other areas of the figure; and in Figure 13.3, by movement from the original inner circle to wider and wider concentric circles.

All contributors, explicitly or otherwise, acknowledge the present political success of behavior therapy. They agree that the field has achieved a sizable following (together, AABT and ABA currently number about 5,000 members), a variety of viable political institutions, third-party payment recognition, and a national image of respectability and participation in the mainstream. In addition, all authors appear to concur that this political success has been in part due to the epistemological and theoretical expansion of the field.

The contributors disagree, however, as to whether behavior therapy's present political success has been worth it, depending on how they evaluate the epistemological and theoretical expansion into constructionism and cognitivism, respectively. This evaluation relates to their views of the type of paradigm in which behavior therapy should be embedded. Thus evaluation of the sociological and political viability of behavior therapy is tied to the epistemological and theoretical models that underlie the field. This then links back to our discussion above of the epistemological and theoretical arenas (see Figures 13.1 and 13.3) and to our consideration below of Kuhnian concepts of paradigm.

Specifically, in terms of behavior therapy's present political viability, Krasner believes that opening up behavior therapy to cognitive models undermined its unique character, created an oxymoron, and ultimately will lead to its death. Eysenck and Rachlin agree, in the main, with Krasner. In sharp contrast, Erwin, Kendall and Bacon, and Rotgers hold that the present cognitive-behavior-therapy and social-learning-theory paradigms provide an excellent conceptual base, whereas Schwartz and Woolfolk see the move toward cognitivism as a conceptual and philosophical step in the right direction that has not gone far enough. Emphasizing technology as the core of the discipline, Fishman views behavior therapy as very healthy. He suggests, however, that a more rational epistemological basis for behavioral technology might be achieved by a reconceptualization of the field in terms of a social constructionist/technological model. Finally, Staats laments the fragmentation and separatism within behavior therapy itself and, more broadly, between behavior therapy and general psychology. To address these problems, he proposes the new, overarching, conceptual framework of paradigmatic behaviorism to help bring integration, coherence, and intellectual cohesiveness to the field.

The Kuhnian Concept of Paradigm

As discussed in Chapter 2 and reflected in Figure 2.1, Kuhn conceives of a paradigm as incorporating, in an integrated manner, the various paradigmatic arenas we have just been reviewing. In terms of the relevance and significance of the Kuhnian concept of "paradigm" for behavior therapy, the views of this volume's contributors cluster into the three historically based groups we originally set forth. We will therefore consider the authors' views in that order.

Conditioning Models

Krasner and Eysenck clearly believe that behavior therapy as developed in the 1950s and 1960s comprised a distinct paradigm in the Kuhnian sense. This paradigm was clearly distinguishable from others in psychology, particularly from the dominant alternative paradigm at that time, psychoanalysis. These two authors differ, however, on the fate of the paradigm after the "cognitive revolution" of the 1970s. In Krasner's view, the essence of behavior therapy's distinctiveness was overwhelmed and destroyed by the incorporation of cognitive and related psychotherapeutic elements. Thus, he calls for:

> a reemergence of the clinical psychologist/behavior therapist/scientist–
> practitioner/participant-observer/prevention/empirical-clinical science/
> social learning/environmental design/utopian role. These terms are delib-
> erately linked together philosophically and historically . . . [I call for the
> re-establishment of] an informal network among individuals with this
> orientation (paradigm), and there are many out there. (p. 41, *this vol.*)

In contrast, Eysenck believes that his paradigm of neobehaviorism can be strengthened and enhanced by the incorporation of certain cognitive elements, which theoretically function as "internal mediators." To accommodate these cognitive components, he replaces the concept of "radical behaviorism," the view that conditioning in animals and humans is an identical process, with the concept of "dialectical behaviorism," which emphasizes differences.

Rachlin also sees the precognitive behavior therapy of the 1960s as a distinct paradigm in the Kuhnian sense. Following Krasner, Rachlin emphasizes the incompatibility of behavior therapy and its behavioristic background with cognitivism. In his view, conditioning principles cannot logically incorporate cognitive or, for that matter, any other "molecular" types of causal variables.

The Cognitive Revolution

Erwin's chapter is, in large part, a critical, comparative discussion of three paradigms in clinical psychology: the behaviorist, cognitivist, and psychoanalytic. Closely following Kuhn's notion of "disciplinary matrix," Erwin defines a *paradigm* as follows:

> A paradigm exists if a scientific group shares an empirical theory, some distinctive philosophical or methodological views, and one or more exemplars (shared examples of a successful research strategy). (p. 109, *this vol.*)

Erwin's only difference from Kuhn is that Erwin does not require a research consensus for the entire discipline of clinical psychology:

> The main reason for using *paradigm* in this nonconsensus sense is that some term is needed to characterize what psychoanalysis, behaviorism, and cognitivists are disagreeing about. The term *theory* is too narrow for this purpose. The disagreements are partly about empirical theories, but they are also about scientific values, the utility of certain exemplars, and philosophical and methodological assumption. (p. 109, *this vol.*)

In Kuhn's terms, Erwin seems to be saying that clinical psychology as a whole is presently in the third, "crisis" stage of science development in which at least three different paradigms are competing for dominance. However, within each paradigm, its adherents tend to function in the second-stage model of "normal science" puzzle solving.

Kendall and Bacon point to Masterman's (1974) elaboration of Kuhn's concept of a pre-paradigmatic discipline into three substages: nonparadigmatic science, when investigators first start to think about some natural phenomenon; multi-paradigmatic science, when there are many competing paradigms; and dual-paradigmatic science, when the number of competitors has been reduced to two. Kendall and Bacon, like Erwin, see present clinical psychology as multiparadigmatic, with behavior therapy or cognitive behavior therapy as one of the paradigms.

Of all the authors, Kendall and Bacon address Kuhnian concepts in most detail. By a careful analysis of Kuhn's writings and the concept of a "scientific community," Kendall and Bacon derive a quantitative perspective on a scientific community and its paradigm. The smallest community is the individual scientist. For any community that is greater than an individual, the community's paradigm can be defined as "the mean set of assumptions or average framework used by the group." Kuhn's concept of paradigm shift is viewed as the aggregate of personal paradigm shifts.

Kendall and Bacon point out that paradigm shifts need not be the dramatic, sudden changes that Kuhn suggests. Rather, there can be more gradual "paradigm drifts." These are based upon cumulative changes arising at the grassroots level, that is, from cumulative decisions to change by different individual scientists in response to the inability of their present paradigm to solve the particular scientific problems with which they are grappling. This is the manner in which Kendall and Bacon view the shift from conditioning-only models in the 60s to cognitive behavior therapy approaches in the 1970s and 80s:

> In behavior therapy we do not see any rapid shifts taking place. Certainly behavior therapy has become broader as it has matured, that is, there has been increased variability around the paradigmatic mean. Rather than a sudden shift, we ... have observed what might be called "paradigm drift" toward cognitively mediated conceptions of behavior, with gradual increase in the number of behavior therapists whose personal paradigms include an emphasis on cognition. (pp. 146–147, *this vol.*)

Woolfolk sees the "cognitive revolution" as a paradigm shift in the Kuhnian sense. He attributes this shift in part to paradigmatic anomalies in "classical behavioral therapy that relied exclusively on analogies from operant and respondent conditioning" (p. 169). In addition, in accord with Kuhn's notion of a paradigm, he suggests that the cognitive shift was

> influenced by factors other than the objective explanatory adequacy of paradigms ... Behavior therapy was unquestionably pulled along by the rest of psychology, which had become, as had all of society, profoundly influenced by the computer and the information-processing metaphor. (pp. 169–170, *this vol.*)

Woolfolk views this shift from conditioning to cognitive behavior therapy as involving changes in fundamental assumptions about "philosophical anthropology," that is, in assumptions about human nature and the human condition. He believes that, while the shift to cognitive behavior therapy led to "philosophical progress" in its conception of the person, it did not go far enough in adequately addressing questions of value and meaning:

> In order to ponder and be affected by questions related to the meaning and purpose of one's existence, or human existence at large, one must possess. ... rather sophisticated second-order self-reflective capacities ... Behavior therapy [including cognitive behavior therapy] has not been

much interested in such concerns, . . . [nor, in a related way, in such] problems as the so-called self disorders, such as borderline and narcissistic personality disorders. (p. 182, *this vol.*)

Conceptualization of such syndromes, and conceptualization of the human condition in the broader sense, requires "relational cognitive propositions—statements that show how different aspects of mental life affect each other and interrelate" (pp. 182–183). To date, Woolfolk posits, cognitive behavior therapy has not systematically considered such propositions. Rather, the field has limited itself to relationships between cognitive variables and observable behaviors.

Integrationist Approaches

Rotgers agrees with Kuhn concerning the presence of nonrational and constructionistic components in the choice of a paradigm. Rotgers argues that such a choice is based to a significant degree not on logical argument, but on personal values and intuitive processes. Consistent with this position, he discusses a number of contemporary philosophers of science (e.g., Secord, Toulmin, and Van Fraassen) whose work represents a reaction against the positivist values and assumptions of traditional behaviorism. These philosophers emphasize:

a greater reliance on social processes in determining what is to be included within the scientific domain; . . . a correspondingly greater emphasis on cognitive processes as causal determinants of scientific knowledge and human behavior; . . . and . . . a movement away from a reliance on rationalism (as exemplified by empiricism and experimental methodology) alone to provide adequate explanations of behavior, with a corresponding shift in the emphasis of science from prediction and control to explanation and understanding. (p. 199, *this vol.*)

Rotgers argues that these postpositivistic values are embodied in social-learning theory and cognitive behavior theory, and thus that these two theories represent a fundamental, paradigm-like shift when compared to classical, conditioning-based behavior therapy.

Staats rejects the relativistic and constructionistic aspects of Kuhn's concept of paradigm. However, Staats does endorse the importance of a unifying epistemological, theoretical, methodological, and political framework for behavior therapy and psychology generally, in order to combat the destructive fragmentation and disunity that presently exists, he argues, both within and between these fields. Staats contends that Kuhn's theory of paradigm development is not in itself sufficient for psychology:

It is necessary to construct a tenable, productive, positivistic philosophy that can be studied using the general—not the specific—methods of science. Further, however, it is necessary to formulate a philosophy of science that deals with what psychology is, what it should become, and what tasks it must complete to make that transition. (p. 218, *this vol.*)

To meet the need for an indigenous philosophy of science, Staats proposes a new variant of positivism, which he calls "unified positivism," as described above. In line with his stress on the need for a unifying framework theory, he proposes a conceptual model called "paradigmatic behaviorism." The use of the term *paradigmatic* emphasizes that this theory is explicitly designed to facilitate unification, both within behavior therapy, specifically, and between behavior therapy and psychology, generally:

> Paradigmatic behaviorism . . . aims to construct a framework that has conditioning as its basic principles but that utilizes and unifies knowledge from the other areas of psychology throughout the range of its theory construction. This is not done in an eclectic way, but in a closely reasoned way. . . . First and foremost, it [paradigmatic behaviorism] requires that its theoretical unifications produce heuristic, theoretical, empirical, applied, and methodological products. (p. 229, *this vol.*)

Fishman supports the usefulness of Kuhn's idea that a scientific discipline consists of a group of individuals who share a body of explicit and implicit assumptions about epistemology, theory, technology, ethics, and sociopolitical organization. Kuhn's description of historical change in the sciences is characterized not by a continuous, linear progression, but rather by sudden abrupt changes, as in the Copernican, Darwinian, and Einsteinian "revolutions." While not passing judgment on the specifics of Kuhn's theory, Fishman points to the consistency of Kuhn's position with the epistemology of social constructionism, which Fishman endorses:

> The "soft," flexible link between scientific concepts and external reality allows for the interplay of political and social dynamics among scientists as they struggle for and negotiate consensus about paradigmatic assumptions. (p. 255, *this vol.*)

Fishman argues that there are problems in the positivist epistemological assumptions of the traditional behavior therapy paradigm. He proposes that the technological accomplishments and capacities of behavior therapy can be better rationalized and practically developed by changing the field's epistemology to a social-constructionist, technological one.

Schwartz views general-systems theory as presenting a new paradigm, both for behavior therapy and science in general:

> Systems theory is more appropriately described as a "metatheory." . . . a metacognitive framework for viewing the whole of nature rather than a framework for viewing a specific discipline per se. Systems theory (i.e., metatheory) represents a broad and far-ranging shift in human perception and conception. As such, it meets all the criteria for reflecting a prototypic shift in paradigm, using Kuhn's (1962) generic meaning of the term. (p. 296, *this vol.*)

Schwartz describes how systems theory can be most easily understood and applied when seen as an organized collection of integrative conceptual tools for theory building in any scientific field. By cutting across the physical, biological, psychological, and social levels of intervention, systems theory can help build transdisciplinary theories and applications, not only in behavior therapy but in all modes of therapy. Schwartz suggests that systems theory might well help behavior therapy and health care in general to evolve into a truly integrative health science. In sum, Schwartz views systems theory as a new Kuhnian paradigm applicable to many areas of science. When brought to bear upon behavior therapy, this paradigm in effect transforms behavior therapy into "systems therapy."

Present and Future Paradigms

All chapter authors express strong endorsement of behavior therapy. All agree that the field has contributed much in the past and that it has a potential for contributing even more in the future. Within this context, each author describes certain assumptions in the dominant paradigm(s) in behavior therapy today and discusses why those components should be maintained or changed for the field's optimal viability and effectiveness. As evident from the present discussion, the major assumptions lie in the arenas of epistemology, and theory. Specifically, the authors take positions concerning the present dominance and continuing desirability for the field of (1) a positivistic as opposed to a constructionistic epistemology, and (2) a conditioning-focused, cognition-focused, or other type theoretical foundation. A summary of these positions is presented in Table 13.1

This table shows general consensus that the dominant epistemology in behavior therapy today is positivism, and the dominant theory, cognitive behavior therapy. There is disagreement, however, on the desired course for the field in the future. In the epistemological arena, four of the authors (Eysenck, Rachlin, Erwin, and Kendall and Bacon) propose a continuation of positivism; four (Krasner, Woolfolk, Fishman, and Schwartz), a change to constructionism; and two, a change to

TABLE 13.1 Authors' Views of Epistemological and Theoretical Paradigmatic Models in Behavior Therapy: Dominant Models Existent Today and Desired Models for the Future

	Existent dominant model today		Desired model for the future	
Author	Epistemology	Theory	Epistemology	Theory
Krasner	Positivism	Cognitive Behavior Therapy (CBT)	Constructionism	"Outer," environmental, social-change model
Eysenck	Positivism	Neobehaviorism	Positivism	Neobehaviorism
Rachlin	Positivism	CBT and Molecular Behaviorism	Positivism	Molar Behaviorism
Erwin	Positivism	CBT	Positivism	CBT
Kendall & Bacon	Positivism	CBT	Positivism	CBT
Woolfolk	Positivism	CBT	Constructionism	Phenomeno logically expanded CBT
Rotgers	Positivism	CBT/Social-Learning Theory	Constructive Empiricism	CBT/Social-Learning Theory
Staats	Positivism	Many different, fragmented sub-theories	Unified positivism (positivism revised to facilitate unification and integration among existent theories)	Paradigmatic behaviorism
Fishman	Positivism	CBT	Constructionism in the form of the Technological Paradigm	Pragmatic Behaviorism
Schwartz	Positivism	CBT (dominance of formistic and mechanistic thinking)	Constructionism	Systems theory (dominance of contextual and organismic thinking)

a mixture of these, labeled "constructive empiricism" (Rotgers) or "unified positivism" (Staats).

The greatest disagreement lies in the theoretical arena. Not surprisingly, the authors generally divide in terms of their chapter groups. Thus, Krasner, Eysenck, and Rachlin advocate a return to the conditioning-focused models of early behavior therapy; Erwin and Kendall and Bacon, a continuation of contemporary cognitive behavior therapy models; and Staats, Fishman, and Schwartz, the adoption of more broadly based, integrative models, labeled "paradigmatic behaviorism," "pragmatic behaviorism," and "systems theory," respectively. The two exceptions to this pattern are Woolfolk, who advocates a phenomenologically based expansion of cognitive behavior therapy, and Rotgers, who advocates a continuation of a combination of cognitive behavior therapy and social-learning theory.

Conclusions: The Process of Paradigmatic Decision Making

From our review of Chapters 3 to 12, it is clear that, while there are some dominant, overarching commonalities and sources of identity within the general field of contemporary behavior therapy, the field also contains a wide diversity of paradigmatic assumptions and positions. An underlying theme throughout concerns the relative gains and tradeoffs of various competing positions. A summary of some of these is presented in Table 13.2.

The table is organized into three columns. The first column lists different paradigmatic issues, with one issue identified for each of the paradigm arenas we have been discussing—the epistemological, scientific/theoretical, technological, ethical, and sociological/political/historical. Under each issue, two or three different positions with respect to it are listed. Some of the main advantages of the position are listed in the second column, and some of the main disadvantages, in the third. Where appropriate, the advantages and disadvantages are numbered in pairs to emphasize the explicit nature of the tradeoffs involved. Sample authors from the earlier chapters are referenced to further link the table to these chapters. Finally, it should be noted that, because the different paradigmatic issues and their associated positions are themselves interrelated, there are some advantages and disadvantages that are multiply listed.

In light of Table 13.2, we suggest that in order to facilitate more rational and balanced decision making about paradigmatic issues, it is useful to consider an analogy between a geographic region and the

TABLE 13.2 Illustrative Tradeoffs in Adopting Particular Paradigmatic Positions in Behavior Therapy

Paradigmatic issue		
Position on issue	Advantages of position	Disadvantages of position

Choice of an epistemology

a. Positivism and the Experimental Paradigm (see Table 11.1)	1. Link to the natural-science tradition, which is associated in the public's mind with objective truth and impressive technological potential (Krasner)	1. Philosophically out of date and discredited by many philosophers of science (Woolfolk; Fishman)
	2. Continuity with the historical roots of behavior therapy (Krasner, Eysenck, Rachlin)	2. Few general, substantive laws have been discovered about which there is disciplinary consensus (Fishman)
	3. Avoids embarking upon the "slippery slope" of vague, metaphysical concepts (Rachlin)	3. Cannot handle such phenomenologically based concepts as "the self as moral agent" and "the lived experience." In a related way, this position is inconsistent with the assumption in behavior therapy that the client has free will in the goal-setting phase of treatment (Woolfolk)
	4. Emphasizes rigor and data-based thinking (Eysenck)	
b. Social constructionism and the Technological Paradigm	1. Explains the lack of consensus upon general laws in the social science field (Fishman)	1. Susceptible to the problems of philosophical "relativism" (Erwin)
	1'.Explains the lack of theoretical consensus in behavior therapy (Fishman)	
	2. Emphasis on context links behavior theory and method to clinical realities and complexities (Fishman)	2. General laws are not viewed as attainable, and so generalization among cases and studies is limited (Fishman)
	3. Retains the quantitative and experimental methods of positivism, without its discredited epistemological assumption of a directly discovered world (Fishman)	3. Cannot easily incorporate such phenomenologically based concepts as "the self as moral agent" and "the lived experience" (Woolfolk)

TABLE 13.2 *(continued)*

Paradigmatic issue		
Position on issue	Advantages of position	Disadvantages of position
c. Social constructionism and the Hermeneutic Paradigm	1. Can handle such phenomenologically based concepts "the self as moral agent" and "the lived experience." In a related way, paradigm is consistent with the assumption in behavior therapy that the client has free will in the goal-setting phase of treatment (Woolfolk)	1. Appears to reject the basic core commitments of behavior therapy to such principles as operational definition, reliability in assessment, and quantification (see Fishman, Table 11.3) 1′.Appears to embark upon the "slippery slope" of subjectivism and metaphysics (Rachlin)
Choice of a theory		
a. Conditioning-only theory	1. Maximizes the maintenance of reliability, specifiability, observability, and manipulability (Krasner, Rachlin)	1. Theoretical and clinical power are limited by the exclusion of cognitive and affective variables. Theoretically cut off from the field of experimental cognitive psychology (Erwin, Kendall and Bacon, Rotgers, Staats) 1′.Out of contact with "the lived experience" of everyday life; too tied to models and metaphors of behavior based on the laboratory rat (Woolfolk)
	2. Maintains a high degree of operationalizability, using concepts involving relatively low inference (Krasner, Rachlin)	2. No consensus that this position can adequately explain language use and ethical judgment. Perhaps conditioning theory's level of inference is *too* low to explain these phenomena (Erwin, Kendall and Bacon, Rotgers, Staats)
	3. Continuity with historical behaviorism (Krasner, Rachlin)	

cont.

TABLE 13.2 *(continued)*

Paradigmatic issue		
Position on issue	Advantages of position	Disadvantages of position
b. Cognitive behavior/ social-learning theory	1. Inclusion of cognitive and affective variables adds theoretical and clinical power to the theory and allows linkage to the field of experimental cognitive psychology specifically and general psychology more broadly (Erwin, Kendall and Bacon, Rotgers, Staats)	1. Since cognitive variables are "inside" the person, they cannot be directly observed or manipulated; some loss in specifiability and operationalizability thus occurs (Krasner, Rachlin)
	1'.Relatively noncontroversial in its ability to explain language and its development (Staats)	
	2. Tied to models and metaphors based upon distinctively human behavior (Erwin, Kendall and Bacon, Woolfolk, Rotgers, Staats)	2. Inconsistent with historical behaviorism (Krasner, Rachlin)
c. General systems theory	1. Board scope and applicability to the biological, individual, group, organizational, and community/ cultural levels of phenomena. Highlights links among these levels (Schwartz)	1. Highly abstract concepts would appear in conflict with the low-inference, observation-based tradition of behavior therapy (Krasner, Rachlin)
		1'.Systems concepts are not well operationalized (Krasner, Rachlin).

TABLE 13.2 *(continued)*

Paradigmatic issue		
Position on issue	Advantages of position	Disadvantages of position

Choice of a primary focus on theory or technology

a. Primary focus on technology	1. Maintains a focus on the pragmatic "bottom line" of any therapeutic endeavor— does it work? (Kendall and Bacon, Fishman) 1'.Avoids tendencies to force clinical data into theoretical procrustean beds (Kendall and Bacon, Fishman) 2. The technological spinoff model for the development of new clinical methods provides an alternative to the derivation of new methods from theory (Kendall and Bacon)	1. The deemphasis of theory can be a loss, for theory can help to understand why certain procedures are not working in a particular case, thus acting as a guide for how to refine ineffective procedures (Erwin)
b. Primary focus on theory	1. Continues a tradition in the field of emphasis upon critical thinking and conceptualization instead of "blindly" following established procedures (Erwin, Rotgers, Staats) 2. Theory can be very useful in the derivation of new or improved clinical treatment procedures (Erwin)	1. There is a danger of becoming theory-driven and losing sight of the ultimate goal of behavior therapy as an applied discipline— namely, helping individuals to increase adaptive, desirable behaviors and to decrease those with the opposite characteristics (Kendall and Bacon, Fishman)

cont.

TABLE 13.2 *(continued)*

Paradigmatic issue		
Position on issue	Advantages of position	Disadvantages of position

Choice of view on the role of ethical values and free will in behavior therapy

a. Exclusion of ethical values and free will: behavior therapy deals only with the facts of behavior in a deterministic framework	1. Consistent with behavior therapy's historical identification with logical positivism and the natural sciences (Eysenck, Rachlin)	1. Inconsistent with the practice of behavior therapy (e.g., see AABT's 1977 code of ethics) in which clients are assumed to have free will in selecting their treatment goals and in contracting with the therapist for a treatment plan (Woolfolk)
b. Integration of ethical values and free will: behavior therapy is based on a postpositivistic epistemology in which free will and determinism are not viewed as mutually exclusive categories, but rather as alternative perspectives on human behavior	1. Consistent with the practice of behavior therapy (e.g., see AABT's 1977 code of ethics) in which clients are assumed to have free will in selecting their treatment goals and in contracting with the therapist for a treatment plan (Woolfolk, Fishman)	1. Inconsistent with behavior therapy's historical identification with logical positivism and the natural sciences (Eysenck, Rachlin)

TABLE 13.2 *(continued)*

Paradigmatic issue		
Position on issue	**Advantages of position**	**Disadvantages of position**

Choice of a political definition of behavior therapy (who should be included as a "behavior therapist"?)

a. A narrow focus, e.g., "a behavior therapist is one who practices applied experimental psychology" (see Figure 11.1, Circles 1 & 2)	1. Consistent with behavior therapy's history (Krasner, Eysenck, Rachlin)	1. Not able to accommodate to change. Thus, unable to gain political power from the wide theoretical spectrum that in fact exists among those identifying themselves as behavior therapists (Rotgers, Staats, Fishman, Schwartz)
b. A broad focus, e.g., "a behavior therapist is one who practices according to the principles of 'pragmatic behaviorism'" (see Figure 11.1, Circle 5)	1. Able to accommodate to change. Thus able to gain political power from the wide theoretical spectrum that in fact exists among those identifying themselves as behavior therapists (Rotgers, Staats, Fishman, Schwartz)	1. In danger of losing the core identity and essence of the behavior therapy movement: sacrificing theoretical principles for political power can be an intellectual "sell out" (Krasner, Eysenck, Rachlin)
	1'.More able to link theoretically with mainstream psychology. Thus more able to develop political alliances with mainstream psychologists (Staats, Schwartz)	

domain of paradigmatic positions. Just as a conventional roadmap helps guide an individual to a particular physical place, so a conceptual roadmap can help an individual route himself or herself to a particular conceptual position. Along the way, the roadmap presents certain choicepoints. The purpose of a conceptual roadmap is to inform the reader as to where the conceptual choicepoints are and what the possible conceptual consequences might be of taking one path rather than another.

In sum, our primary goal here is not to argue for the merits of one paradigm over another. Rather, our intent is to give the reader a guide to the topography of paradigmatic issues in the behavior therapy field, as well as to the conceptual hills, valleys, and even hazards that could emerge out of these different paradigmatic positions. The development of a detailed conceptual roadmap for paradigmatic decision making in behavior therapy is a demanding and complex task. It is our hope that this book will motivate others to recognize the need for such a roadmap and thereby contribute to its further development.

References

AABT (Association for Advancement of Behavior Therapy). (1977). Ethical issues for human services. *Behavior Therapy, 8,* v-vi.

Barbrack, C.R. (1985). Negative outcome in behavior therapy. In D.T. Mays & C.M. Franks (Eds.), *Negative outcome in psychotherapy and what to do about it* (pp. 76–105). New York: Springer.

Erwin, E. (1978). *Behavior therapy: Scientific, philosophical and moral foundations.* New York: Cambridge University Press.

Foa, E.B., & Emmelkamp, P.M.G. (1983). *Failures in behavior therapy.* New York: Wiley.

Franks, C.M., & Rosenbaum, M. (1983). Behavior therapy: Overview and personal reflections. In M. Rosenbaum, C.M. Franks, & Y. Jaffe (Eds.), *Perspectives on behavior therapy in the eighties* (pp. 3–14). New York: Springer.

Krasner, L., & Houts, A.C. (1984). A study of the "value" systems of behavioral scientists. *American Psychologist, 39,* 840–850.

Masterman, M. (1974). The nature of a paradigm. In I. Lakatos & A. Musgrave (Eds.), *Criticism and the growth of knowledge* (pp. 59–89). New York: Cambridge University Press.

Messer, S.B., & Winokur, M. (1980). Some limits to the integration of psychoanalytic and behavior therapy. *American Psychologist, 35,* 818–827.

Paul, G.L. (Ed.). (1979). New assessment systems for residential treatment, management, research, and evaluation. *Journal of Behavioral Assessment, 1* (Whole Issue No. 3).

Paul, G.L., & Lentz, R.J. (1978). *Psychosocial treatment of chronic mental patients.* Cambridge, MA: Harvard University Press.

Pepper, S.C. (1942). *World-hypotheses.* Berkeley: University of California Press.

Spiegler, M.D. (1983). *Contemporary behavioral therapy.* Palo Alto, CA: Mayfield Publishing Company.

Woolfolk, R.L., & Richardson, F.C. (1984). Behavior therapy and the ideology of modernity. *American Psychologist, 39,* 777–786.

Subject Index

Name Index